GENESIS RABBAH
Volume II

Program in Judaic Studies
Brown University
BROWN JUDAIC STUDIES
Edited by
Jacob Neusner,
Wendell S. Dietrich, Ernest S. Frerichs,
Calvin Goldscheider, Alan Zuckerman

Project Editors (Project)

David Blumenthal, Emory University (Approaches to Medieval Judaism)
William Brinner (Studies in Judaism and Islam)
Ernest S. Frerichs, Brown University (Dissertations and Monographs)
Lenn Evan Goodman, University of Hawaii (Studies in Medieval Judaism) (Studies in
Judaism and Islam)
William Scott Green, University of Rochester (Approaches to Ancient Judaism)
Ivan Marcus, Jewish Theological Seminary of America
(Texts and Studies in Medieval Judaism)
Marc L. Raphael, Ohio State University (Approaches to Judaism in Modern Times)
Norbert Samuelson, Temple University (Jewish Philosophy)
Jonathan Z. Smith, University of Chicago (Studia Philonica)

Number 105
GENESIS RABBAH
The Judaic Commentary to the Book of Genesis
A New American Translation
by
Jacob Neusner

GENESIS RABBAH:
THE JUDAIC COMMENTARY TO
THE BOOK OF GENESIS:
A NEW AMERICAN TRANSLATION

Volume II:
Parashiyyot Thirty-four through Sixty-seven
on Genesis 8:15 to 28:9

Jacob Neusner

Studies in Judaism

University Press of America,® Inc.
Lanham · Boulder · New York · Toronto · Oxford

Copyright © 1985 by
Brown University

University Press of America,® Inc.
4501 Forbes Boulevard
Suite 200
Lanham, Maryland 20706
UPA Acquisitions Department (301) 459-3366

PO Box 317
Oxford
OX2 9RU, UK

Library of Congress Cataloging-in-Publication Data

Midrash rabbah.   Genesis.   English.
Genesis rabbah.

(Brown Judaic studies ; 104-106)
Includes index.
Contents: v. 1. Parashiyyot 1 through 33 on Genesis 1:1 to 8:14—v. 2.
Parashiyyot 34 through 67 on Genesis 8:15 to 28:9—v. 3. Parashiyyot
68 through 100 on Genesis 20:10 to 50:26.
1.   Midrash rabbah. Genesis—Commentaries. 2. Bible. O.T. Genesis—
Commentaries. I. Neusner, Jacob, 1932— . II. Title. III. Series: Brown
Judaic studies ; no. 104-106.
BM517.M65A3   1985   296.1'4   85-22085
ISBN-13: 978-0-89130-934-5 (paperback : alk. paper)
ISBN-10: 0-89130-934-9 (paperback : alk. paper)

For my hosts at

Åbo Academy

with thanks for their gracious hospitality
to my family and to me
and for their careful hearing of my ideas

Karl-Johan Illman
Karl-Gustav Sandelin
Nils Martola

their wives and families

and

their many friendly colleagues
and students
in the faculties of
Theology
and of
History of Religions

CONTENTS

Preface

Genesis Rabbah presents a deeply religious view of Israel's historical and salvific life, in much the same way that the Mishnah provides a profoundly philosophical view of Israel's everyday and sanctified existence. Just as the main themes of the Mishnah evoke the consideration of issues of being and becoming, the potential and the actual, mixtures and blends and other problems of physics, all in the interest of philosophical analysis, so Genesis Rabbah presents its cogent and coherent agendum as well. That program of inquiry concerns the way in which, in the book of Genesis, God set forth to Moses the entire scope and meaning of Israel's history among the nations and salvation at the end of days.

In a few words we may restate the conviction of the framers of the document: We now know what will be then, just as Jacob had told his sons, just as Moses had told the tribes, because everything exists under the aspect of a timeless will, God's will, and all things express one thing, God's program and plan. Our task as Israel is to accept, endure, submit, and celebrate. So, as I said, in the Mishnah, we take up the philosophy of what we now call Judaism, and, in the polemical and pointed statements of the exegete-compositors of Genesis Rabbah, we confront the theology of history of that same Judaism.

Genesis Rabbah came to closure, all scholars generally concur, at the end of the fourth century and the beginning of the fifth. The document in its final form therefore emerges from that momentous century in which the Rome empire passed from pagan to Christian rule, and, in which, in the aftermath of Julian's abortive reversion to paganism, Christianity adopted that politics of repression of paganism that rapidly engulfed Judaism as well. The issue confronting Israel in the Land of Israel therefore proved immediate: the meaning of the new and ominous turn of history, the implications of Christ's worldly triumph for the other-worldly and supernatural people, Israel, whom God chooses and loves. The message of the exegete-compositors addressed the circumstance of historical crisis and generated remarkable renewal, a rebirth of intellect in the encounter with Scripture, now in quest of the rules not of sanctification -- these had already been found -- but of salvation. So the book of Genesis, which portrays how all things had begun, would testify to the message and the method of the end: the coming salvation of patient, hopeful, enduring Israel.

Genesis Rabbah presents the first complete and systematic Judaic commentary to the book of Genesis. In normative and classical Judaism, that is, the Judaism that reached its original expression in the Mishnah, ca. A.D. 200, and came to final and full statement in the Talmud of Babylonia, ca. A.D. 600, Genesis Rabbah therefore takes an important position. Specifically, this great rabbinic commentary to Genesis, generally thought to have been closed ("redacted") at ca. A.D. 400, provides a complete and authoritative account of how Judaism proposes to read and make sense of the first book of the Hebrew Scriptures.

The interest and importance of their reading of Genesis transcend the age in which the sages did their work. For how the great Judaic sages of that time taught the interpretation of the stories of Genesis would guide later Judaic exegetes of the same biblical book. So when we follow the work before us, we gain entry into the way in which Judaism in its normative and classical form, from that day to this, would understand the stories of the creation of the world. These concern Adam's sin, Noah, and, especially, the founding family of Israel, in its first three generations, Abraham, Isaac, and Jacob, as well as Joseph. In an age in which the book of Genesis attracts remarkable interest and in which a literal mode of reading enjoys the authority of true religion, the supple and creative approach of the ancient rabbis, founders of Judaism, provides a valuable choice. The sages show the profound depths of the story of the creation of the world and Israel's founding family. How so? They systematically the history of the people Israel to the lives and deeds of the founders, the fathers and the mothers of this book of the Torah.

Once we have read Genesis the way "our sages of blessed memory" teach us to, we gain the freedom to follow our imagination as they arouse it. We no longer need to deal with those who claim to dictate how in what they deem a literal and fundamental sense we must receive the story of the creation of the world and of Israel. What to some proves fundamental to us, having heard the story as the third and fourth century sages of Israel retell it, appears shallow. What these sages find in the text opens our minds to possibilities beyond imagining.

Sages' way of reading the first book of the Bible shows that faithful exegetes may uncover deep layers of meaning and discover truth entirely consonant with the concerns of a given age. That is so, whether it is the fourth century, in which our sages did their work, or the twenty-first century, to which, with God's help, I hope to hand on these books of mine. Let me now spell out the character of this translation and what I hope to contribute by doing it.

This translation of Bereshit Rabbah takes as its text and systematic commentary J. Theodor and Ch. Albeck, *Midrash Bereshit Rabba. Critical Edition with Notes and Commentary* (Berlin and Jerusalem, 1893-1936) I-III. That text is critical, so far as contemporary Judaic scholarship can produce a critical text, and I have treated it as authoritative in every detail. I have furthermore had the advantage of an excellent translation, already available, and have made ample use of it. I systematically consulted H. Freedman, *Genesis*, in *Midrash Rabbah. Translated into English with Notes, Glossary, and Indices,* ed.

by H. Freedman and Maurice Simon (London, 1939: Soncino Press) I-II. Where I have adopted Freedman's translation verbatim or nearly so, I have indicated by adding his name in square brackets. But I have taken full account of his rendering of nearly every line. I learned from him on each occasion on which I consulted him. It is a splendid piece of work. As to the translation of verses of Scripture, I took an eclectic approach, sometimes copying Freedman's, sometimes relying on the fine English of the RSV, and sometimes making up my own translation.

Let me now explain why I have undertaken a fresh translation of the text at hand. In this translation, I hope to accomplish several things.

First, I have aimed at a more colloquial and American English than Freedman, in the nature of things, provided.

Second, and of far greater importance, I have systematically divided the text up into its sense-units, something no one has ever done in any language.

Third, I have provided a commentary with stress on issues of composition, proportion, redaction, and, above all, sustained polemic. No prior commentary pursuing those interests has ever appeared, nor do I expect any is likely to appear in any language.

In general work on this, as on other compilations of scriptural exegesis produced by the ancient and medieval rabbis, devotes extensive attention to the meaning of words and phrases. Higher critical interests have yet to penetrate circles in which these compilations find students. My principal interest in the present text, by contrast, focuses upon the authors' or compositors' recurrent points of polemic. I take for granted that where there are problems in the meanings of words and phrases, Freedman and the commentators whom he follows have given us as likely an account of the sense of a passage as we are apt to have. In any event the studies I plan on the basis of this translation will not rest on proof provided by a particular meaning imputed to a given word or phrase. So the things that do seem to me important -- as distinct from questions I believe either successfully settled by earlier scholarship, classical and modern, or essentially trivial -- has now to be made very clear.

What I wish to learn is how the people who made the document as we know it made an important statement through both what they presented and how they presented it. How so?

Genesis Rabbah is a composite document, as I said, generally regarded as the work of compilers of the period ca. A.D. 400. Much of the material in the compilation, however, can be shown to have been put together before that material was used for the purposes of the late fourth century compilers. Many times we shall see, for example, that a comment entirely apposite to a verse of Genesis has been joined to a set of comments in no way pertinent to the verse of Genesis at hand. Proof for a given syllogism, furthermore, will derive from a verse of Genesis as well as from verses of other books of the Bible. Such a syllogistic argument therefore has not been written for exegetical purposes particular to the verse at hand. It must follow that the composition before us has been created without special interest in the particular and distinctive exegetical task of working out the meaning of a passage of Genesis. The ones who selected that completed composition made the decision, hence spoke through their selection and there alone. That is what I mean by my stress on the work of selection and ordering, rather than on the original authorship or composition. We find in the work of redaction, and only in that aspect of the text before us, our point of entry into the mind and imagination of the compositors of Genesis Rabbah. So if we want to know about the mind and imagination of fourth-century rabbis in the Land of Israel, we have to pay close attention to what the sages at hand have selected, to how they have arranged the document at hand, and to the points of stress and emphasis they repeatedly locate in the verses that are subject to their explanation.

Let me consequently state the question of this project as simply as I can:

1. Who speak through Genesis Rabbah?

2. What is their message?

To amplify these simple questions: do we hear only from those who selected and arranged completed units of discourse? Or may we derive a message, also, from the authors of the bits and pieces of which the composite is made up? Can we identify recurrent problems and themes, points of emphasis, polemical arguments? Or is the document essentially miscellaneous and unfocused? As I shall argue, the ultimate compositors of the document, the people who selected and arranged available materials, speak through the document. They do deliver a striking, repeated and emphatic, message.

Thus I propose in the present volumes to lay the groundwork for a set of studies on the message and meaning of Genesis Rabbah for the age in which the document reached closure: who speaks what message? The ultimate redactors or compositors of the composition, Genesis Rabbah as we now have are the people who selected an available composition and made use of it in connection with their set of comments on passages of the book of Genesis. I hope to venture into the inner life, the world-view, of Israel's sages in the Land of Israel in a critical age. For at the time at which our document reached closure, the Roman empire in general, and the Land of Israel in particular, went from pagan to Christian rule. The political situation of the Jews and of the Judaism presented by the sages of the document at hand and of the canon of which it forms a part radically changed. That is the context in which I want to know whether the responsible authorities repeatedly stressed a given viewpoint or problem. Let me explain what is at stake here. It is this: how did they propose to read the book of Genesis for purposes important in their circumstance and context? When we know the answer to that question, we may gain entry into the way in which the sages at hand thought about, and responded to, the world in which they lived.

Why do I stress that the document in certain aspects reliably testifies only to the mind of its ultimate arrangers and organizers? The answer is simple. We do not know whether what is attributed to the cited authorities of our document really was said by them. We cannot demonstrate that stories told about them record things that actually happened. What we cannot show we do not know. The mere appearance of a sage's name in a saying or story does not prove that the saying or story reached closure at the time the named sage lived. Hence we do not know whether the story tells us about a period before the time of ultimate closure. So much for the negative.

What do we know with some certainty? While in the nature of things we cannot identify passages in the document before us deriving from the long centuries prior to the period of redaction, the document as we read it does tell us what a handful of sages picked and chose, and how, in their selection and arrangement of comments on the book of Genesis, they made a comment on matters of special concern to them. And we do know what that comment was. So the task of this fresh translation and the exegesis of traits of composition of Genesis Rabbah -- its points of proportion, arrangement, and stress -- is to try to listen to people who used what they had inherited to speak, also, for themselves.

My plan of studies to follow rests to begin with on the analyses worked out in the present composition. Since, for what I propose to do, I had to retranslate the entire text and so to satisfy myself that I have made some sense of every line, as best I could, I saw good reason to bring out a fresh reading of the marvelous composition at hand.

But no one has to apologize for retranslating a classic text. On the contrary, all of the great works of the human mind and spirit, the Bible, the writings of Plato, the classics of literature and philosophy, through fresh translation gain access to age succeeding age. Why not the monuments of the Judaic spirit as well? I provided the first translation into English of the Tosefta, the Yerushalmi, parts of the Sifra, several of Aphrahat's demonstrations on Judaism, several chapters of the Shkand Gumanik Vicar from Pahlavi (Pazend), and other documents. I have done the second complete translation into English of the Mishnah, of five tractates of the Bavli, of Genesis Rabbah and of Leviticus Rabbah (though in fact mine is the first of Leviticus Rabbah in Margulies' wonderful text). I hope to translate for the first time parts of Sifre to Numbers as yet untranslated, and to retranslate other parts of the same document. If all goes well, I shall leave this world having given to the American reader access to every important rabbinic document of late antiquity. Nothing would please me more than to see my translations replaced by better ones. Let each generation improve on what it has received, as mine assuredly has done better in this and other aspects than its precedessors. Fresh translations of rabbinic texts, each new translation with its particular point of interest and sustained analysis, testify to the vitality of learning. Such translations, in the nature of things, also constitute commentaries. For good reason, therefore, they should appear not only in American English, the principal language of Judaic studies today, but also in living Hebrew (surely not the same as the Hebrew of our text) and in European languages as well.

My brief commentary of course is entirely new, since the points of interest to me have not occupied prior exegetes of this text, at least, not in a systematic and sustained way. And, it must be said, what interested them, which was mainly the exegesis of words and phrases, does not interest me. I am satisfied that we understand the basic sense of the text as well as we are likely to. Since earlier generations have carried out the bulk of the text-critical and philological work sufficiently well to allow other sorts of inquiries to commence, we might as well build upon the solid foundations already laid a new construction. In any event if we translate a word long thought to mean garlic as onion, or corn-bread as barley-bread, I do not think our historical insight will be vastly enriched or deepened. Nor can I get terribly excited about titles of Roman officers, though I should be happy to keep them straight.

Let me state one further contribution I believe I make in these volumes. All analytical work depends upon the possibility of comparing and contrasting the bits and pieces of evidence, *inductively construed.* Here for the first time I have provided the document at hand with a complete system for identifying its smallest whole components of thought. I have made it possible to identify and classify those minima -- the bits and pieces of evidence. In providing the most primitive requirements of analysis, I make it possible to move beyond the preliminary stage. This I have done by making up an adequate system for identifying each complete component, each sentence of the document, and not only those large blocks of undifferentiated type with which the earlier printers of the Hebrew text as well as translators have presented us.. Indeed, I should claim that I have made that same unique contribution to the more important documents of the rabbinic canon, specifically, the Mishnah, the Tosefta, the Yerushalmi, and the Bavli (for the five tractates I have translated), as well as some less important documents.

Of course I do not claim that my system, now applied to nearly the whole of the rabbinic canon of antiquity, lacks flaws. But at least it is a system, and we no longer have to refer to a passage as "Chapter Five, at the end," or "Page ll8a, in the middle." We also can differentiate one whole unit of thought, beginning, middle, and end, from some other whole unit of thought -- and compare the two. Until now we have had slight guidance for the reference to a given statement, sentence or verse. Without such a well differentiated reference system, all sorts of literary taxonomic exercises simply cannot be contemplated. The beginning of all analysis lies in the provision of a systematic scheme of differentiating one thing from something else. In breaking up long columns of undifferentiated type into the smallest whole units of thought, I believe I have made it possible to read the components of the canon of Judaism in that precise way in which, in our day, all classical literature is read. Prior analysis rests on an imperfect system of differentiation and hence has to be redone.

My system is quite simple. I have labeled each sentence, paragraph, and larger composite, so as to facilitate ready reference to the entire document. The first Roman numeral refers to the *parashah*, or chapter; the second, to the paragraph of the *parashah*. These two matters are already signified in the printed text and in Freedman's translation. Many of the so-called paragraphs in fact are made up of two or more complete and autonomous thoughts. In my use of an Arabic numeral after the Roman, I indicate the divisions within paragraphs as I propose to differentiate them. I then indicate, by a letter, each individual stich, that is, the smallest whole unit of thought. Thus I:I.1.A stands for the first *parashah*, the first paragraph of the first *parashah*, the first complete composition of the first paragraph of the first *parashah*, and the first sentence of the first complete composition of the first paragraph of the first *parashah* -- and so on.

Before closing, let me specify the several projects that led me to work on Genesis Rabbah. My hope is to offer the four projects. The following are of a scholarly and analytical character:

1. *Comparative Midrash: Genesis Rabbah and Leviticus Rabbah.* Atlanta, 1986: Scholars Press for Brown Judaic Studies.

In addition, I am publishing two anthologies, for diverse audiences:

2. *Reading Scriptures: An Introduction to Rabbinic Midrash. With special reference to Genesis Rabbah.* Chappaqua, 1986: Rossel. This will be an anthology with an introduction on how the sages read the book of Genesis.

3. *Genesis and Judaism: The Perspective of Genesis Rabbah.* Atlanta, 1986: Scholars Press for Brown Judaic Studies. An analytical anthology. The structure of values rabbis brought to the biblical text, as portrayed in Genesis Rabbah, together with analysis of the categories at hand.

Finally, I plan to turn to the larger historical question that, to begin with, brought me to the writings that reached closure in the fourth and early fifth centuries:

4. *Christianity and the Birth of Judaism* (Tentative title.) This work will treat the formation of Judaism in reply to the Christian challenge of the fourth century: canon and Torah, Christ and rabbi, Israel and Esau. It will present a point-by-point comparison of principal doctrines of the Jews and Judaism in writings of fourth century Christian thinkers, and a construction of rabbis' responses to these controverted points, based on the third and fourth century canonical writings, e.g., the Yerushalmi, Sifra and the like.

My former student, Professor Howard Eilberg-Schwartz, Indiana University, was kind enough to read the first draft and correct errors of omission and commission alike. I am grateful for this generous assistance, continuing the amiable tradition he began in graduate school.

Jacob Neusner

Program in Judaic Studies
Brown University
Providence, Rhode Island

July 28, 1985
My fifty-third birthday.

Chapter One

Parashah Thirty-Four.   Genesis 8:15-9:7

XXXIV:I.

1. A. "Then God said to Noah, 'Go forth from the ark, you and your wife and your sons and your sons' wives with you'" (Gen. 8:15):

   B. "Bring my soul out of prison, that I may give thanks to your name; the righteous shall crown themselves because of me; for you will show me goodness" (Ps. 142:8).

   C. "Bring my soul out of prison" speaks of Noah, who was locked up in the ark for twelve months.

   D. "That I may give thanks to your name" means offering words of thanksgiving to your name.

   E. "The righteous shall crown themselves because of me" means that the righteous shall glory in me.

   F. "For you will show me goodness"[refers to the fact that] you showed me goodness in saying, "Go forth from the ark" (Gen. 8:15).

The intersection of the verse from Psalms with the base verse is aptly spelled out. But the point the exegete wishes to make does not emerge, because it is not spelled out. What we have is simply the identification of the situation of Noah with the sentiments of the Psalm at hand. The point of course is that emerging from the ark was like coming out of prison, and Noah's feelings correspond on that account to the sentiments of the cited verse of Psalms.

XXXIV:II.

1. A. "The Lord tries the righteous, [but the wicked and him who loves violence his soul hates" (Ps. 11:5)]:

   B. Said R. Jonathan, "A potter does not test a weak utensil, for if he hits it just once, he will break it. So the Holy One, blessed be he, does not test the wicked but the righteous: 'The Lord tries the righteous' (Ps. 11:5)."

   C. Said R. Yose bar Haninah, "When a flax maker knows that the flax is in good shape, then the more he beats it,the more it will improve and glisten. When it is not of good quality, if he beats it just once, he will split it. So the

Holy One, blessed be he, does not try the wicked but the righteous: 'The Lord tries the righteous' (Ps. 11:5). "

D. Said R. Eleazar, "The matter may be compared to a householder who has two heifers, one strong, one weak. On whom does he place the yoke? It is on the one that is strong. So the Holy One, blessed be he, does not try the wicked but the righteous: 'The Lord tries the righteous' (Ps. 11:5).

2. A. Another interpretation:"The Lord tries the righteous" (Ps. 11:5) refers to Noah.

B. "Then the Lord said to Noah, 'Go into the ark, you and all your household, for I have seen that you are righteous before me in this generation'" (Gen. 7:1).

I assume that the compositor chose this item because of the correspondence of going into the ark and coming out of it. The point is that Noah was found able to withstand the trial and so was proved righteous. That is made explicit at 2.B, accounting for the selection of the intersecting verse. But the base verse is Gen. 7:1, not Gen. 8:15. The compositor has used the passage to call to mind, at the end of the ordeal, Gen. 8:15, the purpose for which the experiment was tried, Gen. 7:1. The selection is a good one, because it prepares the way for an exercise in praising Noah. XXXIV:III-V present precisely that kind of discourse, so the compositor, has usual, has signaled his intentions clearly.

XXXIV:III.

1. A. R. Yudan in the name of R. Aibu commenced [discourse by citing the following verse]: "'In the transgression of the lips is a snare to the evil man' (Prov. 12:13):

B. "On account of the rebellion of the generation of the Flood against the Holy One, blessed be he, their downfall came.

C. "'But the righteous comes out of trouble' (Prov. 12:13) refers to Noah: 'Go forth from the ark' (Gen. 8:5)."

The contrast between Noah's obedience, going into the ark when told, coming out when told, explains why he survived the flood, while the rebels, who did not accept God's word, perished.

XXXIV:IV.

1. A. "If the spirit of the ruler rise up against you, do not leave your place" (Qoh. 10:4):

B. This verse speaks of Noah. Said Noah, "Just as I entered the ark only with permission, so I shall leave only with permission."

C. Said R. Judah bar Ilai, "If I were there, I should have broken down the door to get out. But Noah said, 'Just as I entered the ark only with permission, so I shall leave only with permission.'

D. "'Come into the ark   and Noah came in...' (Gen. 7:1). 'Go forth from the ark' (Gen. 8:15). 'So Noah went forth' (Gen. 8:18)."

Noah waited for God to tell him when the time had come to leave the ark, another mark of his obedience. The point is made twice, A-B, C-D. The proof-texts are entirely direct and apt. The intersecting text now is read to stress that one should wait for instructions from the ruler. We see that the message of the exegete is uniform from the beginning of the *parashah*.

XXXIV:V.

1. A. "Wisdom is a stronghold to the wise man more than ten rulers" (Qoh. 7:19):

B. This verse speaks of Noah. [How so?]

C. "More than ten rulers" refers to the ten generations from Adam to Noah.

D. Among all of them, I spoke with none except with you: "And God spoke to Noah, saying ..." (Gen. 8:15).

Each point of distinction, singling Noah out from his predecessors and contemporaries, is underlined. Now it is the language that God spoke to Noah. It does not occur with any prior figure, beyond the first man.

XXXIV:VI.

1. A. "To every thing there is a season and a time to every purpose" (Qoh. 3:1).

B. There was a season for Noah to enter the ark, "Come into the ark, with all your household"" (Gen. 7:1),

C. and there was a time for him to leave the ark: "Go forth from the ark" (Gen. 8:15).

2. A. "Go forth from the ark" (Gen. 8:15): [Why did God have to order Noah to leave the ark?] This matter may be compared to the case of an administer who went away and left someone else in his place. When he came back, he said to him, "Leave your office." But the replacement did not agree to leave. [Freedman, p. 270, n. 2: Similarly, for twelve months Noah was in charge of the only creatures that were destined to live and thus acted, as it were, as God's

regent. Now he was to leave this exalted position.] [That is why he had to be instructed to leave the ark.]

B. He said, "Should I go forth and procreate only for a curse [and produce children who will be subject to divine wrath]?"

C. Only when the Holy One, blessed be he, took an oath to him that he would never again bring a flood, as it is said, "For this is the waters of Noah to me, for as I have sworn that the waters of Noah should no more go over the earth,' (Is. 54:9), [did Noah agree to leave the ark,] and then he engaged in further acts of procreation.

In yet another way at No. 1 the correspondence between the entry and the exit is demonstrated. No. 2 contradicts the spirit of the foregoing by indicating that God had to order Noah to leave the ark, thus indicating that Noah did not wish to leave and had to be told to do so. It was now not a mark of obedience to God but of Noah's own independent judgment. In point of fact there is a disjuncture between 2.B and 2.A, since 2.B seems to flow from a different statement from that at 2.A, and 2.A demands different continuation from that at 2.B-C.

XXXIV:VII.

1. A. "You and your wife" (Gen. 8:15):

B. R. Judah bar Simon and R. Hanan in the name of R. Samuel bar R. Isaac: "From the time that Noah got into the ark, sexual relations were forbidden for him [and his wife]. That is in line with the formulation of this verse: 'You shall come into the ark, you, your sons'-- by yourselves, 'your wife and your sons' wives' -- by themselves.

C. "When he left the ark, sexual relations once more were permitted. That is in line with the formulation of this verse: 'Go out of the ark, you and your wife' (Gen. 8:16)."

2. A. Said R. Abin, "'They were lonely in want and famine' (Job 30:3). If you see scarcity come to the world and famine come to the world, 'be lonely,' that is, regard your wife as though she were set apart [in her menstrual period]."

B. Said R. Muna, "It is written, 'And to Joseph were born two sons' (Gen. 41:50). When did this take place? 'Before the year of famine came' (Gen. 41:50)."

The point is familiar, another careful reading of the formulation of the instructions for going into the ark and leaving it. The present unit is repeated because it carries forward the point of the proceeding. But it is the choice of the compositor at hand, since the present passage occurs without the materials of XXXIV:VI.

XXXIV:VIII.

1. A. "Bring forth with you every living thing that is with you of all flesh, birds and animals and every creeping thing that creeps on the earth" (Gen. 8:15):

   B. Said R. Yudan, "What is written is, 'Go forth,' and what is read is, 'Put them out' [by force if necessary]."

   C. "That they may breed abundantly on the earth" (Gen. 8:17) and not in the ark.

   D. "And be fruitful and multiply on the earth" (Gen. 8:17) and not in the ark."

2. A. "Every beast, every creeping thing, and every bird, everything that moves upon the earth went forth by families out of the ark" (Gen. 8:19):

   B. R. Aibu said, "The word for 'every creeping thing' is fully spelled out [and not written in abbreviated form]."

3. A. "By families" serves to forbid hybridization and serves to exclude emasculation.

4. A. The children of Noah received seven commandments, specifically those prohibiting idolatry, fornication, murder, blasphemy,

   B. enjoining the establishment of good government,

   C. prohibiting stealing and cruelty to animals ["cutting a limb off a living beast"].

   D. R. Haninah said, "There also was a prohibition against eating blood drawn from a living beast."

   E. R. Eleazar said, "They also were forbidden hybridization."

   F. R. Simeon said, "They also were forbidden the practice of witchcraft."

   G. R. Yohanan said, "They also were forbidden to emasculate males."

   H. R. Issi said, "The children of Noah were forbidden to do any of the things that are written in the following section: 'There shall not be found among you any one who makes his son or his daughter pass through the fire' (Deut. 18:10)."

Nos. 1, 2 comment on the mode of writing out the cited words. Whether these comments produce lessons is not entirely clear. Because No. 3 refers to hybridization in the context of exegesis of the cited verse, No. 4's important discussion is attached on account of 4.E, G.

XXXIV:IX.

1. A. "Then Noah built an altar to the Lord" (Gen. 8:20):

    B. What is written is "he understood" [that is, the word is so spelled out that it can be read as "understood" rather than "built"], with the implication that he thought matters out in this way: "What is the reason that the Holy One, blessed be he, ordered me to take more clean than unclean animals?

    C. "Is it not that he wanted me to offer up animals of the clean classification?"

    D. Forthwith: "And he took of every clean animal" (Gen. 8:20).

2. A. "And offered up burnt offerings on the altar" (Gen. 8:20):

    B. R. Eliezer b. Jacob said, "It was on the great altar in Jerusalem, the same place at which the first man made his offering: 'And it shall please the Lord better than a bullock that has horns and hoofs' (Ps. 69:32)."

3. A. "And when the Lord smelled the pleasing odor" (Gen. 8:21):

    B. R. Eleazar and R. Yose bar Hanina:

    C. R. Eleazar says, "The children of Noah [when they made offerings] offered their sacrifices in the status of peace-offerings. [They kept portions of the sacrificial beast, e.g., the hide, and burned up on the fire only the minimal sacrificial parts.]"

    D. R. Yose bar Hanina said, "They prepared them in the status of whole-offerings [burning up the entire animal and not keeping any portions for the sacrificer and sacrifier (he who benefits from the offering)]."

    E. R. Eleazar objected to the view of R. Yose bar Hanina, "And is it not written, 'And of their fat portions' (Gen. 4:4)? It was an offering in the status of one, the fat portions of which are burned up on the altar [and not eaten by the sacrificer]."

    F. How does R. Yose bar Hanina treat this passage? He interprets it to refer to the fat animals [and not to the portions of those that were offered up, but only to "the best of the flock"].

    G. R. Eleazar objected to the view of R. Yose bar Hanina, "And lo, it is written: 'And he sent the young men of the children of Israel, who offered burnt offerings and sacrificed peace offerings of oxen unto the Lord' (Ex. 24:5)? [This was before revelation, and hence would indicate that the children of Noah, into the category of which the Israelites fell at that time, prior to the giving of the Torah, offered not only whole offerings but also peace offerings, just as Eleazar maintains]."

H. How does R. Yose bar Hanina treat this verse? He interprets the reference to "peace-offerings" to mean that they offered up the beasts with their hides, without flaying them and cutting them into pieces. [So even though the verse refers to peace offerings, in fact the animals were offered up as whole offerings, hide and all.]

I. R. Eleazar objected to R. Yose bar Hanina, "And is it not written, 'And Jethro, Moses' father-in-law, took a burnt-offering and sacrifices' (Ex. 18:12)? [The reference to a burnt offering would suffice, so the inclusion of the further reference to "sacrifices" indicates that there was an offering made in a different classification, hence, peace-offerings.]"

J. How does R. Yose bar Hanina deal with this verse? He accords with the view of him who said that Jethro came to Moses after the giving of the Torah, [at which point Jethro was in the status of an Israelite. Hence the type of offering Jethro gave would indicate only what Israelites did when they made their sacrifices and would not testify to how children of Noah in general offered up their animals.]

K. [We shall now deal with the point at which Jethro rejoined Moses.] Said R. Huna, "R. Yannai and R. Hiyya the Elder differed on this matter."

L. R. Yannai said, "It was prior to the giving of the Torah that Jethro came."

M. R. Hiyya the Elder said, "It was after the giving of the Torah that Jethro came."

N. Said R,. Hanina, "They did not in fact differ. The one who said that it was prior to the giving of the Torah that Jethro came holds that the children of Noah offered peace-offerings [in addition to offerings in accord with the rules governing the classification of whole-offerings]. The one who maintains that it was after the giving of the Torah that Jethro came takes the position that the children of Noah offered up animals only in the status of whole-offerings."

O. The following verse supports the view of R. Yose bar Hanina, "Awake, O north wind" (Song 4:16) refers to the whole offering, which was slaughtered at the north side of the altar. What is the sense of "awake"? It speaks of something that was asleep and now wakes up.

P. "And come, you south" (Song 4:16) speaks of peace-offerings, which were slaughtered [even] at the south side of the altar. And what is the sense of "come"? It speaks of a new and unprecedented practice. [Hence the rules governing peace-offerings constituted an innovation. Freedman, p. 184, n. 1: Thus it was only now, after the giving of the Torah, that the practice of sacrificing peace-offerings was introduced.]

Q. R. Joshua of Sikhnin in the name of R. Levi: "Also the following verse supports the view of R. Yose bar Hanina: 'This is the torah governing the preparation of the whole-offering, that is the whole-offering [of which people already are informed]' (Lev. 6:2) meaning, that whole-offering that the children of Noah used to offer up.

R. "When by contrast the passage speaks of peace-offerings, it states, 'And this is the law of the sacrifice of peace-offerings' (Lev. 7:11), but it is not written, '*which they offered up*,' but rather, 'which they *will* offer up' (Lev. 7:11), meaning, only in the future. [Hence peace-offerings' rules, allowing the sacrificer and sacrifier a share in the animal that is offered up, represented an innovation, not formerly applicable, in support of the view of R. Yose bar Hanina that such offerings' rules constituted an innovation.]"

4. A. "And when the Lord smelled the pleasing odor,[the Lord said in his heart, 'I will never again curse the ground because of man, for the imagination of man's heart is evil from his youth']" (Gen. 8:21):

B. He smelled the fragrance of the flesh of Abraham, our father, coming up from the heated furnace.

C. He smelled the fragrance of the flesh of Hananiah, Mishael, and Azariah, coming up from the heated furnace.

D. The matter may be compared to the case of a king, whose courtier brought him a valuable present. It was a fine piece of meat on a lovely plate [following Freedman].

E. His son came along and brought him nothing. His grandson came along and brought him a present. He said to him, "The value of the gift you brought is equivalent to the value of the gift your grandfather brought."

F. So God smelled the fragrance of the sacrifice of the generation of persecution.

5. A. R. Shillum in the name of R. Menahama bar R. Zira: "The matter may be compared to the case of a king who wanted to build a palace by the sea, but did not know where to build it. He came across a flask of perfume and followed its scent and built the palace on that spot.

B. "That is in line with this verse: 'For he has founded it upon the seas' (Ps. 24:2). On whose account? On account of those of whom the following speaks: 'Such is the generation of those that seek after him, that seek your face, even Jacob, Selah (Ps. 24:6)."

No. 1 completes the discourse on Noah's preparation of the sacrifice;this will not dominate what follows. No. 2 opens with the explicit link between the site of Noah's sacrifice and the altar at Jerusalem. At issue now is the relationship between the sacrifices of humanity at large and those of Israel. That accounts for the introduction of No. 3, a familiar item better situated (if it belongs at all) with the story of Abel's sacrifice, at which it is at least tangentially relevant. No. 3 goes its own way, taking up an issue to which the exegesis of the cited passage is peripheral. The discourse is fully spelled out, but in no way adds to the interpretation of the present passage. But the relevance to Gen. 8:21 cannot be missed, since at issue is whether God prefers a sacrifice in which the entire beast is burned up or one in which part of the beast is shared by the priest and the sacrifier. Nos. 4, 5 now take up the important link between the sacrifice of Noah and the cult of Israel. The true sacrifices to God come from those who give their lives for his name. Now in context we address those who accepted death by burning, equivalent to the burning up of the animals that produces the sweet smell God likes. So the blood-sacrifice is turned into a symbol for Israel's sacrifice of itself in God's name. The effect of the composition exceeds the contribution of the several discrete parts. For the point of the compositor is, first, Israel's sacrifices, offered at Jerusalem, succeed those of Noah, and, second, that those sacrifices really derive from the flesh and blood of the children of Israel, who offer themselves for God's name. The intersection of Israel's cultic history with the sacrifice of Noah so proves the main point to be read at the present passage, a substantial and important proposition indeed. But the proposition concerns not the cult in times past but the sacrifice of Israel in the present, as is made explicit at Nos. 4, 5.

XXXIV:X.

1. A. "The Lord said to his heart, ['I will never again curse the ground because of man, for the imagination of man's heart is evil from his youth']" (Gen. 8:21):

    B. [Reading the word "to his heart" to refer to someone in control of his heart, we interpret as follows:] The wicked act at the whim of their heart.

    C. "The fool has said *in* his heart" (Ps. 14:1). "And Esau said *in* his heart" (Gen. 27:41). "And Jeroboam said in *his* heart" (1 Kgs. 12:25). "Now Haman said *in* his heart" (Est. 6:6).

    D. But the righteous maintain their heart subject to their own control [speaking *to* their heart, as God does, and telling their heart what to do, rather than be governed by their heart's impulses, thus]:

    E. "Now Hannah spoke upon her heart" (1 Sam. 1:13). "And David said to his heart" (1 Sam. 27:1). "But Daniel placed upon his heart" (Dan. 1:8).

    F. "And the Lord said to his heart" (Gen. 8:21).

2. A. "I will not again curse the ground [and I shall never again destroy every living creature as I have done]" (Lev. 8:21):

B. Enough is enough.

C. And rabbis say, "'I shall not again' do so with reference to the children of Noah in particular, 'and I shall never again' do so, for all generations."

3. A. "For the imagination of man's heart is evil from his youth" (Gen. 8:21):

B. Said R. Hiyya the elder, "Miserable is the dough concerning which the baker herself testifies that it is no good: 'For the imagination of man's heart is evil from his youth.'"

C. Abba Yose the potter said, "Miserable is the yeast concerning which the one who kneaded it testifies that it is no good: 'For he knows our evil passions, he remembers that we are dust' (Ps. 103:14)."

D. Rabbis say, "Miserable is the planting when the one who planted it testifies that it is no good: 'For the Lord of hosts, who planted you, has spoken ill of you' (Jer. 11:17)."

4. A. Antoninus asked our rabbi, "At what point is the impulse to do evil placed in the human being?"

B. He said to him, "From the moment that the human being is formed."

C. He said to him, "If that were so, then the foetus would dig through the walls of the womb and come forth right away. Rather, it must be at the moment that the foetus comes forth."

D. Then Rabbi concurred with him, for what he said conformed to the statement of Scripture: "For the imagination of man's heart is evil from his youth" (Gen. 8:21).

E. R. Yudan said, "'From his youth' is written, 'from his awakening, that is, 'when he awakes to the world' [Freedman]."

F. He further asked him, "At what point is the soul placed in the human being?"

G. He said to him, "At the point at which the human being emerges from his mother's womb."

H. He said to him, "Put meat out without salt for three days. Will it not rot? Rather, it must be at that moment at which the human being is remembered [and God determines the life-story of the person, which is while the person is still in the womb]."

I. Then Rabbi concurred with him, for what he said conformed to the statement of Scripture: "All the while my soul is in me, and the spirit of God is in my nostrils" (Job 27:3), and it is written, "And your providence has preserved my spirit" (Job 10:12). "At what point did you put the soul in me? It is when you remembered me."

Nos. 1, 2 interpret the language of the cited verses. The comment of No. 3 takes up the substance of the verse, the situation in which God, who made man, registers so negative a judgment of him. No. 4 is included because of its reference to the verse at hand, though, obviously, the issue is not the interpretation of the language or sense of the verse. So we move from interest in the formulation to concern with the content, then, third, essentially miscellaneous observations in which the verse figures only tangentially.

XXXIV:XI.

1. A. "While the earth remains, seedtime and harvest, cold and heat, summer and winter, day and night shall not cease" (Gen. 8:22):

    B. R. Yudan in the name of R. Aha: "What were the children of Noah thinking? Was it that the covenant with them ['neither will I again destroy every living creature,' Gen. 8:21)] would last forever? Rather, only so long as heaven and earth lasted would the covenant with them endure. But when that day should come concerning which it is written, 'For the heavens shall vanish away like smoke, and the earth shall be worn out like a garment, (Is. 51:6), then: 'And [the covenant] will be broken in that day' (Zech. 11:11)."

2. A. Said R. Aha, "'What is it that made them rebel against me? Was it not because they sowed but did not reap, produced offspring and did not have to bury them?

    B. "Henceforward: 'Seedtime and harvest,' meaning that they will give birth and then have to bury their children.

    C. "'Cold and heat,' meaning they have have fever and ague.

    D. "'Summer and winter,' meaning: 'I shall give the birds the right to attack their summer crops,' in line with this verse, 'And the ravenous birds shall summer upon them and all the beasts of the earth shall winter upon them' (Is. 18:6)."

3. A. The story concerns one of the great authorities of the generation who had a headache. Some say it was R. Samuel b. Nahman.

    B. He said, "What has the generation of the flood done to us." ["Heat" referred to the high temperature behind his headache (Freedman, p. 276, n. 6).]

4. A. Another interpretation: "While the earth remains, [seedtime and harvest, cold and heat, summer and winter, day and night, shall not cease]" (Gen. 8:22):

    B. R. Yudan in the name of R. Aha: "What were the children of Noah thinking? Was it that the covenant with them ['neither will I again destroy every living creature,' Gen. 8:21)] would last forever? Rather, only so long as day and night endured, would the covenant with them endure.

C. "But when that day comes, concerning which it is written, 'And there shall be one day which shall be known as the Lord's, which is not day and not night' (Zech. 14:7), then: 'And it will be broken in that day' (Zech. 11:11)."

5. A. Said R. Isaac, "'What is it that made them rebel against me? Was it not because they sewed but did not reap?'"

B. For R. Isaac said, "Once every forty years they would sow a crop, and as they made their trip they would travel from one end of the world to the other in a brief span and cut down the cedars of Lebanon . And the lions and leopards made no more of an impression on them than did a louse on their skin."

C. How so? The climate for them was like the climate from Passover to Pentecost.

D. R. Simeon b. Gamaliel said in the name of R. Meir, and so said R. Dosa, "The latter half of Tishre, Marheshvan, and the first half of Kislev are for sowing, the second half of Kislev and Tebet and the first half of Shebat are winter, the latter half of Shebat and Adar and the first half of Nisan are the cold season, the second half of Nisan and Iyyar and the first half of Sivan are the harvest season, the second half of Sivan and Tammuz and the first half of Ab are summer, and latter half of Ab and Elul and the first half of Tishre are the hot season."

E. R. Judah counts from Marheshvan.

F. R. Simeon counts from Tishri.

6. A. Said R. Yohanan, "The planets did not function the entire twelve months [in which the flood took place] [and that means they had rest, in line with Noah's name]."

B Said R. Jonathan to him,"They served but they made no impression."

C R. Eleazer said, "'They shall not cease' (Gen. 8:22) indicates that they had never ceased.'"

D. R. Joshua said, "Since it says, 'They shall not cease' [in the future] it means they had ceased [in the past]."

Two distinct readings of the statement of Gen. 8:22 present themselves. The first emphasizes the limitations of the covenant made with humankind, that is, that covenant lasts up to the end-time but not beyond. The second reads the statement as essentially a curse, namely, humankind had rebelled under conditions of prosperity, so now they will have to endure "hot and cold," "seedtime and harvesttime," interpreted as misfortunes. The former of the two readings makes its appearance at Nos. 1, 4, and the latter, at Nos. 2-3, 5+6.

XXXIV:XII.

1.   A. "And God blessed Noah and his sons and said to them, 'Be fruitful and multiply and fill the earth'"(Gen. 9:1):

    B. [Since at Gen. 8:17, God has already told the inhabitants of the ark to be fruitful and multiply, what we have is a fresh blessing, now] on account of the sacrifices.

2.   A. "The fear of you and the dread of you [shall be upon every beast of the earth and upon every bird of the air, and upon everything that creeps on the ground and all the fish of the sea; into your hand they are delivered]" (Gen. 9:2):

    B. The fear and dread [Gen. 1:28) did come back, but dominion over the natural world [conferred at Gen. 1:28] did not return.

    C. At what point then did human dominion over the animals come back? It was in the time of Solomon: "For he had dominion over all the region" (1 Kgs. 5:4).

3.   A. [Contrasting the fear and dread of animals for living persons with their indifference to corpses,] R. Simeon b. Eleazar taught on Tannaite authority: "In the case of a one-day-old infant, people violate the Sabbath on his account [to save his life]. But in the case even of David, king of Israel, lying dead, people may not violate the Sabbath on his account."

    B. And so did R. Simeon say, "In the case of an infant one day old, who is alive, people do not have to keep from him rats and snakes, so that they will not bite his eyes [because they are afraid of him]. If a lion sees him it will flee, and if a snake sees him, it will flee. But in the case even of Og, king of Bashan, lying dead, people do have to guard his corpse.

    C. "For so long as a man is alive, fear of him is upon all other creatures, but when he is dead, fear of him is taken away from all other creatures.

    D. "That is in line with this verse: "Fear of you, so long as you are alive, shall be upon...' (Gen. 9:2) [a meaning imputed by a shift in vowels for the same consonants]."

Nos. 1 goes over the points of repetition among several versions of the story at hand, or of the present set of events, and explains why a given detail occurs more than once. No. 2 notes the absence of another anticipated detail and explains when it recurs, essentially a rerun of the former question. No. 3 then presents a rereading of the base verse in proof of a proposition distinct from the present passage. So No. 3 is syllogistic, in no way exegetical.

XXXIV:XIII.

1. A. "Every moving thing that lives shall be food for you, and as I gave you the green plants, I give you everything. Only you shall not eat flesh with its life, that is, its blood" (Gen. 9:3-4):

B. R. Yose b. R. Abin in the name of R. Yohanan: "The first man, who was not permitted to eat meat as a matter of mere appetite [and was permitted to eat only vegetables] was not admonished concerning not removing a limb from a living beast.

C. "But the children of Noah, who were permitted to eat meat as a matter of appetite, were admonished about not eating a limb cut from a living beast. [They were likely to want to cut a limb off a beast in order to eat the meat. They did not have to avoid all meat other than that produced by the sacrificial cult, but could eat meat whenever they wished. So the admonition was necessary.]."

2. A. "And surely your blood of your lives I will require" (Gen. 9:5):

B. The use of the word "and," which is understood to encompass an otherwise unstated category, serves to include one who hangs himself [so that a suicide is punishable]. [That is, God will not only punish someone for eating an animal's blood, Gern. 8:3-4, but also will punish someone who hangs himself.]

C. Is it possible that a suicide of someone *in extremis* such as Saul, would be encompassed?

D. Scripture accordingly uses the word "surely."

E. Is it possible that someone in the category of Hananiah, Mishael, and Azariah should be included in the prohibition of suicide [since they willingly gave up their lives for the sanctification of God's name]?

F. Scripture accordingly uses the word "surely."

3. A. "At the hand of every beast will I require it" (Gen. 9:5)

B. This refers to the four kingdoms [Babylonia, Media, Greece, and Rome, who are answerable for murders that they commit.]

C. "At the hand of man" (Gen. 9:5):

D. Said R. Levi, "That means, from the hand of the Edomite."

E. "Even at the hand of every man's brother" (Gen. 9:5). "Deliver me, I pray you, from the hand of my brother, from the hand of Esau" (Gen. 32:12).

F. "Will I require the life of man" (Gen. 9:5). This refers to Israel. "And you my sheep, the sheep of my pasture, are men" (Ez. 34:31).

The exegetes go over the verses, one by one, in each case imputing to a clause a meaning not visible to the untutored eye. I see no sustained polemic, nor is there cogency among the several observations. But Israel's history figures, both with regard to the sacrifice of one's life for God's sanctification and the role of the four kingdoms, with Esau/Edom/Rome at the climax. They are answerable for the blood that they shed. So even in what seems a neutral exposition, the fundamental polemic of the compositors makes its appearance.

XXXIV:XIV.

1. A. "Whoever sheds the blood of man, by man shall his blood be shed" (Gen. 9:6):

B. Said R. Haninah, "All of the following are laws that govern trials of children of Noah [as distinct from trials of Israelites accused of murder]:

C. "Such a person may be condemned on the testimony of a single witness, by the judgment of only one judge, without admonition in advance of the crime, for murder committed through an agent, and for murder of a foetus.

D. "[How do we know that such a trial may receive the testimony of] a single, unsubstantiated witness before a single judge? As it is said, 'Whoever sheds the blood of man, by man shall his blood be shed'
(Gen. 9:6).

E. "Without admonition in advance of the crime: 'Whoever sheds the blood of man, by man shall his blood be shed' (Gen. 9:6).

F. "For murder committed through an agent: 'Whoever sheds the blood of man, by man shall his blood be shed' (Gen. 9:6)-- meaning, 'by means of another person shall his blood be shed.'

G. "For the murder of a foetus: 'Whoever sheds the blood of man, by man shall his blood be shed' (Gen. 9:6)."

H. R. Yudah bar Simon said, "Also one who commits murder by strangling,

I. "and also one who strangles himself: 'Whoever sheds the blood of man, by man shall his blood be shed' (Gen. 9:6)."

2. A. Said R. Levi, "Lo, if someone murdered someone but was not himself put to death, when will he be put to death? When a man comes [that is, the last man, at the last judgment]:

B. "'Whoever sheds the blood of man, by [the last] man shall his blood be shed' (Gen. 9:6)."

3. A. R. Aqiba gave the following exposition: "Whoever sheds blood is regarded by Scripture as if he had diminished the image of God. What is the scriptural basis for that statement?

B. "'Whoever sheds the blood of man, by man shall his blood be shed' (Gen. 9:6).

C. "And on the basis of what further verse of Scripture: 'For God made man in his own image' (Gen. 9:6)."

D. R. Eleazar b. Azariah gave the following exposition: "Whoever gives up procreating is regarded by Scripture as if he had diminished the image of God.

E. "What is the scriptural basis for that statement? 'For God made man in his own image' (Gen. 9:6). And immediately thereafter it is written, 'And you, be fruitful and multiply, bring forth abundantly on the earth and multiply in it' (Gen. 9:7)."

F. Ben Azzai gave the following exposition: "Whoever gives up procreating is regarded by Scripture as if he had shed blood and diminished the image of God.

G. "What is the scriptural basis for the statement that it is as if he shed blood? 'Whoever sheds the blood of man...' On what account? 'For God made man in his own image' (Gen. 9:6). And immediately thereafter it is written, 'And you, be fruitful and multiply, bring forth abundantly on the earth and multiply in it' (Gen. 9:7)."

H. Said to him R. Eleazar, "Words are nice when they are spoken by people who really carry them out. Ben Azzai talks a good game but he doesn't do a thing."

I. He said to him, "It is because my soul lusts after the Torah. It is entirely possible for the world to be kept going by other people."

No. 1 links the passage at hand to laws governing the murder trial of a gentile, laws significantly more strict than those governing an Israelite's trial. That is to say, it is easier to convict a gentile than an Israelite. The exegesis links the rules to one word after another.

No. 2 is somewhat enigmatic, and my translation (following Freedman) is mere conjecture. No. 3 presents a closely related sequence of exegeses of the juxtapositions of Gen. 9:6 and 9:7, as cited. I see no real tie among the three units of exegesis of Gen. 9:6.

XXXIV:XV.

1. A. "And you, be fruitful and multiply, bring forth abundantly on the earth and multiply in it" (Gen. 9:7):

B. Said R. Simeon b. Laqish, "A covenant has been worked out even among diverse climates [to permit humanity to produce crops everywhere]. [Freedman, p. 281, n. 4: God has implanted in man a love of his native soil even in bad climates.]"

C. R. Simeon b. Laqish was laboring over Torah-study in a little forest in Tiberias. Two women came out of there. One said to the other, "Thank God we got out of that terrible air."

D. He called to them, "Where do you come from?"

E. One of them said to him, "From Mazga."

F. He said to them, "I know Mazga, and that town has only two dwellings."

G. He then said, "Blessed is he who has endowed with grace in the eyes of the locals the town in which they live."

2.   A. A disciple of R. Isi was in session before him. The master explained a matter to him, but he could not grasp it. He said to him, "Why cannot you grasp things?"

B. He said to him, "I am in exile from my place."

C. He said to him, "Where do you come from?"

D. He said to him, "From Gabat Shammai."

E. He said to him, "And what is the climate there?"

F. He said to him, "When a baby is born there, we have to crush spices and rub them on his head so that the mosquitos will not be able to eat him alive."

G. He then said, "Blessed is he who has endowed with grace in the eyes of the locals the town in which they live.

H. "And so in the future: 'And I will take away the stony heart out of your flesh and I will give you a heart of flesh (BSR)' (Ez. 36:26), meaning, 'a heart that does not envy (BSR) his fellow's portion.'"

The two stories clearly are meant to illustrate Simeon b. Laqish's statement, that people like the place in which they live. That is, they are satisfied with what they have. But I find at the conclusion a quite stunning link to the discourse on murder. That is, we have just been told that murder will be punished. Now we are further informed that at the eschatological finis, in the age to come, people will not envy one another. I see here the underlying notion that people murder out of envy. People in the end of time will accept and be happy with what they have, in whatever part of the earth they live, and so at that time the issue of Gen. 9:6-7 will be resolved. So an eschatological theme comes out of a this-worldly discourse on civilized colonization of the earth.

Chapter Two

Parashah Thirty-Five.   Genesis 9:8-17

XXXV:I.

1. A. "Then God said to Noah and his sons with him, 'Behold I establish my covenant with you and your descendants after you'" (Gen. 9:8-9):

    B. R. Judah said, "Because he violated the religious instruction [to procreate when he left the ark, and did not do so, but rather, planted a vineyard], therefore he was disgraced."

    C. R. Nehemiah said, "He [not only kept the religious instruction he had received but] added to it and behaved in sanctity. Therefore he and his sons enjoyed the merit of God's direct speech with them: 'And God said to Noah and his sons with him' (Gen. 9:8)." [Freedman explains Nehemiah's view: It was a more scrupulous observance of God's command. While God had forbidden marital relations in the ark only, Noah subdued his desires even after leaving the ark.]

    I take it the passage is inserted here, where it is out of phase with the biblical narrative, because of the proof text that serves Nehemiah, namely, Gen. 9:8. But that verse has not yet been subjected to explanation. In fact the compositors have nothing to say about the verse read on its own and not in some other connection.

XXXV:II.

1. A. "And God said, 'This is the sign of the covenant which I make between me and you and every living creature that is with you for all future generations'" (Gen. 9:12):

    B. Said R. Yudan, "What is written for 'generations' lacks the consonant that stands for the plural when it is fully spelled out, hence [there is an exclusion, and] what is excluded is two generations, the generation of Hezekiah and the generation of the men of the great assembly. [Those generations required no such sign, because they were righteous on their own.]"

    C. R. Hezekiah deletes the generation of the men of the great assembly and in their place introduces the generation of R. Simeon b. Yohai.

2.   Elijah, of blessed memory, and R. Joshua b. Levi were in session and repeating traditions together. They came to a teaching in the name of R. Simeon b. Yohai. They said [in response to a point that was unclear,"Let the master of the teaching come forth so that we can ask him our question."

B. Elijah of blessed memory went to join him in session.

C. [Simeon] said to him, "Who is with you?"

D. He said to him, "One of the great men of the generation, R. Joshua b. Levi."

E. [Elijah] said to him, "Has the rainbow ever appeared in his time? And if it has appeared, then he is not worthy of having me receive him [since he cannot be truly righteous]."

3.   A. R. Hezekiah in the name of R. Jeremiah: "So did R. Simeon b. Yohai say, 'Valley, valley! Be filled with golden denars!' And it filled up with golden denars."

4.   A. R. Hezekiah in the name of R. Jeremiah: "This is what R. Simeon b. Yohai said, "If he wants. Abraham can [Freedman:] intercede from his time to mine, and I can intercede from mine to the king-messiah.

B.   "'But if he does not want, then Ahijah the Shilnoite can join with me, and we together can intercede in behalf of all generations from Abraham to the king-messiah.""

5.   A. R. Hezekiah in the name of R., Jeremiah, "So too did R. Simeon b. Yohai say, 'The world never lacks thirty-six righteous men in the classification of Abraham. If they are three, my son and I are two of them. If they are twenty, my son and I are two of them. If they are ten, my son and I are two of them. If they are five, my son and I are two of them. If they are only two, my son and I are they.

B.   "'If only one remains, it is I.'"

1.C explains the insertion of the sequence of Simeon-b.-Yohai-sayings, all of which make the same point. The exegesis of the verse falls by the wayside. In this case we have no reason to doubt that Nos. 2ff. had joined 1.C prior to the insertion of the entire composition. Otherwise there is no reason for the composition to take the direction that it does.

XXXV:III.

1. A. "[God said, 'This is the sign of the covenant which I make between me and you and every living creature that is with you for all future generations.] I set my bow in the cloud, [and it shall be a sign of the covenant between me and the earth]'" (Gen. 9:12-13):

    B. The consonants for the word "bow" may be read as "likeness," thus [the verse may be interpreted as follows]: "My likeness, something that may draw an analogy to me."

    C. Is such a thing possible? [Surely not.]

    D. Rather, just as straw looks like grain, so [the bow looks like God].

2. A. "When I bring clouds over the earth, and the bow is seen in the clouds, I will remember my covenant which is between me and you and every living creature of all flesh, and the waters shall never again become a flood to destroy all flesh.] When the bow is in the clouds, [I will look upon it and remember the everlasting covenant between God and every living creature of all flesh that is upon the earth" (Gen. 9:15-16):

    B. R. Yudan in the name of R. Judah in the name of R. Simon, "This is analogous to one who had in his hand hot flour. He tried to give it to his son, but gave it to his servant." [Freedman: In his anger he was going to pour it on his son, but instead restrained himself and gave it to his servant. So too, God promises to bring the clouds on the earth, but not on humanity.]

    C. There was this incident. R. Isaac, R. Jonathan, and R. Yudan bar Giori went to listen to the exposition of a passage of the Torah by R. Simeon b. Yohai. There are those who say that it was the passage that deals with libations. They took their leave of him and waited there yet another day. They then said, "We have once again to take our leave of him."

    D. [Explaining why it was necessary once more to get permission from the master to leave,] one of them expounded, "'So Joshua blessed them and sent them away, and they went into their tents' (Josh. 22:6). Why then does Scripture further state, 'Moreover when Joshua sent them away to their tents, he blessed them' (Josh. 22:7)?

    E. "At the time that the Israelites were in the process of conquering and dividing the land, the tribe of Reuben and Gad were with them, laboring with them for fourteen years in the conquest and division of the land. After fourteen years they took their leave of Joshua, gaining permission to return to their tents. But they remained there another few days, so they returned and took their leave of him yet another time. That is why it is written, 'Moreover, when Joshua sent them away' (Josh. 22:7)."

    F. Said R. Yudan, "The tribes of Reuben and Gad formed part of the extended family of Joshua, so he accompanied them to the Jordan. When they saw that his extended family had now diminished in number, they then went and accompanied him back to his house. [Therefore they took their leave of Joshua a second time. This is why] the second blessing, then, was greater than the first, in line with this statement of Scripture: 'And he spoke to them, saying, "Return with much wealth to your tents"' (Josh. 22:8)."

G. Another of them gave the following exposition: "It is written, 'On the eighth day he sent the people away, and they blessed the king' (1 Kgs. 8:66). If so, why is it further stated, 'And on the twenty-third day of the seventh month he sent the people away and they blessed the king' (1 Chr. 7:10)? It is because they took their leave waited for a few days, and then, before leaving, went and took their leave yet a second time. On that account it is written, 'And on the twenty-third day of the seventh month he sent the people away and they blessed the king' (1 Chr. 7:10)."

H. Said R. Levi, "It is written, 'For they kept the dedication of the altar for seven days and the feast [of Tabernacles [for seven days' (1 Chr. 7:9). Now there is not a week prior to Tabernacles which does not contain both the Sabbath and the Day of Atonement. Those seven days, however, the Israelites ate and drank and made merry and lit candles. At the end of the week they were pained by the matter. They said, 'Is it possible that we have been guilty of the sin of profaning the Sabbath and also of eating on the Day of Atonement?' So as to make them feel better, making sure they knew that the Holy One, blessed be he, had approved what they had done, an echo came forth and said to them, 'All of you are destined to inherit the age to come.' So the latter blessing was greater than the former: 'On the eighth day he sent the people away, and they blessed the king. And they returned to their tents happy and glad of heart.' (1 Kgs. 8:66)."

I. Said R. Isaac, "'They were happy' because they found their wives in a state of cleanness [and so able to have sexual relations when they got home] 'and glad of heart' because the wives became pregnant with male children.'"

J. Said R. Levi, "An echo came forth and declared, 'All of you are destined for the age to come.'"

K. Yet another gave this exposition [to prove the same point, that yet again they have to get permission to leave:] "'So she went from him' (2 Kgs. 4:5) [speaking of the woman for whom Elisha had performed the miracle of making more oil than she originally had]. Why then does Scripture say, 'Then she came and told the man of God [that the miracle had taken place]' (2 Kgs. 4:7)? [Since it is said,] 'And the oil lasted' (2 Kgs. 4:6), it indicated that the price of oil had gone up, so she came to ask whether or not she should sell. For this reason the latter blessing was greater than the former: 'And you live and your sons of the rest' (2 Kgs. 4:7), that is, until the resurrection of the dead.'"

L. When [Simeon b. Yohai] recognized that these were men of such well-established learning, he sent with them a pair of disciples to find out what they were discussing on the way. One of them gave this exposition: "'And the angel of God, who went before the camp of Israel, left and went behind' (Ex. 14:19). Then why is it further stated, 'And the pillar of cloud went from before them and stood behind them' (Ex. 14:19)? What it means is that measure of strict justice that the Holy One, blessed be he, had originally stretched out against Israel did he reverse himself and stretched forth against the Egyptians."

M. Another of them gave this exposition: "'When the bow is in the clouds, I will look upon it and remember the everlasting covenant between God and every living creature of all flesh that is upon the earth' (Gen. 9:16). When the verse says, 'between God,' it refers to the measure of strict justice that is above, 'and every living creature of all flesh' refers to the measure of strict justice that is below, on earth. The measure of strict justice that applies above is more strict than the measure of strict justice that applies below, which is more gentle."

N. Another of them gave this exposition: "One verse of Scripture says, 'For wisdom is better than rubies, and all things desirable are not to be compared to her' (Prov. 8:11). Another verse says, 'And all your desirable things are not to be compared to her' (Prov. 3:15). 'Desirable things' speaks of the carrying out of religious duties and also supererogatory good deeds. 'Your desirable things' refers to precious stones and pearls."

O. R. Aha in the name of R. Tanhuma bar Hiyya: "'My desirable things and your desirable things' are not compared to her, since [it is said,] 'But let him who glories glory in this, that he understands and knows me' (Jer. 9:23)."

The entire composition is inserted because of L. Here is a fine example of how the compositors make use of available materials, sometimes with good effect, other times not.

Chapter Three

Parashah Thirty-Six.   Genesis 9:18-27

XXXVI:I.

1. A. "The sons of Noah who went forth from the ark were Shem, Ham, and Japheth. [Ham was the father of Canaan. These three were the sons of Noah, and from these the whole earth was peopled]" (Gen. 9:18):

   B. "When he gives quietness, who then can condemn? [When he hides his face, who can set him right, whether it be a nation or a man? that a godless man should not reign, that he should not ensnare the people]" (Job 34:29).

   C. [In Leviticus Rabbah, the following, at Lev.R. V:I.1.Aff., serves Lev. 4:3:] R. Meir interpreted the matter as follows: "'When he is quiet' in his world, 'when he hides his face' in his world.

   D. "The matter may be compared to the case of a judge who draws a veil inside [over his face] and so does not see what goes on outside."

   E. They said to him, "That's enough from you, Meir."

   F. He said to them, "What is it that is written? 'When he is quiet, who can condemn? When he hides his face, who can set him right?'[So the people of the generation of the flood thought: "The thick clouds will cover him, so he will not see what we do" (Job 22:14)."]

   G. "They thought, 'Since he gave tranquillity to the generation of the flood, who could come and condemn them?'

   H. "And what sort of tranquillity did he give them? 'Their children are established in their presence, and their offspring before their eyes. [Their houses are safe from fear, and no rod of God is upon them]' (Job. 21:8). [We shall now explain the meaning of that sort of prosperity and tranquillity.]"

2. A. "They send forth their little ones like a flock" (Job 21:11):

   B. R. Levi said, "In three days their wives would become pregnant and give birth. Here it is said, 'established,' and elsewhere, the same word appears in this way: 'Be established in three days' (Ex. 19:15). Just as the word, 'established' used there involves a span of three days, so the word 'established' used here means a span of three days."

- 25 -

C. Rabbis say, "In a single day a woman would get pregnant and give birth. Here the word 'established' is used and elsewhere: 'And be established in the morning' (Ex. 34:2). Just as the word 'established' stated there involves a single day, so the word established used here involves a single day."

3. A. "And their children before their eyes" (Job 21:8): for they saw children and grandchildren.

B. "They send forth their little ones like a flock, [and their children dance]" (Job 21:11):

C. [The word for children means 'their young,' for] said R. Levi, "In Arabia for children they use the word 'the young.'"

D. "And their children dance" (Job 21:11) like devils, in line with this verse: "And satyrs will dance there" (Is. 13:21).

4. A. When one of them would give birth by day, she would say to her son, "Go and bring me a flint, so I can cut your umbilical cord."

B. If she gave birth by night, she would say to her son, "Go and light a lamp for me, so I can cut your umbilical cord."

C. There was a case in which a woman gave birth by night and said to her son, "Go and light a lamp for me, so I can cut your umbilical cord."

D. When he went out to get it, [a devil,] Asmodeus, [head of the spirits], met him and said to him, "Go, boast to your mother that the cock has crowed, but if the cock had not crowed, I would have beaten and killed you."

E. He said to him, "Go and boast to your mother that my mother had not yet cut my umbilical cord, for if my mother had cut my umbilical cord, I would have beaten and killed *you*."

F. [This is in line with the following verse:] "Their houses are safe from fear" (Job 21:9), meaning, from destructive spirits.

G. "And no rod of God is upon them" (Job 21:9) meaning that they are free of suffering.

H. But when God hid his face from them, who can come and say to him, "You have not done right"?

I. And how indeed did he hide his face from them? [It was when he brought the flood on him:] "Whether it be to a nation or a man together" (Job 34:29). "To a nation" refers to the generation of the flood. "To a man together" refers to Noah, from whom the world was established.

J. And he can perfectly well rebuild his world from a nation or he can rebuild it from a single individual: "And the sons of Noah..." (Gen. 9:18).

The intersection with the story of the Flood is familiar: reading passages of Job. The larger polemic of the construction as a whole is not entirely articulated. Reviewing the entire construction as it appears in Lev. R. V:I-III, we know the point. It is that, if for a while, the wicked enjoy prosperity, in the end they suffer. Meir refers to God's failure to intervene, and the remainder, to the end, stresses that the generation of the Flood had every reason to suppose they would not be punished for their wickedness. But they were punished. So to begin with God is quiet, but, later on, hiding his face, he punishes. From our viewpoint the interesting side is the introduction of Noah. God can rebuild humanity from a single individual, Noah. But, the passage concludes, God can also rebuild the world from a nation.

My sense is that, as before the exegete-compositor wishes to say that Israel forms the counterpart to the salvific figures in times past, and that God can, and will, destroy and rebuild the world, now substituting Israel, the people, for Noah. That does not seem to me farfetched.

In the present case, if we compare the utilization of the construction in Leviticus Rabbah with that before us, we find a quite different purpose for the inclusion of the discourse. At Leviticus Rabbah, with reference to the priest who brings guilt on the people, Lev. 4:3, Noah serves as the counterpart and opposite. That is why Noah is introduced. That is, one may bring guilt upon the entire people, but one also may bring merit to the entirety of humanity, as Noah was such a one. But whatever polemic operates in Leviticus Rabbah is not fully exhausted in the passage at hand, since the exegesis runs on for several more units (Lev. R. V:I-III). The climax there, at Lev. R. V:III.13, defines a clear point of intersection with Lev. 4:3.

So we see that the compositors take a vigorous role in reshaping received materials and giving them that character and purpose that the compositors, not the original framers or authors, wished to emphasize.

XXXVI:II.

1. A. "Mighty men do evil that is unfathomable" (Job 34:24):

    B. The men of the generation of the Flood did evil deeds.

    C. "That is unfathomable" means that there was no limit to their wicked actions.

    D. "And he sets others in their stead" (Job 34:24), meaning the children of Noah: "And the sons of Noah" (Gen. 9:18). [They took the place of the wicked.]

2. A. "Yes, since the day was I am he, and there is none who can deliver out of my hand" (Is. 43:13):

    B. No one can save the nations of the world out of my hand.

C. "I shall act, and who can reverse it" (Is. 43:13);

D. "As to all the deeds and plans that I worked out with regard to the generation of the Flood, who can say to me, 'You did not do things rightly.'"

E. For truly Noah went in whole and came out whole: "And the sons of Noah..." (Gen. 9:18).

3. A. "And Ham is the father of Canaan" (Gen. 9:18), the source of degradation.

4. A. "These three were the sons of Noah, and from these the whole world was peopled" (Gen. 9:19), to be compared to the case of a large fish that scattered its eggs and filled the world.

Nos. 1 and 2 treat the sons of Noah as the counterpart of humanity, that had been wiped out in the flood. No. 3 makes an episodic comment, and No. 4 spells out the plausibility of the statement of Scripture.

XXXVI:III.

1. A. "Noah began to till the soil. He planted a vineyard" (Gen. 9:20):

B. [Since the word for "began" uses consonants that can produce the word for "become profane," we interpret the cited verse in this way:] He was made common [no longer holy] and became profane.

C. Why? "Because he planted a vineyard."

D. Ought he not to have planted something valuable, such as a young fig-shoot or olive shoot? Instead: "He planted a vineyard" (Gen. 9:20). [Wine causes degradation; Noah made a poor choice.]

2. A. Where did he get it?

B. R. Abba bar Kahana said, "He brought in shoots [e.g., of vines] for the elephants, shrubbery for the deer, glass for the ostriches."

C. [The version at hand omits the following: R. Levi said, "He brought vine shoots for vine plantings, fig shoots for fig trees, olive shoots for olive trees." In the view of R. Abba bar Kahana, the meaning of, "and it shall serve as food for you and for them" means that it must be both for you and for the animals. In the view of R. Levi, "'And it shall serve as food for you and for them" means that you are the principal concern, and they are secondary.] That is in line with the following verse of Scripture: "And gather it for you" indicates that someone gathers something only if he needs it later on.

[Freedman, p. 248, n. 1: He understands "gather" to mean store, hence, it means for future use.]"

3. A. "The first tiller of the soil" (Gen. 9:20):

B. There were three who lusted after the soil, and no good ever came of them: Cain, Noah, and Uzziah.

C. Cain: "Cain a tiller of the ground" (Gen. 4:2).

D. Noah: "Noah the tiller of the soil" (Gen. 9:20).

E. Uzziah: "For he loved husbandry" (2 Chr. 26:10). [Freedman, p. 181, n. 6: Cain became a murderer, Noah a drunkard, and Uzziah a leper.]

4. A. "Tiller of the soil" [Hebrew: man of the earth]:

B. He was called by that title because, on his account the earth was saved, and also because his descendants covered the face of the earth.

C. "Man of the earth:" in the way in which the guard of a fortress bears the name of that fortress.

5. A. Said R. Berekhiah, "Moses was more beloved than Noah. Noah once was called 'a righteous man' (Gen. 6:9), but in the end was called 'a man of the earth.'

B. "But Moses at first was called, 'An Egyptian man' (Ex. 2:19), but in the end was called, 'A man of God' (Deut. 33:1).

C. "[So he was more beloved] than Noah, who in the end was castrated."

6. A. "He planted a vineyard" (Gen. 9:20):

B. When he was going out to plant the vineyard, the demon, Asmodeus, met him, saying to him, "You can join me in this partnership, but be very careful not to come into my share of the deal, and if you do come into my share of the deal, I am going to clobber you."

No. 1 makes a negative comment on what Noah did, finding the basis in the cited passage. No. 2 answers an obvious question. No. 3 goes over the same point as No. 1, now introducing an independent construction to express the same negative evaluation of what Noah did. No. 4 explains why Noah was given the title, "man of the earth." No. 5 predictably introduces the comparison of Noah and Moses, reading the verses that speak of each as "a man of..." and then pointing to the striking difference in formulation, a good piece of specific exegesis to make a general point. No. 6 introduces an extraneous item.

XXXVI:IV.

1. A. "And he drank of the wine and became drunk" (Gen. 9:20):

    B. He drank without restraint [beyond the proper measure] and so became drunk and was shamed.

    C. Said R. Hiyya, "On that same day he planted the vineyard, drank the wine, and suffered shame."

2. A. "And he lay uncovered in his tent" (Gen. 9:21):

    B. R. Judah bar Simon, R. Hanan in the name of R. Samuel b. R. Isaac: "What is written is not 'lay uncovered' but 'uncovered himself,' and [since the consonants of the word for 'uncover' can yield the meaning, 'exile,' we may read the passage to indicate that it was that sort of drunkenness that] brought about both for himself and generations to come the penalty of exile.

    C. "The ten tribes were exiled only on account of wine, in line with this verse: 'Woe to those who get up early in the morning to follow strong drink' (Is. 5:11).

    D. "The tribes of Judea and Benjamin went into exile only on account of wine, in line with this verse: 'But these also erred through wine' (Is. 28:7)."

3. A. "...and lay uncovered in his tent" (Gen. 9:21):

    B. The word for "his tent" is written as if it were to be read "in her tent," namely, in the tent of his wife.

    C. Said R. Huna in the name of R. Eliezer, "When Noah went out of the ark, a lion mauled him and mutilated his sexual organs, so that, when he had sexual relations, his seed scattered and on that account he was shamed."

4. A. Said R. Yohanan, "You should never lust for wine, for through the passage that deals with wine, the word 'woe' is written [through appropriate consonantal arrangements] no fewer than fourteen times [in that the combination of WY appears in various words, as follows:]

    B. "'And Noah was the first tiller of the soil. He planted a vineyard, and he drank of the wine and became drunk and lay uncovered in his tent. And Ham, the father of Canaan, saw the nakedness of his father and told his two brothers outside. Then Shem and Japheth took a garment, laid it upon both their shoulders, and covered the nakedness of their father; their faces were turned away, and they did not see their father's nakedness. When Noah awoke from his wine and knew what his youngest son had done to him, he said, "Cursed be Canaan"' (Gen. 9:20-25)."

No. 1 seems to me simply to state the gist of the story. No. 2 links the story to the history of Israel, finding the downfall of the Northern, then the Southern kingdom to fit the paradigm of Noah's humiliation. No. 3 introduces another recurrent motif, namely, sexual misdeed. No. 4 then provides a general thematic statement, drawing on the passage at hand for facts in support of the announced syllogism.

XXXVI:V.

1. A. "And Ham, the father of Canaan, saw the nakedness of his father, and told his two brothers outside" (Gen. 9:22):

B. He said to them, "The first man had two sons, and one of them went and killed the other. Now this one has three and he wants to produce a fourth."

C. "He told them" means "he persuaded them" [Freedman].

2. A. Said R. Jacob bar Zabedi, "What is the verse of Scripture that indicates that a slave goes forth free if the master knocks out his tooth or his eye?

B. "It is the following: 'He saw..and he told...' (Gen. 9:22). [He saw with his eye, he reported with his mouth. Since he is the prototype of the slave, he goes free when he has received his punishment for seeing and telling.]"

The gap in the biblical account, which omits reference to what, exactly, Ham told the brothers, is filled. The comment weaves a common narrative out of diverse snippets. But the effort to link the story at hand, in its details, to other laws and stories, persists.

XXXVI:VI.

1. A. "Then Shem and Japheth took a garment, laid it upon their shoulders, walked backward, and covered the nakedness of their father" (Gen. 9:23):

B. Said R. Yohanan, "Shem undertook the religious duty first, then Japheth came and concurred in his action. Therefore Shem [who stands for Israel] had the merit of wearing the fringed cloak [*tallit*], while Japheth [who stands for Greece] got the *pallium*. [Freedman, p. 292, n. 1: The reward of Shem, the ancestor of the Jews, was the precept of fringes,(Num. 15:38), while that of Japheth, the Greek, was the *pallium*, a cloak betokening his dignity.]"

2. A. "They laid it upon both their shoulders" (Gen. 9:23):

B. Since the verse explicitly states, "They walked backward and covered the nakedness of their fathers," may we not conclude that "they did not see their father's nakedness"?

C. What the formulation teaches is that they put their hands over their faces and walked backward [while facing Noah, so as not to turn their backs on him, which would have been disrespectful], and so [while preserving his dignity,] they paid him that respect that is owing for the father by the son.

D. Said the Holy One, blessed be he, to Shem, "You covered up the nakedness of your father. By your life, I shall pay you a just reward: 'When these men are bound in their cloaks...' (Dan. 3:21). [Freedman, p. 292, n. 4: 'When Shadrach, Mesach, and Abed-nego your descendants are cast into the fiery furnace, I will save them.']"

E. R. Yudan and R. Huna:

F. R. Yudan said, "As to the meaning of the word for 'in their cloaks,' it means, 'In their official robes.'"

G. [Reverting to the discourse of D, broken off at E-F:] Said the Holy One, blessed be he, to Japheth, "You covered up the nakedness of your father. By your life, I shall pay you a just reward: 'It shall come to pass in that day that I will give to Gog a place fit for burial in Israel' (Ez. 39:11)."

H. Said the Holy One, blessed be he, to Ham, "You treated with scorn your father's nakedness. By your life, I shall pay you back a just reward: 'So shall the king of Assyria lead away the captives of Egypt and the exiles of Ethiopia, young and old, naked and barefoot, and with buttocks uncovered to the shame of Egypt' (Is. 20:4)."

The effect of Yohanan's comment, No. 1, is to restate the link between Israel's everyday way of life -- in this case, the wearing of fringes upon the garment -- and the story of the history of humanity. No. 2 supplies a sizable discourse on the future history of the three brothers.

XXXVI:VII.

1. A. When Noah awoke from his wine" (Gen. 9:24):

   B. having sobered up.

2. A. "He knew what his smallest son had done to him" (Gen. 9:24):

   B. "The smallest son" means "the son who was useless," in line with this verse: "Because the brazen altar that was before the Lord was too small to receive the burned offering" (1 Kgs. 8:64).

3. A. "He said, 'Cursed be Canaan'" (Gen. 9:25):

   B. Should Ham be the one who sinned yet Canaan [his descendant] be cursed?

C. R. Judah and R. Nehemiah:'

D. R. Judah said, "It is because it is said, 'And God blessed Noah and his sons' (Gen. 9:1). Now there cannot be a cursing where there has been a blessing. Accordingly, he said, 'Cursed be Canaan.' [He could not curse Ham, so he cursed his descendant.]"

E. R. Nehemiah said, "It was Canaan who saw and informed the others. Therefore the curse is assigned to the one who is ruined."

4. A. "Said R. Berekhiah, "Noah in the ark was most distressed that he had no young son to take care of him. He said, 'When I shall get out of this ark, I shall produce a young son to take care of me.'

B. "When Ham had done the disgraceful deed, he said, 'You are the one who stopped me from producing a young son to to take care of me, therefore that man himself [you] will be a servant to his brothers.'"

C. R. Huna in the name of R. Joseph: "'You are the one who prevented me from producing a fourth son, therefore I curse your fourth son [corresponding to the fourth son I never had].'"

D. R. Huna in the name of R. Joseph: "'You are the one who stopped me from doing something that is done in darkness, therefore your seed will be ugly and dusky.'"

5. A. Said R. Hiyya, "Ham and a dog had sexual relations in the ark. Therefore Ham came forth dusky, and the dog, for his part, has sexual relations in public [both being marks of what they had done in private]."

B. Said R. Levi, "The matter may be compared to the case of someone who coined his own coins [showing his visage] doing so in the very residence of the king himself. The king declared, 'I decree that his effigy be defaced and his coins declared counterfeit.'

C. "So too, Ham and the dog had sexual relations in the ark and both of them were smitten."

Nos. 1, 2 explain the sense of Scripture and point to the meaning of its word choices. The remaining compositions explain the curse of Canaan. No. 3 asks the urgent question and supplies an answer credible in context. No. 4 pursues the same line of thought. Ham's deeds in regard to his father provoked the curse. Then No. 5 introduces a different approach to answering the same question. Now it is what Ham himself did in sexual misconduct that marked his descendants.

XXXVI:VIII.

1. A. "He also said, 'Blessed by the Lord my God be Shem, and let Canaan be his slave. God enlarge Japheth, and let him dwell in the tents of Shem; and let Canaan be his slave'" (Gen. 9:26-27):

B. The blessing of Japheth refers to Cyrus, who decreed that the house of the sanctuary be rebuilt.

C. Nonetheless: "Let him dwell in the tents of Shem" (Gen. 9:27).

D. The presence of God comes to rest only in the tents of Shem.

2. A. [Explaining the reference to Japheth's living in the tents of Shem in a different way,] said Bar Qappara, "Let words of Torah in the language of Japheth [Greek] be spoken in the tents of Shem." [It is proper to study the Torah in Greek.]

B. R. Yudan said, "On the basis of this verse we have evidence that the translation of the Scripture into other languages is permissible:

C. "'And they read in the book, in the Torah of God' (Neh. 8:8). That passage refers to Scripture. 'Distinctly' refers to a translation. 'And they gave the sense' speaks of the punctuation. 'And caused them to understand the reading' speaks of the beginnings of the verses" [all: Freedman].

D. R. Hiyya bar Luliani said, "This refers to the grammatical sequence of words" [Freedman].

E. Rabbis of Caesarea say, "On the basis of that reference, we find the legitimacy of following the received text [in a vocalization not in accord with the text as it is written out]."

3. A. R. Zira and R. Hananel in the name of Rab: "Even though someone is sufficiently fluent in the Torah as to rival Ezra, he should not recite Scripture from memory and so write it down [but should only copy what is written]."

B. But has it not been taught on Tannaite authority: There was the case of R. Meir, who was in Assya, and, finding no scroll of Esther available, he recited it from memory and wrote it down?

C. There [in Babylonia] they say that he wrote out two scrolls, the first of which was put into storage, and the second approved for use [since the second was copied from a written scroll, namely, the first].

No. 1 makes explicit the relationship of the blessing of Japheth, meaning Greece, to the history of Israel. No. 2 then moves into a less concrete range of interest, asking about the relationship between the translation of the Torah into Greek and the life of the house of Shem, namely, Israel. Translation is approved. Obviously, the exegetes cannot read the passage at hand out of relationship to the history of Israel, since they find explicit the reference to Israel in the name of Shem. No. 3 expands on 2.E. Clearly No. 3 had joined No. 2 before the whole found its position here.

Chapter Four

Parashah Thirty-Seven.   Genesis 10:2-30

XXXVII:I.

1. A. "The sons of Japheth: Gomer, Magog, [Madai, Javan, Tubal, Meshech, and Tiras]" (Gen. 10:2):

    B. Said R. Samuel bar Ammi, "[Reference is made to] Africa, Germany, Media, Macedonia, and Mysia."

    C. "And Tiras" (Gen. 10:2);

    D. R. Simon said, "Persia."

    E. Rabbis say, "Thrace."

2. A. "The sons of Gomer: Ashkenaz, Riphath, and Togarmah" (Gen. 10:3):

    B. Assya, Adiabene, and Germania.

    C. R. Berekhiah said, "Germanica."

3. A. "The sons of Javan: Elishah, Tarshish, Kittim, and Dodanim" (Gen. 10:4):

    B. Hellas, Taras, Italia, and Dardania.

    C. One verse of Scripture speaks of "Dodanim," while at another passage it is "Rodanim" (1 Chr. 1:7).

    D. R. Simon said, "It is 'Dodanim,' [the word for uncle is *dod*] because they descend from Israel's relations, and 'rodanim' [the word for oppress is *rodeh*] because they come and oppress them [the roots being DD and RD, respectively]."

    E. Said R. Hanan, "When Israel is on the rise, they call themselves 'children of your uncle,' but when they are on the decline, they come and oppress them."

The exegete identifies various descendants with particular regions and peoples inhabiting those regions. No. 3 links the whole to Israel's history.

XXXVII:II.

1. A. "The sons of Ham: Cush, Egypt, Put, and Canaan" (Gen. 10:6):

     B. Said R. Simeon b. Laqish, "We might have imagined that the family of Put was assimilated [into other families, since they are not spelled out as are those of Cush, Egypt, and Canaan,] so Ezekiel came along and spelled out who they are: 'Ethiopia and Put and Lud and all the mingled people...shall fall' (Ez. 30:5)."

2. A. "Cush became the father of Nimrod; he was the first on earth to be a mighty man" (Gen. 10:8).

     B. That is in line with this verse: "Shiggaon of David, which he sang to the Lord, concerning Cush, a Benjaminite" (Ps. 7:1).

     C. R. Joshua b. R. Nehemiah in the name of R. Hinena bar Isaac: "This corresponds to the podium of that wicked man [Esau].

     D. "Now was Esau an Ethiopian? [Certainly not.] But what happened is that he did the things that Nimrod did, [that is, hunting people down, and so was regarded as his descendant]. That is in line with this verse: '*Like* Nimrod, a mighty hunter before the Lord' (Gen. 10:9).

     E. "What is written is not 'a mighty hunter was Nimrod,' but rather 'was *like* Nimrod.' Just as that one acted like a hunter in catching people by slips of the tongue, so this one acts like a hunter in snaring people by slips of the tongue.

     F. "[For example, the prosecutor says,] 'So you did not steal, but who was the thief with you?' 'So you did not kill, but who was the murderer who was with you?' [Reveal your accomplice.']"

     No. 1 clarifies the cited passage, and No. 2 builds a lesson on the basis of a somewhat abbreviated exegesis. The main point is to identify Esau, that is Rome, with those who hunt people down, like Nimrod. This seems somewhat far-fetched, except as part of the on-going search for links among all the peoples to the history of Israel.

XXXVII:III.

1. A. "He was a mighty hunter" (Gen. 10:9):

     B. When the word "he" is used with stress, as in this case, in five instances it speaks of an evil person, and in five, a good one.

     C. The five times that the use of "he" with emphasis indicates a wicked character are as follows:

D. "He was a mighty hunter" (Gen. 10:9).   "He is Esau, father of the Edomites" (Gen. 36:43). "He is that Dathan and Abiram" (Num. 26:9). "He is the same king, Ahaz" (2 Chr. 28:22). "He is Ahasuerus" (Est. 1:1).

E. The five times the use of he" with emphasis indicates a good character are as follows:

F. "Abram, he is the same as Abraham" (1 Chr. 1:27). "He is Moses and Aaron" (Ex. 6:27). "He is Aaron and Moses" (Ex. 6:26). "He is Hezekiah" (2 Chr. 32:30). "He is Ezra, who went up" (Ezra 7:6).

G. R. Berekhiah in the name of the rabbis over there [in Babylonia} said, "There is another, best of all: 'He is the Lord our God' (Ps. 105:7), indicating that the measure of his mercy is forever."

The syllogism utilizes the verse at hand, but obviously is not constructed with the exegesis of the present verse as focus. But the point -- a negative judgment on the principal character -- is consistent with the foregoing, which is why the compositor selected the passage.

XXXVII:IV.

1. A. "The beginning of his kingdom was Babel, Erech, and Accad, all of them in the land of Shinar" (Gen. 10:10):

    B. The verse speaks of Edessa, Nisibis, and Ctesiphon.

    C. "In the Land of Shinar" (Gen. 10:10) refers to Babylonia.

2. A. "The word 'Shinar' indicates that the land is emptied out of [the possibility of doing various] religious duties [a play on the root used in the name Shinar]; for example, there is no possibility there [outside of the Holy Land] of carrying out the religious duty of separating the priestly rations from the crop, of designating tithes out of the crop, or of observing the rules of the Seventh Year.

    E. The word Shinar further indicates that when the people die there, it is in agony, without light, without a bath.

    F. The word Shinar further means that the princes there die young [a play on the root used in the name Shinar, meaning young].

    G. The word Shinar finally means that the princes there trample on the Torah while they are young. [The exilarch was reputed to be ignorant of the Torah.]

3. A. "From that land he went into Assyria [and built Nineveh, Rehoboth-Ir, Calah, and Resen, between Nineveh and Calah, that is the great city]" (Gen. 10:11-12):

B. From the counsel [to build a great city, Gen. 11:1-9] Assyria separated himself.

C. When he saw that the others were coming to take issue with the Holy One, blessed be he, he left his country. Said the Holy One, blessed be he, to him, "You abandoned four places [Babylonia, Erech, Accad, and Calneh], so, by your life, I shall give you four places: 'He built Nineveh, Rehoboth-Ir, Calah, and Resen, between Nineveh and Calah' (Gen. 10:12)."

D.. "Resen" is the same as Talsar.

E. But [Assyria] did not do [what he had planned, and he did join in a conspiracy against God]. When he came and allied himself with those who were destroying the house of the sanctuary, the Holy One, blessed be he, said to him, "Yesterday you were a fledgling, but today you have gone back to being a mere egg. Yesterday you flew about on wings of religious duties and good deeds. But now you are closed off like an egg. Therefore: 'They have been an arm to the children of Lot' (Ps. 83:9), that is, 'a curse' [a play on the name of Lot]"

4. A. "Resen, between Nineveh and Calah; that is the great city" (Gen. 10:12):

B. We do not know, in the cited verse, whether Resen is the great city or Nineveh is the great city. When the Scripture states, "And Nineveh was a great city," (Jonah 3:5), we must conclude that the reference to "great" here speaks of Nineveh.

As before, we work our way through the verses by explaining them at two levels. First comes a factual level at which we identify a given place or people with a known point in the world of the exegete. Then we turn to a moralizing exegesis, imputing to the name certain traits of character. No. 1 provides the former, No. 2 the latter. No. 3 proceeds to draw an explicit link between the verse at hand and Israel's history. No. 4 provides a minor clarification of the sense of a component of the verse. The order is fairly uniform throughout, as we notice.

XXXVII:V.

1. A. "Egypt became the father [of Ludim, Anamim, Lehabim, Nephtuhim, Pathrusim, Casluhim, whence came the Philistines, and Caphtorim]" (Gen. 10:13-14):

B. Said R. Abba bar Kahana, "All of the coinage of Egypt is only debased.

C. "[Following Freedman:] the name 'Pathrusim' denotes degradation, Casluhim, shame ."

D. Said R. Abba bar Kahana, "The men of Pathrusim and Casluhim organized bazaars. They snatched one another's wives, and what came of them? Philistines and Caphtorim. The Philistines were giants, the Caphtorim, dwarfs."

The identification jumps directly to the moral matter.

XXXVII:VI.

1. A. "Canaan became the father of Sidon,[his firstborn, and Heth, and the Jebusites, the Amorites, the Girgashites, the Hivites, the Arkites, the Sinites, the Arvadites, the Zemarites, and the Hamathites]" (Gen. 10:15-18):

   B. "The Hivites" refers to those who live in Hildin.

   C. "The Arkites" speaks of Arkas of the Lebanon.

   D. "The Sinite" speaks of Orthosia.

   E. "The Arbadites" refers to Aradus.

   F. "The Zemarites" refers to Hamats.

   G. Why are they called "the Zemarites"? Because wool [which shares the consonants of the word Zemar] comes from there.

   H. "The Hamathites" refers to Epiphania.

   I. "The the territory of the Canaanites extended from Sidon [in the direction of Gerar as far as Gaza, and in the direction of Sodom, Gomorrah, Admah, and Zeboiim] as far as Lashah" (Gen. 10:19):

   J. As far as Callirrhoe.

All we have is the first layer of exegesis, with some minor expansions.

XXXVII:VII.

1. A. "To Shem also, the father of all the children of Eber, the elder brother of Japheth, children were born" (Gen., 10:21).

   B. We do not, on the basis of the statement at hand, know whether Shem was the oldest or Japheth was the oldest.

   C. On the basis of what is written: "These are the generations of Shem. Shem was a hundred years old and was the father of Arpachshad, two years after the flood" (Gen. 11:10) we learn that Japheth was the elder. [Freedman, p. 299, n. 4: For Noah begot his first child at the age of 500, while the Flood occurred in his 600th year. Now his children are enumerated thus: Shem, Ham, and Japheth. Consequently, if these were in the order of birth, Shem would have been 102 years old two years after the Flood, not 100. Hence we must assume that they are enumerated in order of wisdom, not of age, Shem being the youngest, Ham a year older, and Japheth the eldest.]

2. A. "To Eber were born two sons, the name of the one was Peleg, for in his days the earth was divided (NPLGH), [and his brother's name was Joktan]" (Gen. 10:25):

B. R. Yose says, "Since the ancients knew their ancestry full well, they would give names in accord with events of some kind. But we, who do not know our genealogy all that well, give names in line with our parentage."

C. Rabban Simeon b. Gamaliel says, "Since the ancients had access to the Holy Spirit [which told them in advance what was going to happen], they would give names in accord with events. But we, who do not have access to the Holy Spirit, give names in line with our parentage."

D. Said R. Yose bar Halaphta, "Eber was a great prophet, because he assigned a name in accord with what was going to happen. That is in line with what is written, 'To Eber were born two sons' (Gen. 10:25)."

3. A. Why was the other son of Eber called Yoktan ["And his brother's name was Yoktan" (Gen. 10:25) that is, "he shall be small"]?

B. For he diminished himself [by his modest actions]. And what on that account did he merit? He had the merit of raising up thirteen families.

C. Now if that is the case with a small person, if a great person diminishes his affairs, how much the more so [will he merit on that account]!

D. Along these same lines: "And Israel put forth his right hand and placed it on the head of Ephraim , while he was the younger" (Gen. 48:14).

E. Said R. Hunia, "Now do we not know on our own the order of the generations [of Joseph's household], that Scripture should have to tell us that he was the younger?!

F. "But rather, he is called 'the lesser' because he diminished himself. And what did he merit on that account? He gained the merit of being awarded the blessing of the first-born. If a great person diminishes his affairs, how much the more so [will he merit on that account]!"

No. 1 clarifies a point of the verse at hand, and Nos. 2 and 3 introduce moral lessons and also link the passage to the history of Israel. Obviously, No. 3 presents a syllogism, not an exegesis, and the text at hand supplies a mere proof-text.

XXXVII:VIII.

1. A. "Yoktan became the father of [Almodad, Sheleph,] Hazarmaveth, [Jerah, Hadoram, Uzal, Diklah, Obal, Abimael, Sheba, Ophir, Havilah, and Jobab; all these were the sons of Yoktan]" (Gen. 10:26-29):

   B. R. Huna said, "The name Hazarmaveth speaks of a place which is called 'the Court of Death' [the meaning of the Hebrew words for the place at hand,] in which people eat leeks, wear clothing made of papyrus, and look forward to death every single day."

   C. Samuel said, "[They are so poor that] they do not have even clothing made of papyrus."

2. A. "The territory in which they lived extended from Mesha [in the direction of Sephar to the hill country of the east]" (Gen. 10:31):

   B. R. Eleazar b. Pappos said, "Mesha is dead [from the viewpoint of genealogy, there having been so many improper marriages among its Jewish population], Media is sick, Elam is dying, Hebel Yama is the choice area of Babylonia, and Susira is the choice area of Hebel Yama."

   C. R. Judah says, "The area of Mesopotamia is in the status of the Exile [of Babylonia] so far as genealogical standing is concerned."

3. A. "Toward Sephar" (Gen. 10:30):

   B. that is, Taphar.

4. A. "To the hill country of the east" (Gen. 10:30):

   B. To the mountains in the east.

No. 1 finds meaning in the place name. No. 2 is introduced because of the reference to Mesha/Mesene, at Gen. 10:30. Nos. 3, 4 lightly gloss the cited verse.

Chapter Five

Parashah Thirty-Eight.   Genesis 11:1-30

XXXVIII:I.

1. A. "Now the whole earth had one language and few words" (Gen.11:1):

    B. R. Eleazar in the name of R. Yose b. Zimra commenced discourse by citing the following verse: "Slay them not, lest my people forget, make them wander to and fro by your power and bring them down, O Lord our shield (Ps. 59:12)."

    C. Rabbis refer the verse to Doeg and Ahitophel.

    D. "Said David, 'Do not slay Doeg and Ahitophel.'

    E. "'Lest my people forget:' lest the coming generations forget.

    F. "'Make them wander to and fro by your power:' throw them around.

    G. "'And bring them down, O Lord our shield:' bring them down from their position of power.

    H. "But as to us:' 'O Lord our shield.'

    I. "'For the sin of their mouth and the words of their lips' (Ps. 59:13):

    J. "This one [Doeg] permitted fornication and murder, and that one [Ahitophel] permitted fornication and murder.

    K. "This one [Ahitophel] permitted fornication and murder:' [For he advised Absalom], 'Go in unto your father's concubines' (2 Sam. 16:21). 'And I will come upon him while he is weary and weak-handed...and I will smite the king' (2 Sam. 17:2)."

    L. "That one [Doeg] permitted [fornication and murder]:"

    M. Nahman b. Samuel said, "He took away the civil rights [of David] and made him an outlaw, as one who was dead. so that it was permitted to shed his blood, and his wife was made available to anyone."

2. A. R. Eleazar in the name of R. Yose b. Zimra interpreted the verse to speak of the generation of the dispersion: "The Israelites said, 'Do not slay' the generation of the dispersion.

    B. "'Lest my people forget,' lest the coming generations forget.

    C. "'Make them wander to and fro by your power:' throw them out.

D. "'And bring them down:' from above to below.

E. "'But as to us:' 'O Lord our shield.'

F. "'For the sin of their mouth:' For the sin which they uttered with their mouth.

G. "They said, 'One time in a thousand six hundred and fifty-six years the firmament totters. Let us go and make supports, north, south, and west, while here we shall set its eastern support.'

H. "'And the word of their lips' (Ps. 59:13): so it is written, 'Now the whole earth had one language and few words' (Gen. 11:1)."

The intersecting verse is read in terms of two distinct incidents, one involving David, the other, the generation of the Dispersion. The polemic in the case of the latter appears to me quite standard. The history of Israel corresponds to the history of humanity.

XXXVIII:II.

1. A. R. Abba bar Kahana commenced discourse by citing the following verse of Scripture: "Though you should bray a fool in a mortar with a pestle among groats" (Prov. 27:22).

B. Said R. Abba b. Kahana, "To be compared to the case of a man who pounds barley in a frame, is the one who tries to improve a fool.

C. "Even as the pestle rises and falls: 'Yet will his foolishness not depart from him' (Prov. 27:22).

D. "So the generation of the flood [had perished] only two years prior to the generation of Separation, as it is written, 'Shem fathered Arpachshad two years after the flood' (Gen. 11:1).

E. "Yet: 'And the whole earth had one language' (Gen. 11:1.) [They had learned nothing: 'Yet will his foolishness not depart from him' (Prov. 27:22)."

The intersecting verse now permits the point to be made that the generation of the Dispersion learned nothing from the experience of the Flood, which had been completed only two years earlier. The analogy then is apt.

XXXVIII:III.

1. A. R. Yohanan commenced discourse by citing the following verse of Scripture: "Whoever rewards evil for good, evil shall not depart from his house" (Prov. 17:13).

B. Said R. Yohanan, "If your fellow has entertained you by serving lentils, while you entertained him by serving meat, nonetheless he has a claim on you. Why so? Because he showed kindness to you first, [and you received him only afterward]."

C. Said R. Simeon b. Abba, "It is not the end of the matter that 'he who repays evil for good' [will suffer], but even as to him who repays evil for evil, 'evil shall not depart from his house' either."

D. Said R. Alexandri, "'Whoever rewards evil for good,' of which the Torah has spoken, is in such a case as this: 'If you see the ass of him who hates you lying under its burden, you shall forbear to pass by him; you shall surely release it with him' (Ex. 23:5). Of such a person, Scripture says, 'Whoever rewards evil for good, evil will not depart from his house' (Prov. 17:13)."

E. R. Berekhiah interpreted the verse to speak of the generations at hand [who were saved by God from the flood but repaid him with evil]. Specifically, the generation of the Flood came before the generation of the Dispersion by only two years: 'Shem was father of Arpachshad two years after the flood' (Gen. 11:10), yet: 'Now the whole earth had one language' (Gen. 11:1)."

The climax of course comes at E; the several expositions of the intersecting verse present no surprises. The members of the generation of the Dispersion not only did not learn the lesson of the Flood but also did not show gratitude to God for having saved them. The lessons to be drawn on the present topic accumulate.

XXXVIII:IV.

1. A. R. Judah b. Rabbi commenced [discourse by citing the following verse of Scripture:] "They do not know nor do they understand for their eyes are covered up so that they cannot see, and their hearts, so that they cannot understand' (Is. 44:18).

B. "That is in line with this verse: 'The Nephilim were in the earth in those days' (Gen. 6:4)."

C. Said R. Judah, "Did not the ones who came later learn from the experience of the ones who came earlier? The generation of the Flood was only two years prior to the generation of the Dispersion:

D. 'Shem was father of Arpachshad two years after the flood' (Gen. 11:10), yet: 'Now the whole earth had one language' (Gen. 11:1)."

The same point is made again, though the sense of B is not clear. The point that is important is simply at A, C-D, that the people were so blind that they could not draw the obvious conclusions.

XXXVIII:V.

1. A. R. Azariah commenced discourse [by citing the following verse of Scripture] "'We would have healed Babylon, but she was not healed' (Jer. 41:9).

B. "'We would have healed Babylon' refers to the generation of Enosh.

C. "'But she was not healed' refers to the generation of the Flood.

D. "'Forsake her, and let us go every one to his own country' (Jer. 51:9). Thus: 'Now the whole earth had one language' (Gen. 11:1)."

The intersecting verse is parsed in line with the established point.

XXXVIII:VI.

1. A. "Now the whole earth had one language and few words" (Gen. 11:1):

B. R. Eleazar said, "'Few words' means that while the deeds of the generation of the Flood were spelled out, the deeds of the generation of the Dispersion were not spelled out [and hence were covered by only a few words]."

2. A. "Few words:" That phrase means that they addressed words against the two who are singular [using the same word as is translated few], against the one of whom it is said, "Abraham was one" (Ez. 33:24), and against, "The Lord, our God, the Lord is one" (Deut. 6:4).

B. [They thus spoke against Abraham and against God.] They said, "This man Abraham is a barren mule, who will never have offspring."

C. "Against 'The Lord our God, the Lord is one:'" "He does not have the power to select the heavenly spheres for himself and hand over to us merely the lower world. So come, let us make a tower for ourselves and put an idol on top of it, and put a sword in its hand, so that it will appear as if it carries on warfare with him."

3. A. Another explanation for the phrase, "Few words [now in the sense of things]:" property held in common.

B. What this one held in his possession was held in the possession of the other.

4. A. Rabbis say, "'One language' may be compared to the case of one who had a wine cellar. He opened the first jar and found it vinegar, the second and found it vinegar, the third and found it vinegar.

B.   "He said, 'Thus I am satisfied that all the barrels are no good.   [Thus they convinced God that they were uniformly unfit (Freedman).]"

5.   A.   Said R. Eleazar, "Who is worse, one who says to the king, 'Either you or I shall live in the palace,' or the one who says to him, 'Neither you nor I shall live in the palace.' It is the one who says, 'Either you or I shall live in the palace.'

B.   "So the generation of the Flood said, 'What is the almighty, that we should serve him' (Job 21:15).

C.   "But the generation of the Dispersion said, [against 'The Lord our God, the Lord is one], 'He does not have the power to select the heavenly spheres for himself and hand over to us merely the lower world. So come, let us make a tower for ourselves and put an idol on top of it, and put a sword in its hand, so that it will appear as if it carries on warfare with him.' [[Thus: either you or I shall live in heaven.]

D.   "Of the former not a remnant survived, while of the latter a remnant survived.

E.   "Now as to the generation of the Flood, because they were stuffed on the returns of thievery, 'They remove the landmarks, they violently take away flocks and feed them' (Job 24:2), not a remnant survived of them. But as to the others, because they [at least] loved one another, 'Now the whole earth had one language and few words' (Gen. 11:1), a remnant of them survived."

6.   A.   Rabbi said, "Great is peace, for even if Israel should worship idols, if there is peace among them, said the Holy One, blessed be he, it is as if I shall not exercise dominion over them [and punish them], as it is said, 'Ephraim is united in idol worship, let him alone' (Hos. 4:17).

B.   "But if they are torn by dissension, what is written concerning them? 'Their heart is divided, now shall they bear their guilt' (Hos. 10:23)."

7.   A.   Another interpretation of "Few words:" They were sharp words that they spoke [using the same consonants as occur in 'few'].

B.   They said, "One time in a thousand six hundred and fifty-six years the firmament totters. Let us go and make supports, north, south, and west, while here we shall set its eastern support.

C.   "['And the word of their lips' (Ps. 59:13)]: so it is written, 'Now the whole earth had one language and few words' (Gen. 11:1)."

The interpretation of "few words" covers a range of possible meanings. The first simply rests on the statement that few words were said about these people.

No. 2 moves on to the sense of the same word as "one," hence those described as one, Abraham and God, are now at issue. No. 3 moves on to the word for "words," which can stand also for "things," and now the exegete has "few" stand for "unified," thus "property held in common." No. 4 presents a play on the word "language," connecting that word with the one for tranquilize or satisfy, so Freedman, p. 305, n. 3. No. 5 and No. 6 go on to contrast the generation of the Flood with the generation of the Dispersion, making the point that the latter proved superior in character to the former, for reasons that are worked out. This yields the emphasis on the harmony imputed to the generation at hand, which stands close to the simple sense of the verse of Scripture with its stress on a single shared language. No. 7 draws us closer to the story that is to follow, since it brings up the matter of a war against God.

XXXVIII: VII.

1. A. And as men migrated from the east, [they found a plain in the land of Shinar and settled there]" (Gen. 11:2):

    B. They traveled from a more easterly point to a less easterly point.

    C. [Interpreting the consonants for "east" to mean "ancient,"] said R. Eleazar b. R. Simeon, "They removed themselves from the Ancient of the world. They declared, 'We want neither him nor his divinity.'"

2. A. "They found a plain [in the land of Shinar and settled there]" (Gen. 11:2):

    B. R. Judah said, "All of the nations of the world came together to find out what valley might contain them all, and, in the end, they found it."

    C. ["They found:"] said R. Nehemiah, "'And they found:' 'If it concerns scorners, he permits them to scorn' (Job 3:34). [Freedman, p. 306, n. 6: God permitted them to find a spot suitable for their purpose.]"

3. A. "They settled there" (Gen. 11:2):

    B. Said R. Isaac, "In every passage in which you find a reference to 'settling,' Satan leaps at the opportunity [because Satan is interested in people who live securely]."

    C. Said R. Helbo, "In every passage in which you find satisfaction, Satan serves as the prosecuting attorney."

    D. Said R. Levi, "In every passage in which you find eating and drinking, that head-thug dances with joy."

As in the treatment of the story of the Flood, so here the exegetes find it necessary to justify God's actions. So, noting in the narrative little basis for

God's punishment, they have provided what was lacking. The points are, first, the generation of the Dispersion rejected God's rule, and, second, they became complacent in their prosperity. No. 1 makes the first point, no. 3 the second.

XXXVIII:VIII.

1. A. "And they said to one another" (Gen. 11:3):

   B. Who spoke to whom?

   C. Said R. Berekhiah, "Egypt spoke to Ethiopia."

2. A. "Come, let us make bricks and burn them thoroughly" (Gen. 11:3):

   B. The word for "burn them thoroughly" is written as if to be read "and we will be burned," meaning: "this people are going to be burned out of the world."

3. A. "And they had brick for stone" (Gen. 11:3):

   B. R. Huna said, "The work went very well for them. If someone planned to lay one, he laid two stones; if he came to plaster one row, he did two. [Freedman: He translates, 'and the brick turned itself for them into stone' (Freedman, p. 307, n. 7)]."

4. A. "Then they said, 'Come, let us build ourselves a city, and a tower [with its top in the heavens, and let us make a name for ourselves, lest we be scattered abroad upon the face of the whole earth]'" (Gen. 11:4):

   B. Said R. Yudan, "The tower they built, the city they did not build."

   C. They objected to him, "But has it not been written: 'And the Lord came down to see *the city* and the tower which the sons of men had built' (Gen. 11:5)?"

   D. He said to him, "Read what is said just after to the cited verse: 'And they left off building *the city* ' (Gen. 11:8). What is not written is 'tower.'"

   E. Said R. Hiyya bar Abba, "This tower that they built -- a third of it sank into the ground, a third was burned up, but a third remains."

   F. Now should you say that it was small, R. Huna in the name of R. Idi: "Whoever goes up to the top sees the palm trees down below him as they were locusts."

5. A. "And let us make a name for ourselves" (Gen. 11:4):

   B. A Tannaite authority of the house of R. Ishmael: "The meaning of the word 'name' can only be 'idol.'"

6. A. "Lest we be scattered abroad upon the face of the whole earth" (Gen. 11:4):

B. Said R. Simeon b. Halputa, "'A fool's mouth is his ruin' (Prov. 18:7). [Freedman, p. 308, n. 1: By saying this they unconsciously prophesied their fate and were themselves responsible for it.]"

The components of the cited verses are systematically explained. The recurrent emphasis maintains that the generation of the Dispersion was responsible for its own fate, which the people predicted; but they enjoyed every assistance, once they had started on the path to their ruin.

XXXVIII:IX.

1. A. "And the Lord came down to see [the city and the tower which the sons of men had built]" (Gen. 11:5):

B. Said R. Simeon b. Yohai, "This is one of the ten passages in the Torah that refer to God's descending."

2. A. "...which the sons of men had built" (Gen. 11:5):

B. Said R. Berekhiah, "What could the passage have said? 'Sons of asses'? 'Sons of camels'? [Why specify these are the sons *of man* who built the city?']

C. "But [God said,] 'They are the true heirs of the first man. Just as in the case of the first man, after all that I lavished on him, he said, "The woman whom *you* gave me [caused the sin, so you are responsible, not I]" (Gen. 3:21), so in the case of the generation of the Dispersion [they learned nothing].'

D. "So the generation of the flood [had perished] only two years prior to the generation of Separation, as it is written, 'Shem fathered Arpachshad two years after the flood' (Gen. 11:1).

E. "Yet: 'And the whole earth had one language' (Gen. 11:1)"

3. A. "And the Lord said, 'Behold they are one people'" (Gen. 11:6):

B. R. Judah said, "Since they are 'one people and they all have one language,' if they repent, I shall accept them back."

C. R. Nehemiah said, "What caused them to rebel against me? Is it not that 'they are one people and they all have one language'?"

4. A. "And now" (Gen. 11:6):

B. Said R. Abba bar Kahana, "This teaches that the Holy One, blessed be he, gave them an opening to repent. 'And now' means only to refer to repentence.

C. "That is in line with the following verse of Scripture: 'And now, Israel, what does the Lord God require of you, but to fear the Lord your God' [an invitation to repentence] (Deut. 10:12)."

5. A But they said, "No."

B. Said the Holy One, blessed be he, "'And nothing that they propose to do will not be impossible for them' (Gen. 11:6)."

C. When a vineyard does not produce a crop, what does the owner do to it? He uproots it.

Nos. 1 2 form links between the present story and others, creating as seamless a narrative as possible. Nos. 3, 4 and 5 all clarify the meaning of phrases at hand. The stress lies upon God's willingness to forgive and the unwillingness of the generation of the Dispersion to be conciliated. So the underlying motif of the exegesis, the guilt of those who were punished, once more guides the interpretation of the passage before the exegetes.

XXXVIII:X.

1. A. "Come, let us go down" (Gen. 11:7):

B. This is one of the passages that the translators of the Greek version of Scripture changed when they presented matters to King Ptolemy, preferring to read as follows:

C. "Come, *I* shall go down and *I* shall confound their language" [so that no one should suppose there is more than one God].

2. A. Said R. Abba, "[The Hebrew words for 'confound their language' may be interpreted as:] 'Out of their own lips I shall turn them into corpses.' [Freedman, p. 309, n. 3: He reads the word for 'confound' as meaning 'destruction,' and the word for 'their language' as referring to 'the words of their lips.']

B. "[We shall now illustrate how the confusion impeded their work.] One of them would ask his fellow, 'Bring me water,' and the other brought him dirt. So he hit him and split his skull.

C. "'Bring me an axe' and he brought a spade, so he hit him and split his skull.

D. "That is in line with the verse: 'Out of their own lips shall I turn them into corpses" (Gen. 11:7)."

3. A. "So the Lord scattered them abroad from there over the face of all the earth" (Gen. 11:8):

B. R. Yudan said, "The Tyrians went to Sidon, the Sidonians to Tyre. The Egyptians held on to their land."

C. Said R. Nehemiah, "All of the lands gathered together [Freedman:] within the angular points, and each absorbed its own original inhabitants. [Freedman, p. 309, n. 6: The idea is as though points were taken on the inner borders of all countries and joined by lines into a huge figure, and the nations entered within this and withdrew each those of its members who had gathered there to build the tower. Thus Nehemiah holds that the people remained in their own countries after the Separation, as they were before they gathered to build the tower.]"

4. A. Rabbis say, "The word for 'scattered' may be read 'swept away.'

B. "The sea came in and swept away thirty families."

C. R. Phineas in the name of R. Levi: "Whenever suffering befalls someone, another party benefits. As to those thirty families, who took their place? From Abraham came sixteen families of the sons of Keturah, and twelve from Ishmael.

D. "As to the missing two: 'And the Lord said to her, "Two nations are in your womb"' (Gen. 25:23)."

Nos. 1 and 2 explain linguistic usages. No. 3 presents a substantive disagreement about the sense of the passage. One party holds that the dispersion brought peoples from their original homeland to some other, and the second authority maintains that each people returned to the place from which it had started. No. 4 introduces the coming theme, namely, Abraham, the first point at which the compositors have provided us with a transition to Abraham. In this way the exegete-compositors join the threads of the story.

XXXVIII:XI.

1. A. "Therefore its name was called Babel, because there the Lord confused the language of all the earth" (Gen. 11:9):

B. A disciple of R. Yohanan was in session before him. The master spelled out a matter, but the disciple did not grasp it. The master said, "What's wrong?"

C. He said, "I am in exile from my place."

D. He said to him, "Where do you come from?"

E. He said to him, "From Borsif."

F. He said to him, "It is not Borsif but Balsif, in line with this verse: 'Because the the Lord confused the language of all the earth' (Gen. 11:9). [Freedman, p. 310, n. 1: Yohanan remarked that the town should be called Balsif, this name being compounded of the words for 'confuse' and 'language' and thus showing its origin.]"

The etymology is clear as explained by Freedman.

XXXVIII:XII.

1. A. "Now these are the descendants of Terah. Terah [was the father of Abram, Nahon, and Haran]" (Gen. 11:27):

B. Said R. Abba bar Kahana, "In every passage in which a name is mentioned twice, [one may be sure that] that person enjoys a share in this age and in the age to come."

C. An objection was raised, "And lo, it is written, 'These are the generations of Terah. Terah [begot Abram]' (Gen. 11:27). Does he have a portion in this age and in the age to come? [Surely not, he was an idolator.]"

D. He said to him, "Even this item does not contradict the point, [for R. Yudan in the name of R. Abba said,] 'What is the meaning of the verse of Scripture, "And even you will come to your fathers in peace" (Gen. 15:15)? They thus informed [Abraham] that his father [Terah] had a portion in the age to come.

E. "'You will be buried in good old age' (Gen. 15:15). They informed him that Ishmael would repent. [Thus Terah indeed did have a portion in the age to come, and Abraham was so informed. So the case supports Abba's proposition.]"'

The syllogism makes use of the verse at hand but does not come to expression as a means of interpreting the verse in particular.

XXXVIII:XIII.

1. A. "Haran died in the presence of his father Terah in the land of his birth, in Ur of the Chaldaeans" (Gen. 11:28):

B. Said R. Hiyya [in explanation of how Haran died in his father's presence], "Terah was an idol-manufacturer. Once he went off on a trip and put Abraham in charge of the store. Someone would come in and want to buy an idol. He would say to him, 'How old are you?'

C. "He said, 'Fifty years old.'

D. "He said, 'Woe to that man, who is fifty years old and is going to bow down to something a day old.' So the man would be ashamed and go his way.

E. "One time a woman came in with a bowl of flour, and said to him, 'Take this and offer it before them.'

F. "He went and took a stick, broke the idols, and put the stick in the hand of the biggest idol.

G. "When his father came back, he said to you, 'Why in the world have you been doing these things?'

H. "He said to him, 'How can I hide it from you? One time a woman came in with a bowl of flour, and said to me, "Take this and offer it before them." Then this idol said, "I'll eat first," and that idol said, "I'll eat first." One of them, the largest, got up and grabbed the stick and broke the others.'

I. "[Terah] said to him, 'Why are you making fun of me! Do those idols know anything [that such a thing could possibly happen]? [Obviously not!]'

J. "He said to him, 'And should your ears not hear what your mouth is saying?' He took him and handed him over to Nimrod.

K. "He said to him, 'Bow down to the fire.'

L. "He said to him, 'We really should bow down to water, which puts out fire.'

M. "He said to him, 'Bow down to water.'

N. "He said to him, 'We really should bow down to the clouds, which bear the water.'

O. "He said to him, 'Then let's bow down to the clouds.'

P. "He said to him, 'We really should bow down to the wind, which disperses the clouds.'

Q. "He said to him, 'Then let's bow down to the wind.'

R. "He said to him, 'We really should bow down to human beings, who can stand up to the wind.'

S. "He said to him, 'You're just playing word-games with me. Let's bow down to the fire. So now, look, I am going to throw you into the fire, and let your God whom you worship come and save you from the fire.'

T. "Now Haran was standing there undecided. He said, 'What's the choice? If Abram wins, I'll say I'm on Abram's side, and if Nimrod wins, I'll say I'm on Nimrod's side. [So how can I lose?]'

U. "When Abram went down into the burning furnace and was saved, Nimrod said to him, 'On whose side are you?'

V. "He said to him, 'Abram's.'

W. "They took him and threw him into the fire, and his guts burned up and came out, and he died in the presence of his father.

X. "That is in line with the verse of Scripture: 'And Haran died in the presence of his father, Terah' (Gen. 11:28)."

The powerful story leads us back to the explanation of the verse at hand, but, of course, the story can stand alone and serve an-other-than exegetical purpose. In fact the point of the story is the polemic against idolatry as fetishism, to which the verse at hand is hardly critical. In the present context, the story links Abram to the story at hand.

XXXVIII:XIV.

1. A. "And Abram and Nahor took wives; [the name of Abram's wife was Sarai, and the name of Nahor's wife, Milcah, the daughter of Haran, the father of Milcah and Iscah]" (Gen. 11:29):

B. Abram was a year older than Nahor. Nahor was a year older than Haran. So Abram was two years older than Haran. There was a year of the pregnancy with Milcah and a year of the pregnancy with Iscah, and it turns out that Haran produced children when he was six years old. And [if Haran could do it,] how then could Abram not produce a child? [Freedman, p. 312, n. 1: Iscah was Sarah. Now Abram was ten years older than Sarah. Since he was two years older than Haran, Sarah's father, Sarah was born when Haran was only eight years old. Again, she was his second daughter, and since the period of pregnancy and child-bearing is roughly a year for each child, Haran must have been six years old when he begot a child. Why could Abram not do as well?]

C. [The fault was Sarai's:] "And Sarai was barren, *she* had no child" (Gen. 11:30).

2. A. ["She had no child" (Gen. 11:30):] said R. Levi, "In any passage in which it is said, 'She had no...,' she eventually would have.

B. "'And Sarai was barren, she had no child' (Gen. 11:30). 'And the Lord remembered Sarah' (Gen. 21:1).

C. "'And Peninah had children but Hannah had no children' (1 Sam. 1:2). 'And she bore three sons' (1 Sam. 2:21).

D. "'She is Zion, there is none who cares for her' (Jer. 30:17). 'And a redeemer will come to Zion and to those who turn from transgression' (Is. 59:20)."

The comment on the fact yielded by the verse at hand, No. 1, gives way to a glorious conclusion. Now there is a direct link between the mundane facts at hand and the redemption of Israel, a point at which the exegetes' eagerness to build bridges between the narrative at and the sacred history of Israel produces a surprising, and therefore stunning, climax.

Chapter Six

Parashah Thirty-Nine. Genesis 12:1-9

XXXIX:I.

1. A. "Now the Lord said to Abram, 'Go [from your country and your kindred and your father's house to the land that I will show you']" (Gen. 12:1):

    B. R. Isaac opened [discourse by citing the following verse of Scripture:] "Hearken, O daughter, and consider and incline your ear; forget also your own people and your father's house" (Ps. 45:11).

    C. Said R. Isaac, "The matter may be compared to the case of someone who was going from one place to another when he saw a great house on fire. He said, 'Is it possible to say that such a great house has no one in charge?'

    D. "The owner of the house looked out and said to him, 'I am the one in charge of the house.'

    E. "Thus since Abraham, our father, [took the initiative and] said, 'Is it possible for the world to endure without someone in charge,' the Holy One, blessed be he, [responded and] looked out and said to him, 'I am the one in charge of the house, the lord of all the world.'

    F. "'So shall the king desire your beauty' (Ps. 45:12), to show how splendid you are in this world.

    G. "'For he is your Lord and do homage to him' (Ps. 45:12): 'Now the Lord said to Abram, Go...' (Gen. 12:1)."

The relevance of the intersecting verse, that the daughter is to leave her family, derives from the reference to leaving one's family, as Abram did. Then each of its elements demand integration with the situation before us, so that the analogy is fully exposed. The metaphor in this case, however, does not really relate to the syllogism. Why not? Because the syllogism stresses that one has to obey God by leaving his family. That is the point of the base-verse. But the metaphor deals with someone who reaches the conclusion, on his own, that, when there is trouble, someone must care about it. God responds to Abraham's remarkable insight. That point does not seem to me well drawn in the present context. By contrast, what follows, F-G, is entirely a propos. Without the metaphor, the intersecting verse works well, while the value of the metaphor to the point of the composition as a whole hardly emerges. Ordinarily, the power

__ ...᷈ ᴍetaphor is to state in highly immediate terms the proposition of the composition as a whole But here that is not the case.

XXXIX:II.

1. A. R. Berekhiah commenced [discourse by citing the following verse of Scripture]: "Your ointments have a good smell" (Song 1:3).

B. Said R. Berekhiah, "To what may Abraham be compared? To flask of myrrh sealed with a tight lid and lying in the corner. The fragrance of that vial does not waft upward. But when the vial is moved about, its fragrance spreads upward.

C. "So said the Holy One, blessed be he, 'Move yourself about from place to place, so that your name may be made great in the world: "Go out" (Gen. 12:1).'"

Why did Abram have to leave his homeland? The metaphor explains. The exegesis focuses upon the purpose of God's instruction to Abram. What Scripture treats as a neutral statement the exegete endows with purpose. Yet all he has done is read Gen. 12:2 into Gen. 12:1, so his contribution is only the analogy, not the syllogism.

XXXIX:III.

1. A. R. Berekhiah commenced discourse by citing the following verse of Scripture]: "'We have a little sister' (Song 8:8). This passage speaks of Abraham, who united the entire world for us. [At hand is a play on the word for 'sister,' the consonants of which can yield the word for 'unite.']"

B. Bar Qappara: "The matter may be compared to someone who sews up a tear [a play on the same two words]."

C. "Little" (Song 8:8): For while he was yet small, he built up a treasury of merit for the religious duties and acts of goodness that he carried out.

D. "And she does not have breasts" (Song 8:8): No breasts gave him suck, neither in acts of religious duty or of goodness [since he had no example from whom to learn].

E. "What shall we do for our sister on the day when she shall be spoken for?" (Song 8:8): [This refers to] the day on which the wicked Nimrod threw him down in the heated furnace.

F. "If she is a wall, we will build upon her" (Song 8:9): If he stands up against Nimrod like a wall, [God] will build upon him.

G. "If she is a door, we will enclose her with boards of cedar" (Song 8:9): If he is poor in merit accruing for doing acts of religious duty and good deeds [a play on the words for door and poor, both of which use the letters DL],

H. "...we will enclose her with boards of cedar" (Song 8:9): and just as a drawing lasts only for a moment, so I shall sustain him only for a time. [The play now is on the words for "enclose" and "drawing."]

[Freedman, p. 314, n. 4: A drawing is easily rubbed off. He translates: We will treat her like a drawing.]

I. He said before him, "Lord of the ages, 'I am a wall' (Song 8:10). I stand up as firmly as a wall.

J. "'And my breasts are like the towers of the wall' (Song 8:10). My sons are Hananiah, Mishael, and Azariah."

K. "Then I was in his eyes as one who found wholeness [peace]" (Song 8:10). He entered whole and came out whole.

L. "Now the Lord said to Abram, 'Go from your country'" (Gen. 12:1).

The systematic reading of Song 8:8-10 in line with Abram works quite well, linking the story of Abram in Nimrod's furnace to Hananiah, Mishael, and Azariah in later times. The power of the identification, of course, lies in linking the story in Daniel, which took place in Babylonia, to the story of Abraham, leaving his family in the same region and going to the Holy Land. H is somewhat jarring; it makes Abram plead with God to stand by him. Then the appeal to Hananiah, Mishael, and Azariah, I-J, and the further reference at K to the shared experience in the fiery furnace, serve as Abram's case for God's continuing support. The net effect of the exegesis at hand is to allude in a fresh and subtle way to the story that we read at the end of XXXVIII:XIII in a simple narrative.

So that story, treated as classic and well known, weaves its way into the embroidery of the larger loom of Scripture.

XXXIX:IV.

1. A. "Wisdom makes a wise man stronger than ten rulers" (Qoh. 7:19):

B. The passage speaks of Abraham.

C. "...than ten...:" [he was stronger] than the ten generations that lived from Noah to Abraham.

D. "Among all of them, I spoke only with you:"

E. "And the Lord said to Abram" (Gen. 12:1).

The exegesis moves on from the general theme of leaving the fiery furnace of Nimrod to the next component of the base verse, which is the statement that the Lord spoke to Abram. The passage does ignore the several statements that God made to Noah, not to mention the stress laid on that fact by our own exegetes.

XXXIX:V.

1. A. R. Azariah commenced discourse [by citing the following verse of Scripture] "'We would have healed Babylon, but she was not healed' (Jer. 41:9).

   B. "'We would have healed Babylon' refers to the generation of Enosh.

   C. "'But she was not healed' refers to the generation of the Flood.

   D. "'Forsake her' refers to the generation of the dispersion.

   E. "'...and let us go every one to his own country' (Jer. 51:9):

   F. "Thus: 'Now the Lord said to Abram, "Go from your country and your kindred...to the land that I will show you"' (Gen. 12:1)."

We now reach the element, "from your country," and explain Abram's leaving Babylonia. Why did God not have him do his work there? God had done the work, with the generation of the Flood and of the Dispersion, and it had done no good. The latter returned to their own countries, so God had Abram leave Babylonia for the Land of Israel. That is the basic view expressed here. Linking Abram's call to the generation of the Dispersion not only ties the threads of the narrative. It also contrasts Israel's loyalty to the Land with the cosmopolitan character of the generation of the Dispersion, shown by its willingness to abandon its ancestral homeland. Whether or not there is a further judgment on the Jews of Babylonia I cannot say.

We recall that, at XXXVIII:V, the same statement, omitting only the strikingly appropriate climax of E-F, served the following verse: "Now the whole earth had one language" (Gen. 11:1). What we see is a shift so important, in an otherwise identical pericope, as to demonstrate the drastic intervention of the redactors in received materials. They were prepared to revise what they had in hand to fit the purposes of a different context. Once more the thesis with which we began, that the document before us speaks for its ultimate compositors, finds substantial illustration.

XXXIX:VI.

1. A. R. Azariah in the name of R. Aha commenced [discourse by citing the following verse of Scripture:] "You have loved righteousness and hated wickedness" (Ps. 45:8).

   B. R Azariah in the name of R. Aha interpreted the verse to speak of our father, Abraham: "When our father, Abraham, stood to seek mercy for the Sodomites, what is written there? 'Far be it from you to do such a thing' (Gen. 18:25)."

C. Said R. Aha, "[Abram said to God,] 'You bound yourself by an oath not to bring a flood upon the world. Are you now going to act deceitfully against the clear intent of that oath? True enough, you are not going to bring a flood of water, but you are going to bring a flood of fire. If so you will not carry out the oath!'"

D. Said R. Levi, "'Will not the judge of all the earth do justly?' (Gen. 18:25). 'If you want to have a world, there can be no justice, and if justice is what you want, there can be no world. You are holding the rope at both ends, you want a world and you want justice. If you don't give in a bit, the world can never stand.'

E. "Said the Holy One, blessed be he, to him, 'Abraham, "You have loved righteousness and hated wickedness. Therefore God, your God, has anointed you with the oil of gladness above your fellows." (Ps. 45:8).

F. "'From Noah to you there are ten generations [that is, that lived from Noah to Abraham.

G. "'Among all of them, I spoke only with you.'"

H. "And the Lord said to Abram, ['Go from your country and your kindred and your father's house to the land that I will show you']" (Gen. 12:1).

The element at issue now is the singling out of Abram, and that is on account of his love for righteousness. On that basis the world can endure -- but also be righteous. Reading the intersecting verse into the base verse becomes possible only at the end, at which point how Abram was singled out justifies the reference. The story by itself, that is, the discourse on Sodom, amply validates selecting Ps. 45:8, since Abram's plea for justice at Sodom draws attention to the cited verse of Psalms. Without the concluding clause of the same intersecting verse, we should have no reason to assign the entire passage to the present locus. At *Parashah* Forty-Nine we shall have occasion to compare the two versions of the same exegesis of an intersecting verse and to see how the compositors have been willing to reshape matters for their larger constructive purpose.

XXXIX:VII.

1. A. Now what is written prior to the passage at hand? It is this verse: "And Terah died in Haran" (Gen. 11:32). Then comes: "And the Lord said to Abram, 'Go [from your country and your kindred and your father's house to the land that I will show you']" (Gen. 12:1).

B. Said R. Isaac, "As to the chronology involved, another sixty-five years are needed [Freedman, p. 315, n. 3: to bring the narrative to the death of Terah. For Terah was seventy years old at Abram's birth, so Gen. 11:26, while Abram departed from Haran at the age of seventy-five, so Gen. 12:4, and so

Terah, whose age at death was two hundred and five, Gen. 11:32, died sixty-five years after this command, and yet it is narrated before].

C. "But to begin with you must interpret the passage to indicate that wicked people are called dead while they are yet alive.

D. "For Abraham was concerned, reckoning, 'If I leave, through me people will execrate the Name of heaven, saying, "He abandoned his father in his old age and went away."'

E. "The Holy One, blessed be he, said to him, 'You in particular I shall free from the responsibility of paying honor to your father and your mother, but I shall never free anyone else from the responsibility of paying honor to his father and his mother. And not only so, but [in order to do so] I shall move up his death to before your departure.'

F. "Accordingly first comes: 'And Terah died in Haran" (Gen. 11:32). Then: 'And the Lord said to Abram, "Go [from your country and your kindred and your father's house to the land that I will show you"]' (Gen. 12:1)."

The exegete now asks about the interplay of the successive verses, in line with the chronology spelled out by Freedman. The result is a strong exegesis on how Abram found it possible to leave his family.

XXXIX:VIII.

1. A. "Go, go" (Gen. 12:1) [the consonants for "Get you" may be read to mean the word, "Go," repeated twice:]

B. R. Judah said, "'Go, go,' two times, indicates that one time he was told to go out of Aram Naharim, and the other time to go out of Aram Nahor."

C. R. Nehemiah said, "'Go, go,' two times, indicates that once he was told to go out of Aram Naharim, and once to fly from 'the covenant between the pieces' [Gen. 15], bringing him to Haran."

2. A. That [base verse] is in line with the following verse of Scripture: "Your people offer themselves willingly on the day of your warfare" (Ps. 110:3).

B. [Since the letters for "your people" may be read "with you," we interpret the verse as follows:] "I was with you when you willingly offered yourself for my Name, going down into the heated furnace."

C. "On the day of your warfare" (Ps. 110:3): [since the letters for "your warfare" may be read "your retinue," we interpret the verse as follows]: "When you gathered for me all of those great populations [to my service].

D. "In the mountains of holiness" (Ps. 110:3): "From the mountain of the world I sanctified you."

E. "From the womb of the dawn" (Ps. 110:3): "From the womb of the world I sought you for myself" [the word "dawn" and "sought" share the same consonants].

F. "Yours is the dew of youth" (Ps. 110:3): Our father Abraham was concerned, saying, "Is it possible that I am responsible for some sort of transgression, for I worshipped idolatry during all of those years!" Said the Holy One, blessed be he, to him, "'Yours is the dew of youth.' Just as dew evaporates, so your sins will evaporate. Just as dew is a sign of blessing for the world, so you are a sign of blessing for the world."

3.   A. [The base verse is in line with the following intersecting verse:] "And I said, 'O that I had wings like a dove, then I would fly away and be at rest'"(Ps. 55:7):

B. Why like a dove?

C. R. Azariah in the name of R. Yudan b. R. Simon: "It is because when all other birds tire, they rest on a rock or a tree, but when a dove tires, it draws in one of its wings and limps along with the other of its wings."

D. "Then I would wander far off" (Ps. 55:8): wandering after wandering, move after move.

E. "I would lodge in the wilderness. Selah" (Ps. 55:8): It is better to abide in the wilderness areas of the Land of Israel than in the palaces abroad. [That applies in particular to Abram's wanderings in the land.]

F. And if you should say, had Abram not hesitated but delighted [to migrate to the Land of Israel], then why did he not go forth sooner than he did? It was because he had not yet received permission.

G. But as soon as he got permission, "So Abram went as the Lord had told him, and Lot went with him" (Gen. 12:4).

4.   A. Said R. Levi, "When Abraham was traveling through Aram Naharim and Aram Nahor, he saw the people eating and drinking and having a good time. He said, 'I hope my portion will not be here!'

B. "When he got to the Ladder of Tyre, he saw the people at work, weeding in weeding time and hoeing in hoeing time. He said, 'I hope that my portion will be in this land.'

C. "Said the Holy One, blessed be he, to him, 'And to your seed I shall give this land' (Gen. 15:18)."

Once we have dealt with the peculiarity of the base-verse, No. ,1 we move directly to two intersecting verses, Ps. 110:3, at No. 2, and Ps. 55:7, at No. 3. Why someone should have found that Abraham's life called for a rereading of these verses in particular I cannot say. But both of them serve very well. Ps. 110:3 once more forms a link to the exegetical interest of the earlier passage on Abraham in the fiery furnace of the Chaldaeans. No. 3 then joins Abraham's life to the history of Israel, with its movement from place to place. That seems to me the likely implication of the passage, first, because in the literature before us Israel commonly is compared to the dove, and, second, there is a specific warrant for the suggestion. It is the wry comment on the fact that Abraham abandoned the advantageous life of Ur for the labor-wracked life of the Land of Israel. That is the stunning stress of No. 3-4. So the whole leads us to the center-piece of the base-verse, which is "to the land that I will show you." That is the fact, even though that component of the base-verse does not appear to be subject to inquiry. If this interpretation of the composition proves sound, then the compositors show considerable subtlety.

XXXIX:IX.

1.   A.   Said R. Levi, "Go, go" (Gen. 21:1) is repeated twice [once in the present context, the other at Gen. 22:1, in going to offer up Isaac at Mount Moriah].

B.   "We do not know which of them is more precious, the first or the second."

2.   A.   Said R. Yohanan, "'Go from your country"(Gen. 12:1), refers to your hyparchy.

B.   "'From your birthplace' refers to your neighborhood.

C.   "'From your father's house' refers literally to the house of your father.

D.   "To the land that I will show you:' but why did he not inform him [in advance where that would be]?

E.   "It was so as to make it still more precious in his view and to give him a reward for each step that he took [in perfect faith and reliance on God]."

F.   That is the view of R. Yohanan, for R. Yohanan said, "'And he said, "Take your son"' (Gen. 22:2).

G.   "'Which son?' 'Your only son.'

H.   "'This one is the only son of his mother, and that one is the only son of his mother.'

I.   "'Whom you have loved' (Gen. 22:2).

J.   "'This one I love, and that one I love. Are there boundaries within one's heart?'

K.   "So he said to him, 'Isaac' (Gen. 22:2).

L.   "And why did he not tell him to begin with whom he wanted?

M. "It was so as to make it still more precious in his view and to give him a reward for each statement that he made [in perfect obedience to and reliance on God]."

3. A. For R. Huna said in the name of R. Eliezer, "He whom the Holy One, blessed be he, puts in doubt and holds in suspense, namely, the righteous, he then informs, explaining his reasoning.

B. "Thus: 'To the land that I will show you' (Gen. 12:1). 'On one of the mountains which I shall tell you' (Gen. 22:2). 'And make to it the proclamation that I shall tell you' (Jonah 3:2). 'Arise, go forth to the plain, and there I will speak with you' (Ez. 3:22)."

The contribution of No. 1 is to link the present story to the binding of Isaac, so strengthening the force of the narrative. The fact that both conversations utilize the same language justifies the exegete. No. 2 carries this matter forward and makes its point articulate. No. 2 and No. 3 do not take shape around Gen. 12:2 in particular, as we see, but the syllogism presented in both compositions fully accords with the exegetical needs of our passage, and No. 1 has prepared us for what is to follow. The point in both cases is made quite articulate. Once again we find the contribution of the compositors to lie in the weaving of a strong fabric, uniting the threads of the stories into a single and important statement. Their own composition provides a model for sustained argument of a single syllogism, worked out through diverse and discrete components. The syllogism, of course, is that God demands perfect submission and unquestioning faith, but then rewards that faith.

XXXIX:X.

1. A. R. Berekhiah b. R. Simon in the name of R. Nehemiah: "The matter may be compared to the case of a king who was traveling from place to place, and a pearl fell out of his crown. The king stopped there and held up his retinue there, collected sand in heaps and brought sieves. He had the first pile sifted and did not find the pearl. So he did with the second and did not find it. But in the third heap he found it. People said, 'The king has found his pearl.'

B. "So said the Holy One, blessed be he, to Abraham, 'Why did I have to spell out the descent of Shem, Arpachshad, Shelah, Eber, Peleg, Reu, Serug, Nahor, and Terah? Was it not entirely for you?'

C. "'And he *found* his heart faithful before you' (Neh. 9:8). [Freedman, p. 319, n. 2: He was the pearl that God found.]

D. "So said the Holy One, blessed be he, to David, 'Why did I have to spell out the descent of Perez, Hezron, Ram, Aminadab, Nachshon, Shalomon, Boaz, Obed, and Jesse? Was it not entirely for you?'

E. "Thus: 'I have *found* David my servant, with my holy oil have I anointed him' (Ps. 89:21)."

Abraham and David compare to one another, one standing at the commencement of Israel's history, the other at the end. The exegete is interested in the reason that Gen. 11 has preceded Gen. 12. But the syllogism again emerges not from exegesis but from a quite separate reflection on the relationship between genealogy and narrative (to state matters in literary terms). Why has the Scripture presented the genealogies at hand? It is to point to the treasure that God found by sifting the sand of the generations. That point, stated on its own, bears considerable power. The parable of the king bears the implication that Abraham and David had fallen from God's head and had to be recovered, but I think we err if we read the parable too closely and too literally. I see here no allusion to the saved savior of some Gnostic systems, for instance. The main point, so far as the exegete is concerned, lies in the sifting of the generations, on the one side, and the match at the start and finish, on the other..

XXXIX:XI.

1. A. "And I will make of you a great nation" (Gen. 12:2):

B. [Abram] said to him, "And from Noah have you not raised up seventy nations?"

C. He said to him, "From you I shall raise up that nation of whom it is written, 'For what great nation is there that has God so near to them' (Deut. 4:7)." [The reference, in both passages, is to a great nation, not merely to a nation.]

2. A. Said R. Berekhiah, "What is written is not, 'I will give you,' or, 'I will set you,' but 'I will make of you,' meaning, 'once I create you in a completely new act of creation, you will be fruitful and multiply.'"

3. A. R. Levi bar Ahyatah, R. Abba: "In the present passage there are three references to greatness and four references to blessings.

B. "In this way God gave Abram the good news that there will be three patriarchs and four matriarchs."

4. A. Said R. Berekhiah, "[Reference to Abram's having many children] is because traveling causes three things. It diminishes the act of procreation, one's financial resources, and one's repute [since one is far from people who know him]. [So God had to say to him,] 'I shall make you a great nation [despite the rigors of travel].'

B. "Since it diminishes the act of procreation: 'I shall make you a great nation' (Gen. 12:2).

C. "Since it diminishes one's financial resources: 'I shall bless you' (Gen. 21:2).

D. "Since it diminishes one's repute: 'I will make your name great' (Gen. 12:2).

E. "And even though people say, 'From house to house, a move costs a shirt, from place to place, a move costs a life,' in your case, however, you will lose neither your life nor your money.'"

5. A. R. Berekhiah in the name of R. Helbo: "[The promise that God will make Abram great] refers to the fact that his coinage had circulated in the world.

B. "There were four whose coinage circulated in the world.

C. "Abraham: 'And I will make you' (Gen. 12:2). And what image appeared on his coinage? An old man and an old woman on the obverse side, a boy and a girl on the reverse [Abraham, Sarah, Isaac and Rebekah].

D. "Joshua: 'So the Lord was with Joshua and his fame was in all the land' (Josh. 6:27). That is, his coinage circulated in the world. And what image appeared on his coinage? An ox on the obverse, a wild-ox on the reverse: 'His firstling bullock, majesty is his, and his horns are the horns of a wild ox' (Deut 33:17). [Joshua descended from Joseph.]

E. "David: 'And the fame of David went out into all lands' (1 Chr. 14:17). That is, his coinage circulated in the world. And what image appeared on his coinage? A staff and a wallet on the obverse, a tower on the reverse: 'Your neck is like the tower of David, built with turrets' (Song 4:4).

F. "Mordecai: 'For Mordecai was great in the king's house, and his fame went forth throughout all the provinces' (Est. 9:4). That is, his coinage circulated in the world. And what image appeared on his coinage? Sackcloth and ashes on the obverse, a golden crown on the reverse."

6. A. Said R. Isaac, "[God said to Abraham,] 'I shall provide a blessing for you in the Eighteen Benedictions,' but you do not know whether 'mine' comes first or 'yours' comes first.'"

B. Said R. Aha in the name of R. Zeira, "[He told him,] 'Yours comes before mine,' since people say first, '...the shield of Abraham,' and only afterward they say, '...who resurrects the dead' [thus referring first to Abraham, then to God]."

7. A. R. Abbahu said in regard to [the verse, "And I will make your name great," (Gen. 12:2) on which the comment is that that is done by adding an H to Abram's name,] "[At Gen. 15:5] what is written is not, 'Look now at the heaven,' but, 'Look, now *to* the heaven,' (Gen. 15:5), thus adding an H at the end of the word. The meaning is, 'With this additional H I created the world. Now lo, I am going to add it to your name [calling you not Abram but Abraham], so you will also be fruitful and multiply.'"

B. Said R. Yudan, "The numerical value of the letters of your name will add up to the numerical value of the word 'I shall bless you.' Just as the numerical value of the letters of the word, 'I shall bless you,' add up to two hundred forty-eight, so the numerical value of the letters of your name add up to two-hundred forty eight."

8. A. [Commenting on Gen. 12:2: "So that you will be a blessing,"] said R. Levi, "No one ever haggled with Abraham about the price of a cow without being blessed, and no one ever gave a price to Abraham to sell him a cow without being blessed.

B. "Abraham would pray for barren women until they conceived, for the sick and they would be healed."

C. R. Huna said, "It was not the end of the matter that Abraham would have to go to the sick person, but if the sick person merely laid eyes on him, he got better."

D. Said R. Haninah, "Even ships that sailed on the ocean would be saved on account of the merit of Abraham."

E. But were they not carrying wine used for libations [and so serving idolatry]?

F. [He replied,] "'Vinegar cheapens wine' -- wherever gentile wine [used for libations to idols] is abundant, Israelite wine also is sold at a cheap price."

G. Said R. Isaac, "God treated Job the same way : 'You have blessed the work of his hands' (Job 1:10): No one took a penny from Job and had to get another penny from him [since the original act of charity sufficed to bring the pauper prosperity]."

9. A. "And you will be a blessing" (Gen. 12:2):

B. [Since the word may be read, "pool of water, what it means is, "Just as a pool of water removes the cultic uncleanness of an unclean person, so you will bring near to God those who are far from him."

10. A. Said R. Berekhiah, "Since the Scripture states, 'I will bless you,' why does it go on to state, 'You will be a blessing'?

B. "He said to him, 'Up to this point I had to give a blessing to my world. From now on, lo, the power of bestowing a blessing is handed over to you. To the person whom you wish to give a blessing, give a blessing.'"

The sizable composition serves to spell out the meaning of God's promise to make Abraham "a great nation." At No. 1 we begin by asking why Abraham, not Noah, is set apart. The difference is that Abraham will be the father of a "great nation," now with reference to Israel in particular, Deut. 4:7. This point is underlined at No. 2, where Abraham is now subjected to a fresh act of creation, the counterpart not to Noah but to the first man, made in the first act of creation. No. 3 moves in a different direction, remaining close, at Nos. 3-4, to the exegesis of the language before us.

No. 5 takes up the interpretation of what greatness is promised. That is the great name involved in circulating one's own coinage. What is striking here is the names on the list: Abraham, Joshua, David, Mordecai, all of them figures in the salvific history of Israel. Abraham began the work, Joshua acquired the Land, David stands for the messianic redemption, and Mordecai, forever the favorite in the salvific repertoire of this composition, represents Israel's conquest of this-worldly power. So the salvific history of Israel works itself out in terms of Israel's own coinage. When we consider the use of the mint to proclaim the theory of the state, the passage becomes rather daring in its implications.

No. 6 proceeds to yet another matter, namely, the reference to a "blessing," which calls to mind the Eighteen Benedictions of the liturgy. No. 7 reads the statement that God will make Abram's name great to mean that he will make his name longer, by adding an H. No. 8 proceeds to the sort of blessing that people got from Abraham, and Nos. 9, 10, focus on the same matter. So the net effect is to lay out a repertoire of meanings to be imputed to the base verse. We note that no intersecting verses are brought to bear; that exercise has been concluded. Exegesis takes a number of forms.

XXXIX:XII.

1. A. "I will bless those who bless you, [and the one who curses you I will curse, and by you all the families of the earth shall bless themselves]" (Gen. 12:3):

B. Said R. Jeremiah b. Eleazar, "The Holy One, blessed be he, imposed a requirement in the case of the honor owing to the righteous man more exacting even than the honor owing to him himself. In respect to the honor owing to him himself, it is written, 'For them that honor me I will honor, and those who despise me shall be disgraced' (1 Sam. 2:30) that is, through what others do.

C. "But with reference to the honor owing to the righteous man: 'I will bless those who bless you, and him who curses you I will curse,' that is, I personally will see to it."

2. A. It has been taught on Tannaite authority: What are the benedictions [of the Eighteen Benedictions] at which one bends the knee? In the first benediction, at the start and at the end; in the benediction beginning, "We give thanks," at the start and at the finish. And if one has bowed on the occasion of the recitation of each of the benedictions, people teach such a person not to do so.

B. R. Isaac bar Nahman in the name of R. Joshua b. Levi, "The high priest does so at the beginning of each blessing, and the king does so at the beginning of each blessing and at the end of each blessing."

C. R. Simon in the name of R. Joshua b. Levi: "Once the king has bent his knee, he does not straighten up until he has completed the entire prayer that he was going to say, in line with this verse: 'And it was so that when Solomon had made an end of praying all this prayer and supplication to the Lord, he arose from before the altar of the Lord, from kneeling on his knees' (1 Kgs. 8:54).

D. What is the difference between one form of bending the knee and another?

E. R. Hiyya the elder indicated to Rabbi how one does the one and he was lamed but later healed. Levi b. Sisi showed him the other, got lame, but never got better.

3. A. "And by you will be blessed" (Gen. 12:3):
   B. Rain and dew will come on account of your merit.

4. A. "And the thing became known to Mordecai, who told it to Esther, the queen" (Est. 2:22):
   B. The one was circumcised, the other not, and yet the former showed concern for the latter?
   C. R. Judah said, "'From my elders I receive understanding' (Ps. 119:100).
   D. "[This verse applies to Mordecai.] For Mordecai thought to himself, 'Jacob blessed Pharaoh: "And Jacob blessed Pharaoh" (Gen. 47:7), and did not Joseph interpret his dreams for him, and did not Daniel interpret the dreams of Nebuchadnezzer? So too shall I do: "And he told Esther the queen" (Est. 2:22).' [In all of these cases a circumcised person helped an uncircumcised one, just as Abraham had taught them to do.]"

5. A. Said R. Nehemiah, "Said the Holy One, blessed be he, to Abraham, 'And by you all the families of the earth shall bless themselves' (Gen. 12:3).

B. "If the reference is to wealth, the gentiles are richer than we are. But it is as to good advice. When they get into trouble, they ask us what to do, and we tell them."

No. 1 provides a straightforward explanation of the blessing that is at hand. God personally blesses Abraham, caring more for that matter than for his own honor. That is simply a close reading of the two proof-texts. Why No. 2 is inserted I cannot say. No.3 explains how the gentiles are blessed by Israel. No. 4 goes over to the same question.

XXXIX:XIII.

1. A. "So Abram went, as the Lord had told him, and Lot went with him" (Gen. 12:4).

B. Lot was a lot of extra baggage for him.

2. A. "Abram was seventy-five years old when he departed from Haran" (Gen. 12:4).

B. "And he brought up Hadassah" (Est. 2:7):

C. Rab said, "She was forty years old."

D. Samuel said, "She was eighty years old."

E. Rabbis of Babylonia say, "She was seventy-five years old."

F. R. Berekhiah in the name of Rabbis: "Said the Holy One, blessed be he, to Abraham, 'You have left your father's house at the age of seventy-five. By your life, I shall raise up a redeemer from you who will be seventy-five years old,' the numerical value of the letters of the name of Hadassah."

No. 1 provides a minor gloss, explaining that Lot was never central to the event. No. 2 refers to the fact of the present verse. The repeated reference to Mordecai raises the question of why he is deemed a critical figure in the typology of Abraham. It seems to me the prominence accorded to Mordecai and Esther derives from their standing as heroes in the this-worldly struggle for Israel's salvation.

XXXIX:XIV.

1. A. "And Abram took Sarai his wife, and Lot his brother's son, and all their possessions which they had gathered, and the soul that they had made..." (Gen. 12:5):

B. R. Eleazar in the name of R. Yose b. Zimra: "If all of the nations of the world should come together to try to create a single mosquito, they could not put a soul into it, and yet you say, 'And the soul that they had made'? [They could not have created souls.] But this refers to proselytes."

C. Then why should not the text say, "The proselytes whom they had converted." Why stress, "whom they had made"?

D. This serves to teach you that whoever brings a gentile close [to the worship of the true God] is as if he had created him anew.

E. And why not say, "That he had made"? Why, "That *they* had made"?

F. Said R. Huniah, "Abraham converted the men and Sarah the women."

The cited clause is subjected to a careful analysis. The activity of Abram and Sarai in creating converts to the one true God comes under repeated stress.

XXXIX:XV.

1. A. "Abram passed through the land to the place at Shechem, to the oak of Moreh. At that time the Canaanites were in the land" (Gen. 12:6):

   B. Up to that point they still had the merit to retain the land.

2. A. "Then the Lord appeared to Abram and said, 'To your descendants I will give this land.' So he built there an altar to the Lord who had appeared to him" (Gen. 12:7):

   B. This was on account of the good news about the Land of Israel.

3. A. "Thence he removed to the mountain on the east of Bethel" (Gen. 12:8):

   B. [Since the word for "east" also can mean "in earlier times," we read:] it used to be called "the house of God" (*beth el*) but now it is called "the house of sin (*beth aven).*"

   C. Said R. Eliezer, "If one does not have the merit of being called 'son of toil,' he is called 'son of dung'. [Freedman, p. 325, n. 2: He who does not earn for himself the epithet, a toiler in the Torah, earns for himself the other epithet.]"

   D. Said R. Isaac bar Nahman, "There [in the land of Israel] a good worker is called 'industrious' but [Freedman:] urine-soaked dung is called by that other epithet."

4. A. "He pitched his tent" (Gen. 12:8):

   B. Said R. Haninah, "The word is so written as to be read, 'his tent.' Once he had pitched Sarah's tent, he pitched his own."

Nos. 1, 2 introduce the theme of the Israelite claim to the land. No. 1 concedes that, in Abram's time, the Canaanites still had not used up all the merit that they had. No. 2 then states that Abram's altar responded to the good news that he would get the land. No. 3 is introduced for its own reasons and makes no point relevant to this context. No. 4 is miscellaneous as well.

XXXIX:XVI.

1. A. "[And pitched his tent with Bethel on the west and Ai on the east]; there he built an altar to the Lord and called on the name of the Lord" (Gen. 12:8):

B. Said R. Eleazar, "He built three altars, one on the occasion of receiving the good news of the coming gift of the Land of Israel, one to mark the right of possession of the land, and one to gain the merit that his descendants not fall at Ai [Joshua 7:6ff.].

C. "So it is written: 'And Joshua tore his clothes and fell to the earth upon his face before the ark of the Lord until the evening, he and the elders of Israel, and they put dust on their heads' (Josh. 7:6)."

D. R. Eleazar b. Shamua said, "In doing so, they began to call to mind the merit attained by our father, Abraham, who said, 'I am but dust and ashes' (Gen. 18:27).

E. "'Did their father not build an altar in Ai only so that his descendants would not fall there?'"

2. A. "And called on the name of the Lord" (Gen. 12:8) by praying.

B. Another interpretation: "And he called" by beginning to make proselytes.

3. A. "And Abram journeyed on, still going toward the Negeb" (Gen. 12:9):

B. He marked out his course toward the future house of the sanctuary.

No. 1 links the altar at Ai, Gen. 12:8-9, to the later battle on the same spot. As we see at No. 3, the effort to link the story of Abram to the later history of Israel guides the exegete throughout. The future sanctuary is always in mind.

Chapter Seven

Parashah Forty. Genesis 12:10-16

XL:I.

1. A. "Now there was a famine in the land" (Gen. 12:10):

   B. "Behold the eye of the Lord is toward those who fear him" (Ps. 33:18).

   C. This refers to Abraham.

   D. "For now I know that you fear God" (Gen. 22:12).

2. A. "Toward those who wait for his mercy" (Ps. 33:18).

   B. "You will show faithfulness to Jacob, mercy to Abraham" (Mic. 7:20).

3. A. "To deliver their soul from death" (Ps. 33:19):

   B. [Referring to Abraham, the verse alludes] to the death that Nimrod [had prepared for] him.

4. A. "And to keep them alive in famine" (Ps. 33:19):

   B. "And there was famine in the land, and Abram went down into Egypt to sojourn there" (Gen. 12:10).,

The compositor presents a wholly unitary statement, in which Ps. 33:18-19 is read in light of the figure of Abraham, reaching its climax in the intersection of Ps. 33:19 and Gen. 12:10. The point of intersection is the reference to being saved from famine. That the composition served a purpose distinctive to the present exegetical setting is self-evident. That is to say, it was because the exegete wished to make an observation about Gen. 12:10 that he went about creating the discourse as a whole. The selection of Ps. 33:18-19 thus derives from the concluding clause, No. 4, as we see.

When we see how the compositors here succeed in the larger work of writing a commentary to the book of Genesis in particular, we recognize how much of what they have given us originally was made up to serve purposes irrelevant to the distinctive redactional-exegetical task at hand. Once more,

Genesis Rabbah emerges as the voice of those who selected and arranged its materials, not those who made them up.

XL:II.

1. A. R. Phineas in the name of R. Hanan of Sepphoris commenced discourse [by citing the following verse]: "'Happy is the man whom you chastise, O Lord' (Ps. 94:12).

B. "And if someone should come to complain [about God's chastisement], 'And teach out of your Torah' (Ps. 94:12). [The Torah provides the correct reply to those who complain against the justice of God's punishment.]

C. "What is written in regard to Abraham? 'And I shall bless you and make your name great' (Gen. 12:2).

D. "When [Abraham] went forth [from Ur], famine seized him, but he did not make a complaint or issue a condemnation, but [in all serenity,] 'Now there was a famine in the land, so Abram went down to Egypt' (Gen. 12:10)." [Abram did not complain but accepted the chastisement happily.]

2. A. R. Joshua b. Levi opened [discourse by citing the following verse of Scripture]: "He has given what is torn [*teref*] to those who fear him, he will be ever mindful of his covenant (Ps. 111:5)."

B. Said R. Joshua b. Levi, "Being torn away [from home, that is, wandering] is what he has given to those who fear him in this world. But in the world to come, 'He will be ever mindful of his covenant' (Ps. 111:5).

C. "What is written with regard to Abraham? 'I shall bless you and make your name great' (Gen. 12:2).

D. "When [Abraham] went forth [from Ur], famine seized him, but he did not make a complaint or issue a condemnation, but [in all serenity,] 'Now there was a famine in the land, so Abram went down to Egypt' (Gen. 12:10)."

The intersecting verse now teaches a distinct lesson, at No. 1, which is that Abram having been commanded to leave Ur and go to the Land made no complaint when he immediately had to leave the Land. Once more the trust and faith of Abram call forth emphasis on the part of the exegetes. The underlying polemic against those who ask how God can both promise the Land and also hinder Israelite access to it certainly is to be noted. But I should not be inclined to see that polemic in the center of the passage. The point of No. 2 is the same, but now the chosen verse yields not the rather general theological observation. Rather, the specific issue, Abram's having to wander after having been told to seek a home in the Land, finds full symbolization in the key-word, "tearing up," which is exploited for its several meanings. The composite of No. 1 and No. 2 certainly forms a fine piece of unitary composition. The fundamental message is clear: Abram was saved by his faith, which was unquestioning and uncomplaining. So too will his children be saved by their trust in God, despite present suffering.

XL:III.

1. A. "Now there was a famine in the land" (Gen. 12:10):

    B. Ten famines came into the world.

    C. One was in the time of the first man [Adam]: "Cursed is the ground for your sake" (Gen. 3:17).

    D. One was in the time of Lamech: "Out of the ground which the Lord has cursed" (Gen. 5:29).

    E. One was in the time of Abraham: "And there was a famine in the land" (Gen. 12:10)

    F. One was in the time of Isaac: "And there was famine in the land, beside the first famine that was in the time of Abraham" (Gen. 26:1).

    G. One was in the time of Jacob: "For these two years has the famine been in the land" (Gen. 45:6).

    H. One was in the time of the rule of judges: "And it came to pass in the days when the judges ruled, that there was a famine in the land" (Ruth 1:1).

    I. One was in the time of David: "And there was a famine in the days of David" (2 Sam. 21:1).

    J. One was in the time of Elijah: "As the Lord, the God of Israel, lives, before whom I stand, there shall not be dew or rain these years" (1 Kgs. 17:1).

    K. One was in the time of Elisha: "And there was a great famine in Samaria" (2 Kgs. 6:25).

    L. There is one famine which moves about the world.

    M. One famine will be in the age to come: "Not a famine of bread nor a thirst for water but of hearing the words of the Lord" (Amos 8:11).

    N. R. Huna and R. Jeremiah in the name of Samuel bar R. Isaac: "In point of fact its principal appearance should have come not in the time of David. It was supposed to come only in the time of Saul, but because Saul was a shoot of a sycamore tree, the Holy One, blessed be he, postponed the famine and assigned it to the time of David."

    O. Will Shilah sin and Yohanan be punished?

    P. Said R. Hiyya, "The matter may be compared to the case of a glass maker who had a basket full of cups and cut glass. When he wanted to hang up the basket, he would bring a peg and drive it in and first suspend himself from the peg [to test it] and only then would suspend his basket.

Q. "That is why all of the famines came not in the time of unimportant men but in the time of heroes who could withstand the test."

R. R. Berekhiah recited in their regard the following verse of Scripture: "He gives power to the faint" (Is. 40:29).

S. R. Berekhiah in the name of R. Helbo: "Two famines came in the time of Abraham." [This would then take Lamech off the list of heroes.]

T. R. Huna in the name of R. Aha: "One indeed was in the time of Lamech, the other in the time of Abraham."

U. The famine that came in the time of Elijah was one of [Freedman:] scarcity, one year yielding and one year not yielding. [Freedman p. 208, n. 5: There was food, but not enough to satisfy.]

V. The famine that came in the time of Elishah was one of panic: "Until an ass's head was sold for fourscore pieces of silver" (2 Kgs. 6:25).

W. As to the famine that came in the time of the judges,

X. R. Huna in the name of R. Dosa: "From two *seahs* of wheat for a *sela* the price went up to one *seah* of wheat per *sela*."

Y. And lo, it has been taught on Tannaite authority: [Since it is a religious duty to dwell in the holy land,] someone should go abroad, leaving the land, only if two *seahs* of wheat go for a *sela*. [How then could the family have left Bethlehem and gone abroad, if the price was not at the level that justified emigration?]

Z. Said R. Simon, "When does this rule apply? It is when one cannot find any to buy [at such a high price], but if one can find some to buy, then even if the price is a *seah* for a *sela*, one should not abandon the land and go abroad."

The passage as a whole is inserted here only because the base-verse finds a place in the larger construction. But, quite obviously, the composition does not take shape around an interest in our verse. The contrast to XL:I is clear. The curse to which the cited verse of Gen. 3:17 makes reference was a famine; the remainder of the composition, intersecting with any of the cited passages at only in an unimportant way, pursues the topic of famines. Its syllogism, about God's testing the strong, requires no comment. It is part of the larger polemic at hand, that is, Abram's faithful acceptance of trials, and underlines the message about him. But the choice of the passage, not its contents, is what serves the exegete-compositors' purpose.

XL:IV.

1. A. "When he was about to enter Egypt, [he said to Sarai, his wife, 'I know that you are a woman beautiful to behold. And when the Egyptians see you, they will say, "This is his wife," and then they will kill me, but they will let

you live. Say you are my sister, that it may go well with me because of you, and that my life may be spared on your account']" (Gen. 12:11-12):

B. Now she had been with him for all those years of their marriage, but only now does he say to her, "I know that you are a woman beautiful to behold"! [Why did he not know that earlier?]

C. The reason is that on account of the travails of journeying a person becomes disheveled, [but Sarai remained exquisite].

2. A. R. Azariah in the name of R. Judah b. R. Simon: "[Abram said to her,] 'We have journeyed throughout Aram Naharaim and Aram Nahor and have never found a woman so beautiful as you.

B. "'But now that we are going into a place in which the people are ugly and swarthy, 'Say, you are my sister, that it may go well with me because of you and that my life may be spared on your account' (Gen. 12:13)."

3. A. R. Phineas in the name of R. Reuben: "Two men had the main role but [humbled themselves and] treated themselves as subordinates, Abraham and Barak.

B. "Barak: 'And she sent and called Barak...and Barak said to her, "If you will go with me, then I will go, but if you will not go with me, then I will not go"' (Judges 4:6ff.)." [Likewise here, Abram humbled himself.]

C. [Explaining the conditional contract,] R. Judah said, "'If you will go with me to Kadesh, I will go with you against Hazor, but if you will not go with me to Kadesh, I will not go with you against Hazor.'"

D. R. Nehemiah said, "'If you will go with me in song, I shall go with you to battle, and if you will not go with me in song, I will not go with you to battle' [Freedman, p., 328, n. 5: 'If you undertake to join me in singing praises to God,' as at Judges 5]."

E. "And she said, 'I will surely go with you, notwithstanding the journey that you take shall not be for your honor'" (Judges 4:9):

F. Said R. Reuben, "The word for 'notwithstanding' is a Greek word that stands for 'let alone.' So the sense of what she said to him is this: 'What are you now supposing? Is it that the glory of the song will be handed over to you for a blessing?'"

G. [Reverting to B,] "So he turned out to be subordinated: 'Then sang Deborah and Barak the son of Abinoam' (Judges 5:10)

H. [Continuing A-B above,] "Abraham held the principal role but treated himself as secondary: 'Say you are my sister' (Gen. 12:13).

I. "And as a result he was made subordinate: 'And he dealt well with Abram on her account' (Gen. 12:16)."

The three explanations of Gen. 12:11 take up different questions. No. 1 asks why all of a sudden Abram remarked about Sarai's beauty, and answers that despite their journeys she had retained her looks. No. 2 gives a more straight-forward explanation. Sarai will appear more beautiful in Egypt, by contrast to the looks of the people there. No. 3 focuses upon the quite separate observation that, since Abram had treated himself as subordinated to Sarai, he was treated by Pharaoh as subordinate. Obviously, No. 3 has been worked out in terms of Judges 4:6ff., since the exposition of its clauses hardly contributes to making the main point of the composition as a whole So No. 3 appears to join two distinct passages, A-B+G-I and the inserted and cogent expansion on the passage in Judges.

XL:V.

1. A. "When Abram entered Egypt, the Egyptians saw that the woman was very beautiful" (Gen. 12:14);

B. Now [if we refer only to Abram's entering Egypt,] where was Sarah?

C. [Abram] had put her into a box and locked her up. When he got to the customs booth, the toll collector said to him, "Pay the toll."

D. He said, "I shall pay it."

E. He said to him, "Clothing is what you are carrying."

F. [Rather than opening the box to reveal Sarai,] Abram said to him, "So I shall pay the customs duties on clothing."

G. He said to him, "Silk is what you are carrying."

H. He said to him, "So I shall pay the duty on silk."

I. He said to him, "Pearls are what you are carrying."

J. He said to him, "So I'll pay the fee for pearls."

K. He said to him, "Nothing goes unless you open the box and show us what is in it."

L. When he had opened the box, the whole land of Egypt sparkled from the luster of Sarai.

2. A. R. Azariah and R. Jonathan in the name of R. Isaac: "The model of the beauty of Eve was handed over to the most beautiful women of the generations to come.

B. "Further on it is written, 'And the damsel was very fair' (1 Kgs. 1:4), that is, she was as fair as the beauty in the model of Eve.

C. "But here: 'The Egyptians saw that the woman was very beautiful' (Gen. 12:14), meaning, still more beautiful than Eve."

3. A. "And when the princes of Pharaoh saw her, they praised her to Pharaoh [and the woman was taken into Pharaoh's house]" (Gen. 12:15):

B. R. Yohanan said, "They out did each other in bidding [for the right to go into the palace with] her. One of them said, 'I shall give a hundred *denars* to go into the palace with her,' and the other, 'I shall give two hundred to go in with her.'

C. "I know that that is the case only when it had to do with their rise. [People are willing to bid up the price to participation in the promotion of a righteous person.] How do I know that they bid up the price for the right to join in their degradation as well? [Freedman, p. 330, n. 3: How do I know that when the righteous are to be humbled and mishandled, people outbid each other for the privilege of doing so?]

D. "'They took Jeremiah and cast him into the pit' (Jer. 38:6). They bid up his price.

E. "I know that that is the case as to this world. How do I know that it applies to the world to come?

F. "'And the peoples shall take them and bring them to their place' (Is. 14:2)."

No. 1 presents a charming story on how Abram tried to keep Sarai hidden, paying any price to do so. No. 2 moves on to a quite separate observation about Sarai's remarkable beauty. So No. 1 deals with Gen. 12:14, "When Abram entered Egypt," and No. 2 with the passage, "The Egyptians saw that the woman was very beautiful." Then No. 3 moves on to Gen. 12:15, "They praised her to Pharaoh, and the woman was taken into Pharaoh's house." It would appear that XL:IV.3 is out of place, since it deals with "And for her sake he dealt well with Abram"" Gen. 12:16), and so should follow the present passage.

XL:VI.

1. A. "And for her sake he dealt well with Abram" (Gen. 12:16):

B. "And Pharaoh gave men orders concerning him, [and they set him on the way, with his wife and all that he had]" (Gen. 12:20).

C. R. Phineas in the name of R. Hoshaiah said, "The Holy One, blessed be he, said to our father, Abraham, 'Go and pave a way before your children.' [Set an example for them, so that whatever you do now, they will do later on.] [We shall now see how each statement about Abram at Gen. 12:10-20 finds a counterpart in the later history of Israel, whether Jacob or the children of Jacob.]

D. "You find that whatever is written in regard to our father, Abraham, is written also with regard to his children.

E. "With regard to Abraham it is written, 'And there was a famine in the land' (Gen. 12:10) In connection with Israel: 'For these two years has the famine been in the land'" (Gen. 45:6).

F. "With regard to Abraham: 'And Abram went down into Egypt' (Gen. 12:10).

G. "With regard to Israel: 'And our fathers went down into Egypt' (Num. 20:15).

H. "With regard to Abraham: 'To sojourn there' (Gen. 12:10).

I. "With regard to Israel: 'To sojourn in the land we have come' (Gen. 47:4).

J. "With regard to Abraham: 'For the famine is heavy in the land' (Gen. 12:10).

K. "With regard to Israel: 'And the famine was heavy in the land' (Gen. 43:1).

L. "With regard to Abraham: 'And it came to pass, when he drew near to enter into Egypt' (Gen. 12:11: 'When he was about to enter Egypt').

M. "With regard to Israel: 'And when Pharaoh drew near' (Ex. 14:10).

N. "With regard to Abraham: 'And they will kill me but you will they keep alive' (Gen. 12:12).

O. "With regard to Israel: 'Every son that is born you shall cast into the river, and every daughter you shall save alive' (Ex. 1:22).

P. "With regard to Abraham: 'Say you are my sister, that it may go well with me because of you' (Gen. 12:13).

Q. "With regard to Israel: 'And God dealt well with the midwives' (Ex. 1:20).

R. "With regard to Abraham: 'And when Abram had entered Egypt' (Gen. 12:14).

S. "Israel: 'Now these are the names of the sons of Israel, who came into Egypt' (Ex. 1:1).

T. "With regard to Abraham: 'And Abram was very rich in cattle, in silver, and in gold' (Gen. 13:23).

U. "With regard to Israel: 'And he brought them forth with silver and gold' (Ps. 105:37).

V. "With regard to Abraham: And Pharaoh gave men orders concerning him and they set him on the way' (Gen. 12:20).

W. "Israel: 'And the Egyptians were urgent upon the people to send them out' (Ex. 12:33).

X. "With regard to Abraham: 'And he went on his journeys' (Gen. 13:3).

Y. "With regard to Israel: 'These are the journeys of the children of Israel' (Num. 33:1)."

This powerful litany carefully links the story of Abram to the history of Israel, showing how the Israelites later on point by point relived the life of Abram. Any claim, therefore, that there were children of Abraham other than Israel ("after the flesh") finds refutation in this statement. The passage forms a striking conclusion to Gen. 12:10-20, because it treats the whole and not merely its segments, one by one, and the cogent statement draws out a message that relates to the entire composition. It would be hard to find a more careful effort to conclude a sustained discussion (whether what has gone before in fact was or was not a sustained discussion). On that basis I follow the current printed texts that at the present point separate Parashah XL from Parashah XLI.

Chapter Eight

Parashah Forty-One.   Genesis 12:17-13:17

XLI:I.

1. A. "But the Lord afflicted Pharaoh and his house with great plagues because of Sarai, Abram's wife" (Gen. 12:17):

   B. "The righteous shall flourish like the palm-tree, he shall grow like a cedar in Lebanon" (Ps. 92:13).

   C. Just as a palm tree and a cedar produce neither crooked curves nor growths, so the righteous do not produce either crooked curves or growths.

   D. Just as the shade of the palm tree and cedar is distant [from the base of the tree] so the giving of the reward that is coming to the righteous seems distant.

   E. Just as, in the case of the palm tree and the cedar, the very core of the tree points upward, so in the case of the righteous, their heart is pointed toward the Holy One, blessed be he.

   F. That is in line with the following verse of Scripture: "My eyes are ever toward the Lord, for he will bring forth my feet out of the net" (Ps. 25:15).

   G. Just as the palm tree and cedar are subject to desire, so the righteous are subject to desire.

   H. And what might it be? What they desire is the Holy One, blessed be he.

2. A. Said R. Tanhuma, "There was the case of a palm tree that stood in Amato and did not produce fruit. A palm-horticulturist passed by and saw it.

   B. "He said, 'This ungrafted palm looks toward [a male palm] at Jericho.' Once he had grafted it, the tree produced fruit." [Only when the righteous are joined to the Holy One, whom they desire, can they produce results.]

3. A. Might one continue the analogy as follows: Just as in the case of a palm tree, people cannot make utensils out of its wood, so in the case of the righteous [nothing good comes of them]?

   B. Scripture says, "like a cedar." [The righteous are like a cedar.]

C. Said R. Huna, "Over there [in Babylonia] people make things out of its wood." [The righteous also produce good things.]

4. A. Might one then argue as follows: just as in the case of a cedar, the tree does not produce fruit, so the righteous [do not produce fruit]?

B. Scripture says, "The righteous shall flourish like a palm tree."

5. A. Just as in the case of a palm tree, there is nothing that is left as refuse, for the dates are eaten, the branches used for reciting the Hallel-psalms [on the festival of Tabernacles], the twigs used for *sukkah* -roofing [on the same festival], the bast is used for ropes, the leaves are used for besoms [Freedman], the planed boards used for making ceilings for rooms,

B. the same is so of Israel. There is none among them who lacks all value. Some of them are masters of Scripture, some masters of Mishnah teachings, some masters of Talmud [study], some of them are masters of lore.

6. A. And just as in the case of a palm tree and a cedar, whoever climbs up to the top and does not watch his step falls and dies, so whoever comes to contend with Israel on their account will in the end get what he has coming to him [Freedman: "receive his deserts on their account"].

B. You may know that that is so, for in the case of Sarah, merely because Pharaoh took hold of her for a single night, he was smitten, both he and his household, with plagues.

C. That is in line with this verse: "But the Lord afflicted Pharaoh and his house with great plagues because of Sarai" (Gen. 12:17).

This is an essentially unitary composition, in which the intersecting verse is systematically worked out and only at the end brought to bear upon the base verse. The goal of the whole is the base verse, but that goal is reached only after a thorough account of the meanings to be imputed to the intersecting one. My division therefore is somewhat misleading, since apart from some fairly obvious interpolations, e.g., Nos. 2, 3.A, the movement is inexorable and uniform. The comparison of trying to top the tree and Pharaoh's conduct with Sarai of course proves somewhat too apt.

XLI:II.

1. A. R. Simeon b. Laqish in the name of Bar Qappara: "Pharaoh was smitten with lupus [Freedman]."

B. Said R. Simeon b. Gamaliel, "An elder afflicted with boils met me in Sepphoris. He said to me, 'There were twenty-four kinds of boils, and you have among them all none for which sexual relations with a woman is bad news except for the matter of lupus. And with that form of boil the wicked Pharaoh was smitten.'"

2. A. "[But the Lord afflicted Pharaoh] and his house" (Gen. 12:17):

   B. Said R. Aha, "Even the beams of his house were smitten."

3. A. Everyone said, "It is 'because of Sarai, Abram's wife' (Gen. 12:17)."

   B. Said R. Berekhiah, "It was because he had the gall to come near even to the shoe of that noble woman."

4. A. And that entire night Sarah lay prostrate in prayer, saying, "Lord of the ages, Abraham went forth on account of trust, and I went forth in good faith. Abraham is outside of prison, so should I be put in prison?"

   B. Said to her the Holy One, blessed be he, "Whatever I am going to do will be on your account."

   C. Everyone said, "It is 'because of Sarai, Abram's wife' (Gen. 12:17)."

   D. Said R. Berekhiah, "It was because he had the gall to come near even to the shoe of that noble woman."

5. A. Said R. Levi, "For that entire night the angel was standing by with a whip in hand. If she said to him, 'Hit,' [the angel] hit, and if she said to him, 'Leave off,' he left off.'

   B. "And why all this? Because she had said to [Pharaoh], 'I am a married woman,' and he did not leave her alone."

6. A. R. Eleazar, and it has been taught in the name of R. Eliezer b. Jacob, "We have heard concerning Pharaoh that he was smitten with *saraat*, and in the case of Abimelech, that he was smitten with constipation.

   B. "How do we know that what applied to the one applied to the other and vice versa?

   C. "It is because the words 'for the sake of' occur in both cases, so serving to establish an analogy between them."

Freedman, p. 333, n. 4, explains the exegesis of Nos. 1-5: "All these statements are deduced from the verse under discussion, 'for the sake of,' which can also mean, 'by the word of.' Hence it is interpreted: by the word of all people, that this was on account of Sarai; again, by the word, that is, the prayer, of Sarah, and, finally, 'by the word of Sarai to the angel.' 'Abram's wife' is superfluous, hence the comment: that he should have dared to approach Abram's wife." (No. 3 obviously is out of place and should be dropped, since its logical place is in No. 4.) That the same observation applies at No. 6 is self-evident. In all, therefore, we move from the exegesis generated by the choice of an intersecting verse to a different kind of exegesis, namely, a systematic reading of the language at hand and expansion upon its implications.

XLI:III.

1. A. ""Now Abram was very rich in cattle, in silver, and in gold" (Gen. 13:2):

    B. That is in line with this verse: "And he brought them forth with silver and with gold, and there was none that stumbled among his tribes" (Ps. 105:37).

2. A. "And he journeyed on [from the Negeb as far as Bethel, to the place where his tent had been at the beginning, between Bethel and Ai]" (Gen. 13:3):

    B. He journeyed on in those same routes that he had originally traveled.

    C. Said R. Eleazar, "He went to collect what was owing to him."

3. A. "And Lot, who went with Abram, also had flocks and herds and tents" (Gen. 13:5):

    B. Four advantages did Lot enjoy owing to Abraham.

    C. "And Lot went with him" (Gen. 12:4).

    D. "And Lot...also..." (Gen. 13:5).

    E. "And he also brought back his brother Lot and his goods" (Gen. 14:16).

    F. "And it came to pass, when God destroyed the cities of the plain, that God remembered Abraham and sent Lot out of the midst of the overthrow [rebellion]" (Gen. 19:29).

    G. Now corresponding to these matters Lot's descendants [the Ammonites and Moabites] ought to have paid us back with acts of decency. And it was not enough for them not to pay us back with acts of decency, but they did deeds of evil to us.

    H. That is in line with these verses of Scripture:

    I. "And he [Moab] sent messengers to Balaam...Come now, therefore, I pray you, curse this people" (Num. 22:5).

    J. "And he gathered to him the children of Ammon and Amalek, and he went and smote Israel" (Judges 3:13).

K. "And it came to pass after this that...the children of Ammon and with them some of the Ammonites came against Jehoshaphat to battle" (2 Chr. 20:1).

L. "The adversary has spread out his hand upon all her treasures" (Lam. 1:10).

M. Their sin is then recorded in four passages:

N. "An Ammonite or a Moabite shall not enter into the assembly of the Lord...because they met you not with bread and water in the way" (Deut. 23:4).

O. "Because they did not meet the children of Israel with bread and water" (Neh. 13:2).'

P. "My people, remember now what Balak, king of Moab, devised" (Mic. 6:5).

Q. Four prophets moreover came and pronounced doom against them, Isaiah, Jeremiah, Ezekiel, and Zephaniah.

R. Isaiah: "The burden of Moab" (Is. 15:1).

S. Jeremiah: "Then I will cause an alarm of war to be heard against Rabbah of the children of Ammon" (Jer. 49:2).

T. Ezekiel: "I will open the flank of Moab...together with the children of Ammon, to the children of the east...and I will execute judgments upon Moab" (Ez. 25:9).

U. Zephaniah: "Surely Moab shall be as Sodom and the children of Amon as Gomorrah" (Zeph. 2:9).

The exegesis of the sequential verses continues in due pace. No. 3 is of a different order, since for the exposition of its message the base verse is merely another piece of evidence. The point of the passage in no way rests upon the verse at hand, nor does the exegesis of the base verse attract sustained interest. So while Nos. 1, 2 continue the exegetical procedure of the preceding, No. 3 presents a quite different approach to the larger interests at hand. What No. 3 wishes to present is a story of how what happened to to the patriarchs provides insight into the history of Israel later on. The important point is that Lot, whom Abram saved, stood behind Ammon and Moab as their ancestor. So while Israel remained loyal to the model of its patriarchs, Ammon and Moab did not draw appropriate lessons from the life of their progenitor. They should have exhibited gratitude to Israel and instead paid back the loyalty of Abram with treachery.

XLI:IV.

1. A. "And Lot...also had flocks and herds and tents" (Gen. 13:5):

B. R. Tobiah b. R. Isaac said, "He had two tents, Ruth, the Moabite, and Naamah, the Ammonite."

C. Along these same lines, "Arise, take your wife and your two daughters that are found" (Gen. 19:15).

D. R. Tobiah b. R. Isaac said, "This refers to two serendipitous discoveries ["finds"], Ruth and Naamah."

2. A. Said R. Isaac, "'I have found my servant, David' (Ps. 89:21).

B. "'Where did I find him? In Sodom [through the line of Lot via Ruth the Moabite, thus in accord with Gen. 19:15].'"

Tobiah's point does not rest upon the base verse alone. The main idea is that from Lot came blessings to Israel, thus in contradiction to XLI:III.3. The compositor has then presented both sides of the matter. No. 2 of course carries forward 1.C-D. The whole was put together prior to insertion in the present setting; not only so, but the composition to begin with did not aim at making a point particular to the verse at hand.

XLI:V.

1. A. And there was strife between the herdsmen of Abram's cattle and the herdsmen of Lot's cattle" (Gen. 13:7):

B. R. Berekhiah in the name of R. Yudah: "The cattle of Abraham would go out muzzled, and those of Lot did not go out muzzled. The herdsmen of Abraham said to them, 'Is it now all right to steal [what does not belong to you? Why then do you leave your cattle unmuzzled]?'

C. "The herdsmen of Lot replied, 'So has the Holy One, blessed be he, said to Abraham, "To your seed I will give this land" (Gen. 12:7). Now Abraham is a barren mule. He is not going to produce an heir. So Lot will inherit the land. Accordingly the cattle are eating what belongs to them.'

D. "The Holy One, blessed be he said to them, 'This is what I said to him, "To your seed I *will* give this land" (Gen. 12:7). When will this be the case? When the seven nations are uprooted from the land [and not yet]. But now: "And the Canaanites and the Perizzites dwelt in the land"' (Gen. 31:7).

E. "'Up to this time they still enjoy a right to the land.'"

What the passage contributes is an account of what is at issue in the reported dispute. The verse under discussion, Gen. 13:7, contributes the reason: there was strife because the Canaanites and Perizzites still dwelt in the land. So the present composition, obviously unitary and smooth, falls into the classification of the close exegesis of the verse under discussion.

XLI:VI.

1. A. "'Then Abram said to Lot, 'Let there be no strife between you and me'" (Gen. 13:8):

   B. R. Azariah in the name of R. Judah: "Just as there was strife between the shepherds of Abraham and the shepherds of Lot, so there was strife between Abraham and Lot.

   C. "'Then Abram said to Lot, "Let there be no strife between you and me" (Gen. 13:8).'"

2. A. "For we are brethren" (Gen. 13:8):

   B. Now was he really his brother? No, he was not. But he looked like him [and therefore was referred to as his brother].

3. A. "Is not the whole land before you? Separate yourself from me, I pray you" (Gen. 13:9):

   B. Said R. Helbo, "What is written is not 'depart' but 'separate' [which contains the same letters as the word for mule].

   C. "Just as the mule does not produce seed, so it is not possible for that man to become associated with the seed of Abraham. [No mixing with the Moabites or Ammonites is possible.]"

4. A. "If you take the left hand, then I will go to the right, or if you take the right hand, then I will go to the left" (Gen. 13:9):

   B. Lot said to Abraham, "If you go to the left, I shall go to the south. If I go to the south, you go to the left, so one way or the other, I shall go to the south." [Freedman, p. 336, n. 5: Translating the second half of the verse: "Or if I take the right hand, then I will make you go to the left."]

   C. Said R. Yohanan. "The matter may be compared to the case of two men who had two piles of grain, one of wheat, the other of barley.

   D. "One said to the other, 'If the wheat is mine, then the barley is yours, if the barley is yours, then the wheat is mine. Under all circumstances the wheat will be mine.'"

   E. Said R. Hinena bar Isaac, "What is written is not, 'I shall go left,' but rather, 'I shall cause you to go to the left.' 'In any event, I shall make that man [you] go to the left.'"

The systematic exegesis of Gen. 13:8-9 proceeds, clause by clause. The exposition makes Lot into a villain, which the text at this point does not suggest. The linkage of Lot to the Ammonites and Moabites, of course, explains the broader interest in defaming the figure of Lot.

XLI:VII.

1. A. "And Lot lifted up his eyes [and saw that the Jordan valley was well watered everywhere, like the garden of the Lord, like the land of Egypt, in the direction of Zoar; this was before the Lord destroyed Sodom and Gomorrah]" (Gen. 13:10):

   B. Said R. Nahman bar Hanan, "Whoever lusts after fornication in the end will be fed with his own flesh [committing incest]." [The word for lust contains letters which form the name of Lot.]

   C. Said R. Yose bar Haninah, "This entire verse speaks of fornication."

   D. "And Lot lifted up his eyes" (Gen. 13:10): "And his master's wife lifted up her eyes to Joseph" (Gen. 39:76).

   E. "And saw all the plain of the Jordan" (Gen. 13:10): "For on account of a harlot a man is brought to a loaf of bread" (Prov. 6:26) [the word for "loaf" and that for "plain" being the same]. [Freedman, p. 337, n. 4: Translation: "and beheld all the loaf, the immorality, of the Jordan."]

   F. "That it was well watered everywhere" (Gen. 13:10: "And he shall make the woman drink" (Num. 5:24) [using the same root.]

   G. "Before the Lord destroyed Sodom and Gomorrah" (Gen. 13:10): "And it came to pass, when he went in unto his brother's wife, that he spilled on the ground" (Gen. 38:9). [The word for "destroyed" and "spilled" being the same.]

2. A. "And saw that the Jordan valley was well watered everywhere like the garden of the Lord,"(Gen. 13:10) in trees,

   B. " like the land of Egypt" (Gen. 13:10) in grain.

3. A. "So Lot chose for himself all the Jordan valley" (Gen. 13:11):

   B. Said R. Yose b. Zimra, "It is like a man who covets his mother's dowry."

4. A. "And Lot journeyed east" (Gen. 13:11):

   B. He removed himself from the Ancient of the world [with the word for "ancient" and "east" using the same root]:

   C. "I want no part of Abraham or of his God."

5. A. "Thus they separated from each other" (Gen. 13:11):

B. Rabbi said, "You have no more evil city than Sodom. When a man is evil, they call him a Sodomite.

C. "And you have no more harsh people than the Amorites. When a man is harsh, they call him an Amorite."

D. R. Issi said, "You have no more beautiful city than Sodom. When Lot traveled among all the cities of the plain, he found none like Sodom.

E. "And those people were the most impressive among them."

6. A. "The men of Sodom were wicked and sinners against the Lord" (Gen. 13:31):

B. "Wicked" to one another.

C. "Sinners" in fornication.

D. "Against the Lord" through idolatry.

E. "Greatly" in committing murder.

No. 1 takes up the prevailing theme that Lot sinned because he was wicked. He settled in Sodom with every reason to acknowledge its true character. The sexual character of the city's sin is now underlined by showing that the description of the area in fact alluded to its immoral character. Nos. 3, 4, and 5 pursue the same point, each making it in its own way. No. 3 portrays Lot as covetous, No. 4 has Lot abandon God by leaving Abram, No. 5 as progenitor of mean and wicked people, No. 6 sums it all up. Only No. 2 seems a neutral point of exposition.

XLI:VIII.

1. A. "The Lord said to Abram after Lot had separated from him, ['Lift up your eyes and look from the place where you are, northward and southward and eastward and westward. For all the land which you see I will give to you and to your descendants forever']" (Gen. 13:14-15):

B. R. Judah said, "There was anger against our father, Abraham, when Lot, his nephew, separated from him.

C. "Said the Holy One, blessed be he, 'Everyone he brings to cleave [to me], but Lot, his nephew, he does not bring to cleave to me!'"

D. R. Nehemiah said, "There was anger against our father, Abraham, when lot, his nephew, went along with him. Said the Holy One, blessed be he, 'I said to him, "To your seed have I given this land" (Gen. 15:18), and yet he brings Lot along with himself. If that is how matters are, let him bring along two ordinary errand boys [Pahlavi: *parastak*, messenger]."

2. A. That is in line with the following verse: "Cast out the scorner" (Prov. 22:10) -- this refers to Lot.

B. "And contention will go out" (Prov. 22:10) -- this refers to the verse, "And there was strife between the herdmen of herdsmen of Abraham" (Gen. 13:7).

C. "Yes, strife and shame will cease" (Prov. 22:10). That is in line with the verse: "Then Abram said to Lot, 'Let there be no strife between you and me'" (Gen. 13:8).

D. "He who loves pureness of heart, who has grace in his lips, the king shall be his friend" Prov. 22:11). "Lift up your eyes and look from the place where you are, northward and southward and eastward and westward. For all the land which you see I will give to you and to your descendants forever" (Gen. 13:14-15).

The dispute at No. 1 does not take shape around the exegesis of the verse at hand. Rather, it is worked out by Judah and Nehemiah in terms of the cited proof-text. The sole contribution of Gen. 13:14 is to register the fact that God spoke to Abram after Lot had gone his way, raising the question of the relevance of Lot's departure to the message that God is about to deliver. No. 2, by contrast, works out a rather elegant intertwining of the secondary verse, Prov. 22:10-11, with the base-verse. And yet, one may make the case that Abram's behavior with Lot, separating from him to avoid strife, is what caused God to make the promise to Abram stated at Gen. 13:14. So thematically the two passages do cleave to the base verse, even though in form they appear distinct from it. In any event No. 1 assuredly has not been worked out for the purpose of an exegesis of Gen. 13:14. Nor do I see a close link between No. 1 and No. 2.

XLI:IX.

1. A. "I will make your descendants as the dust of the earth" (Gen. 13:16):

B. Just as the dust of the earth is from one end of the world to the other, so your children will be from one end of the world to the other.

C. Just as the dust of the earth is blessed only with water, so your children will be blessed only through the merit attained by study of the Torah, which is compared to water [hence: through water].

D. Just as the dust of the earth wears out metal utensils and yet endures forever, so Israel endures while the nations of the world come to an end.

E. Just as the dust of the world is treated as something on which to trample, so your children are treated as something to be trampled upon by the government.

F. That is in line with this verse: "And I will put it into the hand of them that afflict you" (Is. 51:23), that is to say, those who make your wounds flow [Freedman].

G. Nonetheless, it is for your good that they do so, for they cleanse you of guilt, in line with this verse: "You make her soft with showers" (Ps. 65:11). [Freedman, p. 339, n. 33: "Words of the same root are used for 'make soft' and 'who afflict you.' The passage understands the former in the sense of making the rain flow and hence the latter too -- to make the wounds flow."]

H. "That have said to your soul, 'Bow down, that we may go over'" (Is. 51:23):

I. What did they do to them? They made them lie down in the streets and drew ploughs over them."

J. R. Azariah in the name of R. Aha: "That is a good sign. Just as the street wears out those who pass over it and endures forever, so your children will wear out all the nations of the world and will live forever."

The metaphor of "dust of the earth" yields quite a fresh meaning for the exegetes. Now it is not a mark that Israel will be numerous, but that Israel will survive the rule of the nations of the world. However humble its condition, Israel in the end will outlast its enemies. Israel's humility therefore testifies to its ultimate triumph. All of this emerges from the lesson of God to the patriarch, once more prefiguring Israel's life later on.

XLI:X.

1. A. "Arise, walk through the length and the breadth of the land, [for I will give it to you]" (Gen. 13:17):

B. It has been taught on Tannaite authority: "If one has walked in a field, whether along its length or its breadth, he has made acquisition of it, up to the place in which he has walked," the words of R. Eliezer, for R. Eliezer says, "The act of walking about in a field effects acquisition."

C. And sages say, "He has not acquired the area in which he has walked until he takes possession of the field."

D. Said R. Jacob, "The scriptural evidence for the view of R. Eliezer: 'Arise, walk through the length and the breadth of the land, [for I will give it to you]' (Gen. 13:17)."

The relevance of the discussion to the cited verse is clear. The verse supplies proof that merely by walking in the area, one effects acquisition of it.

Chapter Nine

Parashah Forty-Two.   Genesis 14:1-13

XLII:I.

1.   A.   "It came to pass in the days of Amraphel, [king of Shinar, Arioch, king of Ellasar, Chedorlaomer, king of Elam, and Tidal, king of Goiim]" (Gen. 14:1):

B.   R. Joshua in the name of R. Levi opened discourse [by citing the following verse]:   "The wicked have drawn out the sword" (Ps. 37:15).

C.   The illustrative case concerns R. Eliezer.   His brothers were ploughing on level ground, and he was ploughing on hilly ground.   His cow fell and broke its leg.   But it was to his advantage that his cow had broken its leg. [For] he fled and went to R. Yohanan b. Zakkai.

D.   He was eating clods of dirt [having no money to buy food] until his mouth produced a bad odor.   They went and told Rabban Yohanan b. Zakkai, "R. Eliezer's breath stinks."

E.   He said to him, "Just as the odor of your mouth stank on account of your studying the Torah, so may the fragrance of your learning pervade the world from one end to the other."

F.   After some days his father came up to disinherit him from his property, and he found him sitting and expounding a lesson with the great figures of the realm in session before him, namely, Ben Sisit Hakkeset, Nicodemus son of Gurion, and Ben Kalba Shabua.

G.   He was giving an exposition of this verse, as follows: "'The wicked have drawn out the sword and have bent the bow' (Ps. 37:14) refers to Amraphael and his allies.

H.   "'To cast down the poor and needy' (Ps. 37:14) refers to Lot.

I.   "'To slay such as are upright in the way' (Ps. 37:14) refers to Abraham.

J.   "'Their sword shall enter into their own heart' (Ps. 37:15) in line with this verse: 'And he divided his forces against them by night, he and his servants, and routed them' (Gen. 14:15)."

K.   His father said to him, "My son, I came up here only to disinherit you from my property.   Now, lo, all of my property is handed over to you as a gift [and not by the law of inheritance, which would not allow me to give you everything]."

L. He said to him, "So far as I am, concerned, the property falls into the category of *herem* [and is forbidden to me]. Rather, divide them equally among my brothers."

2. A. Another matter: "The wicked have drawn out the sword" (Ps. 37:14) refers to Amraphel and his allies, as it is written, "And it came to pass in the days of Amraphel" (Gen. 14:1).

No. 2 shows us the bare bones of the composition, simply two verses, the intersecting one and the base one. The full statement of the same matter is at 1.G-J. I do not see any close tie between the narrative setting and the exegetical substance, and there probably is none. Indeed, the narrative itself consists of three elements, first, Eliezer's flight, second, the success at Torah-study, acknowledged by prestigious persons, third, the father's intent to disinherit Eliezer turned into the desire to give him as a gift all of his property, thus disinheriting the (in this story, hapless) brothers. Since the brothers are not cast as villains, the intersecting verse cannot derive from some element in the story about Eliezer. So the whole must be seen as two distinct elements, the narrative composition, the exegetical syllogism.

The selection of the intersecting verse rests upon the notion that "the wicked" who have declared war are Amraphel and his allies, and the one who was upright in his way -- along the lines of Gen. 13:17, "Arise, walk through the length and breadth of the land" -- was Abram. The contrast must come between Gen. 13:18 and Gen. 14:1, Abram builds an altar, while the kings are making war. So the contrast between the one and the other generates the syllogism that contrasts Temple worship with making war.

XLII:II.

1. A. R. Samuel commenced [discourse by citing the following verse]: "And this also is a grievous evil, that in all points as he came so shall he go" (Qoh. 5:15).

B. Said R. Samuel, "Just as he came, namely, with slops, so shall he leave [the world], namely, with slops."

2. A. Said R. Abin, "Just as [Israel's history] began with the encounter with four kingdoms, so [Israel's history] will conclude with the encounter with the four kingdoms.

B. "'Chedorlaomer, king of Elam, Tidal, king of Goiim, Amraphel, king of Shinar, and Arioch, king of Ellasar, four kings against five' (Gen. 14:9).

C. "So [Israel's history] will conclude with the encounter with the four kingdoms: the kingdom of Babylonia, the kingdom of Medea, the kingdom of Greece, and the kingdom of Edom."

3. A. R. Phineas said in the name of R. Abun, "'But they do not know the thoughts of the Lord, nor do they understand his counsel, for he has gathered them as the sheaves to the threshing floor' (Mic. 4:12).

B. "Why did 'all these join forces' (Gen. 14:3)? So that they might come and fall by the hand of Abraham: 'And it came to pass in the days of Amraphel' (Gen. 14:1)."

No. 1 is included only because it is joined to No. 2. But by itself it does not intersect with the present passage, so Nos. 1 and 2 were put together before being inserted here. The point of No. 2, of course, is to draw the analogy between the beginning and the ending (just as Samuel has done for the life of the private person). Just as Israel's history began with Abraham's encounter with the four kings, so it will end with a similar encounter. Accordingly, the fourth monarchy, namely Rome, marks the end. No. 3 presents a distinct and fresh point, that people do not know why God does things, or why they do them at God's initiative. But there is a solid reason. The message of the reading, all together, is that Israel may not know the meaning of its history, but God does know and have a plan, and things will work out in the end. The upshot is that Israel's later history finds its counterpart in the initial event in the public life of Abram, so, once more, the powerful motif of finding a counterpart between the life of Israel and the lives of the patriarchs makes its impact.

XLII:III.

1. A. R. Tanhuma and R. Hiyya the Elder state the following matter, as does R. Berekhiah in the name of R. Eleazar [the Modite], "The following exegetical principle we brought up from the exile.

B. "Any passage in which the words, 'And it came to pass' appear is a passage that relates misfortune."

C. Said R. Samuel bar Nahman, "There are five such passages marked by the words, 'and it came to pass,' that bear the present meaning.

D. "'And it came to pass in the days of Amraphel, king of Shinar...these kings made war with Bera, king of Sodom' (Gen. 14:1).

E. "The matter [of Abram's defending the local rulers] may be compared to the ally of a king who came to live in a province. On his account the king felt obligated to protect that entire province. Barbarians came and attacked him. Now when the barbarians came and attacked him, the people said, 'Woe, the king is not going to want to protect the province the way he used to [since it has caused him trouble]. That is in line with the following verse of Scripture, 'And they turned back and came to En Mishpat [source of justice], that is Kadesh [holy] [and subdued all the country of the Amalekites]' (Gen. 14:7)." [This concludes the first of the five illustrations.] [Lev. R. XI:VII.2.E adds: So too, Abraham was the ally of the King, the Holy One, blessed be he, and in his regard it is written, 'And in you shall all the families of the earth be blessed' (Gen. 12:4). So it was on his account that the Holy One, blessed be he, felt obligated to protect the entire world.]

F. Said R. Aha, "They sought only to attack the orb of the Eye of the world. The eye that had sought to exercise the attribute of justice in the world did they seek to blind: 'That is Kadesh' (Gen. 14:7)."

G. Said R. Aha, "It is written, 'that is...,' meaning, that is the particular one who has sanctified the name of the Holy One, blessed be he, by going down into the fiery furnace."

H. [Reverting to the discourse suspended at the end of E:] When the barbarians came and attacked, they began to cry, "Woe, woe!"

I. "And it came to pass in the days of Amraphel" (Gen. 14:1).

2. A. "And it came to pass in the days of Ahaz" (Is. 7:1):

B. "The Aramaeans on the east and the Philistines on the west devour Israel with open mouth" (Is. 9:12):

C. The matter [of Israel's position] may be compared to the case of a king who handed over his son to a tutor, who hated the son. The tutor thought, "If I kill him now, I shall turn out to be liable to the death penalty before the king. So what I'll do is take away his wet-nurse, and he will die on his own."

D. So thought Ahaz, "If there are no kids, there will be no he-goats. If there are no he-goats, there will be no flock. If there is no flock, there will be no Shepherd, if there is no Shepherd, there will be no world."

E. So did Ahaz plan, "If there are no children, there will be no adults. If there are no adults, there will be no disciples. If there are no disciples, there will be no sages. If there are no sages, there will be no elders. If there are no elders, there will be no prophets. If there are no prophets, the Holy One, blessed be he, will not allow his presence to come to rest in the world." [Lev. R.: ...Torah. If there is no Torah, there will be no synagogues and schools. If there are no synagogues and schools, then the Holy One, blessed be he, will not allow his presence to come to rest in the world.]

F. That is in line with the following verse of Scripture: "Bind up the testimony, seal the Torah among my disciples" (Is. 8:16).

G. R. Huna in the name of R. Eleazar: "Why was he called Ahaz? Because he siezed (ahaz) synagogues and schools."

H. R. Jacob in the name of R. Aha: "Isaiah said, 'I will wait for the Lord, who is hiding his face from the house of Jacob, and I will hope in him' (Is. 8:17). You have no more trying hour than that moment concerning which it is written, 'And I shall surely hide my face on that day' (Deut. 31:18).

I. "From that hour: 'I will hope in him' (Is. 8:17). For he has said, 'For it will not be forgotten from the mouth of his seed' (Deut. 31:21).

J. "What good did hoping do for Isaiah?

K. "'Behold I and the children whom the Lord has given me are signs and portents in Israel from the Lord of hosts who dwells on Mount Zion' (Is. 8:18). Now were they his children? Were they not his disciples? But this teaches that they were precious to him so that he regarded them as his children."

L. [Reverting to G:] Now since everyone saw that Ahaz had seized the synagogues and schools, they began to cry out, "Woe, woe!' Thus: "And it came to pass [marking the woe] in the days of Ahaz" (Is. 7:1).

3. A. "And it came to pass in the days of Jehoiakim, son of Josiah" (Jer. 1:3).

B. "I look on the earth and lo, it was waste and void" (Jer. 4:23).

C. The matter may be compared to the case of royal edicts which came into a province. What did the people do? They took the document, tore it up and burned the bits in fire. That is in line with the following verse of Scripture: "And it came to pass, as Jehudi read three or four columns, that is, three or four verses, the king would cut them off with a penknife and throw them into the fire in the brazier until the entire scroll was consumed in the fire that was in the brazier" (Jer. 36:23).

D. When the people saw all this, they began to cry out, "Woe, woe."

E. "And it came to pass in the days of Jehoiakim" (Jer. 1:3).

4. A. "And it came to pass in the days in which the judges ruled" (Ruth 1:1). "There was a famine in the land" (Ruth 1:1).

B. The matter may be compared to a province which owed taxes in arrears to the king, so the king sent a revenuer to collect. What did the inhabitants of the province do? They went and hung him, hit him, and robbed him. They said, "Woe is us, when the king gets word of these things. What the king's representative wanted to do to us, we have done to him."

C. So too, woe to the generation that has judged its judges.

D. "And it came to pass in the days in which the judges themselves were judged" (Ruth 1:1).

5.   A. "And it came to pass in the days of Ahasuerus" (Est. 1:1). "Haman undertook to destroy, to slay, and to annihilate all the Jews, young and old, women and children, in one day" (Est. 3:13).

B. The matter may be compared to the case of a king who had a vineyard, and three of his enemies attacked it. One of them began to clip off the small branches, the next began to take the pendants off the grapeclusters, and the last of them began to uproot the vines altogether.

C. Pharaoh [began by clipping off the small branches]: "Every son that is born will you throw into the river" (Ex. 1:22).

D. Nebuchadnezzar [began to clip off the pendants of the grapeclusters,] deporting the people: "And he carried away captive the craftsmen and smiths, a thousand" (2 Kgs. 24:16).

E. R. Berekhiah in the name of R. Judah and rabbis:

F. R. Berekhiah in the name of R. Judah: "There were a thousand craftsmen and a thousand smiths."

G. Rabbis say, "This group and that group all together added up to a thousand."

H. The wicked Haman began to uproot the vines altogether. "To destroy, to slay, and to annihilate all the Jews" (Est. 3:13).

I. When everybody saw that [Ahasuerus had sold and Haman had bought the Jews], they began to cry, "Woe, woe."

J. "And it came to pass in the days of Ahasuerus" (Est. 1:1).

6.   A. R. Simeon b. Abba in the name of R. Yohanan: "Any context in which the words, 'And it came to pass...,' appear serves to signify either misfortune or good fortune. If it is a case of misfortune, it is misfortune without parallel. If it is a case of good fortune, it is good fortune without parallel."

B. R. Samuel b. Nahman came and introduced this distinction: "Any context in which the words, 'And it came to pass...' occur signifies misfortune, and any context in which the words, 'And it shall come to pass...' are used signifies good fortune."

C. They objected [to this claim], "And God said, 'Let there be light,' and it came to pass that there was light" (Gen. 1:3).

D. He said to them, "This too does not represent good fortune, for in the end the world did not enjoy the merit of actually making use of that light."

E. R. Judah [b. R. Simeon] said, "With the light that the Holy One, blessed be he, created on the first day of creation, a person could look and see from one side of the world to the other. When the Holy One, blessed be he, foresaw that there would be wicked people, he hid it away for the [exclusive use of the] righteous. 'But the path of the righteous is as the light of the dawn that shines more and more to the perfect day' (Prov. 4:18)."

F. They further objected, "And it came to pass that there was evening and morning, one day" (Gen. 1:5).

G. He said to them, "This too does not signify good fortune. For whatever God created on the first day of creation is destined to be wiped out. That is in line with the following verse of Scripture: 'For the heaven shall vanish away like smoke, and the earth shall wax old like a garment' (Is. 51:6)."

H. They further objected, "And it came to pass that there was evening and it came to pass that there was morning, a second day..., a third day..., a fourth day..., a fifth day..., a sixth day..." (Gen. 1:8, 13, 19, 23, 31).

I. He said to them, "This too does not signify good fortune. For everything which God created on the six days of creation was incomplete and would require further processing. Wheat has to be milled, mustard to be sweetened, [lupine to impart sweetness]."

J. They further objected, "And it came to pass that the Lord was with Joseph, and Joseph was a prosperous man" (Gen. 39:2).

K. He said to them, "This too does not signify good fortune, for on this account that she-bear [Potiphar's wife] came his way."

L. They further objected, "And it came to pass on the eighth day that Moses called Aaron and his sons for consecration in the priesthood" (Lev. 9:1).

M. He said to them, "This too does not signify good fortune, for on that same day Nadab and Abihu died."

N. They further objected, "And it came to pass on the day on which Moses made an end of setting up the tabernacle" (Num. 7:1).

O. He said to them, "This too does not signify good fortune. For on the day on which the Temple was built, the tabernacle was hidden away."

P. They further objected, "And it came to pass that the Lord was with Joshua and his fame was in all the land" (Joshua 6:27).

Q. He said to them, "This too does not signify good fortune, for he still had to tear his garments [on account of the defeat at Ai, Joshua 7:6]."

R. They further objected, "And it came to pass that the king dwelt in his palace, and the Lord gave him rest round about" (2 Sam. 7:1).

S. He said to them, "This too does not signify good fortune. On that very day Nathan the prophet came to him and said, 'You will not build the house' (1 Kgs. 8:19)."

T. They said to him, "We have given our objections, now you give your proofs about good fortune."

U. He said to them, "'And it shall come to pass in that day that living waters shall go out of Jerusalem' (Zech. 14:8). 'And it shall come to pass in that day that a great horn shall be blown' (Is. 27:13). 'And it shall come to pass in that day that a man shall rear a youngling' (Is. 7:21). 'And it shall come to pass in that day that the Lord will set his hand again a second time to recover the remnant of his people' (Is. 11:11). 'And it shall come to pass in that day that the mountains shall drop down sweet wine' (Joel 4:18). [All of these represent good fortune without parallel.]"

V. They said to him, "'And it shall come to pass on the day on which Jerusalem is taken...' (Jer. 38:28)."

W. He said to them, "This too does not signify misfortune but good fortune [without parallel], for on that day the Israelites received a full pardon for all their sins.

X. "That is in line with what R. Samuel b. Nahman said, 'The Israelites received a full pardon for all their sins on the day on which the Temple was destroyed. That is in line with the following verse of Scripture, "The punishment of your iniquity is completed, daughter of Zion, and he will no more take you away into exile" (Lam. 4:22).'"

The fundamental syllogism, not stated at all, is that Israel's history follows rules that can be learned in Scripture. Nothing is random, all thing connected, and fundamental laws of history dictate the sense and meaning of what happens. These laws are stated in the very language of Scripture. The long discussion obviously is constructed independent of any of the verses used as proof-texts. It serves equally well in any number of contexts, not only here but also at Lev. R. XI:VII, as indicated. The differences in the versions of Gen. R. and Lev. R. are minor and signify nothing of consequence. The sole point of intersection is at No. 1.

XLII:IV.

1. A. "And it came to pass in the days of Amraphel" (Gen. 14:1):

B. He had three names, Kush, Nimrod, and Amraphel.

C. Kush, because he was in fact a Kushite.

D. Nimrod, because he made the world rebel (MRD).

E. Amraphel, for he [Freedman:] made a declaration (*amar imrah*) , "I will cast down."

F. [Freedman translates the words that follow in this way:] [Another interpretation is] that he made sport of the world, also that he made sport of Abraham, again, that he ordered Abraham to be thrown into the furnace. [Freedman, p. 346, n. 3: "The translation is conjectural. Neither the text nor its meaning is certain."]

2. A. "Arioch, king of Ellasar" (Gen. 14:1):

B. Said R. Yose of Milhayya, "How come hazel nuts are called *elsarin* ? Because they come from Ellasar."

3. A. "Chedorlaomer king of Elam and Tidal king of Goiim" (Gen. 14:1):

B. Said R. Levi, "There is a place there which in Latin bears that name. The people took a man and made him king over them."

C. Said R. Yohanan, "'Tidal' was his name."

4. A. Another matter: "And it came to pass in the days of Amraphael, king of Shinar" (Gen. 14:1) refers to Babylonia.

B. "Arioch, king of Ellasar" (Gen. 14:1) refers to Greece.

C. "Chedorlaomer, king of Elam" (Gen. 14:1) refers to Media.

D. "And Tidal, king of Goiim [nations]" (Gen. 14:1) refers to the wicked government [Rome], which conscripts troops from all the nations of the world.

E. Said R. Eleazar bar Abina, "If you see that the nations contend with one another, look for the footsteps of the king-messiah. You may know that that is the case, for lo, in the time of Abraham, because the kings struggled with one another, a position of greatness came to Abraham."

Obviously, No. 4 presents the most important reading of Gen. 14:1, since it links the events of the life of Abraham to the history of Israel and even ties the whole to the messianic expectation. I suppose that any list of four kings will provoke inquiry into the relationship of the entries of that list to the four kingdoms among which history, in Israel's experience, is divided. There are difficult readings in Nos. 1 and 3, and No. 2 is trivial.

XLII:V.

1. A. "These kings made war with Bera [king of Sodom, Birsha, king of Gomorrah, Shinab, king of Admah, Shemeber, king of Zeboiim, and the king of Bela, that is Zoar]" (Gen. 14:2):

B. R. Meir would give expositions of names [such as those at hand]: "'Bera' because he was a bad son.

C. "'Birsha' because he was the son of a wicked man.

D. "'Shinab' because he lusted after money.

E. "'Shemeber' because he would fly about and get money.

F. "'Bela' because the inhabitants of that town were swallowed up."

2. A. "And all of these joined forces in the valley of Siddim, that is, the Salt Sea" (Gen. 14:3):

B. That valley had three names: the valley of Siddim, the valley of Shaveh, and the valley of Sukkot [Gen. 5:17: "valley of Shaveh," and Ps. 60:8, valley of Sukkot].

C. The valley of Shiddim: for oak trees were growing there, that it was divided into fields, and that it gave suck to its children like breasts [*saddanim, sadim, shadayyim*, respectively].

D. "The valley of Shaveh:"

E. R. Berekhiah and R. Helbo in the name of R. Samuel b. Nahman: "For there all of the nations of the world came to an agreement [using the same root as the word *shaveh*, meaning, holding a single view], and they cut down cedars and made a high platform and seated [Abraham] on top of it, praising him and saying, 'Hear us, my lord, you are a prince of God among us, in the choice...'" (Gen. 23:16).

F. "They said to him, 'You are king over us, you are God over us.'

G. "He said to them, 'The world does not even now lack for its king, and the world does not lack for its God."

H. "The valley of Sukkot:" for it was shaded [using the same root] by trees.

I. Said R. Tanhuma, "The vine, the fig tree, the pomegranate, nuts, almonds, apples, and peach trees."

3. A. "[In the valley of Siddim,] that is the Salt Sea" (Gen. 14:3):

B. Said R. Aibu, "There was no sea there, but the rocks on the banks of the river were broken and turned into a sea.

C. "That is in line with this verse of Scripture: 'He cuts out channels among the rocks' (Job 28:10)."

Nos. 1 and 2 explain the names for the kings and the valley, respectively. No. 3 presents a minor clarification.

XLII: VI.

1. A. "Twelve years [they had served Chedorlaomer, but in the thirteenth year they rebelled]" (Gen. 14:14):

B. R. Yose and R. Simeon b. Gamaliel:

C. R. Yose says, "Twelve years and [then] thirteen years, lo, twenty-five years in all."

D. R. Simeon b. Gamaliel says, "In total there were thirteen years. And how do I explain 'the fourteenth year'? That refers to their rebellion."

2. A. "In the fourteenth year Chedorlaomer and the kings who were with him came [and subdued the Rephaim in Ashteroth-karnaim, the Zuzim in Ham, the Emim in Shaveh-kiriathaim, and the Horites in their Mount Seir as far as El-paran on the border of the wilderness]" (Gen. 14:5):

B. "The one who owns the beam has to carry its weight." [Freedman, p. 348, n. 2: Since they had served Chedorlaomer, he had to be in the forefront now, his allies playing a subordinate part.]

3. A. "And the kings who were with him...in Ashteroth-karnaim" (Gen. 14:5):

B. In Ashtarta that was lying between the horns, [that is, between two mountains (*karnaim*)].

4. A. "And the Zuzim in Ham" (Gen. 14:5):

B. The most illustrious among them [a play on the Hebrew words here].

5. A. "And the Emim in Shaveh-kiryathaim" (Gen. 14:5): They were twin cities, both called Shaveh [Freedman].

B. This refers to Eleutheropolis [Freetown].

C. And why was it called Freetown [Eleutheropolis]? It is because the people had chosen it and had gone forth to freedom in the generation of dispersion.

6. A. "As far as El-paran on the border of the wilderness" (Gen. 14:6):

B. By the plain of Paran.

The systematic parsing of the verses at hand serves only to supply mildly interesting information. I see no polemic or sustained argument.

XLII:VII.

1. A. "Then they turned back and came to En-Mishpat, that is Kadesh, and subdued all the country of the Amalekites and also the Amorites who dwelt in Hazazon-tamar" (Gen. 14:7):

B. Said R. Aha, "They sought only to attack the orb of the Eye of the world. The eye that had sought to exercise the attribute of justice in the world did they seek to blind: 'That is Kadesh' (Gen. 14:7)."

C. Said R. Aha, "It is written, 'that is...,' meaning, 'that is the [particular] one who has sanctified the name of the Holy One, blessed be he, by going down into the fiery furnace.'"

2. A. "And they subdued all the country of the Amalekites" (Gen. 14:7):

B. Amalek had not yet arisen, and yet you say, "And they subdued all the country of the Amalekites"? [Is this not an anachronism?]

C. But: "He declares the end from the beginning" (Is. 46:10).

3. A. ""And also the Amorites who dwelt in Hazazon-tamar" (Gen. 14:7):

B. It was in En-gedi of the palm-trees.

4. A. "Then the king of Sodom, the king of Gomorrah, the king of Admah, the king of Zeboiim, and the king of Bela, that is Zoar, went out and they joined battle in the valley of Siddim with Chedorlaomer, king of Elam, Tidal, king of Goiim, Amraphel, king of Shinar, and Arioch, king of Ellasar, four kings against five" (Gen. 14:8-9):

B. Four kings went to war against five and beat them.

5. A. "Now the Valley of Siddim was full of bitumen pits, and as the kings of Sodom and Gomorrah fled, some fell into them and the rest fled to the mountain" (Gen. 14:10):

B. it was an area full of pits that yielded asphalt.

6. A. "And as the kings of Sodom and Gomorrah fled, some fell into them, and the rest fled to the mountain" (Gen. 14:10):

B. R. Judah says, "'And they fell there' refers to the troops, 'and they that remained fled to the mountain' speaks of the kings."

C. R. Nehemiah says, "'And they fell there' refers to the kings, while 'and they that remained fled to the mountain' speaks of the troops."

D. In the view of R. Judah there are no problems. [Freedman, p. 349, n. 4: The kings escaped. So it stated in Gen. 41:17: "And the king of Sodom went out to meet him."]

E. But in the view of R. Nehemiah, [an explanation is required].

F. R. Azariah, R. Jonathan in the name of R. Isaac: "When our father, Abraham, went down into the fiery furnace and was saved, there were nations that believed, and there were those that did not believe. When the king of Sodom went down into the asphalt and was saved, the disbelievers began retrospectively to believe in Abraham."

7. A. "So [the enemy] took all the goods of Sodom and Gomorrah and all their provisions and went their way" (Gen. 14:11):

    B. R. Judah said, "Was it not considerable labor to take 'all their provisions'?"

    C. Said R. Nehemiah, "This refers to the dry dates [which are easy to carry yet highly esteemed (Freedman, p. 350, n. 1)]."

8. A. "They also took Lot, the son of Abraham's brother, who dwelt in Sodom and his goods and departed" (Gen. 14:12):

    B. This is what they did to Lot: they bound him and took him with them.

    C. And why all this? Because "He dwelt in Sodom" (Gen. 14:12).

    D. This serves to show the meaning of the following verse of Scripture: "He who walks with wise men shall be wise, but the companion of fools shall smart for it" (Prov. 13:20).

Only Nos. 6, 8 make points that go beyond the simple explanation of words, phrases, or names. No. 6 links the matter to Abraham's earlier proselytism, and No. 8 makes an obvious point that Lot should never have taken up residence in Sodom. This point of course will recur.

XLII: VIII.

1. A. "Then one who had escaped came and told [Abram the Hebrew, who was living by the oaks of Mamre, the Amorite, brother of Eshcol and of Aner; these were allies of Abram]" (Gen. 14:13):

    B. R. Simeon b. Laqish in the name of Bar Qappara: "This one who escaped refers to Og, and why was he called Og? Because he came and found Abraham sitting and carrying out the religious duty of preparing unleavened bread [since it was the time of Passover].

    C. "[Og] did not have the intention of serving Heaven, but he said, 'This fellow, Abraham, is vindictive. Now I shall tell him that Lot has been taken captive, and he will go to war and be killed, and I shall take Sarai.'

    D. "Said the Holy One, blessed be he, to him, 'By your life! You will get the reward only of the steps that you have taken, in that you will have a long life in the world. But because you planned to kill the righteous man, you will live to see a thousand thousands of his children, and your destiny will be to fall by the hand of his children:

E.   "'And the Lord said to Moses, "Fear him not, for I have delivered him into your hand"' (Num. 21:34)."

2.   A.   "And told Abram the Hebrew" (Gen. 14:13):

B.   The whole world was on one side [using the same consonants as the word for Hebrew], and he was on the other side.

C.   R. Nehemiah said, "It was because he came from Eber."

D.   Rabbis say, "It is because he came from across the river, that he spoke the language of Hebrew."

3.   A.   "...who was living by the oaks of Mamre the Amorite, brother of Eshcol and of Aner; these were allies of Abram" (Gen. 14:13):

B.   R. Judah said, "It was on the plain of Mamre."

C.   R. Nehemiah said, "It was in the palace of Mamre."

D.   In the opinion of R. Judah it was a place by the name of Mamre.

E.   In the opinion of R. Nehemiah, it was a man whose name was Mamre."

F.   And why [from Nehemiah's viewpoint] was he called "Mamre"?

G.   R. Azariah in the name of R. Judah: "Because he rebuked [himrah] Abraham.

H.   "When the Holy One, blessed be he, said to Abraham to circumcise himself, he went and got the advice of his three allies.

I.   "Said Aner to him, 'You are already a hundred years old, and are you going to inflict pain on yourself?'

J.   "Said Eshkol to him, 'Now are you going to go and through circumcision make yourself different from your enemies?'

K.   "Said Mamre to him, 'Where did he not stand up for you? [Everywhere he stood up for you:] In the fiery furnace, in the famine, and in the matter of the kings. Now should you not obey him in this matter?'

L.   "Said the Holy One, blessed be he, to him, 'You gave him good advice about getting circumcised. By your life, I shall appear to him only in your palace. That is in line with this verse: 'And the Lord appeared to him in the palace of Mamre' (Gen. 18:1)."

Nos. 1 and 3 present a striking contrast in identifying the unnamed figures here, the messenger, Gen. 14:13, and Mamre. In the former case the one who escaped did the right thing for the wrong reason. In the latter, the ally gave sound advice about relying upon God. No. 2 presents a minor clarification, dealing with the meaning of the word "Hebrew," by taking up its several possible meanings, based on other words that use the same consonants, "side," "Eber," and "crossing over."

Chapter Ten

Parashah Forty-Three.   Genesis 14:14-17

XLIII:I.

1. A. "When Abram heard that his brother was taken captive" (Gen. 14:14).

    B. "He shall not be afraid of evil reports, his heart is steadfast, trusting in the Lord" (Ps. 112:7).

    C. "And found his heart faithful before you" (Neh. 9:8).

    D. "His heart is established, he shall not be afraid" (Ps. 112:8).

    E. "Fear not, Abram" (Gen. 15:1).

    F. "Until he gaze upon his adversaries" (Ps. 112:8).

    G. "So: "And he divided himself against them by night" (Gen. 15:15).

I see no systematic exposition of the intersecting verse, Ps. 112:7-8, either by itself or in line with the base verse. I take it the main point is that Abram was not afraid. The proposition is that the children of Abraham must not fear but must have confidence in God.

XLIII:II.

1. A. "When Abram heard" (Gen. 14:14).

    B. "He stops his ears from hearing of blood" (Is. 33:15).

2. A. "He led forth his trained men, born in his house, three hundred and eighteen of them, and went in pursuit as far as Dan" (Gen. 14:14):

    B. [Since the word for "led forth" uses the same consonants as the word for "turn an angry face,"] R. Judah said, "They showed an angry face to Abraham. They said, 'Five kings could not beat them, and shall we be able to stand against them?'"

    C. R. Nehemiah said, "Abraham showed *them* an angry face. He said, 'I shall go forth and fall for the sake of the sanctification of the name of the Holy One, blessed be he.'" [Freedman, p. 352, n. 2: Both Judah and Nehemiah interpret the word, "he made pale in anger." Judah holds that he made his servants' faces pale, that is, they opposed him, while in Nehemiah's opinion he made himself pale by defying them.]

D. R. Abba bar Zabeda said, "It was with weapons of war that he made their faces pale, in line with this verse: 'Burnish also the spear and the battle axe against them that pursue me; say to my soul, I am your salvation' (Ps. 35:3)."

E. R. Simeon b. Laqish said, "With precious stones and pearls he made their faces pale, in line with this verse: 'With the shimmer of gold' (Ps. 68:14)."

F. R. Levi said, "He emptied their ranks [using the same root but assigning to it a different meaning] by reading to them the passage of the guards [who pass through the ranks and take out the frightened troops], as it is said, 'Who is the man who is fearful and faint-hearted' (Deut. 20:8). [In this way he polished them by taking away those who would weaken the force.]" [Abraham thus carried out the law of the Torah before it was given.]

3. A. "Born in his house" (Gen. 14:14):

B. They all had his name, being called Abram, like him. [Converted by Abram, they adopted his name.]

4. A. "Three hundred and eighteen" (Gen. 14:14):

B. R. Simeon b. Laqish said, "It was, in point of fact, only Eliezer. The numerical value of the letters of the name of Eliezer is three hundred eighteen."

5. A. "And he went in pursuit as far as Dan" (Gen. 14:14):

B. Idolatry hits both beforehand and afterward.

C. Before hand: "He went in pursuit as far as Dan [but could not go further than that]" (Gen. 14:14).

D. Afterward: "The snorting of his horses is heard from Dan" (Jer. 8:15). [Freedman, p. 353, n. 4: The meaning is that the evil effects of idolatry are felt both before and after it is actually practiced. Because Jeroboam was destined to set up a golden calf at Dan (1 Kgs. 12:19), Abraham was weakened now when he came to that place and so could pursue them no further. Similarly, even after it was destroyed, Jeremiah speaks of terror raging in Dan.]

No. 1 presents only the intersecting and the base verse, without spelling out any point to be derived from the matter. No. 2 presents a sustained inquiry into the meaning of a key-word of the cited verse. Nos. 3, 4 comment on details. No. 5 then draws a more general conclusion from the fact that Abram got as far as Dan but went no further. I see no theme running through the comments before us.

XLIII:III.

1. A. "And the night was divided against them" (Gen. 14:15) [following Freedman's translation of the verse, which, in RSV, reads, "And he divided his forces against them by night"]:

B. R. Benjamin b. Japheth in the name of R. Yohanan: "The night divided on its own."

C. And rabbis say, "Its creator divided it.

D. "Said the Holy One, blessed be he, 'Abraham worked with me at midnight [in going to rescue the captives], so I shall work with him at midnight.'

E. "When did this take place? In Egypt, as it is said, 'And it came to pass at midnight' (Ex. 12:29)."

F. Said R. Tanhuma, "There are those who report the statement in another formulation.

G. "Said the Holy One, blessed be he, 'Their father went forth at midnight, so I shall go forth with his children at midnight, as it is said, 'Thus says the Lord, "At about midnight I will go forth"' (Ex. 11:4)."

2. A. "He routed them and pursued them to Hobah, north of Damascus" (Gen. 14:15):

B. Does someone pursue those who have already been killed?

C. Said R. Phineas, "Those who had pursued our father, Abraham, were [regarded as though they had been] killed, as it is said, 'For they pursue him whom you have smitten' (Ps. 69:27)."

3. A. It is written, "Who has raised up one from the east, Righteousness calling him to his feet" (Is. 41:2):

B. It is the Life of the Ages who gave light for him in every place in which he walked. [Freedman, p. 354, n. 3: By a play on the words to awaken, raise up, is connected the word for to illumine.]

C. Said R. Berekhiah, "It was the star Righteousness [Jupiter] that gave light for him."

D. Said R. Reuben, "Righteousness cried out and said, 'If Abraham does not carry out what I represent, there will be no one who ever will carry out what I represent." [Freedman, p. 354, n. 5: Rendering: Righteousness personified summoned him to his feet, that is, to do it.]

4. A. It is written, "He gives nations before him and makes him rule over kings, his sword makes them as the dust, his bow as the driven stubble" (Is. 41:2):

B. R. Judah and R. Nehemiah:

C. One of them said, "Abraham threw dust at them and it turned into swords, he threw straw and it turned into arrows."

D. The other said, "What is written is not 'he makes dust' but 'he makes *them* as the dust.' They threw swords at Abraham, but the swords turned into dust, and arrow, which turned into straw."

5. A. It is written, "He pursues them and passes on safely" (Is. 41:3):

B. R. Levi and R. Eleazar in the name of R. Yose: "Each footstep taken by Abraham was three *mil* s in length." [Freedman, p. 354, n. 6: The word for "safely" is read as an abbreviation of "three mils."]

C. R. Judah bar Simon said, "It was one *mil*, as it is said, 'The way with his feet he treads not' (Is. 41:3)."

No. 1 links the story of Abraham to the later history of Israel, an important motif throughout. No. 2 clarifies the language of the cited verse. Then Nos. 3, 4, and 5 work on the intersecting verse of Is. 41:23-3, which is read to speak of Abraham's war. The work is systematic and, within the system at hand, persuasive.

XLIII:IV.

1. A. "Then he brought back all the goods and also brought back his kinsman Lot with his goods and the women and the people" (Gen. 14:16):

B. Said R. Yudan, "The men and the women he brought back, but the children were not brought back. They went and converted and cut off 'the reproach of their fathers' [becoming circumcised].

C. "That is in line with this verse: 'Wherefore I will bring the worst of the nations' (Ez.7:24)."

D. Who are the "worst of the nations"?

E. R. Judah said, "They are the men of Sodom: 'The men of Sodom were wicked and sinners' (Gen. 13:13)."

The net effect is once more to link the tale at hand to the history of Israel. We further tie in the story of Sodom.

XLIII:V.

1. A. "[After his return from the defeat of Chedorlaomer and the kings who were with him,] the king of Sodom went out to meet him [at the Valley of Shaveh, that is, the King's Valley]" (Gen. 14:17):

    B. R. Abba bar Kahana said, "He began to wag his tail at him [as a mark of friendliness]. He said to him, 'Just as you went down into the fiery furnace and were saved, so I went down into the asphalt and was saved.'"

2. A. "At the Valley of Shaveh, that is, the King's Valley" (Gen. 14:17)

    B. R. Berekhiah and R. Helbo in the name of R. Samuel b. Nahman: "For there all of the nations of the world came to an agreement [using the same root as the word *shaveh*, meaning, holding a single view], [and they cut down cedars and made a high platform and seated Abraham on top of it, praising him and saying, 'Hear us, my lord, you are a prince of God among us, in the choice...' (Gen. 23:16)].

    C. "They said to him, 'You are king over us, you are God over us.'

    D. "He said to them, 'The world even now does not lack for its king, and the world even now does not lack for its God."

The passage goes over familiar material to augment the cited verses.

I follow Theodor-Albeck, p. 420, in treating what follows as Parashah Forty-Three, so breaking the passage in two. This will serve the convenience of readers following the text supplied by Theodor-Albeck.

Chapter Eleven

Parashah Forty-Three (Concluded)
Genesis 14:18-24

XLIII:VI.

1. A. "And Melchizedek, king of Salem, brought out bread and wine; he was priest of God Most High" (Gen. 14:18):

   B. "And, O daughter of Sor, the richest of the people shall entreat your favor with a gift" (Ps. 45:13).

   C. "Daughter of Sor" speaks of Abraham, who vexed kings and was vexed by kings. [This is a play on the letters in the word *Sor*, treating them as not the name of a place but as the root for the word to vex or distress (Freedman).]

   D. "They shall entreat your favor with a gift" (Ps. 45:13).

   E. "And Melchizedek, king of Salem, brought out bread and wine" (Gen. 14:18).

2. A. "*Melchi* [king] *Zedek* [righteous]": This place [namely, Jerusalem, that is, the Salem of which Gen. 14:18 speaks] justifies the people who live there [hence, he was king over righteous people].

3. A. "And the king of *Zedek*" (Gen. 14:18):

   B. "The Lord of *Zedek*" (Joshua 10:7).

   C. Jerusalem is called "righteousness" [*Zedek*]: "Righteousness lodged in her" (Is. 1:21).

4. A. "King of Salem" (Gen. 14:18):

   B. [Reading the word for Salem as *shalom*, meaning whole, we interpret in the following way:] R. Isaac the Babylonian said, "It is because he was born circumcized."

5. A. "Brought out bread and wine" (Gen. 14:18):

B. R. Samuel bar Nahman: "He handed over to him the laws governing the priesthood.

C. "The bread stands for the show-bread, and the wine stands for the drink-offerings."

D. Rabbis say, "He revealed the Torah to him: 'Come, eat of my bread and drink of the wine which I have mingled' (Prov. 9:5)."

6. A. "He was priest of God Most High" (Gen. 14:18):

B. R. Abba bar Kahana: "Every reference to wine that is mentioned in the Torah makes its mark except for the present reference. [That is, wine always causes trouble, but for the present case.]"

C. Said R. Levi, "Even this one is no exception. For on this basis it was revealed to him, 'And they shall serve them and they shall afflict them' (Gen. 15:13)." [Freedman, p. 356, n. 12: "This was Abraham's punishment for complying with the request of the king of Sodom, 'Give me the persons,' Gen. 14:21, instead of converting them to the true faith. Levi perhaps holds that this complaisance was due to the convivial and friendly mood induced by the drinking of wine."]

No. 1 begins discourse with the introduction of an intersecting verse, read in line with the base-verse. Nos. 2, 3, and 4 go over the name of the king. No. 5 then links the present passage to the later history of Israel, for it is taken for granted that "Salem" and Jerusalem are one and the same place. So Melchizedek was the priest of Jerusalem even before the Temple was built. Once more the history of Israel is joined to the life of Abraham. One recalls that in the fourth century numerous places in the Holy Land found association, if only after the fact, with the life and deeds of Jesus. But we need not suppose the view of Salem and Jerusalem began only in the time of the composition of our document. No. 6 makes its own point, independent of the cited verse.

XLIII:VII.

1. A. "And he blessed him and said, 'Blessed be Abram by God Most High, who has effected acquisition of heaven and earth; [and blessed be God Most High, who has delivered your enemies into your hand]!'" (Gen. 14:19):

B. From whom did God acquire them? [Is there some authority above God?]

C. R. Abba said, "It is like the case of a man who said, 'So and so has beautiful eyes and lovely hair.' [The sense of the statement is descriptive and attributive, namely, that God is in possession of heaven and earth. The meaning is not that God has acquired heaven and earth from some other authority.]"

D. Said R. Isaac, "Abraham would receive passersby and once they had eaten and drunk, he would say to them, 'Say a blessing.'

E. "They would say to him, 'What should we say?'

F. "He would say to them, 'Blessed is the God of the world, of whose food we have eaten.'

G. "Said the Holy One, blessed be he, to him, 'As for me, my name was not known among those whom I had created, but you made it known among those whom I have created. I regard it in your respect as if you were a partner with me in the creation of the world.

H. "That is in line with this verse: 'And he blessed him and said, "Blessed be Abram by God Most High, who [namely Abram] has effected acquisition of heaven and earth"' (Gen. 14:18)."

We have two theories in explanation of the reference to God "who has made acquisition of heaven and earth." The first excludes the view that there was someone else in charge before God took possession, and so "acquired" is attributive. The latter treats the reference as descriptive of Abram, not of God, thus, "Blessed of God Most High be Abram, who has acquired heaven and earth." This is an example of a close and fruitful reading of a verse. The sense of the statement in the first explanation is seen as descriptive and attributive, namely, that God is in possession of heaven and earth, not that God has a higher authority to whom he was subject. The second treats the reference as descriptive of Abram, not of God, thus, "Blessed of God Most High be Abram, who has acquired heaven and earth."

XLIII:VIII.

1. A. "And blessed be God Most High, who has delivered your enemies into your hand" (Gen. 14:20):

B. [Since the word for "deliver" yields the letters that serve for the word for plans or schemes,] R. Huna said, "It is that he turned your plans against your enemies."

C. R. Yudan said, "How many schemes did I work out to place them under your hand. They were friendly with one another, sending one another dry dates and other gifts. But I made them rebel against one another so that they would fall into your hand."

2. A. "And Abram gave him a tenth of everything" (Gen. 14:20):

B. R. Judah in the namne of R. Nehorai: "On the strength of that blessing the three great pegs on which the world depends, Abraham, Isaac, and Jacob, derived sustenance.

C. "Abraham: 'And the Lord blessed Abraham in *all* things' (Gen. 24:1) on account of the merit that 'he gave him a tenth of *all* things' (Gen. 14:20).

D. "Isaac: 'And I have eaten of *all*' (Gen. 27:33), on account of the merit that 'he gave him a tenth of *all* things' (Gen. 14:20).

E. "Jacob: 'Because God has dealt graciously with me and because I have all' (Gen. 33:11) on account of the merit that 'he gave him a tenth of *all* things' (Gen. 14:20).

3. A. Whence did Israel gain the merit of receiving the blessing of the priests?

B. R. Judah said, "It was from Abraham: '*So* shall your seed be' (Gen. 15:5), while it is written in connection with the priestly blessing: '*So* shall you bless the children of Israel' (Num. 6:23)."

C. R. Nehemiah said, "It was from Isaac: 'And I and the lad will go *so* far' (Gen. 22:5), therefore said the Holy One, blessed be he, '*So* shall you bless the children of Israel' (Num. 6:23)."

D. And rabbis say, "It was from Jacob: 'So shall you say to the house of Jacob' (Ex. 19:3) (in line with the statement, '*So* shall you bless the children of Israel' (Num. 6:23)."

4. A. When shall "I magnify your children like the stars"?

B. R. Eleazar and R. Yose bar Hanina:

C. One of them said, "When I shall be revealed to them with the word '*so* :' 'So shall you say to the house of Jacob' (Ex. 19:3).

D. The other said, "When I shall be revealed to them through their leaders and give a message invoking the word '*so* :' 'So says the Lord, Israel is my son, my firstborn' (Ex. 4:22)."

No. 1 works out a play on the root for "deliver," thereby explaining exactly what God contributed to the salvation of Abram. No. 2 once more links the blessing at hand with the history of Israel. Now the reference is to the word "all," which joins the tithe of Abram to the blessing of his descendants. Since the blessing of the priest is at hand, No. 3 treats the origins of the blessing. But I see no clear point of intersection with the verse at hand. No. 4 is attached because of its discussion of Ex. 19:3, and not because of its relevance to the matter at hand. Therefore Nos. 3 and 4 were joined before the whole was inserted here.

XLIII:IX.

1. A. "And the king of Sodom said to Abram, 'Give me the persons, but take the goods for yourself.' But Abram said to the king of Sodom, 'I have raised

up my hand [RSV: sworn] [to the Lord God Most High, maker of heaven and earth, that I would not take a thread or a sandal-thong or anything that is yours, lest you should say, "I have made Abram rich"']" (Gen. 14:22-23):

B. [The reference of raising up the hand is now explained.] R. Judah said, "He had raised up heave-offering [out of the spoil], in line with this verse: 'Then you shall raise up part of it as a heave-offering gift to the Lord' (Num. 18:26)."

C. R. Nehemiah said, "He had taken an oath, in line with this verse: 'And he lifted up his right hand and his left hand to heaven and swore' (Den. 12:7)."

D. And rabbis say, "He sang a song on account of it, in line with this verse: 'My father's God, and I will raise him up' (Ex. 15:2)."

E. R. Berekhiah in the name of R. Eleazar: "Moses said, 'Using the same language that father did, when he said, 'I have raised up,' I shall sing my song" 'My father's God and I will raise him up' (Ex. 15:2)."

2. A. "...that I would not take a thread or a sandal-thong [or anything that is yours, lest you should say, "I have made Abram rich"']" (Gen. 14:22-23):

B. Said R. Abba bar Mammel, "Said the Holy One, blessed be he, to him, 'You have said, "a thread..." By your life, I shall give your descendants the religious duty of putting fringes on their garments, in line with this verse: "And that they put with the fringe of each corner a thread of blue" (Num. 15:38), that is, a thread of blue wool.

C. "[God continues,] "'or a sandal-thong..." By your life, I shall give your descendants the religious duty of the rite of the deceased childless brother's widow, involving as it does the sandal-thong, in line with this verse: "Then shall she loose his shoe from his foot" (Deut. 25:9).'"

3. A. Another matter [interpreting the verse: "...that I would not take a thread or a sandal-thong [or anything that is yours, lest you should say, "I have made Abram rich"'" (Gen. 14:22-23)]:

B. "A thread" refers to the altar, which is ornamented with blue and purple wool.

C. "Nor a sandal thong" refers to the badger skins.

4. A. Another matter [interpreting the verse: "...that I would not take a thread or a sandal-thong [or anything that is yours, lest you should say, "I have made Abram rich"'" (Gen. 14:22-23)]:

B. "A thread" refers to the sacrifices, in line with what we have learned in the Mishnah: **A thread of scarlet ran around the altar at the middle (M. Middot 3:1).**

C. "Or a sandal thong" refers to the feet of the pilgrims, in line with this verse: "How beautiful are your steps in sandals" (Song 7:2).

5. A. "I will take nothing but what the young men have eaten and the share of the men who went with me; [in addition, even those who did not go with me should have a share, specifically] let Aner, Eshcol, and Mamre take their share" (Gen. 14:24):

B. "Then answered all the wicked men and base fellows, of those who went with David, and said, 'Because they did not go with us, we shall not give them any of the spoil.' Then said David, 'You shall not do this, my brothers. For as is the share of him who goes down to battle, so shall be the share of him who waits by the baggage; they shall all share alike.' And so it was from that day and above, that he made it a statute' (1 Sam. 30:22-25)."

C. Said R. Judah, "What is written is not 'onward,' but, 'from that day and above,' for from whom did David learn the rule? It was from Abraham, his forefather, who had said, 'I will take nothing but what the young men have eaten and the share of the men who went with me; [in addition, even those who did not go with me should have a share, specifically] let Aner, Eshcol, and Mamre take their share" (Gen. 14:24)."

No. 1 deals with the language of the statement, "raise up my hand." The first two treatments of the matter, Judah's and Nehemiah's, focus on the simple sense of the verse, while rabbis as before take an interest in the linkage of the events in the life of Abraham to the history of Israel later on. No. 2 does a still better job of linking the matter at hand with Israel's history. What is important is the effort to demonstrate a link between Abram and the religious duties revealed only later on in the Torah. Nos. 3, 4 revert to the matter of the altar, in line with the view that at hand is Jerusalem and its cult. No. 5 establish yet another link, this time drawing a parallel between Abram's conduct here and David's rule later on.

Chapter Twelve

Parashah Forty-Four.   Genesis 15:1-21

XLIV:I.

1. A. "After these things the word of the Lord came to Abram in a vision" (Gen. 15:1):

    B. "As for God, his way is perfect, the word of the Lord is tried" (2 Sam. 22:31).

    C. If his *way* is perfect, how much the more so is he!

    D. Rab said, "[Since the word for 'tried' yields the meaning 'purify,' we may conclude that] the religious duties were given only to purify humanity. For what difference does it make to the Holy One, blessed be he, if one slaughters a beast at the throat or at the nape of the neck? Lo, the sole purpose is to purify humanity."

2. A. Another matter: "His way is perfect" (2 Sam. 22:31) refers to Abraham, for it is written in his regard, "You found [Abraham's] way faithful before you" (Neh. 9:8).

    B. "The word of the Lord is tried" (2 Sam. 22:31): For the Holy One, blessed be he, tried him in the fiery furnace.

    C. "He is a shield to all them that take refuge in him" (2 Sam. 22:31). "Fear not, Abram, I am your shield" (Gen. 15:1).

The intersecting verse reaches the base verse at hand in No. 2, a successful exercise in reading one matter in the light of the other. The point of No. 1 is made through the play on the word for purify/test. I do not see a direct connection between No. 1 and No. 2.

XLIV:II.

1. A. "A wise man fears and departs from evil" (Prov. 14:16):

    B. "You are wise and depart from evil, yet still are afraid?" "Fear not, Abram, I am your shield" (Gen. 15:1).

2. A. "Be not wise in your own eyes, fear the Lord" (Prov. 3:7):

B. "Do not be too smart about what you see with your own eyes. You ask whether you will produce a child or not produce a child? 'Fear the Lord' (Prov. 3:7)."

C. So it is written: "Fear not, Abram, I am your shield" (Gen. 15:1).

3. A. R. Abin in the name of R. Hanina opened [discourse by citing the following verse of Scripture]: "'The wicked does work of falsehood, but he who sows righteousness has a sure reward' (Prov. 11:18).

B. "'The wicked does work of falsehood' refers to Nimrod, whose deeds were those of falsehood.

C. "'But he who sows righteousness has a sure reward' (Prov. 11:18) refers to Abraham: 'Those who keep the way of the Lord to do righteousness and justice' (Gen. 18:19).

D. "'Has a sure reward.' 'Fear not, Abram, I am your shield. Your reward shall be very great' (Gen. 15:1)."

The point of No. 1 is that a wise man who fears sin does not have to be afraid. No. 2 introduces the notion that Abram feared he would have no children, thus answering the question of what it was that God told Abram not to fear. No. 3 reads Nimrod and Abram into the intersecting verse, thus bringing us back to the base verse with a sure hand.

XLIV:III.

1. A. "But you, Israel, my servant, Jacob whom I have chosen, the seed of Abraham, my friend, you whom I have taken hold of from the ends of the earth" (Is. 41:8): from Mesopotamia and its environs.

B. "And called you from its nobles" (Is. 41:8): from the distinguished men in the area I designated you.

C. "I have chosen you and not cast you away" (Is. 41:8): "I have chosen you" as Abram, "and I did not cast you away" as Abraham.

D. "Fear not, for I am with you, be not dismayed, for I am your God" (Is. 41:10).

2. A. Said R. Hoshaia, "When Isaac said to Jacob, 'Draw near, so that I may feel you' (Gen. 27:21), water poured down on his legs and his heart melted like wax. The Holy One, blessed be he, provided him with two angels, one at his right hand, the other at the left hand, and they held on to him by his elbows, so that he would not fall down.

B. "So he said to him, 'Do not be dismayed,' meaning, 'do not be like wax' [using the same letters]. 'For I am your God. I strengthen you, yes, I help you, yes, I uphold you with my victorious right hand (Is. 41:10).

C. "'Behold, they shall all be ashamed and confounded that were incensed against you' (Is. 41:10) refers to those who are hostile to you.

D. "'Those who strove with you shall be as nothing and shall perish' (Is. 41:10) refers to those who conduct war against you.

E. "'You shall seek them and shall not find them, even those who contended with you' (Is. 41:12) speaks of those who conduct fights with you.

F. "'For I the Lord your God hold your right hand, who say to you, fear not' (Is. 41:13), as it is written, 'Fear not, Abram' (Gen. 15:1)."

No. 1 intertwines Is. 41:8, which refers to Jacob, with statements about Abram. I take it the passage is included here because. Gen. 15:1 has God refer to Abram by that name. The intersecting verse at No. 2 is given an extensive exegesis concerning Jacob, but then it too refers back to Abram at the end. My view is that No. 1 accounts for the selection of Is. 41:8-12, and then No. 2, originally independent of No. 1 in fact dealt with Jacob. When it was joined to No. 1, the composition as a whole was then closed with the reference at F as part of the redactor's revision of the whole. The fundamental message of course simply underlines the statement of the base verse.

XLIV:IV.

1. A. [As to the statement, "Do not fear, Abram," (Gen. 15:1)], R. Levi made two statements concerning the matter, while rabbis stated only one.

B. R. Levi said, "It was because Abraham feared, saying, 'Perhaps it is the case that among those troops whom I killed there was a righteous man or a God-fearer.'

C. "The matter may be compared to the case of a straw-dealer who was passing by the king's orchards. He saw bundles of thorns and dismounted and collected them. The king looked out and saw him. The man began to hide from him. The king said to him, 'Why are you trying to hide. I needed workers to collect them, but now that you have collected them for me, come and take your fee.' So the Holy One, blessed be he, said to Abraham, 'Among those troops whom you killed were only 'thorns that already had been cut down:' 'And the peoples shall be as the burnings of lime, as thorns cut down that are burned in the fire' (Is. 33:12)."

D. R. Levi made yet a second statement, "It was because Abraham feared, saying, 'Perhaps it is the case that the children of those kings whom I killed will collect troops and come and make war against me. Said the Holy One, blessed be he, to him, 'Do not fear, Abram, I am your shield" (Gen. 15:1).

E. "'Just as a shield takes all sorts of spears and stands up against them, so shall I stand by you.'"

F. Rabbis say, "It was because Abraham was afraid, saying, 'I went down into the fiery furnace and was saved, underwent famine and war and was saved. Perhaps now I already have received my reward in this world and will have nothing in the age to come.'

G. "Said to him the Holy One, blessed be he, 'Do not fear, Abram, I am your shield' (Gen. 15:1).

H. "'I am a gift of grace to you' [using the same letters as those for the word for shield]. Everything that I did for you in this world adds up to nothing. In the world to come, 'Your reward shall be very great' (Gen. 15:1). That is in line with this verse: 'Oh how abundant is your goodness, which you have laid up for those who fear you' (Ps. 31:20)."

The exegesis remains close to the verse at hand, answering the obvious question of why Abram was afraid. The answer is that Abram recognized how much had already been done for him, so he feared that he had used up in this world the merit he had attained. Or he feared that those he had killed might have been worthy. Or he feared that those whom he had killed would be avenged. In all the exegete-compositors link one story to the next and do so in a powerful and complex way.

XLIV:V.

1. A. "After these things" (Gen. 15:1):

B. R. Yudan and R. Huna both in the name of R. Yose b. R. Yudan:

C. The former said, "In any passage in which the word 'after' occurs in the spelling, *ahare*, the sense is, 'forthwith and in consequence,' while when the word 'afterward' occurs with the spelling, *ahar*, it does not mean there is a connection between what follows and what has preceded."

D. R. Huna said, "When the word occurs as *ahar*, it means, in consequence of, and where it occurs as *ahare*, it means there is no connection."

2. A. "After these things" (Gen. 15:1): There were some second thoughts.

B. Who had second thoughts? Abraham did. He said before the Holy One, blessed be he, "Lord of the ages, you made a covenant with Noah that you would not wipe out his children. I went and acquired a treasure of religious deeds and good deeds greater than his, so the covenant made with me has set aside the covenant made with him. Now is it possible that someone else will come along and accumulate religious deeds and good deeds greater than mine and so set aside the covenant that was made with me on account of the covenant to be made with him."

C. Said the Holy One, blessed be he, "Out of Noah I did not raise up shields for the righteous, but from you I shall raise up shields for the righteous. And not only so, but when your children will fall into sin and evil deeds, I shall see a single righteous man among them who can say to the attribute of justice, 'Enough.' Him I shall take and make into the atonement for them all."

The placing of No. 1 is somewhat odd, since it takes up the opening clause of Gen. 15:1. No. 2 makes its own point, once more explaining why Abram was afraid, now setting the matter squarely into the setting of Israel's moral life. The merit of Abraham will protect Israel in time to come, and, in future ages, there will be someone in the model of Abraham, who will serve as atonement for Israel.

XLIV:VI.

1. A. "[After these things] the word of the Lord came to Abram in a vision" (Gen. 15:1):

B. It is called by ten names: prophecy, vision, exhortation, speech, saying, command, burden, parable, metaphor, and enigma.

C. And which of them is the most weighty?

D. R. Eleazar said, "It is vision, as it is said, 'A weighty vision is declared to me' (Is. 21:2)."

E. R. Yohanan said, "It is speech, as it is said, 'The man, the lord of the land, spoke weightily with us' (Gen. 42:30)."

F. Rabbis say, "It is the burden, as it is said, 'As a heavy burden' (Ps. 38:5)."

G. Great is the power of Abraham, for with him [God] spoke in both a vision and in speech.

The systematic exposition of the word-choice of the base-verse is underway. That fact once more suggests the slight disorder in the earlier units of the parashah, which treat the question of what Abram feared, that is, the third element in the base-verse.

XLIV:VII.

1. A. "Fear not, Abram" (Gen. 15:1):

B. On what account was he afraid?

C. R. Berekhiah said, "He was afraid of Shem [for he had killed his descendants, Chedorlaomer and his sons], as it is said, 'The isles saw and feared' (Is. 41:5).

D. "Just as islands are distinct in the sea, so Abraham and Shem were distinguished in the world.

E. "'...and were afraid:' This one [Abraham] feared that one [Shem], and that one feared this one.

F. "This one [Abraham] feared that one, thinking, 'Perhaps he has a gripe against me, because I killed his descendants.'

G. "That one [Shem] feared this one, thinking, 'Perhaps he has a gripe against me, because I produced wicked descendants.'

H. "'The ends of the earth' (Is. 41:5): This one lived at one end of the world, and that one lived at the other end of the world.

I. "'They drew near and came' (Is. 41:5): this one drew near that one, and that one drew near this one.

J. "'They helped each one his neighbor' (Is. 41:6): this one helped that one, and that one helped this one.

K. "This one helped that one by means of blessings: 'And he blessed him and said, "Blessed be Abram"' (Gen. 14:19).

L. "And that one helped this one by means of gifts: 'And he gave him a tenth of all' (Gen. 14:20).

M. "'So the carpenter encouraged' (Is. 41:7) refers to Shem, who made the ark.

N. "'The refiner' refers to Abraham, whom the Holy One, blessed be he, refined in the fiery furnace.

O. "'And he that smoothes with the hammer him that smites the anvil' (Is. 41:7): he smoothed with the hammer and beat all of those who pass through the world into a single path.

P. "'Saying of the join, it is good' (Is. 4t:7) refers to the nations of the world, who say, 'It is better to cleave to the God of Abraham and not to the idolatry of Nimrod.'

Q. "'And he strengthens it with nails' (Is. 41:7): Abraham strengthened Shem through the practice of religious duties and good deeds, so that 'he shall not be moved' (Is. 41:7), meaning, Abraham."

No. 1 introduces the exegesis of Is. 41:5f. in terms of the relationship between Abram and Shem, represented by Melchizedek. Then the events of Gen. 14 are linked to the beginning of Gen. 15, as is clear. Once the exegesis of Is. 41:5 in line with Shem is introduced, the matter is carried forward rather effectively. This is a masterpiece of sustained reading of a verse in line with a completely independent theme. It furthermore succeeds in tying together the elements of the narrative into a sustained story.

XLIV:VIII.

1. A. "But Abram said, 'O Lord, God, what will you give me, [for I continue childless, and the heir of my house is Eliezer of Damascus]?'" (Gen. 15:2):

    B. Said R. Jonathan, "There were three who were allowed to ask, Solomon, Ahaz, and the King Messiah.

    C. "Solomon: 'Ask what I shall give you' (1 Kgs. 3:5).

    D. "Ahaz: 'Ask a sign for yourself' (Is. 7:11).

    E. "The king messiah: 'Ask of me' (Ps. 2:8)."

    F. R. Berekiah and R. Ahi in the name of R. Samuel b. Nahman: "We may produce two more, based on lore: Abraham and Jacob.

    G. "Abraham: 'What will you give me.' He could never have said, 'What will you give me?' unless God had already said to him, 'Ask.'

    H. "Jacob: "And of all that you shall give me' (Gen. 28:22). He could never have said, 'Of all that you shall give me' (Gen. 28:22) unless he had already said to him, 'Ask.'"

The composite draws upon the base verse only as part of a larger syllogism. But the point is that Israel's history is marked by occasions on which rulers are permitted to ask something of God, as specified. The mixture of Solomon, Ahaz, and the Messiah seems odd.

XLIV:IX.

1. A. R. Yudan and R. Aibu in the name of R. Yohanan: "Two men said the same thing, Abraham and David.

    B. "Abraham said, "'O Lord God'" (Gen. 15:2). He said before him, 'Lord of the age, If I am going to produce children who will cause you anger, it is better for me "that I go childless" (Gen. 15:2).'

    C. "David said, "'Search me God and know my heart, try me and know my thoughts" (Ps. 139:23). Know my branches. [Thus the word for thoughts is read as the word for branches.] "See if there be any way in me that is grievous, and lead me in the way everlasting" (Ps. 139:24). Lord of the Universe, If I am going to produce children who will cause you anger, it is better for me that you lead me in the everlasting path [of death].'"

2. A. "For 1 continue childless, and the heir of my house is Eliezer of Damascus" (Gen. 15:2):

B. R. Eleazar in the name of R. Yose b. Zimra: "'My house' refers to Lot, whose greatest desire is to inherit me.

C. "'Dameseq Eliezer [Eliezer of Damascus]' for it was on his account that I went in pursuit after kings as far as Damascus, and God helped me.".

D. R. Simeon b. Laqish in the name of Bar Qappara: "'The son of my household' means my steward [and not Lot].

E. "'Dameseq Eliezer:' for it was with his help that I pursued kings as far as Damascus, and Eliezer was in fact his name as it is said, 'He led forth his trained men, three hundred and eighteen' (Gen. 14:14), and the numerical value of the letters of the name Eliezer is three hundred and eighteen."

No. 1 makes the same point in its interpretation of the statements of Abram and David. Obviously, the composition did not come forth to serve as a verse by verse exegesis of the book of Genesis in particular. It makes its own point, which is more or less the opposite of the point of Gen. 15:2. It is better not to have children than to produce faithless ones. No. 2 explains the new name at hand, Eliezer, by identifying that name with Lot and showing how the identification can be made to stick. This view is rejected and the linkage is effected in another way.

XLIV:X.

1. A. "And Abram said, 'Behold, you have given me no offspring, and a slave born in my house will be my heir'" (Gen. 15:3):

B. Said R. Samuel bar Isaac, "A planet has taken hold of my fate and announces, 'Abram will not have children.'

C. "Said the Holy One, blessed be he, to him, 'That is indeed as you say. [How so?] Abram and Sarai will not have children, but Abraham and Sarah will have children.'"

The colloquy between Abram and God is worked out, so making the point that Israelites are not subject to the dictates of the stars, a common polemic. By changing Abram's name, his horoscope will be altered.

XLIV:XI.

1. A. "And behold, the word of the Lord came to him, ['This man shall not be your heir; your own son shall be your heir']" (Gen. 15:4):

B. R. Yudan and R. Eleazar in the name of R. Yose: "'The sentence at hand yields these statements: 'The Lord...to him,' 'the word of the Lord came to him,' 'and behold the word of the Lord came to him.'

C. "The meaning is that angel after angel, angel after angel, statement after statement, statement after statement. I and three angels have appeared to you and say to you, 'Lot is subject to a curse; he shall not inherit Abraham's estate.'"

D. R. Huna and R. Eleazar in the name of R. Yose: "It is written, 'And behold the Lord...' meaning that he in person came and spoke with him [and not through angels]."

At issue is whether God spoke through angels and other intermediaries or directly. The polemic, as before is to set aside the notion that some other power, e.g., astrological or angelic, intervenes between Abram and God.

XLIV:XII.

1. A. "And he brought him outside [and said, 'Look toward heaven and number the stars, if you are able to number them']" (Gen. 15:5):

B. R. Joshua in the name of R. Levi, "Now did he bring him outside of the world, that the text should say, 'And he brought him outside'? But the sense is that he showed him the open spaces of heaven, in line with this verse: 'While as yet he had not made the earth nor the open spaces' (Prov. 8:26)."

C. R. Judah b. R. Simon in the name of R. Yohanan: "He brought him above the vault of heaven. That is in line with the statement, 'Look toward heaven and number the stars,'and the meaning of the word 'look' is only 'from above to below.' [Hence he looked downward from above the vault of heaven.]"

D. Rabbis say, "You are a prophet, not an astrologer, as it is said, 'Now, therefore, restore the man's wife, for he is a prophet' (Gen. 20:7)."

2. A. In the time of Jeremiah the Israelites wanted to take up this principle [of astrology], but the Holy One, blessed be he, did not allow them to do so, in line with this verse: "Thus says the Lord, 'Do not learn the way of the nations, and do not be dismayed at the signs of heaven'" (Jer. 10:2).

B. "Abraham, your forefather, wanted to take up this principle, but [God] did not allow him to do so."

3. A. Said R. Levi, "While the sandal is on your foot, step on the thorn. Someone who is placed below them should fear them, but you are placed above them, so should trample them down."

4. A. R. Yudan in the name of R. Eleazar: "Three things annul an evil decree [that is foreseen by astrology], and these are they: prayer, acts of charity, and

repentence.   And all three of them may be located in a single verse of Scripture:

B.   "'If my people, upon whom my name is called, shall humble themselves and pray [and seek my face, and turn from their evil ways, then I will forgive their sin]' (2 Chr. 7:14).

C.   "'If my people, upon whom my name is called, shall humble themselves and pray' refers to prayer.

D.   "'...and seek my face' refers to acts of charity, in line with this verse: 'I shall behold your face in acts of charity' (Ps. 17:15).

E.   "'...and turn from their evil ways' refers to repentence.

F.   "Then: 'I will forgive their sin.'"

G.   R. Huna in the name of R. Joseph: "Also changing one's name and the doing of a good deed will have the same effect. We know that changing a name makes a difference from the case of Abraham and Sarah. [That has just been specified.]

H.   "We know that doing a good deed makes a difference from the case of the men of Nineveh, as it is said, 'And God saw their works, that they turned from their evil ways' (Jonah 3:10)."

I.   Some say, "Also changing one's place of domicile, as it is said, And the Lord said to Abram, "Get you out of your country"' (Gen. 12:1)."

J.   R. Mana said, "Also fasting [has the same effect], as it is said, 'The Lord answer you in the day of distress [interpreted here to mean the day of fasting]' (Ps. 20:20)."

K.   Raba bar Mehasia and R. Hama bar Guria in the name of Rab: "Fasting is as good for a dream as fire for stubble."

L.   Said R. Joseph, "That is so if it is done on the same day [as the dream], even if that is the Sabbath [on which it is ordinarily forbidden to fast]."

No. 1 carries forward the anti-astrological polemic, invited by the reference of Gen. 15:5 to looking at the stars. The purpose of looking at the stars is not to validate the claims of astrology, so far as these pertain to Israel, because God, not the stars, governs the fate of Israel. Nos. 2,3, and 4 go over the same ground.

XLIV:XIII.

1.   A.   "And he believed the Lord, and he reckoned it to him as righteousness. And he said to him, 'I am the Lord who brought you from Ur of the Chaldeans to give you this land to possess'" (Gen. 15:6-7):

B.   R. Eliezer b. Jacob: "Michael went down and saved Abraham from the furnace."

C. Rabbis say, "The Holy One, blessed be he, himself saved him, in line with this verse: 'I am the Lord who brought you from the furnace [Ur] of the Chaldeans.'

D. "And when was it that Michael [not God in person] went down? It was in the case of Hananiah, Mishael, and Azariah."

The issue here is distinct from the passage at hand. Once more the stress is that God is the one who governs Abraham's fate, not intervening merely through angels or messengers. That point stands on its own and merely draws facts from the verse at hand. So the composition was not made with the exegesis of the cited verse in mind. But the statement also links the story at hand to the one in the book of Daniel.

XLIV:XIV.

1. A. "But he said, 'O Lord God, how am I to know that I shall possess it?'" (Gen. 15:8):

B. R. Hama bar Haninah said, "It was not as though he were complaining, but he said to him, 'On account of what merit [shall I know it? That is, how have I the honor of being so informed?]'

C. "He said to him, 'It is on account of the merit of the sacrifice of atonement that I shall hand over to your descendants.'"

2. A. "And he said to him, 'Bring me a heifer three years old, a she-goat three years old, a ram three years old, a turtledove and a young pigeon'" (Gen. 15:9):

B. He showed him three kinds of bullocks, three kinds of goats, and three kinds of rams.

C. Three kinds of bullocks, the bullock of the day of atonement, the bullock that is brought on account of the inadvertent violation of any of the religious duties, and the heifer whose neck is to be broken.

D. He further showed him three kinds of goats, the goats to be offered on the festivals, the goats to be offered on the occasion of the new moons, and the goat to be offered for an individual.

E. He further showed him three kinds of rams, the one for the guilt offering that is brought in a case of certainty [that one is liable to such an offering], the one that is to be brought as a suspensive guilt offering, and the lamb that is brought by an individual,.

F. "...a turtledove and a young pigeon" (Gen. 15:9): that is as is stated, a turtle dove and a young pigeon [stated in Aramaic].

3. A. "And he brought him all these" (Gen. 15:10):

B. R. Simeon b. Yohai says, "All the forms of atonement did the Holy One, blessed be he, show to Abraham, but the tenth-*ephah* of fine flour he did not show to him [since it is omitted in the cited verse]."

C. Rabbis say, "He even showed him the atonement-rite involving the tenth-*ephah* of fine flour. [How do we know it?] Here it is stated, 'All *these* ' and elsewhere: 'And you shall bring the meal-offering that is made of these *things* ' (Lev. 2:8). [The word *these* occurs in both passages, and the latter refers to the tenth-*ephah* of fine flour.]"

4. A. "But he did not cut the birds in two" (Gen. 15:10):

B. The Holy One, blessed be he, showed him that an act of division of the carcass is carried on out in the case of the burnt-offering made of a bird, while an act of division is not carried out in the case of the sin-offering made of a bird.

Any implication that Abram's conversation with God was captious now is removed at No. 1. Nos 2-4 make the point that God showed Abram the rules of the cult, when he made his sacrifice at Jerusalem. So the origin of the cult is assigned to Abram and the story serves to explain why Jerusalem is the cult-center of Israel.

XLIV:XV.

1. A. Another matter: "Bring me a heifer three years old, [a she-goat three years old, a ram three years old, a turtledove, and a young pigeon]" (Gen. 15:9):

B. "Bring me a heifer three years old" refers to Babylonia, that produced three [kings important in Israel's history], Nebuchadnezzar, Evil Merodach, and Balshazzar.

C. "...a she-goat three years old" refers to Media, that also produced three kings, Cyrus, Darius, and Ahasuerus.

D. "...a ram three years old" refers to Greece.

E. R. Eleazar and R. Yohanan:

F. R. Eleazar said, "Greece conquered every point on the compass except for the east."

G. R. Yohanan said to him, "And indeed so, for is it not written, 'I saw the ram pushing westward and northward and southward, and no beasts could stand before him' (Dan. 8:4)?"

H. That indeed is the view of R. Eleazar, for the verse at hand does not refer to the east.

I. "...a turtledove, and a young pigeon" (Gen. 15:9) refers to Edom. It was a turtle-dove that would rob.

2. A. "And he brought him all these" (Gen. 15:10):

B. R. Judah said, "He showed him the princes of the nations."

C. R. Nehemiah said, "It was the princes of Israel that he showed him."

D. In the view of R. Judah, [the statement, "He laid each half over against the other" indicates that] he set the throne of one opposite the throne of another. [Freedman, p. 371, n. 2: He showed him the hostility of the nations toward each other, in contrast with which the bird, symbolizing Israel, was not to be divided but united.]

E. In the view of R. Nehemiah, [laying each half over against the other symbolized the fact that] there, [in Jerusalem] the great sanhedrin of Israel [seated in semi-circles, so each half could see the other] was in session and laying down the laws of Israel.

3. A. "But he did not cut the birds in two" (Gen. 15:10):

B. R. Abba bar Kahana in the name of R. Levi: "The Holy One, blessed be he, showed him that whoever stands against the wave is swept away by the wave, and whoever does not stand against the wave is not swept away by the wave."

No. 1 now links the sacrifices to the particular stages in Israel's history with the nations. So the dual link, one with the cult, the other with Israel's history, is forged. No. 2 takes up the same task. No. 3 then draws out the important lesson, which is that Israel, symbolized by the bird, has to ride out the waves of history (Freedman, p. 371, n. 5).

XLIV:XVI.

1. A. "And when birds of prey came down upon the carcasses, Abram drove them away" (Gen. 15:11):

B. Said R. Assi, "Abraham took a staff and beat them, but they were not beaten. Nonetheless: 'Abram drove them away' by means of repentence." [Freedman, p. 372, n. 1: The birds of prey represent the nations swooping down on Israel. Abram tried to beat them off by physical force but without success, and it is only when Israel turns to God in penitence that his enemies are driven off.]

C. Said R. Azariah, "When our children become corpses, lacking sinews and bones, your merit will sustain them." [Freedman, p. 372, n.2: When

Israel is defeated and despoiled, then Abraham's merit will disperse the birds of prey.]

Following Freedman, we find here a reference to Israel's history in later time. Only submission to God will save Israel, a recurrent theme.

XLIV:XVII.

1. A. "And it came to pass, as the sun was going down, [a deep sleep fell on Abram, and lo, a dread and great darkness fell upon him]" (Gen. 15:12):

  B. R. Joshua of Sikhnin in the name of R. Levi: "The beginning of downfall is sleep. When one sleeps, he does not labor in Torah-study or do work. [Freedman, p. 136, n. 1: His point is that one causes man to fall through sleep.]"

2. A. Rab said, "There are three kinds of repose: there is the repose of sleep, the repose of prophecy, and the repose of unconsciousness [as in a trance].

  B. "The repose of sleep: 'So the Lord God caused a deep sleep to fall upon the man' (Gen. 2:21).

  C. "The repose of prophecy: 'And as the sun set, a deep repose fell on Abram' (Gen. 15:12).

  D. "The repose of unconsciousness: 'And no man saw it or knew it, neither did any awake, for they were all asleep, because a deep sleep from the Lord had fallen upon them' (1 Sam. 26:12)."

  E. Rabbis say, "Also there is the repose of [drunken] silliness, as it is written, 'Stupefy yourselves and be stupid...for the Lord has poured out upon you the spirit of deep sleep' (Is. 29:10)."

3. A. R. Hinena bar Isaac said, "There are three kinds of partial realization [of a complete experience].

  B. "The partial realization of the experience of death is in sleep.

  C. "The partial realization of the experience of prophecy is in a dream."

  D. "The partial realization of the world to come is in the Sabbath."

  E. R. Abin added two more: "The partial realization of light from above is in the orb of the sun, and the partial realization of wisdom from on high is the Torah."

4. A. "[And it came to pass, as the sun was going down,] lo, a deep sleep fell on Abram, and lo, a dread and great darkness fell upon him" (Gen. 15:12):

B. "...lo, a dread" refers to Babylonia, as it is written, "Then was Nebuchadnezzar filled with fury" (Gen. 3:19).

C. "...and darkness" refers to Media, which darkened the eyes of Israel by making it necessary for the Israelites to fast and conduct public mourning.

D. "...great..." refers to Greece.

E. R. Simon said, "The kingdom of Greece set up one hundred and twenty commanders, one hundred and twenty hyparchs, and one hundred and twenty generals."

F. Rabbis said, "It was sixty of each, as it is written, 'Serpents, fiery serpents, and scorpions' (Gen. 8:15). Just as the scorpion produces sixty eggs at a time, so the kingdom of Greece set up sixty at a time."

G. "...fell upon him" refers to Edom, as it is written, "The earth quakes at the noise of their fall" (Jer. 49:21).

H. Some reverse matters:

I. "...fell upon him" refers to Babylonia, since it is written, "Fallen, fallen is Babylonia" (Is. 21:9).

J. "...great..." refers to Media, in line with this verse: "King Ahasuerus did make great" (Est. 3:1).

K. "...and darkness" refers to Greece, which darkened the eyes of Israel by its harsh decrees.

L. "...lo, a dread" refers to Edom, as it is written, "After this I saw...,a fourth beast, dreadful and terrible" (Dan. 7:7).

Nos. 1-3 form a completed composition on the syllogism at hand, to which the cited verse contributes a mere illustration. No. 4 successfully links the cited passage once more to the history of Israel. I cannot imagine a more successful exploration of that theme.

XLIV:XVIII.

1. A. "Then the Lord said to Abram, 'Know of a surety [that your descendants will be sojourners in a land that is not theirs, and they will be slaves there, and they will be oppressed for four hundred years; but I will bring judgment on the nation which they serve, and afterward they shall come out with great possessions']" (Gen. 15:13-14):

    B. "Know" that I shall scatter them.

    C. "Of a certainty" that I shall bring them back together again.

    D. "Know" that I shall put them out as a pledge [in expiation of their sins].

    E. "Of a certainty" that I shall redeem them.

    F. "Know" that I shall make them slaves.

G. "Of a certainty" that I shall free them.

2. A. "...that your descendants will be sojourners in a land that is not theirs and they will be slaves there, and they will be oppressed for four hundred years:"

B. It is four hundred years from the point at which you will produce a descendant. [The Israelites will not serve as slaves for four hundred years, but that figure refers to the passage of time from Isaac's birth.]

C. Said R. Yudan, "The condition of being outsiders, the servitude, the oppression in a land that was not theirs all together would last for four hundred years, that was the requisite term."

No. 1 parses the cited verse and joins within its simple formula the entire history of Israel, punishment and forgiveness alike. No. 2 parses the verse to follow, trying to bring it into line with the chronology of Israel's later history.

XLIV:XIX.

1. A. "But I will also bring judgment on the nation which they serve" (Gen. 15:14):

B. Said R. Helbo, "Rather than, 'and that nation,' the passage states, 'But I will *also* bring judgment on the nation which they serve' (Gen. 15:14). Also they, also Egypt and the four kingdoms who will enslave you [will God judge]."

2. A. "I will bring judgment" (Gen. 15:14):

B. R. Eleazar in the name of R. Yose: "With these two letters, namely, the letters that form the word for 'judge,' the Holy One, blessed be he, promised our ancestor that he would redeem his children. But should they carry out an act of repentence, he will redeem them with seventy-two letters [and not only with two]."

C. Said R. Yudan, "The verse that follows presents seventy-two letters [in illustration of the foregoing statement]: 'Or has God tried to go and take him a nation from the midst of another nation, by trials, by signs, and by wonders, and by war, and by a mighty hand, and by an outstretched arm, and by great terrors' (Deut. 4:34). Here there are seventy-two letters. But if you propose that there are seventy five, not seventy-two, take off the three letters that make up the second reference to the word 'nation,' which does not count."

D. R. Abin said, "It is by his name that he will redeem them, and the name of the Holy One, blessed be he, contains seventy-two letters."

No. 1 deals with the object of the verb "judge," and No. 2 presents its own proposition on the character of ultimate redemption. The issue here is not particular to the verse at hand. The proposition is that God has unconditionally promised to redeem Israel, but if Israel repents, then the redemption will come with greater glory.

XLIV:XX.

1. A. "And afterwards they shall come out with great possessions" (Gen. 15:14):

B. Said R. Aha, "What is written is not 'after' but 'afterwards,' meaning, only after I shall have brought on them ten plagues, then 'they shall come out with great possessions.'"

2. A. [Abraham] said, "Shall I also be subjugated?"

B. He said to him, "'As for yourself, you shall go to your fathers in peace; you shall be buried in a good old age' (Gen. 15:15)."

3. A. Said R. Simeon b. Laqish, "There are three concerning whom 'good old age' is stated:

B. "Abraham , and he had it coming,

C. "David, and he had it coming,

D. "but Gideon did not have it coming.

E. "Why not? Because 'Gideon made an ephod thereof' (Judges. 8:27) for idolatry."

Nos. 1 and 2 clarify the sense of the verses of Scripture at hand. No. 3 then makes its own point, for its facts referring to this passage among others.

XLIV:XXI.

1. A. "When the sun had gone down and it was dark, [behold a smoking fire pot and a flaming torch passed between these pieces]" (Gen. 15:17):

B. That was intense darkness [in Aramaic].

2. A. "...behold a smoking fire pot and a flaming torch passed between these pieces" (Gen. 15:17):

B. Simeon bar Abba in the name of R. Yohanan: "He showed him four things, Gehenna, the [four] kingdoms, the giving of the Torah, and the sanctuary. He said to him, 'So long as your descendants are occupied with these latter two, they will be saved from the former two. If they abandon two of them, they will be judged by the other two.'

C. "He said to him, 'What is your preference? Do you want your children to go down into Gehenna or to be subjugated to the four kingdoms?'"

D. R. Hinena bar Pappa said, "Abraham chose for himself the subjugation to the four kingdoms."

E. R. Yudan and R. Idi and R. Hama bar Hanina: "Abraham chose for himself Gehenna, but the Holy One, blessed be he, chose the subjugation to the four kingdoms for him."

F. That [statement of Hinena b Papa] is in line with the following: "How should one chase a thousand and two put ten thousand to flight, except their rock had given them over"" (Deut. 32:30). That statement refers to Abraham.

G. "But the Lord delivered them up" (Deut. 32:30) teaches that God then approved what he had chosen.

3. A. R. Huna in the name of R. Aha: "Now Abraham sat and puzzled all that day, saying, 'Which should I choose?'

B. "Said the Holy One, blessed be he, to him, 'Choose without delay.' That is in line with this verse: 'On that day the Lord made a covenant with Abram' (Gen. 15:18)."

C. This brings us to the dispute of R. Hinena bar Pappa with R. Yudan and R. Idi and R. Hama bar Haninah.

D. R. Hinena bar Pappa said, "Abraham chose for himself the subjugation to the four kingdoms."

E. R. Yudan and R. Idi and R. Hama bar Haninah said in the name of a single sage in the name of Rabbi: "The Holy One, blessed be he, chose the subjugation to the four kingdoms for him, in line with the following verse of Scripture: 'You have caused men to ride over our heads' (Ps. 66:12). That is to say, you have made ride over our heads various nations, and it is as though 'we went through fire and through water' (Ps. 66:21)."

F. R. Joshua said, "Also the splitting of the Red Sea he showed him, as it is written, 'That passed between these pieces' (Gen. 15:17), along the lines of the verse, 'O give thanks to him who divided the Red Sea in two' [in which the same word, the letters for pieces, occurs as 'in two'] (Ps. 86:13)."

The main interest at Nos. 2 and 3 is in linking the history of Israel to the passage at hand. That exegesis surely is invited by the substance of the cited verses. But the special interest of the exegetes is in Israel's suffering later on, with the particular stress on God's choosing subjugation to the nations as the appropriate penalty for Israel's failures to come. In fact Abraham is made party to the entire future history of Israel, even choosing, in dealing with God, the penalty for their sin and their mode of atonement.

XLIV:XXII.

1. A. ""On that day the Lord made a covenant with Abram, [saying, 'To your descendants I give this land']" (Gen. 15:18):

   B. R. Yudan: "Rabban Yohanan ben Zakkai and R. Aqiba:

   C. "One of them said, 'This world he revealed to him, the world to come he did not reveal to him.'

   D. "The other said, 'This world and the world to come he revealed to him.'"

   E. R. Berekhiah said, "R. Eleazar and R. Yose b. R. Hanina:

   F. "One of them said, 'Up to this day he revealed to him.'

   G. "The other of them said, 'From this day forward he revealed to him.' [Freedman, p. 376, n. 4: The discussion turns on the implication of 'in that day.' Berekhiah apparently states that one held that God revealed Israel's future to Abraham only until that day, that is, when Israel would leave Egypt, while the other held that he revealed the future to him from the Exodus until Messiah's coming.]"

2. A. "To your descendants I give this land" (Gen. 15:18):

   B. R. Huna and R. Dosetai in the name of R. Samuel b. Nachman: "Even the mere statement of the Holy One, blessed be he, constitutes a concrete deed.

   C. "For it is said, 'To your descendants I give this land.' What is written is not 'I *shall* give' but rather, 'I *have* given.' [Merely saying what God *will* do constitutes an actual deed.]"

   D. R. Yudan in the name of R. Abba: "'What is written is not, 'So let the redeemed of the Lord say whom he *redeems*,' but 'whom he *has* redeemed' (Ps. 107:3). [It is as if it has already been carried out.]

   E. R. Abin said, "What is written is not, 'For the Lord *ransoms* Jacob, ' but, 'For the Lord *has ransomed* Jacob' (Jer. 31:11))."

   F. Rabbis say, "What is written is not, 'I will hiss for them and gather them for I *will redeem* them,' but 'For I *have redeemed* them' Zech. 10:8).

   G. R. Joshua said, "What is written is not, 'And the Lord *will* create,' but,' And the Lord *has* created ...a cloud and smoke by day' (Is. 4:5), that is, 'it had been created and was then ready.'"

   No. 1 takes up the extent of the revelation contained in the covenant of Gen. 15:18. The point of No. 2 does not rest on the verse at hand, which supplies a fact for the proof of the larger syllogism.

XLIV:XXIII.

1. A. "The land of the Kenites, the Kenizzites, [the Kadmonites, the Hittites, the Perizzites, the Rephaim, the Amorites, the Canaanites, the Girgashites, and the Jebusites]" (Gen. 15:20):

   B. R. Dosetai in the name of R. Samuel b. Nahman: "Since the passage at hand does not make mention of the Hivites [who do occur in Deut. 7:1], the author introduces the Rephaim in their place."

2. A. R. Helbo in the name of R. Abba in the name of R. Yohanan: "In point of fact the Holy One, blessed be he, originally contemplated giving Israel an inheritance of ten nations, but he gave them only seven. The other three are: 'The Kenites, the Kenizzites, and the Kadmonites' (Gen. 15:20)."

   B. Rabbi said, "They are Aravayya, Shalamayya, and Nabatayya."

   C. R. Simeon b. Yohai says, "They are the area around Damascus, Asayya, and Aspamayya."

   D. R. Eliezer b. Jacob said, "They are Asayya, Turqi, and Qartegina. [Freedman: Asia Minor, Thrace, and Carthage.]"

   E. Rabbis say, "They are Edom, Moab, and the head of the children of Ammon. They are the three that he did not give to them in this world, as it is said, 'For I will not give you of their land' (Deut. 2:5).

   F. "But in the age of the Messiah they are going to belong to Israel, so as to carry out the word of the Holy One, blessed be he.

   G. "Now, in any event, he has given them the territory of seven [listed here], as it is said, 'Seven nations greater and mightier than you' (Deut. 7:1)."

3. A. Said R. Isaac, "The pig grazes with ten of its young, but the sheep does not graze with one of its young. Thus: 'The Kenite, the Kenizzite,' and so on [were promised to Abraham's children], but still: 'Now Sarai, Abram's wife, bore him no children' (Gen. 16:1)."

No. 1 clarifies a minor point in the comparison of ,the present list with that at Deut. 7:1. No. 2 proceeds to identify the nations that will be given later on. No. 3 then builds a bridge between the present passage and what is to follow, representing Gen. 16:1 as a contrast to Gen. 15:20. The solitary condition of Sarai comes under consideration. Freedman notes, p. 378, n. 3: "The unclean swine is always surrounded by a large litter of its offspring, whereas the clean sheep is alone."

Chapter Thirteen

Parashah Forty-Five. Genesis 16:1-14

XLV:I.

1. A. "Now Sarai, Abram's wife, bore him no children. [She had an Egyptian maid, whose name was Hagar; and Sarai said to Abram, 'Behold now, the Lord has prevented me from bearing children; go in to my maid; it may be that I shall obtain children by her']" (Gen. 16:1):

   B. "A woman of valor who can find? For her price is far above rubies" (Prov. 31:10).

   C. What is the meaning of the word translated "price"?

   D. R. Abba bar Kahana said, It refers to her pregnancy, in line with this verse: 'Your origin and your nativity' (Ez. 16:3) [in which the word for origin uses the same letters as the word for price]."

2. A. Abram was a year older than Nahor. Nahor was a year older than Haran. So Abram was two years older than Haran. There was a year of the pregnancy with Milcah and a year of the pregnancy with Iscah, and it turns out that Haran produced children when he was six years old. And [if Haran could do it,] how then could Abram not produce a child? [Freedman, p[. 312, n. 1: Iscah was Sarah. Now Abram was ten years older than Sarah. Since he was two years older than Haran, Sarah's father, Sarah was born when Haran was only eight years old. Again, she was his second daughter, and since the period of pregnancy and child-bearing is roughly a year for each child, Haran must have been six years old when he begot a child.]

   B. [The fault was Sarai's:] "And *Sarai* was barren, *she* had no child" (Gen. 11:30).

3. A. "She had born him no children" (Gen. 16:1):

   B. R. Judah says, "'To him,' that is, to Abram in particular she had not produced a child, but if she had been married to someone else, she would have produced a child."

   C. R. Nehemiah says, "Neither for him nor for anyone else [could she produce a child]."

D. How then does R. Nehemiah interpret the verse, "She had born him no children"? Explain the passage to mean, "To him and to her," so, she did not bear "for herself" on Sarai's account, or "for him" on Abram's account.

4. A. "She had an Egyptian maid" (Gen. 16:1):

B. She was a serving woman in the status of *melog* -property [literally, property that may be plucked, that is, harvested, by the husband. The *melog* - property was part of the wife's dowry; in the case of that property, the husband enjoyed the usufruct but was not liable for loss of its value. By contrast, "iron flock" property is that portion of the dowry which the husband must return intact, at its full original value, so he is liable for the upkeep of "iron-flock" property but not for *melog*-property -- his for the plucking.]

C. He was liable for support for the maid but he had no right to sell her.

D. People asked before R. Simeon b. Laqish, "What is the meaning of the classification of slaves in the category of 'slaves that may be plucked'?"

E. He said to them, "What you pluck, you pluck [and do not have to pay back]."

5. A. Said R. Simeon b. Yohai, "Hagar was daughter of Pharaoh. When he saw the wonderful deeds that were done for Sarah when she was in his house, he took his daughter and gave her to Sarai, saying, 'It is better that my daughter should be a servant girl in this household, rather than a matron in some other house.' That is in line with this verse of Scripture: 'She had an Egyptian maid, whose name was Hagar' (Gen. 16:1). The sense of 'Hagar' is, 'Here is your reward' [a play on the word for Hagar and for reward, *agar*].

B. "So too Abimelech, when he saw the wonders that were done for Sarah when she was in his house took his daughter and gave her to her, saying, 'It is better that my daughter should be a servant girl in this household, rather than a matron in some other house.' That is in line with the following verse of Scripture: 'Kings' daughters are among your favorites' (Ps. 45:10). That is to say, the daughters of kings.

C. "'At your right hand stands the queen in gold of Ophir' (Ps. 45:10), speaking of Sarai."

No. 1 works out the point of intersection of the cited verse, Prov. 31:10, treating as the priceless gift of a woman her capacity to become pregnant. No. 2 goes over familiar ground, now focused on the base verse alone. No. 3 imposes a close reading on the cited verse. I am not sure why No. 4 reaches the conclusion that it does. No. 5 is more to the point, and the play on words accounts for how Hagar came to be Sarai's serving woman.

XLV:II.

1. A. "And Sarai said to Abram, 'Behold now, the Lord has prevented me from bearing children; go in to my maid; it may be that I shall obtain children by her'" (Gen. 16:2):

   B. She said, "I know the source for my malady. It is not as people say, 'She needs a talisman, she needs a charm.' Rather: 'Behold now, *the Lord* has prevented me from bearing children' (Gen. 16:2)."

2. A. "...it may be that I shall obtain children by her'" (Gen. 16:2):

   B. It has been taught on Tannaite authority:

   C. Whoever does not have a child is as though he were dead and destroyed.

   D. As though dead: "And she said to Jacob, 'Give me children or else I am dead'" (Gen. 30:1).

   E. As though destroyed: "...it may be that I shall obtain [literally: built up, hence, rebuilt] children by her" (Gen. 16:2). Building up takes place only in the case of destruction.

3. A. "And Abram hearkened to the voice of Sarai" (Gen. 16:2):

   B. R. Yose says, "It was to the voice of the holy spirit, in line with the following verse: 'Now therefore hearken to the voice of the words of the Lord' (1 Sam. 15:1)."

No. 1 presents a close reading of the base verse. No. 2 makes its own point, for which the base verse provides a fact. No. 3 interprets Abram's obedience to Sarai's statement as compelled by the holy spirit. The three passages do not fall into a single classification. But No. 3 surely provides an excuse for Abram's consorting with the slave-woman. It also removes the suspicion that Abram obeyed a woman's orders.

XLV:III.

1. A. "And Sarai Abram's wife took Hagar the Egyptian, her maid, and gave her to Abram her husband as a wife" (Gen. 16:3):

   B. She drew her along with persuasive words, saying to her, "Happy are you, that you will cleave to that holy body."

2. A. "So after Abram had dwelt ten years in the land of Canaan" (Gen. 16:3):

   B. R. Ammi in the name of R. Simeon b. Laqish: "How on the basis of Scripture do we know that rule that we have learned in the Mishnah: **If one has married a woman and lived with her for ten years and not** produced a child, he is not allowed to remain sterile [but must marry someone else] [M. Yeb. 15:6]? Proof derives from this verse: 'So after Abram had dwelt ten years ' The statement, '...in the land of Canaan...' further proves that the years of marriage spent outside of the Land of Israel do not count."

3. A. "She gave her to Abram her husband" (Gen. 16:3) -- and not to anyone else.

B. "...as a wife" (Gen. 16:3) --and not as a concubine.

No. 1 provides an interpretation for the word, "take" used at Gen. 16:3, explaining that Hagar acted voluntarily. This again cleans up the picture. No. 2 draws upon the verse at hand to prove the cited proposition. No. 3 then provides a close reading of the language at hand.

XLV:IV.

1. A. "And he went in to Hagar and she conceived" (Gen. 16:4):

B. R. Levi bar Hiyyata said, "She got pregnant from the first act of sexual relations [at which point she loses her virginity]."

C. Said R. Eliezer, "A woman never gets pregnant from the first act of sexual relations."

D. They raised an objection from the following statement: "Thus were both daughters of Lot with child by their father" (Gen. 19:36).

E. Said R. Tanhuma, "They exercised great self-control and removed their own virginity and so became pregnant by the first act of sexual relations."

F. Said R. Haninah b. Pazzi, "Thorns are not weeded nor sown. They grow and sprout up on their own. But how much work and labor are needed to make wheat grow. [Freedman, p. 381, n. 7: Thus Hagar conceived immediately, while Sarah had to wait a long time.]"

2. A. Now why were the matriarchs barren?

B. R. Levi in the name of R. Shila, R. Helbo in the name of R. Yohanan: "The Holy One, blessed be he, lusts after their prayer and mediation: 'O my dove, you are as the clefts of the rock' (Song 2:14).

C. "'Why did I make you barren? So that "I might see your countenance, hear your voice" Song 2:14).'"

D. R. Azariah in the name of R. Hinena: "It was so that they should depend upon their husbands despite their beauty [since they would want to have sexual relations to produce children]."

E. R. Hunah, R. Jeremiah in the name of R. Hiyya bar Abba, "It was so that they might live out the greater part of their years without the subjugation [of child raising]."

F. R. Huna, R. Idi, R. Abin in the name of R. Meir: "It was so that their husbands should have pleasure with them. For so long as a woman receives pregnancies, she loses her looks and lacks grace. For all of those ninety years before Sarah had a child, she was as beautiful as a bride in her marriage-canopy."

3. A. The ladies would come and ask how she was. And Sarah would say to them, "Go and ask how that wretched woman is."

B. And Hagar would say to him, "My mistress, Sarai, is not on the inside what she is on the outside. She looks like a righteous woman, but she really isn't. For if she were a righteous woman, look how many years have passed and she has not become pregnant, but I got pregnant in a single night. [She must have displeased God.]"

C. And Sarah would say, "Should I get involved with this woman and engage in debate with her? Hardly! I shall deal with her master!"

No. 1 explains the base verse, noting that the verse indicates Hagar became pregnant after a single act of intercourse. This generates the question raised at No. 2. No. 3 continues No. 2 by adding a dramatic point of its own. This prepares us for Gen. 16:5. Overall there is a polemic in favor of Sarai and Abram, in each case removing implications negative for them.

XLV:V.

1. A. "And Sarai said to Abram, 'May the wrong [done to me be on you. I gave my maid to your embrace, and when she saw that she had conceived, she looked on me with contempt. May the Lord judge between you and me!]'" (Gen. 16:5):

B. R. Yudan in the name of R. Judah: "'You wrong me with words. Why so? Because you hear me humiliated and say nothing.'"

2. A. R. Berekhiah in the name of R. Abba: "'I have a case against you.'

B. "The matter may be compared to the case of two men who were in prison. The king went by. One of them said, 'Do justice for me.' The king said to let him go. The other said to him, 'I have a case against you. If you had said, "Do justice for *us*," just as he let you out, so he would have let me out. But since you said, "Do justice for me," only you were released. I was not released.'

C. "Similarly [Sarai speaks,] 'If you had said, "*We* go childless," then, just as [God] gave you a child, so he would have given me one. And what you said was, "And I go childless" (Gen. 15:2), so he gave you a child, but to me he gave no child.'

D. "The matter may further be compared to the case of two men who were going to borrow seed from the king. One of them said, 'Let me borrow seed.' The king gave orders to give it to him. His fellow said to him, 'I have a case against you. If you had said, "Let us borrow some seed from you," just as he gave seed to you, so he would have given it to me. But since you said, "Let *me* borrow some seed," to you he gave, but to me he did not give.'

E. "Along these same lines, [Sarai speaks], 'If you had said, "Behold to us you have given no seed," then, just as he gave to you so he would have given to me. But what you said was, "Behold, to *me* you have given no seed"' (Gen. 15:3)."

3. A. R. Menahama in the name of R Abun: "[When the text says, 'My wrong be upon you' (Gen. 16:5) the meaning is,] 'She scratched his face' [since the word for 'wrong' and 'scratch' share the same letters. Thus (Freedman:) 'my scratch be upon you.']"

4. A. Rabbis say, "Four traits apply to women. They are greedy, nosy, lazy, and envious.

B. "Greedy: 'And she took of the fruit thereof and did eat' (Gen. 3:6).

C. "Nosy: 'Sarah heard in the tent door' (Gen. 18:10).

D. "Lazy: 'Make ready *quickly* three measures of fine meal' (Gen. 18:6).

E. "Envious: 'Rachel envied her sister' (Gen. 30:1)."

F. R. Joshua b. Nehemiah said, "Also they scratch and blab.

G. "Scratch: 'And Sarai said to Abram, "My scratch be upon you"' (Gen. 16:5).

H. "Blab: 'And Miriam spoke against Moses' (Num. 12:1)."

I. R. Levi said, "They are also thieves and gadabouts:

J. "Thieves: 'And Rachel stole the teraphim' (Gen. 31:19).

K. "Gadabouts: 'And Dinah went out' (Gen. 34:1)."

5. A. "May the Lord judge between you and me!" (Gen. 16:5):

B. R. Tanhuma in the name of R. Hiyya the Elder, R. Berekhiah in the name of R. Eleazar: "Whoever jumps into litigation does not come out untouched.

C. "Sarah was worthy of reaching the ripe old age that Abraham reached, but because she said, 'May the Lord judge between you and me!' forty-eight years were removed from her life."

6. A. Said R. Hoshaiah, "The word for 'you' is written as if it were 'your son.'

B. "[What actually happened?] Since it is written, 'And he went in to Hagar and she conceived' (Gen. 16:4), why is it also stated, 'Behold, you are with child and shall bear a son' (Gen. 16:11)? [It indicates that she had become pregnant but had lost the first child, and the appearance of the later verse] teaches that the evil eye had gone into her and made her abort her baby."

C. R. Haninah said, "If Elisha the prophet had told her this through the Holy Spirit, it would have been enough for her! [Freedman, p. 384, n. 4: How much greater then was the honor conferred upon her in that an angel spoke to her]."

No. 1 extends the statement of Sarai. No. 2 supplies Sarai with a persuasive case against Abram, thus explaining why she accused him of wronging her. This makes a better case than Yudan at No. 1. No. 3 provides yet another interpretation for the cited word. No. 4 adduces the base verse in behalf of its exposition of the broader syllogism at hand. To that syllogism our verse is simply another piece of evidence. The comments on Gen. 16:5 at Nos. 5 and 6 make two separate points. The former teaches the syllogism that one should avoid litigation, using the case of Sarai's formulation of a case against Abram. No. 6 makes the quite important observation that the text at hand contains two statements about Hagar's becoming pregnant. Since we cannot deal with an imperfect text, let alone two versions of the same story, we are left with the picture drawn by Hoshaiah.

XLV:VI.

1. A. "But Abram said to Sarai, 'Behold your maid is in your power. [Do to her as you please.' Then Sarai dealt harshly with her and she fled from her]" (Gen. 16:6):

B. He said, "It is important to me to do her neither good nor evil. It is written, 'You shall not deal with her as a slave, because you have humbled her' (Deut. 21:14). As to this one, after we have given her anguish, shall we now make her a slave again?

C. "It is important to me to do her neither good nor evil. It is written, 'Then Sarai dealt harshly with her and she fled from her' (Gen. 16:6).' It is further written, 'To sell her to a foreign people he shall have no power, seeing that he has dealt deceitfully with her' (Ex. 21:8). As to this one, after we made her a mistress of the house, shall we turn her again into a slave-woman?

D. "It is important to me to do her neither good nor evil. It is written, 'Then Sarai dealt harshly with her and she fled from her' (Gen. 16:6)."

2. A. [Explaining what the harsh treatment was,] R. Abba said, "She deprived her of sexual relations."

B. R. Berekhiah said, "She slapped her face with a shoe."

C. R. Berekhiah in the name of R. Abba: "Water buckets and towels she gave to her charge for the bath [so humiliating her]."

The exegesis of Gen. 16:6 now involves Abram's discourse with Sarai, filling an obvious gap in the narrative. What is important is the invocation of later laws of the Torah to account for Abram's thinking. So once more we see that Abram kept the Torah before it was given. No. 2 adds a minor detail, so enriching the rather stark narrative.

XLV:VII.

1. A. "And the angel of the Lord found her by a spring of water in the wilderness, the spring on the way to Shur" (Gen. 16:7).

B. It was on the road to the town of Hilsah.

2. A. "And he said, 'Hagar, maid of Sarai, where have you come from and where are you going?' She said, 'I am fleeing from my mistress Sarai.'" (Gen. 16:8):

B. There is a parable: "If one person says to you, 'You have the ears of an ass, don't believe him. If two tell you so, order a halter for yourself."

C. So Abraham said, "[But Abram said to Sarai,] 'Behold your *maid* is in your power' (Gen. 16:6). "

D. Then the angel said to her, "Hagar, *maid* of Sarai" (Gen. 16:7).

E. "She said, 'I am fleeing from my *mistress* Sarai.'" (Gen. 16:8).

3. A. "The angel of the Lord said to her, 'Return to your mistress and submit to her.' The angel of the Lord also said to her, 'I will so greatly multiply your descendants that they cannot be numbered for multitude.'" (Gen. 16:10):

B. How many angels dealt with her [since there are several references to the angel of the Lord, while one would have sufficed, followed by "he said"]?

C. R. Hama bar Hanina said, "There were five, each one being represented by reference to 'he said.'"

D. Rabbis say, "Four, each one being represented by a reference to the word 'angel.'"

4. A. Said R. Hiyya, "Come and take note of the difference between the former generations and the latter generations. Note what Manoah said to his wife: 'We shall surely die, for we have seen God' (Judges 13:22). But the handmaiden, Hagar, saw five angels, but she was not afraid of them!"

B. Said R. Aha, "The fingernail of the patriarchs, not the belly of the descendants."

C. Said R. Isaac, "'She sees the ways of her household' (Prov. 31:27) [since such things were commonplace in Abram's household].

D. "Members of Abraham's household were seers, and she was used to the sight of [angels]."

No. 1 makes a minor gloss. No. 2 points to a peculiarity of the phrasing of the text, since Hagar is made to refer to herself as a slave-woman. But that is after prior references on the part of other actors. No. 3 pursues its own interest, and No. 4 follows up.

XLV:VIII.

1. A. "And the angel of the Lord said to her, 'Behold you, are with child, and shall bear a son, you shall call his name Ishmael, because the Lord has given heed to your affliction'" (Gen. 16:11):

B. Said R. Isaac, "There were three who were called by name before they were formed: Isaac, Solomon, and Josiah.

C. "In the case of Isaac, what does it say? 'And God said, "No, but Sarah your wife shall bear you a son, and you shall call his name Isaac"' (Gen. 17:19).

D. "In the case of Solomon: 'Behold, a son shall be born to you, who shall be a man of rest, and I will give him rest from all his enemies round about, for his name shall be Solomon' (1Chr. 22:9).

E. "In the case of Josiah: 'And he cried against the altar by the word of the Lord: "O altar, altar, thus says the Lord, behold, a son shall be born to the house of David, Josiah by name"' (1 Kgs. 13:2)."

F. Some say, "Also Ishmael among the nations [belongs on this list]: 'And the angel of the Lord said to her, "Behold you, are with child, and shall bear a son, you shall call his name Ishmael, [because the Lord has given heed to your affliction]"' (Gen. 16:11)."

The syllogism draws upon the verse at hand. The case proves that not only Israelites, but also gentiles, represented by Ishmael, fall under the same classification.

XLV:IX.

1. A. "He shall be a wild ass of a man, [his hand against every man and every man's hand against him, and he shall dwell over against all his kinsmen]" (Gen. 16:12):

   B. R. Yohanan and R. Simeon b. Laqish:

   C. R. Yohanan said, "[The term is used figuratively.] For most people grow up in a settled community, while he grew up in the wilderness."

   D. R. Simeon b. Laqish said, "'A wild ass of a man' is meant literally, for most people plunder property, but he plundered lives."

2. A. "...his hand against every man and every man's hand against him" (Gen. 16:12):

   B. [Reading the consonants for "every...against him" with different vowels, we produce the meaning:] His hand and the hand of his dog were alike. Just as his dog ate carrion, so he ate carrion.

3. A Said R. Eleazar, "When is it the case that 'his hand is against every man and every man's hand against him'?

   B. "When he comes concerning whom it is written: 'And wheresoever the children of men, the beasts of the field and the fowl of the heaven dwell, has he given them into your hand' (Dan. 2:38). [Freedman, p. 386, n. 2: In the days of Nebuchadnezzar, whose ruthless policy of conquest aroused the whole world against him.]

   C. "That is in line with the following verse of Scripture: 'Of Kedar and of the kingdoms of Hazor, which Nebuchadnezzar smote' (Jer. 49:28). His name is spelled, 'Nebuchadnezzar' because he shut them up in the wilderness and killed them. [Freedman, p. 386, n. 4: A play on the name, which, with the present spelling, ends in *asar*, spelled with an *alef*, as though it were *asar*, spelled with an *ayin* and yielding the meaning, shut up.]"

4. A. ["...and he shall dwell over against all his kinsmen]" (Gen. 16:12):

   B. Here the word-choice is "dwell" while later on it is "he fell" (Gen. 25:18).

   C. So long as Abraham was alive, "he [Ishmael] shall dwell." Once he died, "he fell." [His father's merit no longer protected him.]

   D. Before he laid hands on the Temple, "he shall dwell." After he laid hands on the Temple, "he fell."

   E. In this world "he shall dwell." In the world to come, "he fell."

No. 1 takes up the interpretation of the metaphor used for Ishmael. No. 2 carries forward the same theme, interpreting the passage in a literal way. Nos. 3-4 move from the figure of Ishmael to those like him, Nebuchadnezzar, then Rome. The Temple was destroyed by each of these persons, in the tradition of Ishmael. The conclusion then provides the hope to Israel that the enemy will perish, at least in the world to come. So the passage is read as both a literal statement and also as an effort to prefigure the history of Israel's suffering and redemption.

XLV:X.

1. A. "So she called the name of the Lord who spoke to her, ['You are a God of seeing,' for she said, 'Have I really seen God and remained alive after seeing him?' Therefore the well was called Beer-lahai roi, it lies between Kadesh and Bered]" (Gen. 16:13-14):

    B. R. Judah [bar Simon] and R. Yohanan in the name of R. Eleazar bar Simon: "On no occasion did the Holy One, blessed be he, ever find it necessary to enter into a conversation with a woman, except with that righteous woman [Sarah] alone, and even on that occasion there was a special reason." [In the case of the woman in the garden, it is alleged , God used an intermediary. We now review all the other possible cases, in addition to the one involving Eve, as these cases unfold in the book of Genesis. The relevance of the case of Hagar is clear: here it was through an angel.]]

    C. R. Abba bar Kahana in the name of R. Biri: "How many roundabout routes did he take in order to enter into conversation with her: 'And he said, "No, but you did laugh"' (Gen. 18:15)."

    D. But it is written, "And she called on the name of the Lord who had spoken with her" (Gen. 16:13) [speaking of Hagar]!

    E. R. Joshua bar Nehemiah in the name of R. Idi: "It was through an angel."

    F. And is it not written, "And the Lord said to her [Rebecca]" (Gen. 25:23)?

    G. R. Levi in the name of R. Hama bar Hanina: "It was through an angel."

    H. R. Eleazar in the name of R. Yose b. Zimri: "It was through Shem."

2. A. "You are a God of seeing" (Gen. 16:13):

    B. R. Aibu said, "You see the humiliation of those who are humiliated."

3. A. "[So she called the name of the Lord who spoke to her, ['You are a God of seeing,'] for she said, 'Have I really seen God and remained alive after seeing him?" (Gen. 16:13):

B. She said, "It was not enough for me that I had the merit of speech [with the angel], but even of royalty [that is coming for my child], in line with this verse: 'That you have brought me thus far' (2 Sam. 7:18) [using the same word at 'thus far' as is used for 'really.' Hence she says that she has seen a throne coming for her child.]

C. "It was not enough for me that I had the merit of speech with my mistress, but even all by myself [I have that same privilege, which means it is coming on my account, not on hers]."

D. Said R. Samuel, "The matter may be compared to the case of a noble lady, to whom the king said, 'Pass before me.' She passed before him, leaning on her handmaiden and pressing her face into the handmaiden [as a mark of modesty]. So the handmaiden saw the king, but she did not see the king. [So Hagar's statement shows the superior modesty of Sarai.]"

No. 1 utilizes the verse at hand to make its own point. No. 2 answers the question of what God sees. No. 3 expands on Hagar's statement, with the effect of linking Hagar to the messianic history of Israel, a familiar motif.

Chapter Fourteen

Parashah Forty-Six. Genesis 17:1-14

XLVI:I.

1. A. "When Abram was ninety-nine years old, [the Lord appeared to Abram and said to him, 'I am God Almighty. Walk before me and be blameless']" (Gen. 17:1).

   B. "I found Israel like grapes in the wilderness, I saw your fathers as the first-ripe in the fig-tree at her first season" (Hos. 9:10).

   C. R. Yudan said, "In the case of a fig-tree, to begin with the fruit is gathered one by one, then two by two, then three by three, until in the end people are able to gather whole basketsful and shovelsful. So too at the beginning there was only Abraham, then there were Abraham and Isaac, and then there were Abraham, Isaac, and Jacob, until: 'And the children of Israel were fruitful and increased abundantly and multiplied' (Ex. 1:7)."

   D. Said R. Yudan, "Just as in the case of a fig-tree, nothing goes to waste except for its stem, and when the stem is taken away the blemish is removed, so did the Holy One blessed be he say to Abraham, 'You have no refuse except for the foreskin. Remove it and the blemish will go away:' 'Walk before me and be blameless' (Gen. 17:1)."

The second interpretation of the intersecting verse brings us back to the base-verse and also explains the pertinence of the circumcision, which removes the one disfiguring trait that afflicted Abraham. The perfection or blamelessness to which Gen. 17:1 then refers is identified as the foreskin. Having explained the blemish, we proceed to the meaning of the reference to Abram's age.

XLVI:II.

1. A. "When Abram was ninety-nine years old, [the Lord appeared to Abram and said to him, 'I am God Almighty. Walk before me and be blameless']" (Gen. 17:1).

   B. "To everything there is a season, and a time to every purpose under the heaven" (Qoh. 3:1):

C. There was a time for Abraham to receive the commandment of circumcision: "That very day Abraham and his son Ishmael were circumcised" (Gen. 17:26).

D. There also was a season when his descendants were expected to neglect that commandment, namely, when they were in the wilderness: "For all the people that came out were circumcised, but all the people that were born in the wilderness by the way as they came forth out of Egypt had not been circumcised" (Joshua 5:5).

2. A. Why did he not circumcise himself at the age of forty-eight, when he first recognized his creator. It was so as not to shut the door before proselytes.

B. Then he should have circumcised at the age of eighty-five, when God spoke with him [during the incident when he commanded Abraham to pass] between the pieces [of an animal that had been sacrificed]. But it was so that Isaac in particular [and not Ishmael] should be born of a holy seed, [that is, of semen of a circumcised penis]

C. Then he should have been circumcised at the age of eighty-six, when Ishmael was born.

D. Said R. Simeon b. Laqish, "[God said,] 'I will plant a cinnamon tree in the world. Just as in the case of a cinnamon tree, so long as you manure and hoe it, it will produce fruit, so in the case of Abraham, even when his blood coagulates and his desire and passion wane, [he shall produce children.' [That is, the circumcision served to renew his virility (Freedman, p. 390, n. 3)]."

No. 1 deals with the specification of the time of circumcision, making the point that the time is not necessarily fixed, and other considerations will come into play. No. 2 then spells out these considerations, as they affected Abraham.

XLVI:III.

1. A. [Abraham] said, "If circumcision is so precious, then why was it not assigned to Adam?"

B. Said to him the Holy One, blessed be he, "Abraham, it is enough for you that you and I should be in the world. [Freedman, p. 390, n. 4: This and the following comments are based on the phrase, I am El Shaddai. By a play on words, Shaddai is derived from the word that means enough.]

C. "If you do not accept on yourself the requirement of circumcision, it is enough for the world to have existed up to now, it is enough for the status of uncircumcision to have existed until now, and it is enough for circumcision that it should have been neglected up to now."

D. He said to him, "Before I was circumcised, people came and joined me [in worshipping you]. Now that I am circumcised, do you think that people will come and join me? [This will be an impediment to proselytism.]"

E. Said to him the Holy One, blessed be he, "Abraham, it is enough for you that I am your God. It is enough for you that I am your sponsor. And it is not for yourself alone that I so view matters, but it is enough for my world that I am its God. It is enough for my world that I am its patron."

2. A. R. Nathan in the name of R. Aha, R. Berekhiah in the name of R. Isaac, "'I am the God who [said,] "Enough"' (Gen. 17:1) [reading *shaddai* as *she-dai*, 'that is enough']."

B. "'I am the one who said to the world, "Enough." I am the one who said to the land, "Enough." For if I had not said "Enough" to heaven, and to earth, "Enough," even up to now they would have continued to spread forth.'"

C. [Freedman, p. 391:] It was taught in the name of R. Eliezer b. Jacob, "It is I whose Godhead outweighs the world and the fulness thereof."

D. Aqilas translated it, "Sufficient and incomparable."

What is interesting at No. 1 is the allusion to the difficulty of making converts in light of the requirement of circumcision. God's answer then is that he is satisfied with what he has. But the further question, if circumcision matters, why was the imperfection created in man, demands attention for polemical purposes. Otherwise creation would be left with an imperfection affecting the crown of creation, man himself. In that context the answer is not very persuasive. No. 2 is an exegesis on the language "enough," as noted at No. 1 by Freedman.

XLVI:IV.

1. A. "Walk before me and be blameless" (Gen. 17:1):

B. Said R. Levi, "The matter may be compared to the case of matron to whom the king said, 'Pass before me.' She passed before him and she grew white with apprehension. She said, 'It may be that some sort of flaw is found in me.' Said the king to her, 'There is only one flaw in you, that the nail of your little finger is a bit long. Cut it off and the blemish will be removed.'

C. "So did the Holy One blessed be he say to Abraham, 'You have no refuse in you except for the foreskin. Remove it and the blemish will go away: 'Walk before me and be blameless' (Gen. 17:1)."

2. A. "And I will make my covenant between me and you and will multiply you exceedingly" (Gen. 17:2):

B. R. Huna in the name of Bar Qappara: "Abraham went into session and argued by analogy. 'Here it is said, "foreskin," and "foreskin" is said with reference to a tree. Just as in the case of the tree, when the word "foreskin" is used, it refers to the place which produces fruit, so here too "foreskin" with reference to man speaks of a place which produces fruit.'"

C. Said to him R. Haninah, "But was the mode of argument through analogy available to Abraham? [Surely not.] Rather: 'And I will make my covenant between me and you and will multiply you exceedingly.'

D. "From the place from which 'I will multiply you exceedingly,' at that place: 'I will make my covenant between me and you.'"

The exposition of the relationship between circumcision and perfection goes over familiar ground, No. 1. No. 2 then explains how Abraham knew that it was through the circumcision of the penis in particular that the covenant would be effected. The two modes of argument are neatly spelled out, B, C-D.

XLVI:V.

1. A. R. Ishmael and R. Aqiba:

B. R. Ishmael says, "Abraham was a high priest, as it is said, 'The Lord has sworn and will not repent, "You are a priest for ever after the manner of Melchizedek"' (Ps. 110:4). And it is said, 'And you shall be circumcised in the flesh of your *orlah* [a word we shall now define]' (Gen. 17:11). [Because Abram was a priest, we have a fact that will explain the place at which the *orlah* is to be found and removed. The argument now proceeds.] Now if he should practice circumcision with the ear, he would not be valid to bring an offering [since the blemish would render him unsuitable to serve at the altar]. If it were done at the mouth, he would not be valid to make an offering, likewise if it were done at the heart. So at what point could he make the mark of circumcision and still remain suitable for bringing an offering? It would have to be the foreskin of the body, that is, of the penis."

C. R. Aqiba said, "There are four matters to which the word *orlah* applies. The word is used in respect to the ear: 'Behold, their ear is uncircumcised (*orlah*)' (Jer. 6:10); the mouth: 'Behold, I am uncircumcised (*aral*) of lips' (Ex. 6:30); the heart: 'For all the house of Israel are uncircumcised (*arle*) in the heart' (Jer. 9:25). He was commanded: 'Walk before me and be without blemish' (Gen. 17:1). Now if he should practice circumcision on the ear, he would not be without blemish, likewise in the case of the mouth and the heart. Where then could he practice circumcision and remain without blemish? It would have to be the foreskin of the body, that is, of the penis."

D. Naqdah said, "'And he who is eight days old shall be circumcised among you, every male' (Gen. 17:12). Now if one should circumcise the ear, he will not hear, if he does so at the mouth, he will not speak, and if he does so at the heart, he will not reckon. At what point may one practice circumcision so that he may be able to reckon? This has to be circumcision of the body."

E. Said R. Tanhuma, "The proof of Naqdah is most reasonable."

2. A. "And the uncircumcised *male* who is not circumcised in the flesh of his foreskin shall be cut off from his people; he has broken my covenant" (Gen. 17:14):

B. Is there such thing as an uncircumcised female? [Why then does the passage specify "male"?]

C. But the sense of the passage is that the place at which one can distinguish whether one is male or female, that is the point at which the circumcision takes place.

The proof that the circumcision is to be of the penis occupies both Nos. 1 and 2. The proof-texts are diverse, and the sole point of intersection with the base verse, Gen. 17:1, is not critical to the larger construction.

XLVI:VI.

1. A. "Then Abram fell on his face [and God said to him, 'Behold, my covenant is with you, and you shall be the father of a multitude of nations']" (Gen. 17:3-4):

B. R. Phineas in the name of R. Levi: "Two times did Abraham fall on his face, on account of the merit of which circumcision was taken away from his sons twice, once in the wilderness and once in Egypt [for on both occasions the Israelites neglected the rite]. [Freedman, p. 393, n. 2: His falling on his face is regarded as an indication of unwilling assent to God's command.]

C. "In Egypt Moses came along and circumcised them, and in the wilderness, Joshua came along and circumcised them."

Linking Abraham's actions to the later history of Israel introduces a familiar theme. We now account for two later references to Israel's uncircumcision.

XLVI:VII.

1. A. "As for me, behold, my covenant is with you, [and you shall be the father of a multitude of nations]" (Gen. 17:4):

B. There is this case: R. Abba, R. Berekhiah, R. Abba bar Kahana, and R. Samuel bar Ammi were in session asking the following question: "How on the basis of the Torah do we have proof for the practice of exegesis by reading a word as an acronym [i.e., a composite of letters, each one of which is regarded as an abbreviation for another word]?

C. "We know it from the following: '...and you shall be the father of a multitude of nations' (Gen. 17:4). The R is lacking in the words 'father of a multitude.' [Freedman: His name was changed from Abram to Abraham, so that it might read: *ab*, father of, and *ham*, an abbreviation of *hamon*, multitude. Hence the R must be ignored in a case where Scripture itself provides the exegesis.]"

The point is clear as spelled out by Freedman. The exegesis proves a point extrinsic to the cited verse.

XLVI:VIII.

1. A. "No longer shall your name be Abram, but your name shall be Abraham, [for I have made you the father of a multitude of nations]" (Gen. 17:5):

B. Bar Qappara said, "Whoever refers to Abraham as Abram violates a religious duty of commission."

C. Said R. Levi, "It is a religious duty of both commission and omission. [How so? Violation of the statement,] 'No longer shall your name be Abram,' represents a religious duty of omission. [Violation of the statement,] '...but your name shall be Abraham' represents a religious duty of commission."

D. But lo, the men of the Great Assembly referred to him as Abram in the verse: "You ...who did choose Abram" (Neh. 9:7).

E. The case is different, for the sense is, "While he was still known as Abram you chose him." [So the context does matter.]

F. And along these same lines, is it the case that he who refers to Sarah as Sarai also violates a religious duty of commission?

G. [Not at all,] for it was only [Abraham] who was commanded in her regard. [He alone was told to use her new name.]

H. And along these same lines, is it the case that he who refers to Israel as Jacob violates a religious duty of commission?

I. It has been taught on Tannaite authority: It is not that the name of Jacob should be entirely abandoned, but that the name Israel should be principal and Jacob secondary.

J. R. Zebida in the name of R. Aha: "In any event, 'Your name is Jacob' with this proviso, that 'but Israel also shall be your name' (Gen. 35:10). It is so that the name Israel should be principal and Jacob secondary.

The discussion of the rule requires close reading of the verse, in that order of precedence. So the composition cannot be called exegetical in original intent. The main point is to derive rules for governing the names of those included here, Abram/Abraham, Sarai, and Jacob/Israel.

XLVI:IX.

1.   A.   "And I will give to you and to your descendants after you [the land of your sojournings, all the land of Canaan, for an everlasting possession; and I will be their God]" (Gen. 17:8):

B.   In this connection R. Yudan made five statements [imputing to God five propositions, which are now spelled out].

C.   R. Yudan said, "[God said,] 'If your descendants accept my divinity, I shall be their patron-God, and if not, I shall not be their patron-God.

D.   "'If your children enter the land, they will receive my divinity, and if they do not enter the land, they will not receive my divinity.

E.   "'If your descendants accept circumcision, they will receive my divinity, and if not, they will not receive my divinity.

F.   "'If your descendants accept circumcision, they will enter the land, and if not, they will not enter the land.' [So the cited verse yields a number of distinct conditions.]"

G.   [As a further example of the association of circumcision to receiving the land,] R. Berekhiah and R. Helbo in the name of R. Abin bar Yose: "It is written, 'And this is the cause that Joshua circumcised' (Joshua 5:4). Joshua spoke a word [using the same letters as 'cause'] to them, then he circumcised them. [Freedman, p. 394, n. 5: "And by this word did Joshua circumcise them.]

H.   "Joshua said to them, 'Now do you really imagine that you will enter the land uncircumcised? So did the Holy One, blessed be he say to Abraham: 'And I will give to you and to your descendants after you the land of your sojournings, all the land of Canaan, for an everlasting possession; and I will be their God' (Gen. 17:8). And that is on this stipulation: 'As for you, you shall keep my covenant, you and your descendants after you throughout their generations' (Gen. 17:9)."

2.   A.   "And God said to Abraham, 'As for you, you shall keep my covenant, you and your descendants after you throughout their generations'" (Gen. 17:9):

B.   R. Huna said Rab and R. Yohanan [made these statements:]

C.   "Rab said, "'And as for you, [someone like] you [shall keep my covenant]" [that is, the verse] is so formulated as to teach the rule that only one who already is circumcised is suitable to perform the rite of circumcision.'

D. "R. Yohanan said, '"He must certainly be circumcised" (Gen. 17:13) teaches the rule that only one who already is circumcised is suitable to perform the rite of circumcision.'"

E. It has been taught on Tannaite authority: An uncircumcised Israelite may not perform the rite of circumcision, all the more so an uncircumcised gentile.

The base verses, given at H, are read at No. 1 as interdependent conditions, both by Yudan and by the authorities cited thereafter. In this way the exegesis of the base verses yields an important lesson. The same classification encompasses No. 2, namely, the derivation of a rule from the formulation of Scripture. The purpose is clear.

XLVI:X.

1. A. "You shall be circumcised in the flesh of your foreskins [and it shall be a sign of the covenant between me and you]" (Gen. 17:11):

B. [Freedman:] The prepuce is like a sore hanging from the body. [Freedman, p. 395, n. 2: "The grammatical form, *unemaltem*, is unusual, and so by a play on words it is read: *numi* , a sore, *maltem* , shall you circumcise."]

2. A. There is the case of Monobases and Izates, sons of king Ptolemy, who were in session and studying the book of Genesis. When they came to this verse, "You shall be circumcised in the flesh of your foreskins [and it shall be a sign of the covenant between me and you]" (Gen. 17:11) this one turned his face to the wall and wept, and that one turned his face to the wall and wept.

B. This one went and circumcised himself, and that one went and circumcised himself.

C. After a while they were in session and studying the book of Genesis. When they came to the verse, "And you will circumcise...," one said to the other, "Woe is you, my brother" [thinking he was not circumcised]. The other said, "Woe is you, not me." Then each revealed the matter to the other.

D. When their mother found out about the matter, she went and told their father, "As to your sons, a sore appeared on their flesh, and the doctor ordered that they be circumcised."

E. He said, "Then let them be circumcised."

F. How did the Holy One, blessed be he, pay him back?

G. Said R. Phineas, "When he went out to battle, the enemy made for him in particular, but an angel came down and saved him."

The story, No. 2, rests upon the point made in No. 1, that the foreskin is like a sore to be removed. The reward, 2.F-G, introduces a separate conception.

XLVI:XI.

1. A. "He who is eight days old among you shall be circumcised; [every male throughout your generations, whether born in your house or bought with your money from any foreigner who is not of your offspring, both he that is born in your house and he that is bought with your money shall be circumcised]" (Gen. 17:13):

B. It has been taught on Tannaite authority: He who purchases the foetus of a gentile's slave-girl--

C. R. Yohanan said, "He is to be circumcised on the eighth day."

D. And it has been taught on Tannaite authority: R. Hama b. R. Yose said, "He is to be circumcised on the eighth day."

E. And it has been taught on Tannaite authority by Samuel along these same lines, for Samuel said, "'For a son or for a daughter' (Lev. 12:6). 'For a son' means under all circumstances, and 'for a daughter' means under all circumstances." [Freedman, p. 396, n. 3: "Whatever the circumstances in which the son is born, and whatever the status of his mother, circumcision must be on the eighth day."]

To the law at hand, the exegesis of the cited verse is critical, since it makes the point that the offspring of a slave is to be circumcised and so brought within the Israelite circle. The rest follows.

XLVI:XII.

1. A. "He shall surely be circumcised" (Gen. 17:13):

B. On the basis of the cited verse we know that the one who performs the rite of circumcision must himself be circumcised.

2. A. "He shall surely be circumcised" (Gen. 17:13):

B. The verse as formulated encompasses the one who is born circumcised [indicating that a rite of circumcision must be performed on him as well].

3. A. It has been taught on Tannaite authority:

B. R. Simeon b. Eleazar says, "The House of Shammai and the House of Hillel did not differ concerning one who was born circumcised, for they concurred that it is necessary to produce a drop of blood signifying the covenant of circumcision, on grounds that such a one is assumed to have a hidden foreskin.

C.   "Concerning what did they differ?   Concerning a proselyte who converted when he had already been circumcised.

D.   "For the House of Shammai say, 'It is necessary to produce a drop of blood signifying the covenant of circumcision.'

E.   "And the House of Hillel say, 'It is not necessary to produce a drop of blood signifying the covenant of circumcision.'"

F.   R. Eleazar, son of R. Eleazar Haqqappar, says, "The House of Shammai and the House of Hillel did not differ either on the one case or the other, agreeing that it is necessary to produce a drop of blood signifying the covenant of circumcision.

G.   "Concerning what case did they differ?   Concerning one who was born circumcised, for whom the eighth day after birth coincided with the Sabbath. [Normally, the requirement of circumcision will override the restrictions of the Sabbath.   But in this case do we invoke that principle, since it is not absolutely necessary to perform the rite?]

H.   "For the House of Shammai say, 'It is necessary to produce a drop of blood signifying the covenant of circumcision.'

I.   "And the House of Hillel say, 'It is not necessary to produce a drop of blood signifying the covenant of circumcision.'"

J.   R. Isaac bar Nahman in the name of R. Hoshaia: "The decided law follows the view of the disciple [=F-H]."

Nos. 1 and 2 set the stage for the disputes at No. 3, which take for granted the results of the prior exegesis.

XLVI:XIII.

1.   A.   "Any uncircumcised male who is not circumcised in the flesh of his foreskin shall be cut off from his people; he has broken my covenant" (Gen. 17:14):

B.   R. Haggai in the name of R. Isaac, R. Berekhiah in the name of R. Isaac: "Is there such thing as an uncircumcised female?

C.   "But the sense of the passage is that the place at which one can distinguish whether one is male or female, that is the point at which the circumcision takes place."

2.   A.   "...he has broken my covenant" (Gen. 17:14):

B.   This speaks of one who draws up the flesh [so as to appear uncircumcised].

C.   It has been taught on Tannaite authority: One who has disguised the mark of circumcision has to be circumcised again.

D.   R. Judah says, "He does not have to be circumcised again, since it is in the status of a concealed foreskin."

E.   They said before R. Judah, "And is it not the case that there were many in the time of ben Kozebah who [in the time of troubles concealed the mark of circumcision and afterward went and] circumcised again, and yet they produced children thereafter?"

3.   A   So it is written, "He shall surely be circumcised" (Gen. 17:13) even four or five times.

B.   "...he has broken my covenant" (Gen. 17:14):

C.   This speaks of one who draws up the flesh [so as to appear uncircumcised].

Nos. 1, 2 go over the elements of the verse, and No. 3 presents a systematic exegesis spelling out what is at issue in different form. The issue of No. 2 is whether we penalize one who has been circumcised but then hid the mark. No. 3 goes over the same ground.

Chapter Fifteen

Parashah Forty-Seven. Genesis 17:15-27

XLVII:I.

1. A. "And God said to Abraham, 'As for Sarai, your wife, you shall not call her name Sarai, but Sarah shall be her name'" (Gen. 17:15):

    B. "A virtuous woman is a crown to her husband" (Prov. 12:4).

    C. Said R. Aha, "Her husband was crowned through her, but she was not crowned through her husband. [Freedman, p. 399, n. 1: He refers this verse to Sarah. Her original name was Sarai, spelled with a Y. The numerical value of Y is 10, while that of H, her new name being spelled with an H rather than a Y, is 5. Thus God took the Y from her name and split it up into two Hs, one for her name, which became Sarah, with an H, and one to be added to Abraham's name, which thus received an H and was changed from Abram to Abraham. Hence Abraham was crowned through Sarah, but Sarah was not crowned through him.]

    D. Rabbis say, "She was master of her husband. In every other context the man gives the orders, but here: 'In all that Sarah says to you, listen to her voice' (Gen. 21:12)."

2. A. "You shall not call her name Sarai, but Sarah shall be her name" (Gen. 17:15):

    B. Said R. Joshua b. Qorha, "The Y that the Holy One, blessed be he, took away from the name of Sarai went fluttering above, before the Holy One, blessed be he, saying, 'Lord of all ages, because I am the smallest of all the letters you took me out of the name of that righteous woman!'

    C. "Said the Holy One blessed be he to it, 'In the past you were in the name of a woman and at the end of the letters of the name. Now I shall put you in the name of a male, and as the first of the letters of his name: "And Moses called Hoshea ben Nun Yehoshua'" (Num. 13:16)."

    D. Said R. Mana, "In the past she was princess for her own people, now she shall be princess for all humankind." [Freedman, p. 400, n. 1: He holds that both Sarai and Sarah denote princess, but that the latter is more comprehensive.]

Both Nos. 1 and 2 work on the meaning of the change in Sarai's name to Sarah. No. 1 presents the view that Sarai lost, as well as the position that she gained. No. 2 then portrays matters from the viewpoint of the transient Y.

XLVII:II.

1.   A.   "I will bless her and moreover I will give you a son by her; [I will bless her and she shall be a mother of nations; kings of peoples shall come from her]" (Gen. 17:16):

   B.   R. Judah says, "'I will bless her' by giving her a son, 'and moreover I will give you a son by her;' 'I will bless her' by giving her the blessing of milk."

   C.   Said to him R. Nehemiah, "And had she already been informed about the matter of milk? But this teaches that the Holy One, blessed be he, restored her youth to her."

2.   A.   R. Abbahu in the name of R. Yose b. R. Hanina: "'I shall place fear of her over all the nations of the world, so that they will not abuse her by calling her barren.'"

   B.   R. Yudan in the name of R. Simeon b. Laqish: "She had no ovary, so the Holy One, blessed be he, formed an ovary for her."

3.   A.   "...and she shall be a mother of nations; kings of peoples shall come from her" (Gen. 17:16):

   B.   Said R. Hama bar Haninah, "From the statement at hand Abraham so reasoned that he took Keturah back. [Keturah is the same as Hagar. 'From her' namely from Sarah he would produce kings, so he might have children from another wife, and those children would not be kings (Freedman, p. 400, n. 3).]"

Nos. 1, 2 work out the meaning of the repeated reference to a blessing, and No. 3 accounts for the entry of Hagar/Keturah into the narrative.

XLVII:III.

1.   A.   "Then Abraham fell on his face" (Gen. 17:17):

   B.   R. Phineas in the name of R. Levi: "Two times did Abraham fall on his face,on account of which circumcision was taken away from his sons twice, once in the wilderness and once in Egypt [for on both occasions the Israelites neglected the rite]. [Freedman, p. 393, n. 2: His falling on his face is regarded as an indication of unwilling assent to God's command.]

C. "In Egypt Moses came along and circumcised them, and in the wilderness, Joshua came along and circumcised them."

2. A. "[Then Abraham fell on his face and laughed] and said to himself, 'Shall a child be born to a man who is a hundred years old? [Shall Sarah, who is ninety years a old, bear a child?]'" (Gen. 17:17):

B. R. Yudan said, "'Shall a child be born to a man who is a hundred years old?' Why [was Abraham surprised]? Because of Sarah: 'Shall Sarah, who is ninety years old, bear a child?' The man does not get old, but the woman gets old!"

C. Said R. Simeon b. Laqish, "A woman is old when people call her 'grandmother,' and she does not mind."

Linking Abraham's actions to the later history of Israel at No. 1 introduces a familiar theme. No. 2 explains the thought that Abraham expressed. 2.C does not belong and was tacked on before the composition found its place here.

XLVII:IV.

1. A. "And Abraham said to God, 'O that Ishmael might live in your sight!'" (Gen. 17:18):

B. R. Judah in the name of R. Yudan, "The matter may be compared to the case of the king's ally, whose stipend the king wished to increase. The king said to him, 'I am planning to double your stipend.' He said to him, 'Do not raise my hopes. Just don't take away from what you have been giving me in the past.'

C. "Along these same lines: 'O that Ishmael might live in your sight!' (Gen. 17:18)."

The sense of Abraham's statement is made articulate.

XLVII:V.

1. A. "God said, 'No, but Sarah your wife [shall bear you a son, and you shall call his name Isaac. I will establish my covenant with him as an everlasting covenant for his descendants after him.] As for Ishmael, I have heard you. Behold, I will bless him and make him fruitful and multiply him exceedingly. He shall be the father of twelve princes, and I will make him a great nation]'" (Gen. 17:19-20).

B. R. Yohanan in the name of R. Joshua b. Hananiah, "In this case the son of the servant-woman might learn from what was said concerning the son of the mistress of the household:

C. "'Behold, I will bless him' refers to Isaac.

D. "'...and make him fruitful' refers to Isaac.

E. "'...and multiply him exceedingly' refers to Isaac.

F. "'...As for Ishmael, I have informed you' through the angel. [The point is, Freedman, p. 401, n. 4, explains, Ishmael could be sure that his blessing too would be fulfilled.]"

G. R. Abba bar Kahana in the name of R. Birai: "Here the son of the mistress of the household might learn from the son of the handmaiden:

H. "'Behold, I will bless him' refers to Ishmael.

I. "'...and make him fruitful' refers to Ishmael.

J. "'...and multiply him exceedingly' refers to Ishmael.

K. "And by an argument *a fortiori* : 'But I will establish my covenant with Isaac' (Gen. 17:21)."

2. A. Said R. Isaac, "It is written, 'All these are the twelve tribes of Israel' (Gen. 49:28). These were the descendants of the mistress [Sarah].

B. "But did Ishmael not establish twelve?

C. "The reference to those twelve is to princes, in line with the following verse: 'As princes and wind' (Prov. 25:14). [But the word for *prince* also stands for the word *vapor* , and hence the glory of the sons of Ishmael would be transient (Freedman, p. 402, n. 2).]

D. "But as to these tribes [descended from Isaac], they are in line with this verse: 'Sworn are the tribes of the word, selah' (Hab. 3:9). [Freedman, p. 402, n. 3: The word for *tribe* and for *staff* or *rod*, in the cited verse, are synonyms, both meaning tribes, both meaning rods, and so these tribes would endure like rods that are planted.]"

3. A. "But I will establish my covenant with Isaac, whom Sarah shall bear to you at this season next year" (Gen. 17:21):

B. R. Huna in the name of R. Idi: "That year was intercalated."

Nos. 1 and 2 take up the problem of the rather fulsome blessing assigned to Ishmael. One authority reads the blessing to refer to Isaac, the other maintains that the blessing refers indeed to Ishmael, and Isaac will gain that much more. No. 2 goes over the same issue, now with the insistence that the glory of Ishmael will pass like vapor, while the tribes of Isaac will endure as well planted rods. The polemic against Edom/Rome, with its transient glory, is familiar. No. 3 makes a minor observation on the time at which the good news came. The point, Freedman explains, is that the news came on Tabernacles, and "this set time" or "season" speaks of Passover, six months later. The year then was intercalated with an extra month, seven between Tabernacles and Passover, allowing for a valid period of gestation.

XLVII:VI.

1. A. "When he was finished talking with him, [God went up from Abraham]" (Gen. 17:22):

B. It has been taught on Tannaite authority: He who takes his leave from his fellow, whether of higher or lower status, has to request permission from him. From whom shall we learn this rule? From Abraham.

C. One time Abraham was speaking with the Holy One, blessed be he. Ministering angels came to speak with him. He said to them, "Let us take our leave from the Presence, which is of higher rank than you are, and afterward I shall speak with you." Once he had spoken with the Holy One, blessed be he, for all the time that he needed to, he said before him, "Lord of all ages, I have to speak [with others]." He said to him, "Take your leave in peace."

D. "God went up from Abraham" (Gen. 17:22).

2. A. Said R. Simeon b. Laqish, "The patriarchs are themselves the chariot [of God]: 'God went up from Abraham' (Gen. 17:22). 'And God went up from upon him' (Gen. 35:13). 'And behold the Lord stood upon him' (Gen. 28:13)."

The statement is entirely cogent, No. 1, and cites the base verse to make its point. No. 2 presents its own point, once more drawing on the base verse among other sources of probative facts.

XLVII:VII.

1. A. "Then Abraham took Ishmael his son and all the slaves born in his house [or bought for his money, every male among the men of Abraham's house, and he circumcised the flesh of their foreskins that very day, as God had said to him]" (Gen. 17:23):

B. Said R. Aibu, "When Abraham circumcised those who were born of his house, he made a mountain of foreskins, and the sun shone on them, and they putrefied. The stench rose to heaven before the Holy One, blessed be he, like the scent of incense.

C. "Said the Holy One, blessed be he, 'When my children will come into bad deeds, I shall remember in their behalf that scent and will be filled with mercy for them."

Israel enjoys the merit of Abraham's actions in the present narrative, a familiar theme. The acts of Abraham bear sacerdotal meaning and prefigure the Temple's sweet savor, rising to heaven.

XLVII:VIII.

1. A. "Abraham was ninety-nine years old when he was circumcised in the flesh of his foreskin. And Ishmael was thirteen years old when he was circumcised in the flesh of his foreskin" (Gen. 17:24):

B. Here the language is "the flesh of his foreskin" and elsewhere the same language is preceded by the accusative particle, *et*. [What is the difference?]

C. In the case of Abraham, because he had become flabby by sexual experience, the statement lacks the accusative particle, while in the case of Ishmael, because he had not become flabby through sexual experience, the statement gains the accusative particle. [Freedman, p. 403, n. 4: His flesh was firmer, and a severer operation was necessary, and that is indicating by the extending particle *et*.]

Since the accusative particle is understood to broaden the reference of a transitive verb, making the verb encompass a larger object than the absence of the *et* would signify, the meaning proposed here is discovered.

XLVII:IX.

1. A. "That very day Abraham and his son Ishmael were circumcised" (Gen. 17:26):

B. Said R. Berekhiah, "'I have not spoken in secret' (Is. 45:19).

C. "Thus said the Holy One, blessed be he, 'If Abraham had circumcised himself by night, then all of his contemporaries would say, "We did not know about it, but if we had known about it, we never should have allowed him to circumcise himself." Rather: 'That very day Abraham and his son Ishmael were circumcised' (Gen. 17:26). Whoever wants to object can make his statement!"

2. A. "...Abraham and his son Ishmael were circumcised" (Gen. 17:26):

B. Said R. Abba, "He felt the rite and was pained by it, so that the Holy One, blessed be he, could double the reward that was coming to him."

C. Said R. Levi, "What is written is not, 'Abraham circumcised himself,' but rather, 'Abraham was circumcised.' That is because he examined himself and found himself already circumcised."

D. Said R. Berekhiah, "That was when R. Abba bar Kahana treated R. Levi lightly. He said to him, 'It is in fact a fraud. For [as just now stated]: He felt the rite and was pained by it, so that the Holy One, blessed be he, could double the reward that was coming to him."

No. 1 explains the emphatic statement that the rite took place by day. The negative view of circumcision among the nations finds expression here. Israel does it in full view of the world, so facing down public opprobrium. There is nothing to hide. No. 2 presents a debate between two authorities on the status of Abraham prior to the day in question. The one emphasizes that Abraham went through the operation, the other that Abraham had been perfect all along.

XLVII:X.

1. A. "And all the men of his house, those born in the house and those bought with money from a foreigner were circumcised with him" (Gen. 17:27):

B. It has been taught on Tannaite authority:

C. People may go to a gentile fair on the intermediate days of a festival to purchase from them houses, fields, vineyards, slaves and slave-girls.

D. R. Ammi in the name of R. Simeon b. Laqish: "It is not the end of the matter that they may do so to purchase slaves that are already circumcised, but it is permitted to go to purchase even uncircumcised ones, because one thereby brings them under the wings of the Presence of God."

E. R. Joshua b. Levi asked before R. Simeon b. Laqish, saying to him, "What is the rule about purchase from a gentile of uncircumcised slaves?"

F. He said to him, "Under what circumstances do you phrase your question? If you refer to a purchase on the festival day, it has been taught on Tannaite authority that it is permitted to do so even on the Sabbath."

G. Hezekiah taught on Tannaite authority, "'You may build bulwarks against the city that makes war with you until it falls' (Deut. 20:20) even on the Sabbath, for so we find that Jericho was conquered only on the Sabbath."

2. A. There are three fairs, the fair of Gaza, the fair of Acre, and the fair of Batanea, and among them the most clearly idolatrous one is that of Batanea.

3. A. Said Abraham, "Before I circumcised myself, people passing by would come to me. Is it possible that, now that I have circumcised myself, they will not come to me any more?"

B. Said the Holy One, blessed be he, to him, "Before you circumcised yourself, uncircumcised men would come to you. Now I in my own glory will appear to you."

C. So it is written, "And the Lord appeared to him [by the oaks of Mamre, as he sat at the door of his tent in the heat of the day]" (Gen. 18:1).

Nos. 1, 2 have nothing to do with the verse at hand but intersect because of their interest in the circumcision of slaves. No. 3 builds a strong bridge to the next unit.

Chapter Sixteen

Parashah Forty-Eight.   Genesis 18:1-16

XLVIII:I.

1. A. "And the Lord appeared to him [by the oaks of Mamre as he sat at the door of his tent in the heat of the day]" (Gen. 18:1).

    B. "You have also given me your shield of salvation and your right hand has held me up, and your condescension has made me great" (Ps. 18:36).

    C. "You have also given me your shield of salvation" refers to Abraham.

    D. "... and your right hand has held me up" in the fiery furnace, the famine, and the encounter with the kings.

    E. "and your condescension has made me great:" What was this act of condescension that the Holy One, blessed be he, lavished on Abraham? That Abraham remained sitting, even while the Presence of God was standing.

    F. That is in line with this verse: "And the Lord appeared to him [by the oaks of Mamre as he sat at the door of his tent in the heat of the day]" (Gen. 18:1).

The intersecting verse is systematically brought into contact with the base verse, so that the main point, God's special favor to Abraham, may be underlined. Because Abraham was still sick in the aftermath of the circumcision, God did not expect him to rise.

XLVIII:II.

1. A. "And when after my skin this is destroyed, then through my flesh shall I see God" (Job 19:26):

    B. Said Abraham, "After I circumcised myself, many proselytes came to join in with this sign. [Freedman, p. 406, n. 4: The verb 'destroy' produces the consonants for the word 'surround,' so proselytes surrounded him as a result of the circumcision.]"

    C. "...And the Lord appeared to him" (Gen. 18:1): "If I had not done so, on what account would the Holy One, blessed be he, have revealed himself to me?"

D. "And the Lord appeared to him" (Gen. 18:1).

The second intersecting verse takes up the concern that the rite of circumcision not repel potential converts to Judaism. It is, indeed, the precondition for seeing God.

XLVIII:III.

1. A. R. Issi opened his statement as follows: "'If I did despise the cause of my manservant or of my maidservant when they contended with me, what then shall I do when God rises up? and when he remembers, what shall I answer him?'" (Job 31:13).

   B. The wife of R. Issi had a quarrel with her servant-woman, and he rejected her complaint in the very presence of the slave. She said to him, "How can you reject my complaint in the presence of my slave?"

   C. He said to her, "And did not Job say, 'If I did despise the cause of my manservant or of my maidservant when they contended with me, what then shall I do when God rises up? and when he remembers, what shall I answer him?' (Job 31:13)."

2. A. Another matter: "If I did despise the cause of my manservant or of my maidservant [when they contended with me, what then shall I do when God rises up? and when he remembers, what shall I answer him?]" (Job 31:13) refers to Abraham: "Then Abraham took Ishmael his son [and all the slaves born in his house or bought with his money, every male among the men of Abraham's house, and he circumcised the flesh of their foreskins that very day]" (Gen. 17:23).

   B. He said, "If I had not done so, on what account would the Holy One, blessed be he, have revealed himself to me? [He would not have done so, had Abraham neglected his slaves.]"

   C. "And the Lord appeared to him" (Gen. 18:1).

The intersecting verse is subject to citation alone in No. 1. At No. 2 makes the familiar point that because Abraham circumcised himself and his menfolk, God appeared to him at Mamre. The verse of Job underlines Abraham,'s virtue in doing as he did.

XLVIII:IV.

1. A. R. Isaac commenced discourse by citing the following verse: "An altar of earth you shall make for me...I will come to you and bless you" (Ex. 20:21).

B. Said R. Isaac, "'Now if to this one, who built an altar for my name, lo, I reveal myself to him and bless him, Abraham, who circumcised himself for my name, how much the more so [shall I reveal myself to him and bless him]?'

C. "And the Lord appeared to him" (Gen. 18:1).

If sacrifices at the altar produce merit, how much the more so Abraham's sacrifice in his circumcision! The same point is made in a new setting. The earlier allusion to the mountain of foreskins is not repeated, but the comparison of the offering is implicit.

XLVIII:V.

1. A. R. Levi opened discourse by citing this verse: "And an ox and a ram for peace-offerings...for today the Lord appears to you" (Lev. 9:4).

B. He said, "If to this one, who offered up an ox and a ram for my name, lo, I reveal myself to him and bless him, Abraham, who circumcised himself for my name, how much the more so [shall I reveal myself to him and bless him]?"

C. "'And the Lord appeared to him' (Gen. 18:1)."

The same point is made yet another time.

XLVIII:VI.

1. A. "Sinners in Zion are afraid" (Is. 33:14):

B. Said R. Jeremiah b. Eleazar, "The matter may be compared to the case of two children who ran away from school. While the one was being thrashed, the other trembled."

C. Said R. Jonathan, "Whenever there is a reference in Scripture to faithlessness, the passage speaks of heretics. The generative case for all of them is in this verse: 'The sinners in Zion are afraid, trembling has seized the ungodly' (Is. 33:14)."

D. Said R. Judah bar Simon, "The matter may be compared to the case of a bandit chief who rebelled against the king. The king said, 'To whoever arrests him I shall give a bounty.' Someone went and arrested him. The king said, 'Hold the two of them over until morning.' The one was trembling about what sort of bounty the king would give to him, and the other was afraid about what sort of judgment the king would mete out to him.

E. "So in the age to come Israel will be afraid: 'And they shall come in fear to the Lord and to his goodness' (Hos. 3:5).

F. "And the gentiles also will be afraid: 'Sinners in Zion are afraid' (Is. 33:14)."

2. A. Said R. Judah, "Why does the prophet refer to them as 'Everlasting burnings' (Is. 33:14)?

B. "For if he gave the nations the power to do so, they would commit the entire world to conflagration."

3. A. "He who walks righteously" (Is. 33:15) refers to Abraham: "To the end that he may command his children that they may keep the way of the Lord to do righteousness and justice" (Gen. 18:19).

B. "And speaks uprightly" (Is. 33:15): "The upright ones love you" (Song 1:4).

C. "He who despises the gain of oppressions" (Is. 33:15): "I will not take a thread or a shoe latchet" (Gen. 14:23).

D. "Who shakes his hands from the holding of bribes" (Is. 33:15): "I have lifted up my hand to the Lord, God Most High" (Gen. 14:22).

4. A. "He shall dwell on high" (Is. 33:16):

B. R. Judah b. R. Simon in the name of R. Yohanan: "'He brought him above the vault of heaven. That is in line with the statement, 'Look toward heaven and number the stars,'and the meaning of the word 'look' is only 'from above to below.' [Hence he looked downward from above the vault of heaven.]"

5. A. "His place of defense shall be the munitions of rocks" (Is. 33:16) speaks of clouds of glory.

B. "His bread shall be given" (Is. 33:16): "While I fetch a morsel of bread" (Gen. 18:5).

C. "His waters shall be sure" (Is. 33:6): "Let a little water be brought and wash your feet" (Gen. 18:4).

D. "Your eyes shall see the king in his beauty" (Is. 33:17):

E. "'And the Lord appeared to him" (Gen. 18:1).

This classic rendition of the exegetical form in which an intersecting verse is systematically and thoroughly worked out, applied to a number of settings or contexts, and only at the end brought into contact with the base verse, has not commonly appeared to us in earlier passages. What we see is a sustained and successful exposition of Is. 33:14-17. Since the points of the successive clauses are worked out in their own terms, and not in terms of Abraham, one might regard the composition as a whole as having been completed prior to its use for the present purpose. When, at the end, the present case is reached, the intersection is not general but quite specific, with reference to the bread and water of Gen. 18:4-5 validating the climactic conclusion with Gen. 18:1.

But a second glance at the two principal components, Nos. 1-2 and 3, 5 provides a different perspective. Nos. 1, 2 speak of the nations of the world and their fear of judgment at the same moment at which Israel looks forward to its final reward. Nos. 3, 5 then speak of Abraham and treat as a prefiguring of the future and fulfillment of the cited verses, Is. 33:15-17, the things that he did in the narrative of Gen. 18:1-5. So viewed from a distance, the two components -- that is, the two approaches to the exegesis of the intersecting verse -- match one another. We speak first of the nations and Israel, then of Abraham and God, making the single point that Abraham prefigures Israel's future vision of God and salvation. If this reading of the composite is sound, then the composite in fact forms a single, pointed and sustained composition, even though bits and pieces clearly have taken shape before the whole formed a single aggregate.

XLVIII:VII.

1. A. "As he sat at the door of his tent in the heat of the day" (Gen. 18:1):

B. R. Berekhiah in the name of R. Levi: "What is written is 'he sat' [and not in the progressive tent, while he *was sitting*]. The point is that he at least tried to get up.

C. "Said the Holy One, blessed be he, to him, 'Remain seated. You thereby serve as a model for your children, for you may remain seated even while the Presence of God is standing.

D. "'So you will remain seated while the Presence of God is standing: "God stands in the congregation of God" (Ps. 82:1).'"

2. A. R. Haggai in the name of R. Isaac: "What is written is not standing but 'stationed at his post' [Freedman], which is to say, 'ready,'

B. "in line with this verse: 'You shall be stationed on the rock' (Ex. 33:21)."

3. A. R. Samuel b. R. Hiyya and R. Yudan in the name of R. Hanina: "In response to each and every statement of praise with which Israel praises the Holy One, blessed be he, he brings his Presence to rest on them.

B. "What is the text that makes that point? 'You are holy, O you who are enthroned upon the praises of Israel' (Ps. 22:4)."

The theme of Abraham's remaining seated provokes the display of a number of passages about sitting and standing. No. 2 extends the exegesis of Ps. 82:1. I do not see any close tie between No. 3 and Nos. 1-2. The intersecting texts are diverse. No case can be made for the essential unity of all three components, though self-evidently No. 2 was tied to No. 1 before the whole was used in the present setting.

XLVIII:VIII.

1. A. "At the door of his tent in the heat of the day" (Gen. 18:1):

   B. [God stated to Abraham,] "You indeed opened a good door for passersby. You opened a good door for proselytes.

   C. "For if it were not for you, I should not have created heaven and earth: 'He spreads them out as a tent to dwell in' (Is. 40:22).

   D. "If it were not for you, I should not have created the orb of the sun: 'In them has he set a tent for the sun' (Ps. 119:5).

   E. "If it were not for you, I should not have created the moon: 'Behold, even for the moon he does not set a tent' (Job 25:5)."

2. A. Said R. Levi, "In the age to come Abraham will sit at the gate of Gehenna, and he will not permit a circumcised Israelite to go down there. Then what will he do for those who sinned too much? He will remove the foreskin from infants who died before they were circumcised and will place it over [Israelite sinners] and then lower them into Gehenna [protected by the skin].

   B. "That is in line with this verse: 'He has sent forth his hands to those that whole. He has profaned his covenant' (Ps. 55:21)."

3. A. "In the heat of the day" (Gen. 18:1):

   B. R. Ishmael taught on Tannaite authority: "'And as the sun waxed hot, it [the mana] melted' (Ex. 16:21). That was at the fourth hour. You say it was at the fourth hour, but perhaps it was only at the sixth? When Scripture says, 'In the heat of the day' (Gen. 18:1), it must speak of the sixth hour.

   C. "But perhaps matters are exactly the opposite? [No, for] at the fourth hour, it is cool in the shade and warm in the sun, but at the sixth hour, the sun and the shade are equally hot." [Freedman, p. 410, n. 5: "In the heat of the day" implies that it was hot everywhere, that condition is fulfilled at noon. But "and as the sun waxed hot" indicates that it was hot only in the sun but not in the shade.]

4. A. Said R. Yannai, "A hole was made in Gehenna [through which heat escaped so that] for a while the whole world was boiling for all of its inhabitants. Said the Holy One, blessed be he, 'My righteous man is suffering pain and should the world be comfortable?' [Surely not. So:]

B. "'In the heat of the day' (Gen. 18:1). [God made it warm so that everyone would be uncomfortable when Abraham was.]

5. A. ["In the heat of the day" (Gen. 18:1)]:

B. On the basis of the cited verse, we know that hot water is good for the wound.

The reference to "tent" calls for No. 1 in its wake a set of verses in which the word "tent" appears. These verses all have to do with creation, yielding the effort to draw a parallel between the life of Abraham and the creation of the world. What must follow is that the world was created for the sake of Israel. But that position is not announced, merely implicit. No. 2 takes up the theme of Abraham's guarding the door, now with a completely original message. Again, Israel's life is prefigured in Abraham's action, now with reference to the individual, not the nation and its history. No. 3 alludes to the verse at hand in the inquiry into its own syllogism. No. 4 makes its own point, extending the sense of "the heat of the day." No. 5 is tacked on.

XLVIII:IX.

1. A. Said Abraham, "Before I circumcised myself, people passing by would come to me. Is it possible that, now that I have circumcised myself, they will not come to me any more?"

B. Said the Holy One, blessed be he, to him, "Before you circumcised yourself, uncircumcised men would come to you. Now I and my retinue will appear to you."

C. So it is written, "And the Lord appeared to him [by the oaks of Mamre, as he sat at the door of his tent in the heat of the day]" (Gen. 18:1).

2. A. ["He lifted up his eyes and looked, and behold, three men stood in front of him" (Gen. 18:3)]: Said R. Haninah, "The names of the months did we bring up with us from Babylonia."

B. R. Simeon b. Laqish said, "Also the names of the angels, Michael, Gabriel, and Raphael."

3. A. Said R. Levi, "One of the men appeared to him in the guise of a Saracen, another as a Nabataean, the third as an Arab.

B. "Abraham thought to himself, 'If I see the Presence of God waiting for them, I shall know that they are all right, and if I see them paying respect to one another, I shall know that they are really fine.'

C. "When he saw them paying respect to one another, he knew that they were really fine."

4. A. Said R. Abbahu, ""The tent of our father, Abraham, was wide open at both sides."

B. R. Yudan said, "It was like a double-gated passage."

5. A. He said, "If I see them turn aside, I shall know that they are coming to me."

B. When he saw that they turned aside, forthwith: "When he saw them, he ran from the tent door to meet them" (Gen. 18:3).

The passage is familiar. No. 1 hardly bears repetition in the present context. No. 2 takes for granted that the three men were the three angels, which is to say the passage rests upon information supplied somewhere else. No. 3 has its own point to make, explaining what it is that Abraham saw. No. 4 is inserted, making its own point about Abraham's tent. No. 5 takes up the thought interrupted by No. 4. In all the conglomerate yields a number of discrete pieces of material on the base verse, nothing more.

XLVIII:X.

1. A. [He lifted up his eyes and looked, and behold, three men stood in front of him. When he saw them, he ran from the tent door to meet them and bowed himself to the earth] and said, 'My lord, if I have found favor in your sight, do not pass by your servant'" (Gen. 18:3):

B. R. Hiyya taught on Tannaite authority, "It was to the most important of them, Michael, that he spoke."

2. A. "Let a little water be brought" (Gen. 18:4):

B. Said to him the Holy One, blessed be he, "You have said, 'Let a little water be brought' (Gen. 18:4). By your life, I shall pay your descendants back for this: 'Then sang Israel this song," spring up O well, sing you to it"' (Num. 21:7)."

C. That recompense took place in the wilderness. Where do we find that it took place in the Land of Israel as well?

D. "A land of brooks of water" (Deut. 8:7).

E. And where do we find that it will take place in the age to come?

F. ""And it shall come to pass in that day that living waters shall go out of Jerusalem" (Zech. 14:8).

G. ["And wash your feet" (Gen. 18:4)]: [Said to him the Holy One, blessed be he,] "You have said , 'And wash your feet.' By your life, I shall pay your descendants back for this: 'Then I washed you in water' (Ez. 16:9)."

H. That recompense took place in the wilderness. Where do we find that it took place in the Land of Israel as well?

I. "Wash you, make you clean" (Is. 1:16).

J. And where do we find that it will take place in the age to come?

K. "When the Lord will have washed away the filth of the daughters of Zion" (Is. 4:4).

L. [Said to him the Holy One, blessed be he,] "You have said, 'And rest yourselves under the tree' (Gen. 18:4). By your life, I shall pay your descendants back for this: 'He spread a cloud for a screen' (Ps. 105:39)."

M. That recompense took place in the wilderness. Where do we find that it took place in the Land of Israel as well?

N. "You shall dwell in booths for seven days" (Lev. 23:42).

O. And where do we find that it will take place in the age to come?

P. "And there shall be a pavilion for a shadow in the day-time from the heat" (Is. 4:6).

Q. [Said to him the Holy One, blessed be he,] "You have said, 'While I fetch a morsel of bread that you may refresh yourself' (Gen. 18:5). By your life, I shall pay your descendants back for this: 'Behold I will cause to rain bread from heaven for you' (Ex. 16:45)"

R. That recompense took place in the wilderness. Where do we find that it took place in the Land of Israel as well?

S. "A land of wheat and barley" (Deut. 8:8).

T. And where do we find that it will take place in the age to come?

U. "He will be as a rich cornfield in the land" (Ps. 82:16).

V. [Said to him the Holy One, blessed be he,] "You ran after the herd ['And Abraham ran to the herd' (Gen. 18:7)]. By your life, I shall pay your descendants back for this: 'And there went forth a wind from the Lord and brought across quails from the sea' (Num. 11:27)."

W. That recompense took place in the wilderness. Where do we find that it took place in the Land of Israel as well?

X. "Now the children of Reuben and the children of Gad had a very great multitude of cattle" (Num. 32:1).

Y. And where do we find that it will take place in the age to come?

Z. ""And it will come to pass in that day that a man shall rear a young cow and two sheep" (Is. 7:21).

AA. [Said to him the Holy One, blessed be he,] "You stood by them: 'And he stood by them under the tree while they ate' (Gen. 18:8). By your life, I shall pay your descendants back for this: 'And the Lord went before them' (Ex. 13:21)."

BB. That recompense took place in the wilderness. Where do we find that it took place in the Land of Israel as well?

CC. "God stands in the congregation of God" (Ps. 82:1).

DD. And where do we find that it will take place in the age to come?

EE. "The breaker is gone up before them...and the Lord at the head of them" (Mic. 2:13).

After No. 1's rather minor improvement, No. 2 presents a sizable and beautifully disciplined construction, making one point again and again. Everything that Abraham did brought a reward to his descendants. The enormous emphasis on the way in which Abraham's deeds prefigured the history of Israel, both in the wilderness, and in the Land, and, finally, in the age to come, provokes us to wonder who held that there were children of Abraham beside Israel. The answer then is clear. We note that there are five statements of the same proposition, each drawing upon a clause in the base verse. The extended statement moreover serves as a sustained introduction to the treatment of the individual clauses that now follow, item by item.

XLVIII:XI.

1. A. "While I fetch a morsel of bread and you may refresh yourselves" (Gen. 18:5):

B. Said R. Isaac, "In the Torah, the Prophets, and the Writings we find that bread refreshes ['stays the heart'].

C. "In the Torah: 'While I fetch a morsel of bread and you may refresh yourselves' (Gen. 18:5).

D. "In the Prophets: 'Stay your heart with a morsel of bread' (Judges 19:54).

E. "In the writings: 'And bread that stays man's heart' (Ps. 104:15)."

2. A. R. Aha said, "What is written is not, 'And stay your heart' [with two Bs, that is, in the fuller spelling] but 'Stay your heart' [with only one B]. [Freedman, p. 413, n. 1: The shorter form is used, and he regards this as a limitation.]

B. "That indicates that the impulse to do evil has no control over angels. [Freedman, p. 413, n. 2: Hence their hearts were all as one, to do good, and they did not have two hearts, as it were, one to do good and the other to do evil.] [So the omission of one of the two Bs.]"

C. That accords with the view of R. Hiyya, for R. Hiyya said, "'Turn your hearts to the dance' [with two Bs] is not what is written, but rather, 'Turn your hearts to the dance' [with only one B] (Ps. 48:17). That indicates that the impulse to do evil does not come back in the world to come."

3.   A. "Since for this purpose you have come to your servant" (Gen. 18:4):

B. Said R. Joshua b. R. Nehemiah, "[Abraham said to them,] 'From the day the the Holy One, blessed be he, created you, you were designated to come to me: "Since for this purpose you have come to your servant" (Gen. 18:4).'

C. "That is in line with this verse: 'So for this purpose the Lord be with you' (Ex. 10:10)."

4.   A. "So they said, 'Do as you have said'" (Gen. 18:5):

B. [The angels said,] "As for us, we do not eat or drink, but as for you, who does eat and drink: 'Do as you have said'" (Gen. 18:5).

C. "And let this day be repeated in honor of the child [who will be born]."

No. 1 simply uses the verse at hand to prove an autonomous syllogism. No. 2 does the same, now imposing a closer reading on the verse.   The proposition, however, does not derive from the verse or its context. No. 3 takes the verse on its own terms and discovers meaning in the language at hand. No. 4 squares the statement about eating with the fact that angels do not eat or drink.

XLVIII:XII.

1.   A. "And Abraham hastened into the tent to Sarah and said, 'Make ready quickly three measures of fine meal, knead it and make cakes'" (Gen. 18:6):

B. R. Abiathar said, "Nine *seah* s in all were baked, three for cakes, three for *habis*, and three for various kinds of pastries."

2.   A. "...knead it and make cakes'" (Gen. 18:6):

B. [Since the word for cakes generally means thin, unleavened ones,] it was before Passover.

3. A. R. Jonah and R. Levi in the name of R. Hama b. R. Hanina: "The wilderness of Sin [Ex. 16:1ff.] and the wilderness of Alush [Num. 33:13] are the same place.

B. "On account of what merit did the Israelites merit having mana given to them? It was because of the statement, 'knead it and make cakes.' [The word for knead is *lushi*, hence because of the kneading of the dough by Sarah, the later Israelites had the merit of receiving mana in the wilderness of Alush which is the same as the wilderness of Sin, where, in the biblical account, the mana came down, so Ex. 16:1ff.]"

The important contribution is at No. 3, at which the merit of Sarah's action stands for the later Israelites. The point-for-point emphasis on that theme presents no surprises. The contributions of Nos. 1, 2 are minor clarifications.

XLVIII:XIII.

1. A. "And Abraham ran to the herd [and took a calf, tender and good, and gave it to the servant, who hastened to prepare it]" (Gen. 18:7):

B. Said R. Levi, "He ran to get there before the nation of whom it is written, 'Ephraim is a heifer well broken, that loves to thresh' (Hos. 10:11)."

2. A. "And took a calf, tender and good, and gave it to the servant, who hastened to prepare it" (Gen. 18:7):

B. Might one think that it was full-grown [therefore tough]? Scripture says, "Tender."

C. If it was tender, might one think that it lacked taste? Scripture says, "And good."

3. A. "...and gave it to the servant, who hastened to prepare it" (Gen. 18:7):

B. The servant was Ishmael, whom Abraham thereby wanted to teach to be prompt in the performance of religious duties [in the present case: hospitality to the stranger].

I do not grasp the point of No. 1. Nos. 2 and 3 amplify the cited verses. Once more the emphasis is on Abraham's keeping the commandments even before the Torah was given.

XLVIII:XIV.

1. A. "Then he took butter and milk" (Gen. 18:8):

B. Said R. Haninah, "The best [butter] is made of a hundredth part of milk [and the rest, cream], the middling, a fortieth, and the cheapest, a twentieth."

2. A. [Since the text does not make it explicit that he gave them bread, but only butter and milk, we ask:] Where was the bread?

B. Ephraim the Contentious, a disciple of R. Meir, in the name of R. Meir: "Sarah's menstrual period began just then, so that the dough was made unclean. [They would not eat bread that was in a state of cultic uncleanness, even though this was not a meal in the Temple.]"

C. Rabbis say, "Indeed he brought bread to them, for if he gave them things that he had not earlier mentioned, such as butter and the like, all the more so did he bring the things [that he had promised in his original invitation]!"

3. A. "And he stood by them under the tree while they ate" (Gen. 18:8):

B. Earlier on it says, "They were stationed by him" (Gen. 18:2).

C. The point is that before they had carried out their obligation, "they were stationed by him." But once they carried out their obligation, "he stood by them."

D. It was a cause of trembling [for the angels] that he stood over them. Michael trembled, Gabriel trembled.

4. A. R. Tanhuma in the name of R. Eleazar, R. Abin in the name of R. Meir: "There is a saying: 'If you go to a town, follow its custom.' Above, where there is no eating, Moses went up and made it his business to look and act like them: 'Then I abode in the mount forty days and forty nights. I did not eat bread or drink water' (Deut. 9:9).

B. "Below, where there is eating: 'And he stood by them under the tree while they ate' (Gen. 18:8).

C. "Now were they really eating? But they appeared as if they were eating. Each course was taken away in its turn."

No. 1 is irrelevant to the matter at hand. No. 2 clarifies a minor problem in the framing of the story, the omitted detail. No. 3 follows the same path in comparing the earlier formulation with the one at hand. No. 4 reverts to the issue of how the angels could have eaten and drunk.

XLVIII:XV.

1. A. "They said to him, 'Where is Sarah, your wife?'" (Gen. 18:9):

B. [In the received text, there are dots written over three of the four Hebrew letters in the word for "to him,' with] a dot over the alef, yud, and vav, but not over the lamed. [The matter requires explanation.]

C. Said R. Simeon b. Eleazar, "In any such passage, containing words with letters dotted on the top, in which you find that the letters written plain, that is, without a dot on top, are more numerous in the word at hand than the letters written with a dot on top, you should interpret the plain letters. If the letters written with a dot in the word are more numerous than those written without a dot on top , you should interpret the letters written with the dot on top.

D. "Here the letters written with the dots on top are more numerous than the others, so you interpret the matter in line with the dotted letters. They then yield the statement, 'Where is Abraham?'"

E. Said R. Azariah, "[The sense then is this:] Just as they asked Abraham, 'Where is Sarah?' so they asked Sarah, 'Where is Abraham?'"

2. A. "[They said to him, 'Where is Sarah, your wife?' And he said,] 'She is in the tent' (Gen. 18:9):

B. That is in line with this verse: "Blessed above women shall Jael be, the wife of Heber the Kenite, above women in the tent shall she be blessed" (Judges 5:24).

C. R. Eleazar said, "[More blessed[] than the women of the generation of the wilderness. They produced children, but if it were not for Jael, the children would have perished."

D. R. Samuel bar Nahman said, "More blessed than the matriarchs. They produced children, but if it were not for Jael, the children would have perished."

No. 1 explains an important feature of the text at hand. No. 2 introduces an intersecting verse and makes a single point about two pentateuchal passages. Obviously, the link to Sarah is the reference to her being "in the tent," hence Jael is blessed above this woman in the tent. The base verse is not cited at the end.

XLVIII:XVI.

1. A. "The Lord said, 'I will surely return [to you in the spring, and Sarah your wife shall have a son.' And Sarah was listening at the tent door behind him]" (Gen. 18:10):

B. "...behind him" refers to Ishmael.

C. "...behind him" refers to the consideration of the woman's not being left alone with a man other than her husband. [So Ishmael had stayed there to protect his mother.]

D. "...behind him:" She realized that a guest had come, [so she stayed to hear the conversation].

2. A. "Now Abraham and Sarah were old, advanced in age" (Gen. 18:11).

B. R. Yohanan said, "Since Scripture states, 'Now Abraham and Sarah were old, advanced in age' (Gen. 18:11), why does [the Torah] proceed to state: 'Now Abraham was old' (Gen. 24:1)?

C. What happened is that the Holy One, blessed be he, restored him to youth. Therefore it was necessary to state second time, 'Now Abraham was old' (Gen. 24:1)."

D. Said R. Ammi, "In the present case we speak of old age in which there was still virility, in the latter passage the old age is one that lacks virility."

3. A. "It had ceased to be with Sarah after the manner of women" (Gen. 18:11):

B. The meaning of the word for "ceased" is, "it had forborne," in line with the usage in this verse: "But if you shall forbear to vow" (Deut. 23:23).

C. A further meaning of the word is, indeed, "ended altogether," as in the verse: "And forbears to keep the passover" (Num. 9:13). [Freedman, p. 416, n. 5: The two meanings are, first, it had refrained, in the sense that her menses were irregular, or, second, they had altogether ceased.]

No. 1 contributes a richer context for the phrase that she remained at the door "behind him." No. 2 notes a repeated detail and draws an important consequence from the repetition. No. 3 explains the meaning of word by producing parallel usages.

XLVIII:XVII.

1. A. "So Sarah laughed to herself, saying, 'After I have grown old and my husband is old, shall I have pleasure?'" (Gen. 18:12):

B. This is one of the passages that the translators did not render literally when they translated Scripture for King Ptolemy.

C. They presented it to him in this way: "Sarah laughed before her relatives, saying...." [Freedman, p. 417, n. 1: They amended the text so that Ptolemy might understand that God was angry with Sarah because she had publicly laughed at the promise, while Abraham had laughed to himself.]

2. A. "...saying, 'After I have grown old and my husband is old, shall I have pleasure?'" (Gen. 18:12):

    B. She said, "While a woman is young, she has ornaments. After I have grown old and my husband is old, shall I have ornaments?"

    C. For the word for "pleasure" also means "ornaments," as in the verse: "I have decked you also with ornaments" (Ez. 16:11).

    D. "While a woman is young, she has her regular period. After I have grown old and my husband is old, I nonetheless shall have my regular period. But [the real problem is]: '...my husband is old.'"

    E. R. Judah said, "He grinds but does not produce [semen]."

    F. Said R. Judah b. R. Simon, "[God said to them,] 'You treat yourselves as young, and treat your Associate [me] as old. But "Am I too old" (Gen. 18:13) to do miracles?'" [We read Gen. 18:13 and 18:14 together. Thus God says both clauses, but the former is treated as a wry observation."Am I too old to do it? Is anything too hard for the Lord?"]

No. 1 makes a point relevant to a different context. No. 2 imparts two meanings to the cited verse, the second being the important one. The rereading of Sarah's statement strengthens the irony of Gen. 18:14, as noted.

XLVIII:XVIII.

1. A. "The Lord said to Abraham, 'Why did Sarah laugh [and say, "Shall I indeed bear a child now that I am old?"]'" (Gen. 18:13):

    B. Bar Qappara said, "The greatness of peace is shown in the fact that even Scripture told a lie so as to bring peace between Abraham and Sarah.

    C. "'Why did Sarah laugh [and say, "Shall I indeed bear a child *and my lord has grown old* '" is not what it says here, but rather, "'*now that I am old* .'" [But that is not the language that Sarah had originally used."

The exegete again deals with a discrepancy between two verses of the same conversation. The discrepancy is deliberate and shows that God wanted to keep peace.

XLVIII:XIX.

1. A. "Is anything too hard for the Lord?" (Gen. 18:14):

    B. R. Judah in the name of R. Yudan bar Simon, "The matter may be compared to someone who had possession of two parts of a lock. He brought them to a smith and said to him, 'Can you repair them?

C. "He said to him, 'To create them to begin with is something I can do, so should I not be able to repair them?'

D. "So too: 'To create them to begin with is something I can do. So should I not be able to restore them to there youth?'"

The sense of God's statement is now spelled out. Assuredly God can do the needed miracle.

XLVIII:XX.

1. A. "But Sarah denied, saying, 'I did not laugh, for she was afraid. He said, 'No, but you did laugh'" (Gen. 18:17):

B. R. Judah [bar Simon] and R. Yohanan in the name of R. Eleazar bar Simon: "On no occasion did the Holy One, blessed be he, ever find it necessary to enter into a conversation with a woman, except with that righteous woman [Sarah] alone, and even on that occasion there was a special reason." [In the case of the woman in the garden, it is alleged in a parallel version, God used an intermediary. We now review all the other possible cases, in addition to the one involving Eve, as these cases unfold in the book of Genesis.]

C. R. Abba bar Kahana in the name of R. Biri: "How many roundabout routes did he take in order to enter into conversation with her: 'And he said, "No, but you did laugh"' (Gen. 18:15)."

D. But it is written, "And she called on the name of the Lord who had spoken with her" (Gen. 16:13) [speaking of Hagar]!

E. R. Joshua bar Nehemiah in the name of R. Idi: "It was through an angel."

F. And is it not written, "And the Lord said to her [Rebecca]" (Gen. 25:23)?

G. R. Levi in the name of R. Hama bar Hanina: "It was through an angel."

H. R. Eleazar in the name of R. Yose b. Zimri: "It was through Shem."

2. A. "Then the men set out from there and they looked toward Sodom, and Abraham went with them to set them on their way" (Gen. 18:16):

B. There is a proverb: Feed [a guest], give him something to drink, and accompany him on the way.

C. So did Abraham : "Abraham went with them to set them on their way" (Gen. 18:16).

No. 1 goes over familiar ground, cf. Gen. R. 45:10. No. 2 explains that Abraham's action shows proper conduct.

Chapter Seventeen

Parashah Forty-Nine. Genesis 18:17-33

XLIX:I.

1. A. "The Lord said, 'Shall I hide from Abraham [what I am about to do, seeing that Abraham shall become a great and mighty nation and all the nations of the earth shall bless themselves by him? No, for I have chosen him that he may charge his children and his household after him to keep the way of the Lord by doing righteousness and justice...']" (Gen. 17:17-19):

   B. R. Isaac opened discussion by citing this verse: "The memory of the righteous shall be for a blessing" (Prov. 10:7).

   C. Said R. Isaac, "Whoever mentions the name of a righteous man and does not say a blessing for him violates a religious duty of commission. What is the biblical text that indicates it? 'The memory of the righteous shall be for a blessing' (Prov. 10:7). [Hence when one mentions the name of a righteous person, a blessing of that name must be recited.]

   D. "And whoever mentions the name of wicked person and does not curse him violates a religious duty of commission. What is the biblical text that indicates it? 'But the name of the wicked shall rot' (Prov. 10:7)."

2. A. Said R. Samuel bar Nahman, "The names of the wicked are like weaver's webs. Just as a web, so long as you use it, remains taut, but if you leave it, it becomes slack, so have you ever heard a man call his son, 'Pharaoh'? 'Sisera'? 'Senacherib'?

   B. "But [people commonly call their children] Abraham, Isaac, Jacob, Reuben, Simeon, Levi, and Judah."

3. A. Rab said, "Cursed is Haman and his sons."

   B. Said R. Phineas, "'Harmboa -- of blessed memory' [is how one should express things]."

4. A. Said R. Samuel bar Nahman, "We have found that the Holy One, blessed be he, mentions the name of Israel and says a blessing for them, as it is said, 'May the Lord bless the mention of our name' (Ps. 115:12)."

B. R. Huna in the name of R. Aha, "I know that that is the case only for the six hundred thousand [mentioned all at once, that is, the nation as a whole is blessed when God mentions their name]. How do I know that when the Holy One, blessed be he, mentions the name of each and every Israelite, he mentions the name and says a blessing for it?

C. "As it is said, 'The Lord said, "Shall I hide from Abraham what I am about to do, seeing that Abraham shall become a great and mighty nation [and all the nations of the earth shall bless themselves by him]?"' (Gen. 18:17). Now it was necessary for him to say only, 'Because the outcry against Sodom and Gomorrah is great [and their sin is very grave, I will go down to see whether they have done altogether according to the outcry which has come to me, and if not, I will know].'

D. "Said the Holy One, blessed be he, 'I have made mention of the name of that righteous man, and shall I not [interrupt my thought only to] say a blessing for him? "Abraham shall become a great and mighty nation [and all the nations of the earth shall bless themselves by him]"' (Gen. 18:17)."

Nos. 1-3 work out the exegesis of Prov. 10:7. But the intersecting verse is well chosen and leads us naturally back to the base verse. The exegete has asked the question of why the text goes into such fulsome praise of Abraham, which breaks up the flow of the narrative with its reference to the nations of the earth blessing themselves by Abraham's name. So the exegete provides a suitable explanation of the matter, drawing on the lesson of Prov. 10:7 to do so. This does represent a case in which the intersecting verse answers an important question in the base verse and the materials in exegesis of the former furthermore illuminate the latter.

XLIX:II.

1. A. [Referring to God's telling Abraham what he is about to do:] "The secret of the Lord is with them who fear him and his covenant to make them know it" (Ps. 25:14).

B. To begin with "The secret of the Lord is with them who fear him" but in the end it was with the upright: "But his secret is with the upright" (Ps. 3:32).

C. Then it is with the prophets: "For the Lord God will do nothing without revealing his secret to his servants the prophets" (Amos 3:7).

D. Said the Holy One, blessed be he, "This Abraham fears God: 'Now I know that you are a God-fearing man' (Gen. 22:12).

E. "This Abraham is upright: 'The upright love you' (Song 1:4).

F. "This Abraham is a prophet: 'Now therefore restore the man's wife, for he is a prophet' (Gen. 20:7).

G. "Shall I not reveal it to him?"

H. "The Lord said, 'Shall I hide from Abraham [what I am about to do, seeing that Abraham shall become a great and mighty nation and all the nations of the earth shall bless themselves by him? No, for I have chosen him that he may charge his children and his household after him to keep the way of the Lord by doing righteousness and justice...']" (Gen. 17:17-19).

2. A. "The Lord said, 'Shall I hide from Abraham [what I am about to do, seeing that Abraham shall become a great and mighty nation and all the nations of the earth shall bless themselves by him? No, for I have chosen him that he may charge his children and his household after him to keep the way of the Lord by doing righteousness and justice...']" (Gen. 17:17-19).

B. Said R. Joshua b. Levi, "The matter may be compared to the case of a king who gave an estate to his ally and then later on the king wanted to cut down from the property five barren trees [for use as wood]. The king said, 'If I had wanted to cut down trees from his inherited property [and not from the property I gave him], he would not stop me. So what difference does it make.' He nonetheless [paid him respect and so] took counsel with him.

C. "So said the Holy One, blessed be he, 'Now I have already given the land as a gift to Abraham: "To your seed have I given this land" (Gen. 15:18). These towns fall within my property. But if they belonged to his inheritance, he would not object. So what difference does it make to me if I ask his permission?'"

3. A. Said R. Judah bar Simon, "The matter may be compared to the case of a king who had three allies and who would do nothing without their knowledge and consent. One time, however, the king wanted to do something without their knowledge and content. He took the first and drove him out and put him away from the palace. He took the second and put him in prison. He put his seal on the prison door. As to the third, who was a special favorite, he said, 'I simply shall do nothing without his knowledge and consent.'

B. "So in the case of the first man: 'So he drove out the man' (Gen. 3:23).

C. "As to Noah: 'The Lord shut him in the ark' (Gen. 7:5).

D. "But when it came to Abraham, who was the special favorite, he said, 'I simply shall do nothing without his knowledge and consent.'"

4. A. Said R. Samuel b. Nahman, "The matter may be compared to the case of a king who had an adviser, without whose knowledge and consent he would do absolutely nothing. One time he considered doing something without his knowledge and consent. Said the king, 'Did I not make him my counsellor only so as not to do anything without his knowledge and consent?'"

B. Said R. Yudan, "So said the Holy One, blessed be he, 'Did I not call him a man of my own counsel only so as not to do anything outside of his knowledge and consent? Lot, his brother's son is with [the Sodomites], and should I not let him know?'"

5. A. Rabbis say, "I have already called him their father: 'For the father of a multitude of nations have I made you' (Gen. 17:5).

B. "Do they judge a son without the knowledge and consent of the father?

C. "I have already revealed to him Gehenna, the revelation of the Torah, and should I not reveal to him the judgment against Sodom?'"

6. A. R. Aha in the name of R. Alexandri, R. Samuel b. Nahman in the name of R. Jonathan: "Even the laws governing the commingling of domain in courtyards [for purposes of creating a single domain for carrying on the Sabbath] did Abraham know."

B. R. Phineas, R. Hilqiah, R. Simon in the name of R. Samuel: "Even the new name that the Holy One, blessed be he, is destined to assign to Jerusalem: 'On that day they will call Jerusalem "the throne of God"' (Jer. 3:17) Abraham knew."

C. R. Berekhiah, R. Hiyya, the rabbis of the other place [Babylonia] in the name of R. Judah: "There is not a single day on which the Holy One, blessed be he, does not create a new law in the court above. What is the scriptural verse that shows it? 'Hear attentively the noise of his voice and the meditation that goes out of his mouth' (Job 37:2). The word meditation speaks only of the Torah, as it is said, 'But you shall meditate therein day and night' (Joshua 1:8). Even those new laws Abraham knew."

No. 1 sets the stage for the articulation of God's thinking in the base verse by proving the God reveals his secret to persons of Abraham's category. That explains the self-evidence of God's question, cited at the end. It is a persuasive exercise. No. 2 is equally effective in expanding the account of God's reasoning in the rhetorical question at hand. No. 3 presents a powerful explanation for the special favor shown to Abraham, underlining how different was his relationship to God from that of Adam and Noah. No. 4 makes the same point in a different way. No. 5 shifts the ground of argument, reverting to Abraham in particular. No. 6 then expands on the theme of how much God revealed to Abraham. This is the point at which the narrative crosses the distinctive history of Israel. Abraham now knows the name of Jerusalem, the new laws of the heavenly academy, and the rules of the commingling of courtyards, that is, a matter quite distinctive to the rabbis and their tradition, at least, as they portray that particular matter. So in all the climax has Abraham know particularly Israelite matters.

XLIX:III.

1. A. "Seeing that Abraham shall surely become..." (Gen. 18:18):

   B. R. Tanhum bar Hus Eli in the name of R. Berekhiah: "He gave him the information that the world will never have fewer than thirty men as righteous as Abraham."

   C. R. Yudan, R. Aha in the name of R. Alexandri found proof for this proposition in the following verse: "Seeing that Abraham shall surely become" (Gen. 18:18), since the numerical value of the letters used in the word "become" is thirty.

Now we turn to a close reading of the words and phrases of individual verses.

XLIX:IV.

1. A. "For I have known him, so that he may charge his children and his household after him to keep the way of the Lord by doing righteousness and justice, so that the Lord may bring to Abraham what he has promised him" (Gen. 18:19):

   B. [Defining the commandment involving righteousness and justice,] R. Aha in the name of R. Alexandri: "This refers to hospitality."

   C. Rabbis say, "It speaks of visiting the sick."

2. A. R. Azariah in the name of R. Judah: "In the beginning it is righteousness [in the sense of charity] and in the end it is justice.

   B. "How so? Abraham would receive passersby. When they had eaten and drunk, he would say to them, 'Say a blessing.'

   C. "They said to him, 'What should we say?'

   D. "He said, 'Blessed is the God of the world, whose food we have eaten.'

   E. "If he agreed to say a blessing, the traveller would eat and drink and go his way. But if not, he would say to him, 'Pay me what you owe.'

   F. "And the other would say to him,l 'What do I owe you?'

   G. "He would say to him, 'One *xestes* of wine costs ten *follera*, a pound of meat is ten *follera*, a loaf of bread is ten *follera*. For in the wilderness who is going to give you wine, in the wilderness who is going to give you meat, in the wilderness who is going to give you bread?'

   H. "Now since the guest saw that he was trapped, he would say, 'Blessed be the God of the world, whose food we have eaten. That is why to begin with the Scripture speaks of righteousness [in the sense of charity[, but in the end of justice."

3. A. "...so that the Lord may bring to Abraham what he has promised him" (Gen. 18:19):

B. It has been taught on Tannaite authority: R. Simeon b. Yohai says, "He who has a son laboring in the study of the Torah is as if he has not died.

C. "What is the verse of Scripture that indicates it? '...so that the Lord may bring to Abraham what he has promised him.' What it says is not, 'What he has promised...,' but 'what he has promised him.'" [But Abraham was not alive when his descendants inherited the land. He is regarded, though, as if he were alive, because his descendants in Joshua's time were studying the Torah.]

No. 1 defines one set of words, leading to No. 2. Once we introduce the theme of hospitality, we turn to the language of charity and justice and relate those words to Abraham's practice of receiving wayfarers. No. 3 makes its own point, using the proof text for a proposition not closely related to the topic at hand.

XLIX:V.

1. A. "Then the Lord said, 'Because the outcry against Sodom and Gomorrah is great [and their sin is very grave, I will go down to see whether they they have done altogether according to the outcry which has come to me, and if not, I will know]'" (Gen. 18:21):

B. R. Haninah said, "'It is growing ever greater' [is the sense of the statement]."

C. R. Berekhiah in the name of R. Yohanan [said], "We know that the generation of the Flood was judged and punished with water, and the Sodomites with fire. How do we know that we should assign what is stated here to the Sodomites, and what is stated in their regard to the generation of the Flood?

D. "Scripture makes use of the word 'great' in both passages, providing for an analogy [between Gen. 6:5 and Gen. 18:29]."

The exegesis serves the purpose, C, of establishing the announced syllogism. We have two interpretations of the word "great."

XLIX:VI.

1. A. "I will go down and see..." (Gen. 18:21):

B. Said R. Simeon b. Yohai, "This is one of the ten passages in the Torah that refer to God's descending."

2. A. Said R. Abba bar Kahana, "The cited passage teaches that the Holy One, blessed be he, gave them every opportunity for repentance: 'I will go down to see whether they have done altogether...,' that is, whether they ought to be destroyed [with the sense of total destruction drawn from the same letters as make up the word 'altogether'].

B. "'...according to the outcry which has come to me, and if not, I will know' (Gen. 18:21), that is, 'I shall inform them concerning the attribute of justice that rules the world.'"

3. A. Said R. Levi, "'Even if I wanted to keep silent, the requirement of justice for a certain girl will not allow me to keep silent.'"

B. There was the case of two girls, who went down to draw water from the well. One said to her friend, "Why are you pale?"

C. The other said, "All the food is gone from our house and we are ready to die."

D. What did the other do? She filled the jug with flour and exchanged it for her own. Each took the one of the other. When the Sodomites found out about it, they took the girl [who had shared the food] and burned her.

E. Said the Holy One, blessed be he, "Even if I wanted to keep silent, the requirement of justice for a certain girl will not allow me to keep silent."

F. What is written is not, "In accord with their cry," but, "According to her cry," referring in particular to the girl.

4. A. Said R. Jeremiah b. Eleazar, "The golden age of Sodom lasted for fifty-two years, and of them, for twenty-five the Holy One, blessed be he, made the mountains quake about them and brought terror on them so that they might repent, but they did not do so.

B. "That is in line with this verse: 'Who removes the mountains and they know it not, when he overturns them in his anger' (Job 9:5)."

No. 1 is an echo of a passage spelled out elsewhere. No. 2 reads the cited verse to make the point that God was just on his own volition, not merely because of Abraham's urging. No. 3 brings evidence of the sort of cry to which God responded. The pertinence is explained at the end, F-G. No. 5 repeats the emphasis that God had given them every opportunity to repent and had done his best to persuade them to do so. So the claim of Abraham, "will not the judge of all the world do justice?" follows the answer to that question.

XLIX:VII.

1. A. "So the men turned from there" (Gen. 18:22).

B. The verse indicates that angels have no backs. [Freedman, p. 425, n. 5: The verse is translated: "And the men went toward Sodom, yet their faces were still looking upon the place whence they came."]

2. A. "And they went toward Sodom. But Abraham still stood before the Lord" (Gen. 18:22):

B. Said R. Simon, "This formulation represents a revision by scribes. In point of fact, it was the Presence of God that was waiting for Abraham."

No. 1 makes a minor observation. No. 2 deals with the problem explained by Freedman, p. 426, n. 1, as follows: "The phrase, 'But Abraham...Lord' implies that he was still at the same place, which is incorrect, since he had accompanied the angels some distance. Hence it really means that the Lord was still standing before Abraham, since he is omnipresent. But it would be derogatory to his honor to say that he was standing before Abraham, as an inferior before his superior. So it is reversed.]

XLIX:VIII.

1. A. "Then Abraham drew near and said..." (Gen. 18:23):

B. R. Judah, R. Nehemiah, and Rabbis:

C. R. Judah said, "This was a drawing near as for battle, as it says, 'So Joab and the people who were with him drew near to battle' (2 Sam. 10:13). [Abraham drew near to fight with God.]"

D. R. Nehemiah said, "It was a drawing near for conciliation, in line with the usage in this verse: 'Then the children of Judah drew near to Joshua' (Joshua 14:6). The purpose was to conciliate him."

E. Rabbis say, "It was a drawing near for prayer, in line with the usage in this verse: 'And it came to pass at the time of the offering of the evening offering, that Elijah the prophet came near and said, "O Lord, God of Abraham, Isaac, and Israel, this day let it be known that you are God in Israel"' (1 Kgs. 18:36)."

F. Said R. Eleazar, "Interpret the verse to bear this encompassing meaning: 'If it is for war, I am coming. If it is for conciliation, I am coming. If it is for prayer, I am coming.'"

2. A. R. Phineas, R. Levi, and R. Yohanan in the name of Menahem of Gallia: "As to one who goes down before the ark [to lead worship service], people do not say to him, 'Come and do the job,' but, 'Come and draw near,'

which is to say, 'Come and carry out our war, come and prepare the offering for the community.'"

B. Said R. Tanhuma, "Why is it in particular in the fifteenth blessing [of the Eighteen Blessings] that the reference to God's hearing prayer, that is, '...who hears prayer,' is located? That corresponds to the fact that the name of God appears fifteen times in the Psalm, 'Ascribe to the Lord, O you sons of might....,' to, '...the Lord sat enthroned at the flood' (Ps. 29), for that is what keeps punishment from visiting the world."

3. A. "Will you indeed destroy the righteous with the wicked?" (Gen. 18:23):

B. R. Huna in the name of R. Aha: "'Will you indeed destroy [the righteous with the wicked]?' (Gen. 18:23): [Since the word for 'indeed' uses the consonants which produce the meaning, anger,'] the sense of the passage is, 'You place limits around anger, and anger does not fence you in.'"

C. Said R. Joshua bar Nehemiah, "[This is the sense of Abraham's statement:] 'With the anger which you bring onto your world will you destroy the righteous along with the wicked? It is not enough that you should not suspend the punishment coming to the wicked on account of the righteous, but you wipe out the righteous with the wicked!'"

4. A. Rabbi and R. Jonathan:

B. Rabbi said, "In the case of a mortal, anger conquers him, but the Holy One, blessed be he, conquers anger: 'The Lord avenges and masters wrath' (Nahum 1:11)."

C. R. Jonathan said, "In the case of mortal man, envy conquers him, but the Holy One, blessed be he, conquers envy: 'The Lord is God over envy and vengeance' (Nahum 1:1)."

5. A. R. Simlai asked R. Jonathan, saying to him, "What is the meaning of the verse: 'But there is one who is swept away without judgment' (Prov. 13:23)?"

B. He said to him, "'Without being affected by the judgment coming to his own town.'"

C. There is the case of one who was sent to collect fines owed by people of Tiberias and Sepphoris. When he was collecting in Tiberias, he saw someone from Sepphoris and went and arrested him.

D. The man said to him, "I am from Sepphoris."

E. He said to him, "I have warrants against Sepphoris-people to make my collection there too."

F. Before he completed collecting what was owing from the people of Tiberias, a remission of the fine was issued for the people of Sepphoris.

G. So the Sepphorean in Tiberias was "swept away" without being subject to the "judgment affecting his own town."

6. A. R. Levi and R. Simon:

B. R. Levi said, "[Abraham's plea was to ask God, 'Is your anger like that of a] bear, who, not finding prey, eats its own?'"

C. R. Simon said, "[Abraham's plea was to ask God, 'Is your anger like] a scythe, which cuts down thorns, then goes on to the roses?'"

No. 1 presents three meanings imputed to the word "draw near," with the satisfying conclusion that Abraham was ready for all purposes. The composite at No. 2 selects the meaning of prayer and by putting together two discrete items makes the important point for our context. It is that Abraham's intent in drawing near was to pray, as we know from No. 1, and the purpose of the prayer was to keep divine punishment from affecting the world, as 2.B indicates. So here is a case in which the topic at hand finds amplification through set-piece insertion of materials on other topics entirely. No. 3 revises the meaning imputed to the word translated "anger." This yields the amplifications of Nos. 3, 4, 5, and 6. The net-effect is to emphasize that God did not act with wrath but only after reflection and deliberation. So Abraham is not the only party to the coming discourse who has a commitment to justice..

XLIX:IX.

1. A. "Far be it from you [to do such a thing, to slay the righteous with the wicked, so that the righteous fare as the wicked. Far be that from you. Shall not the Judge of all the earth do justly?]" (Gen. 18:25):

B. [Interpreting the consonants for the word "far be it from you," in diverse ways,] said R. Yudan, "'It is a profanation for you, it is alien from you.'"

C. Said R. Aha, "The word 'far be it' [yielding the sense of 'profanation'] is used two times, meaning, 'It is a profanation of the name of heaven, it is a profanation of the name of heaven.'"

2. A. Said R. Abba, "What is written is not, 'from doing the thing,' but rather, 'from doing such a thing,' [that is, 'an act like this act.'] [Abraham's meaning is,] 'Not this act, and not an act like this act, and not an act of even less severe consequences.'"

3. A. R. Levi said, "Two men said the same thing, Abraham and Job.

B.   "Abraham said, 'Far be it from you to do such a thing, to slay the righteous with the wicked, [so that the righteous fare as the wicked. Far be that from you. Shall not the Judge of all the earth do justly?]' (Gen. 18:25).

C.   "Job said, 'It is all one, therefore I say, "He destroys the innocent and the wicked"' (Job 9:22).

D.   "Abraham received a reward on account of making that statement, while Job was punished on that account.

E.   "The difference is that Abraham said it with confidence [that God would never do such a thing], while Job said it as a complaint: 'Is it all one?'"

4.   A.   R. Hiyya bar Abba said, "What we have here is a collection of answers.

B.   "Abraham said, 'Far be it from you,' and the Holy One, blessed be he answered, 'So shall the wicked be as the righteous.' [The sense of this reply of God's is as follows:] 'Should the punishment coming to the wicked be suspended on account of the righteous? But the righteous themselves are fakers.'"

C.   That judgment is in line with the observation that R. Yohanan made, "Every time the word 'righteous' is stated in connection with Sodom, it is written as though it were to be read 'Their righteousness,' that is, defectively [hence the righteousness was fake]."

D.   This is further in line with the approach of R. Yohanan, for R. Yohanan said, "'And our elders and all the inhabitants of our country spoke to us' (Joshua 9:11). The word for 'elders' is written defectively, which indicates that these were elders who gave leadership for doing wrong, elders for giving counsel in doing wickedness. [Freedman, p. 429, n. 2: In wickedness and evil too they were elders.]"

5.   A.   Said R. Joshua b. Levi, "[Abraham made this plea:] 'Combine the various good deeds and you will get up to the number of fifty.'" [Freedman, p. 429, n. 2: If you combine the good of all, it will be equivalent to that of fifty righteous men.]"

B.   Said R. Judah, "'Are you not the Righteous one of the world? Join yourself with them and you will get up to the number of fifty.'"

C.   Said R. Judah bar Simon, "'In the case of mortals, one can make an appeal from the commander to the regional governor, and from the regional governor to the head of state. But as to you, since there is no appeal from your judgment, "will you [the judge of all the world] not do justly?"'"

D.   Said R. Judah, "'When you wanted to judge your world, you handed it over to two such as Romulus and Remus. The upshot was that if one of them wanted to do something, his colleague could hold him back. But as to you, since there is no one who can hold back anything you want to do, "will you not do justice"?'"

6. A. [R. Azariah in the name of R. Aha interpreted the verse to speak of our father, Abraham: "When our father, Abraham, stood to seek mercy for the Sodomites, what is written there? 'Far be it from you to do such a thing' (Gen. 18:25)."] Said R. Aha, "[Abraham said to God,] 'You bound yourself by an oath not to bring a flood upon the world. Are you now going to act deceitfully against the clear intent of that oath?

B. "'True enough, you are not going to bring a flood of water, but you are going to bring a flood of fire.

C. "'If so, you will not faithfully carry out the oath!'"

D. Said R. Levi, "'Will not the judge of all the earth do justly?' (Gen. 18:25). 'If you want to have a world, there can be no justice, and if justice is what you want, there can be no world. You are holding the rope at both ends, you want a world and you want justice. If you don't give in a bit, the world can never stand.'

E. "Said the Holy One, blessed be he, to him, 'Abraham, "You have loved righteousness and hated wickedness. Therefore God, your God, has anointed you with the oil of gladness above your fellows" (Ps. 45:8).

F. "'From Noah to you there are ten generations [that is, that lived from Noah to Abraham].

G. "'Among all of them, I spoke only with you.'"

No. 1 explains the sense of the word "far be it," reading the consonants to mean, "it is a profanation." Then Abraham's meaning is reconstructed. No. 2 again concentrates on interpreting the language at hand. No. 3 broadens the matter to compare the cases of Abraham and Job, both of whom took up the same proposition. But the upshot still is to remain within the limits of the verse at hand and to point up a dimension of its meaning. No. 4 falls into the same category, in which several verses are illuminated by the same principle. The compositor of No. 5 has presented a series of strong pleas to God, and, we now realize, the purpose of the bulk of the composition is to present a range of pleas that Abraham made to God. No. 6, familiar from its own context, then produces the climactic statement that God honored Abraham for making his plea.

XLIX:X.

1. A. "And the Lord said, 'If I find at Sodom [fifty righteous in the city, I will spare the whole place for their sake]'" (Gen. 18:26):

B. R. Judah bar Simon in the name of R. Joshua b. Levi: "'For it is for God to have said, "I have forgiven"' (Job 34:31).

C. "So: 'I will spare the whole place for their sake' (Gen. 18:26)."

D. "I shall not take a pledge" (Job 34:31) means, "I shall not exact a surety," in line with the use of the same root in this verse: "If you take your neighbor's garment as a pledge" (Ex. 22:25).

E. [Speaking in the name of God:] "Yet people complain [using the consonants for the word for exact a surety] against me, claiming that I do not judge rightly."

F. "Apart from me, I will see" (Job 34:32): [God speaks:] "Even without me, you go and examine my judgment. If I have made a mistake, 'You teach me' (Job 34:32), and 'if I have committed an injustice' to the earlier generation, 'I will not do it again' to the later generations."

2. A. "To him will I keep silence, and to his branches" (Job 41:4): [God further speaks to Abraham:] "For you I shall keep silent, and for the branches that come forth from you."

B. This is addressed to Abraham, who said, "Far be it from you to do such a thing" (Gen. 18:25).

C. It is further addressed to Moses, who said, "Lord, why are you angry against your people" (Ex. 32:11).

D. ...to Joshua, who said, "Why have you brought this people over the Jordan" (Joshua 7:7).

E. ...to David, who said, "Why do you stand afar off, O Lord" (Ps. 10:1).

3. A. "Or his proud talk, or his fair array of words" (Job 41:4):

B. Grace infused [Abraham's] extended speech when he sought mercy for the Sodomites.

The two intersecting verses drawn from Job, Job 34:31 and 41:4, cast fresh light on Abraham's statement at hand. No. 1 assigns a long response to God, in which he accepts Abraham's plea. No. 2 assembles a range of examples of Abraham's descendants' following his example, and No. 3 reverts to the case at hand. This is a striking and successful amplification of a base verse and its case through the invoking intersecting verses. The upshot is to introduce into Abraham's discourse the entire history of Israel.

XLIX:XI.

1. A. "And Abraham answered, 'Behold, I have taken upon myself to speak to the Lord, I who am but dust and ashes'" (Gen. 18:27):

B. He said, "If I had been killed by Nimrod, would I not have been turned into dust, and if he had burned me up, would I not now be ashes?"

C. Said the Holy One, blessed be he, to him, "You have said, 'I am but dust and ashes.' By your life, I shall give your descendants a means of atonement through [dust and ashes], as it is said, 'And for the unclean they shall take the ashes of the burning of the purification from sin' (Num. 19:17). 'And a man who is clean shall gather up the ashes of the heifer' (Num. 19:9)."

2. A. We have learned in the Mishnah: **What is the rite for the conduct of a fast? People bring the ark out into the public square and put burned ashes on the ark [M. Ta. 2:1].**

B. R. Yudan bar Menasseh and R. Samuel bar Nahman:

C. One of them said, "It is on account of the merit attained by Abraham, as it is said, 'I who am but dust and ashes' (Gen. 18:27)."

D. The other said, "It is on account of the merit attained by Isaac." But the latter memorized the statement of the Mishnah so that it referred only to ashes and not dust.

E. A ruling of R. Yudan b. Pazzi stands at issue with this formulation [of C].

F. For R. Yudan b. Pazzi would announce in the community, saying, "Whoever has not been reached by the leader of the congregation for the pouring of ashes on his head should take ashes and pour them on his head on his own." [Hence he did not require both dust and ashes, but only ashes.]

G. The ruling of R. Yudan b. Pazzi treats dust and ashes as the same thing [so it does not prove that he differs from C's position].

Once more, at No. 1, statements of Abraham are treated as paradigms for Israel's holy life. The reference now is to the ashes of the red cow, which serve as a means of purification from corpse-uncleanness. No. 2 is tacked on because it gives an example of the concrete action that expresses the viewpoint of No. 1.

XLIX:XII.

1. A. "Suppose five of the fifty righteous are lacking? [Will you destroy the whole city for lack of five?]" (Gen. 18:28):

B. Said R. Hiyya bar Abba, "Abraham really wanted to jump directly from fifty to five in his argument. [Freedman, p. 432, n. 1: Perhaps there will not be fifty but only five.]"

C. "Said the Holy One, blessed be he, 'Slow down.'"

2. A. Said R. Levi, "It is like a water-clock used in courts of justice for measuring the time given for argument [Freedman, p. 432, citing Jastrow].

B. "So long as it has water in it, the defense attorney may continue his case. But there are occasions on which the judge wants the defense attorney to continue, so he will say, 'Put more water into it.'" [The point is that God wanted Abraham to prolong his plea, which is why he had him work by fives.]

No. 2 complements the point made at No. 1, which is that God wanted Abraham to proceed step by step, so as to prolong the appeal for mercy.

XLIX:XIII.

1. A. "Then he said, 'Oh let not the Lord be angry, and I will speak again but this once. Suppose ten are found there'" (Gen. 18:32):

B. Why was the figure ten chosen?

C. It would then be a number sufficient to form a quorum [of righteous] to pray in behalf of all of them.

2. A. Another matter:

B. Why was the figure ten chosen?

C. Because [Abraham realized that] out of the generation of the flood eight righteous people had survived, and yet the world had not had its punishment suspended on account of the merit that they had attained [that is, Noah, his sons and their wives, eight in all].

3. A. Another matter:

B. Why was the figure ten chosen?

C. Because Abraham was thinking that there were ten righteous people there [counting] Lot, his wife, and his four daughters and their husbands.

4. A. R. Yudan bar Simon and R. Hanan in the name of R. Yohanan: "Here ten were required, while in the case of Jerusalem even one would have been enough: 'Run to and fro in the streets of Jerusalem and see whether you can find a man, if there be any one who does justly' (Jer. 5:1).

B. "So too: 'Adding one thing to another to find out the account' (Qoh. 7:27)."

C. Said R. Isaac, "To what extent can the reckoning be drawn out? Even to a single one."

Nos. 1-3 answer the obvious question in explaining the text. No. 4 then broadens the range of discourse. The explanation of the figure ten draws upon a range of motifs, all of them bearing messages. The effect is not only to deepen the narrative but also to link its elements, both those involving Noah and Lot, on the one side, and also those involving the history of Israel, on the other.

XLIX:XIV.

1. A. "And the Lord went his way when he had finished speaking to Abraham and Abraham returned to his place" (Gen. 18:33):

    B. A judge waits while the defense attorney lays out his case. Once the defense attorney falls silent, the judge rises.

    C. Thus: "And the Lord went his way when he had finished speaking" (Gen. 18:33).

    D. So too, a defense attorney continues pleading his case so long as the judge shows him favor. When the judge rises, the defense attorney falls silent. So: "And the Lord went his way when he had finished speaking to Abraham and Abraham returned to his place" (Gen. 18:33).

    E. So long as the defense attorney is laying out his case and the judge shows him favor, the prosecutor waits it out. When the judge rises and the defense attorney falls silent, the prosecuting attorney goes and carries out his mission. Thus: "And the Lord went his way when he had finished speaking to Abraham and Abraham returned to his place" (Gen. 18:33). "The two angels came to Sodom at the evening" (Gen. 19:1).

The point of the composition is fully exposed. The several clauses are read from three perspectives.

Chapter Eighteen

Parashah Fifty.   Genesis 19:1-23

LI:I.

1. A. "The two angels came to Sodom in the evening" (Gen. 19:1):

   B. "And the living creature ran and returned as the appearance of a flash of lightning" (Ez. 1:14):

   C. Said R. Aibu, "What is written is not the word for 'running' but the word for 'eager, in the sense that they are eager to carry out their mission. [So too were the angels.]"

2. A. "...as the appearance of a flesh of lightning" (Ez. 1:14):

   B. R. Judah bar Simon in the name of R. Levi bar Parta: "[Freedman:] [Like the flames breaking forth] when one scatters olive refuse in a stone."

   C. R. Hiyya bar Abba said, "Like a wind driving sparks."

   D. Rabbis said, "Like a lightning flash in the eye."

3. A. [The angels] left Abraham at the sixth hour but reached Sodom only in the evening? [The distance was not that considerable, and, in any case, as we just said, angels travel like a flash of lightning when they do the mission of the Lord].

   B. But they were angels of mercy and were holding back. They thought, "Perhaps Abraham will find some grounds for merit for them."

   C. When he did not found grounds for merit for them: "The two angels came to Sodom in the evening" (Gen. 19:1).

   Nos. 1, 2 prepare the way for No. 3, and here is a case in which the intersecting verse is chosen to open the base verse to a question otherwise not present. The compositor has done his work in a subtle way.

L:II.

1. A. "The two angels came to Sodom in the evening" (Gen. 19:1):

B. "But he is at one with himself and who can turn him? and what his soul desires, even that he does" (Job 23:13).

C. It has been taught on Tannaite authority:

D. One angel does not carry out two missions, and two angels do not carry out one mission. And yet you have said that they were two angels?

E. But Michael stated his news and went his way. Then Gabriel was sent to overturn Sodom, and Raphael to save Lot.

F. "The two angels came to Sodom in the evening" (Gen. 19:1).

2. A. "He sent forth upon them the fierceness of his anger, wrath, indignation, and trouble, a sending of messengers of evil" (Ps. 78:49) [who bear the names of anger, wrath, indignation, trouble, thus four,] so how can you say they were only "two angels" (Gen. 19:1)?

B. But Michael stated his news and went his way. Then Gabriel was sent to overturn Sodom, and Raphael to save Lot.

C. "The two angels came to Sodom in the evening" (Gen. 19:1).

3. A. Here [at Gen. 19:1] you call them angels, but earlier [at Gen. 18:2] they are called men.

B. In that former passage, when the Presence of God was over them, they were men. But when the Presence of God had gone up from them, they put on the form of angels.

C. Said R. Levi, "Because Abraham had great power, they appeared to him as men. But because Lot had little power, they appeared to him as angels."

D. Said R. Hunia, "Before they had carried out their mission, they were men. After they had carried out their mission, they were angels."

E. Said R. Tanhuma, "The matter may be compared to the case of someone who received the power of government from the king. Before he came to the place in which he would rule, he went along like an ordinary person.

F. "Before they had carried out their mission, they were men. After they had carried out their mission, they were angels."

No. 1 carries forward the earlier interest in the rules governing the angels, their travel and how they perform their mission. No. 2 goes over the same ground. No. 3 raises a question to explain the obvious contradiction in the texts at hand.

L:III.

1. A. "To Sodom" (Gen. 19:1):

B. [Since the word is spelled with an additional H at the end,] It has been taught on Tannaite authority in the name of R. Nehemiah: "In any case in which there should be an L at the beginning of a word, to signify place or direction, [e.g., L, that is, to, Sodom] an H added to the end of the word serves the same purpose, e.g., Sodom with an added H, Seir with an added H, Egypt with an added H, Haran with an added H.

C. It was objected: "And lo, it is written, 'The wicked will return to Sheol' (Ps. 9:18), with an L at the beginning of the word and an H at the end!"

D. R. Abba bar Zabedah said, "The sense is that it is to the lowest compartment of hell."

2. A. "[The two angels came to Sodom] in the evening" (Gen. 19:1):

B. The evening of Sodom had come, and the sun of Sodom was setting, and the decree of judgment against it was sealed.

3. A. Said R. Levi, "The Holy One, blessed be he, judges the nations of the world only by night, at the time at which they are asleep and so not committing transgression. [This puts them in the best light.]

B. "And he judges Israel only by day, at the time when they are taken up with the practice of religious duties. [This puts them in the best light too.]

C. "That is in line with this verse: 'He will judge the world in righteousness, he will minister judgment to the peoples with equity' (Ps. 9:9)."

4. A. "And Lot was sitting in the gate of Sodom" (Gen. 19:1):

B. What is written is "sat" in the sense of "sat that one time." The sense is that it was on that very day that the city had appointed him chief justice. [The gate is normally where matters of law are adjudicated by the elders. Hence "sitting in the gate" implies that Lot was one of the judges (Eilberg-Schwartz).]

5. A. There were five chief justices in Sodom: False-Principles, Lyings-Speech, Cad, Justice-Perverter, and Man-Flayer [all: Freedman].

B. And Lot was the chief justice of them all!

C. When he said something that they wanted to hear, they would say to him, "Go further" (Gen. 19:9), meaning, "take a higher seat," and when he said something that they did not want to hear, they said to him, "This one came in to sojourn and he will now play the judge" (Gen. 19:9).

No. 1 makes a grammatical observation. Nos. 2 interprets the word "in the evening" in a pointed way. Since the punishment of Sodom took place in the daytime, not at night, the relevance of No. 3 is not obvious to me. The only point of contact I can see with the present passage is that the proof-text, Ps. 9:9, occurs in the same Psalm as is cited at No. 1. But there is no connection in the sense of the statement. My best guess, therefore, is that the reference to the evening made the compositor wish to introduce the notion that the judgment of Sodom was about to take place. Eilberg-Schwartz, however, observes that the judgment or decision occurred at night. The angels came to Sodom immediately after God and Abraham had debated Sodom's future. This seems a sensible alternative. No. 4 makes a minor grammatical point testify to a major event. No. 5 then then completes the thought. It seems to me that No. 5 is out of place in the unfolding exposition of the passage and was joined to No. 4, which does belong at just this point, before the whole was inserted.

L:IV.

1. A. "When Lot saw them, he rose to meet them and bowed himself with his face to the earth and said, 'My lords, turn aside, I pray you, to your servant's house and spend the night and wash your feet; then you may rise up early and go on your way'" (Gen. 19:1-2):

    B. R. Yudan said, "[He said,] 'Even though I am unworthy, as to you, divert your path for me.'"

    C. R. Huna said, "[He said,] 'Divert your path for me, so that you will not be seen coming to me.'"

2. A. "... and spend the night and wash your feet..." (Gen. 19:1-2):

    B. Abraham put washing before spending the night, while in his address to the guests, Lot put spending the night before washing.

    C. Abraham was meticulous about the filth adhering on account of idolatry, while Lot was not meticulous.

    D. And some say that this too Lot did appropriately. It was so that when they went forth in the morning, there would be dust on their feet, and people would not say, "Where did they spend the night?"

3. A. "They said, 'No, we will spend the night in the street'" (Gen. 19:2):

    B. People may decline the hospitality of an ordinary person, but they may not decline the hospitality of a great person.

4. A. "And he urged them strongly" (Gen. 19:3):

B. [The word for "urge" contains the letters for the words for "anger" and "trouble," hence] through them he brought anger and trouble.

5. A. "And they turned aside to him and entered his house and he made them a feast" (Gen. 19:3):

B. That statement [that they turned aside, that is, took a circuitous path] supports the view of R. Huna [at No. 1]: "'Divert your path for me, so that you will not be seen coming to me.'"

6. A. "...and he made them a feast" (Gen. 19:3):

B. As someone who had grown up in the house of Abraham, he received guests [in a proper way].

7. A. "...and he baked unleavened bread and they ate" (Gen. 19:2):

B. [Reading the letters of the word for "unleavened bread" with different consonants, we derive the meaning of" contention," hence] said R. Isaac, "There was a big fight about salt, for he said to her [his wife], 'Give the guests some salt.'

C. "She replied, 'Even that lousy practice [that you learned from Abraham] do you want to teach here?'"

Nos. 1 and 2 lay stress on what is to come, namely, the inhospitality of the Sodomites. Each statement Lot made is now read in light of what follows later on. No. 1 gives Lot two different intentions, one honorable, the other not. No. 3 contrasts the response of the angels to Abraham and their response to Lot. No. 4 contributes a minor interpretation of a word-choice. No. 5 reverts to the earlier issue, a good example of the compositors' effort to present a tight fabric. No. 6 assigns to Abraham credit for whatever good Lot did. I am baffled by the polemic of No. 7. Perhaps the exegete prepares us for turning Lot's wife into a pillar of salt. Or perhaps she attributes to Abraham the practice now followed by Lot. But otherwise the passage bears no relevance I can discern.

L:V.

1. A. "But before they lay down, [the men of the city, the men of Sodom, both young and old, all the people to the last man, surrounded the house, and they called to Lot: 'Where are the men who came to you tonight? Bring them out to us, that we may know them'"] (Gen. 19:1-2):

B. [The angels] began peppering him with questions, saying to him, "What sort of people live in this city?"

C. He said to them, "Everywhere [in all other towns] there are good and bad, but here, most of them are bad."

2. A. "...the men of the city, the men of Sodom, both young and old, all the people to the last man..." (Gen. 19:2):

B. Not one of them entered an objection.

3. A. "... and they called to Lot: ['Where are the men who came to you tonight? Bring them out to us, that we may know them']" (Gen. 19:1-2):

B. R. Joshua b. Levi in the name of Bar Pedaiah: "For that entire night, Lot pleaded for mercy for the Sodomites, and the angels permitted him to plead for them. But when the people said, 'Bring them out to us, so that we may know them' (Gen. 18:5), meaning to have sexual relations with them, the angels said, 'Have you anyone here besides...' (Gen. 19:12). 'Up to now, you could plead for mercy for them, but from now on you have no right to do so.'"

All three entries provide amplifications of phrases or clauses of the base verses.

L:VI.

1. A. "Lot went out of the door to the men, shut the door after him, and said, 'I beg you, my brothers, do not act so wickedly. Behold, I have two daughters, who have not known man. Let me bring them out to you and do to them as you please. Only do nothing to these men, [for they have come under the shelter of my roof]" (Gen. 19:6-8):

B. [Interpreting the word "these," which uses the consonants that also serve for the word for God, we explain that Lot said,] "These men are strong gods."

2. A. "...for they have come under the shelter of my roof" (Gen. 19:6):

B. "They did not come on account of merit I have accrued, but on account of the merit attained by Abraham."

3. A. "'...for they have come under the shelter of my roof'" (Gen. 19:6):

B. This [reference to the shelter of *my* roof, thus *mine* and not my wife's] teaches that [Lot's wife] had split up the house on their account, saying to him, "If you want to receive them, receive them in your half."

Nos. 2, 3 play out the two themes that whatever Lot did right was because of Abraham, and that his wife was wicked. We are now prepared for the fate of Lot's wife.

L: VII.

1. A. "But they said, 'Stand back'" (Gen. 19:9):

   B. "Get out of the way."

2. A. "And they said, 'This fellow came to sojourn, and he would play the judge!'" (Gen. 19:9):

   B. "The judgment that the ancestors have laid down you wish to pervert. [We only wish to practice our tradition.]"

3. A. R. Menahama in the name of R. Bibi: "This is what the Sodomites had stipulated among themselves.

   B. "They said, 'As to any wayfarer who comes here, we shall have sexual relations with him and take away his money.'

   C. "They said to him, 'Even him concerning whom it is written, "That you may keep the way of the Lord to do righteousness and justice" (Gen. 18:19), we shall have sexual relations with him and take away his money.'"

Nos. 1 and 2 present light glosses. No. 3 expands and makes its explicit that even Abraham would have been abused by the Sodomites, and that they said so.

L: VIII.

1. A. "But the men put forth their hands and brought Lot into the house to them and shut the door. And they struck with blindness the men who were at the door of the house, [both small and great, so that they wearied themselves groping for the door]" (Gen. 19:10-11):

   B. [The ones by the door were struck first, for] the one who began the sin begins to receive punishment first of all.

   C. Along these same lines: "And he blotted out every living substance" (Gen. 7:22), for the one who began the sin begins to receive punishment first of all.

   D. "And her belly shall swell and her thigh shall fall away" (Num. 5:27), for the limb that began the sin first begins to receive punishment of all.

2. A. "...so that they wearied themselves groping for the door" (Gen. 19:11):

B. They were foolish, as in the following verse: "For my people is foolish" (Jer. 4:22).

No. 1 makes a general point, using the cited verse as proof for the syllogism. No. 2 explains the meaning of a word by citing a parallel usage.

L:IX.

1. A. "Then the men said to Lot, 'Have you any one else here? Sons-in-law, sons, daughters, or any one you have in the city, bring them out of the place: for we are about to destroy this place'" (Gen. 19:13):

   B. R. Levi in the name of R. Samuel: "Because the ministering angels revealed the mystery of the Holy One, blessed be he, [telling Lot what he was about to do], they were sent into exile from their appropriate dwelling for a hundred and thirty eight years."

   C. R. Tanhuma stated it in the word for "stalk," which contains the letters of a numerical value adding up to 138.

   D. Said R. Hama bar Hanina, "It was because they puffed themselves up, saying, 'for *we* are about to destroy this place' (Gen. 19:13)."

2. A. "So Lot went out and said to his sons-in-law, who were to marry his daughters,['Up, get out of this place, for the Lord is about to destroy the city.' But he seemed to his sons-in-law to be jesting]" (Gen. 19:14):

   B. [The language implies that] he had four daughters, two married and two betrothed. "Those who had taken" is not what is written, but rather, "Those who are going to take." [Therefore the words "sons-in-law" must refer to men who had already married his daughter, whereas "those who were to marry his daughters" refers to future sons-in-law (Freedman, p. 439).]

3. A. "... But he seemed to his sons-in-law to be jesting" (Gen. 19:14):

   B. They said, "The city is full of organ-grinders and street-bands, and is it going to be overthrown?"

The successive clauses of the cited verse are glossed. What is noteworthy to the exegete at No. 1 is the angels' statement that they are in charge. This is not the language of agents. No. 3 explains why the sons-in-law thought Lot was joking.

L:X.

1. A. "When morning dawned, [the angels urged Lot, saying, 'Arise, take your wife and your two daughters who are found here, lest you be consumed in the punishment of the city']" (Gen. 19:15):

   B. Said R. Haninah, "It was from the time that the morning star arose until the eastern sky was bright, during which a person can walk four *mil* s. [That is the distance involved in the escape.]

   C. "For it is written, 'When morning dawned' (Gen. 19:15). 'The sun had risen on the earth when Lot came to Zoar' (Gen. 19:23)."

   D. But from Sodom to Zoar is it only four *mil* s?

   E. Said R. Zeira, "The angel levelled the road before them."

   F. So how do we know that one can walk four *mil* s in the time from the rising of the morning star until the sun sparkles?

   G. [Freedman:] "And as" is written, intimating that one period is equal to the other. [Freedman, p. 440, n. 4: "And as" is regarded as an extension; hence two periods are envisaged, "and as" intimating that they are both alike.]

2. A. Said R. Yose bar Abin, "If someone should say to you that the morning star is the same as the morning dawn, he is a liar.

   B. "There are times that it is earlier, and there are times that it is later. But something like rays of light come out and light up the world."

3. A. "...the angels urged Lot, saying, 'Arise, take your wife and your two daughters who are found here, [lest you be consumed in the punishment of the city']" (Gen. 19:15):

   B. [Treating the word "found" in the sense of a "happy find," we proceed:] R. Tobiah b. R. Isaac said, "He had two such happy finds, Ruth, the Moabite, and Naamah, the Ammonite [both nations being descended from Lot]."

   C. R. Isaac said, "'I have found David my servant' (Ps. 89:21). Where did I find him? In Sodom [through Lot's daughter]."

Nos. 1-2 take up a syllogism to which the exegesis of the verse at hand is not relevant. The verse supplies a fact for the study of scientific questions. No. 3 bears the same relationship to the cited verse, which simply serves to prove a proposition. 3.C makes the matter explicit in relationship to Sodom.

L:XI.

1. A. "But he lingered" (Gen. 19:16):

B. There was one delay after another. He said, "What a loss of silver and gold and precious stones and pearls."

C. That is in line with this verse: "Riches kept by their owner to his detriment" (Qoh. 8:12).

D. R. Joshua b. Levi said, "This refers to Lot."

E. R. Samuel bar Nahman said, "It refers to Korah."

F. R. Judah bar Simon said, "This refers to Naboth."

G. R. Levi said, "It speaks of Haman."

H. R. Isaac said, "It refers to the tribes of Reuben and Gad."

I. The rabbis said, "It speaks of the tribe of Levi, which lost its wealth but later on got it back."

2. A. "So the men seized him and his wife and his two daughters by the hand" (Gen. 19:16):

B. Which one did the seizing? It was Raphael.

C. This objection was raised: "And when *they* brought them forth..." (Gen. 19:17) [indicating that it was more than one].

D. The reply is as follows: Note what comes afterward. What is written is not, "And they said," but: "...*he* said, ['Flee for your life, do not look back or stop anywhere in the valley, flee to the hills, lest you be consumed']" (Gen. 19:17).

E. If so, why is it written, "And when *they* brought them forth..." (Gen. 19:17) [indicating that it was more than one]? It refers to the merit accrued by Abraham [he is the "one"], along with the involvement of Raphael.

3. A. "[And when they brought them forth, he said, 'Flee for your life, do not look back or stop anywhere in the valley,] flee to the hills, [lest you be consumed]'" (Gen. 19:17):

B. That is, on account of Abraham [who is likened to a hill].

4. A. "...lest you be consumed" (Gen. 19:17):

B. In the sin of the city.

5. A. "And Lot said to them,['Oh, no, my lords, behold your servant has found favor in your sight, and you have shown me great kindness in saving my life; but I cannot flee to the hills, lest the disaster overtake me and I die']" (Gen. 19:19):

B. R. Berekhiah, R. Levi in the name of R. Hama bar Hanina: "Two people made the same statement, Lot and the woman of Zarephath.

C. "The woman of Zarephath said, 'Before you [Elijah] came to me, the Holy One, blessed be he, looked at my [good] deeds and the deeds of the people of my town, and my deeds were more numerous than the deeds of the people of my town. Now that you have come to me, you have called to mind my sin [since my merit no longer protects me] and so you have killed my son.'

D. "Lot said, 'Before I went to Abraham, the Holy One, blessed be he, looked at my deeds and the deeds of the people of my town, and my deeds were more numerous than the deeds of the people of my town. Now that I have gone to Abraham, his deeds are more numerous and I cannot stand his burning coal.' So [Lot said,] '"I cannot flee to the hill"' (Gen. 19:19). [That is to say, 'I cannot flee to Abraham.']"

6. A. R., Berekhiah in the name of R. Levi, "How on the basis of Scripture do we know, **Just as a hovel puts one to the test, so a mansion puts one to the test [M. Ket. 3:10]?**

B. "On the basis of this verse: '...but I cannot flee to the hills [lest the disaster overtake me and I die]' (Gen. 19:19).

C. "He was living in a valley, and they told him to go to a mountain, and this is how he answers! That indicates that moving from a hovel to a mansion [is not good], for **a mansion also puts one to the test.**"

7. A. "'Behold, yonder city is near enough to flee to, and it is a little one. Let me escape there -- is it not a little one? -- and my life will be saved.' He said to him, 'Behold, I grant you this favor also, that I will not overthrow the city of which you have spoken'" (Gen. 19:20-21):

B. Said R. Tahalipa of Qetiriah, "Now if, because Lot had honored the angel, he 'granted this favor,' to you shall I not show favor, on your account and on account of your ancestors? 'The Lord lift up his countenance to you and give you peace' (Num. 6:26)."

No. 1 again disparages Lot's character, now explaining in the most negative possible light why he tarried. The attached identifications serve the cited verse of Qohelet and were included before the entire composite was given its place here, since most of the identifications have no relationship to this context. Nos. 2-4 supply light glosses. No. 5 links the story at hand to the proposition that Lot recognized the superior virtue of Abraham. No. 6 reverts to the use of the verse at hand to make its own point, and the same is so at No. 7.

L:XII.

1. A. "'Make haste, escape there, for I can do nothing until you arrive there'" (Gen. 19:22):

   B. Said R. Levi, "The matter may be compared to the case of a town that had two patrons, one who came from a city, the other who came from a village. Now the king became angry and proposed to punish the the townspeople in general. Said the king, 'If I inflict the punishment in the presence of the man from the city, the people will say, "If the fellow from the village had been here, he would have protected us." And if it is in the presence of the villager, the people will say, "If the fellow from the city had been here, he would have protected us."'

   C. "So too, since some of the Sodomites worshipped the sun, and some the moon, the Holy One, blessed be he, said, 'If I punish them by day, they will say, "If the moon had been out, it would have protected us." If I punish them by night, they will say, "If the sun had been out, it would have protected us."'

   D. "So he did it on the sixteenth of Nisan, when the sun and the moon were both visible in the heaven. That is in line with this verse: 'The sun had risen on the earth when Lot came to Zoar' (Gen. 18:23)."

The proposition is a striking one. The only thing out of line is that the base verse, Gen. 19:22, is ignored. That is probably a copyist's error.

Chapter Nineteen

Parashah Fifty-One. Genesis 19:24-37

LI:I.

1. A. "Then the Lord rained on Sodom and Gomorrah brimstone and fire from the Lord out of heaven" (Gen. 19:14):

   B. "Let them by like a snail which melts and passes away, like the untimely births of a woman that have not seen the sun" (Ps. 58:9).

   C. They are to be compared to [Freedman:] a snail, a slug which dissolves in excrement, like a mole which does not see the light before it returns to the dust,

   D. like a woman who is "taken forth" [to be punished for adultery], who is ashamed for her child to be discerned, so disposes of it by night, before it sees the sun.

   E. That is in line with this verse: "The sun had risen on the earth [when Lot came to Zoar]" (Gen. 19:23).

   F. "Then the Lord rained on Sodom and Gomorrah brimstone and fire from the Lord out of heaven" (Gen. 19:14).

The point of the intersecting verse is to exploit the reference to the fact that the cities of the plain never again saw the sun. Then the verse of Psalms is expounded, and the base verse, Gen. 19:24, is read in light of Gen. 19:23. This is a fine piece of exposition.

LI:II.

1. A. "Then the Lord rained on Sodom [and Gomorrah brimstone and fire from the Lord out of heaven]" (Gen. 19:14):

   B. The matter may be compared to the case of two cities which rebelled against the king. The king had one burned down at its own expense and the other to be burned down on the public budget.

   C. So further on: "And the streams thereof shall be turned into pitch, and the dust thereof into brimstone" (Is. 34:9) [so the land had to supply its own fuel).

D. Here by contrast: "Then the Lord rained on Sodom [and Gomorrah brimstone and fire from the Lord out of heaven]" (Gen. 19:14). [God supplied it from heaven.]

2. A. Said R. Abin, "The matter may be compared to the case of a servant-woman who was baking bread in the oven. Her son came along and took a piece of bread, and she gave it to him. The son of her mistress came along and took burning coals, and she gave them to him.

B. "So later on: 'Then the Lord said to Moses, "Behold, I will cause bread to rain from heaven for you"' (Ex. 16:4),

C. "while here by contrast: 'Then the Lord rained on Sodom [and Gomorrah brimstone and fire from the Lord out of heaven]' (Gen. 19:14)."

3. A. Abbah Hilpai bar Samqi in the name of R. Judah: "'Then the Lord rained on Sodom [and Gomorrah brimstone and fire]' refers to Gabriel.

B. "'...from the Lord out of heaven]' (Gen. 19:14) refers to the Holy One, blessed be he."

4. A. Said R. Eleazar, "Any passage in which it is said, 'And the Lord,' refers to him and his court. [In this way we may understand the double reference to the Lord in the base verse, Gen. 19:14.]"

B. Said R. Isaac, "In the Torah, in the Prophets, and in the Writings, we find that an ordinary person mentions his own name twice in a single verse [as we have here a reference to the Lord twice in the cited verse].

C. "In the Torah: 'And Lamech said to his wives, Adah and Zillah hear my voice.' What is said is not, 'my wives,' but, 'You wives of Lamech' (Gen. 4:23).

D. "In the Prophets: 'And the king said to them, "Take with you the servants of your lord and cause Solomon my son to ride on my own mule"' (1 Kgs. 1:33). What is said is not, 'Cause the king's son to ride on my mule,' but, 'Cause Solomon *my* son to ride on *my* mule.'

E. "In the Writings: 'For the writing which is written in the king's name' (Est. 8:8).

F. "Is there any reason for surprise, then, that the Holy One, blessed be he, should make mention of his name two times in a single verse of Scripture?'

What strikes the exegetes, No. 1, is the fact that God provided the fire and brimstone, while in other passages, that is not the case. No. 2 draws a still more interesting contrast, between the heavenly punishment here and the heavenly gift to Israel. So the contrast between Israel and the nations is drawn quite explicitly. Nos. 3, 4 turn to the repetition of God's name and make sense of that peculiarity of style.

LI:III.

1. A. "Brimstone and fire" (Gen. 19:24):

   B. "Upon the wicked he will cause coals to rain" (Ps. 11:6), meaning, coals and snares, "fire and brimstones" (Ps. 11:6).

   C. Said R. Yudan, "When a person smells brimstone, his soul is repelled by it. Why? Because the soul knows that in the future it will be judged thereby."

2. A. "The portion of their cup" (Ps. 11:6);

   B. R. Ishmael bar Nahman in the name of R. Jonathan: "It is like a double dose of poterion after a bath [Freedman, p. 446, n. 1: so does a spirit of trembling await the wicked in full measure.]"

3. A. Said R. Haninah b. Pazzi, "Something bad never comes from above."

   B. The following objection was entered: "Lo, it is written, 'Fire and hail, snow and vapor, stormy wind, fulfil his word' (Ps. 148:8)."

   C. He said to them, "Only the 'stormy wind' carries out his word."

   D. A statement of R. Simeon b. Laqish differs. For R. Simeon b. Laqish said, "'The Lord will open to you his good treasure' (Deut. 28:12). That indicates that he has other than good 'treasures' too."

4. A. "...from the Lord out of heaven" (Gen. 19:14):

   B. Like a blow from a weight-lifter.

Nos. 1, 2 work out the intersecting verse. I do not see more than an intensification of details. No. 3 works out its own syllogism, relevant to the passage at hand but, of course, contradicted by it (which is why our base verse is not cited). No. 4 introduces a minor gloss.

LI:IV.

1. A. "And he overthrew those cities [and all the valley and all the inhabitants of the cities and what grew on the ground]" (Gen. 19:25):

   B. R. Levi in the name of R. Samuel bar Nahman: "Those five cities were situated on a single rock. The angel put out its hand [onto the rock] and turned the cities over.

C. "That is in line with this verse: 'He puts forth his hand upon the flinty rock, he overturns the mountains by the roots' (Job 28:9)."

D. Two Amoraim on this matter, one maintains that the verse means, "With a fifth of his hand" and the other, "With a fifth of his finger."

2. A. "...and what grew on the ground" (Gen. 19:25):

B. Even the growths on the ground were smitten.

C. Said R. Joshua b. Levi, "Even to this very day if someone collects moisture from the air at Sodom and pours it out over a furrow somewhere else, nothing will grow."

No. 1 introduces a verse only to prove the stated proposition. No. 2 presents a minor gloss.

LI:V.

1. A. "But Lot's wife behind him look back and she became a pillar of salt" (Gen. 19:26):

B. R. Isaac said, "It is because she sinned through the argument about salt."

The matter is as we surmised above.

LI:VI.

1. A. "So it was that, when God destroyed the cities of the valley, God remembered Abraham and sent Lot out of the midst of the overthrow, when he overthrew the cities in which Lot dwelt" (Gen. 19:29):

B. What was it about [what Lot had done for] Abraham that God remembered?

C. It was the silence that [Lot] kept when Abraham said concerning Sarah, "She is my sister." He knew the truth but said nothing.

2. A. "...and sent Lot out of the midst of the overthrow, when he overthrew the cities in which Lot dwelt" (Gen. 19:29):

B. R. Samuel bar. Nahman said, "The sense is that Lot had lived in all of those cities."

C. Rabbis say, "It is because he lent money on interest in all of them."

No. 1 interprets the verse to refer to something Lot had done in connection with Abraham. The exegete cannot imagine that there is any other merit associated with Lot. No. 2 spells out why the verse refers to Lot's dwelling in more than one city. He is tied up with all of the wicked cities, explaining why not only Sodom but the others were overturned.

LI:VII.

1. A. "Now Lot went up out of Zoar and dwelt in the hills with his two daughters" (Gen. 19:30):

    B. "For the leader, al tashheth. A Psalm of David. Michtam. When he fled from Saul, in the cave" (Ps. 57:1).

    C. He said before him, "Lord of all ages, even before I came into the cave, you did an act of mercy for others on my account. Now that I am hidden in the case, may it be pleasing to you: 'do not destroy' [al tashheth.]"

Freedman (p. 447, n. 5) explains the reference: "Before I [David] was born you spared Lot because I was to come from him." So, as before, the exposition of the story is on a broad scale, since we have now had a reference to L:IV and to L:X.

LI:VIII.

1. A. "And the first-born said to the younger, 'Our father is old, and there is not a man on earth [to come in to us after the manner of all the earth. Come, let us make our father drink wine, and we will lie with him , that we may preserve offspring through our father]'" (Gen. 19:31-32):

    B. It is because the girls imagined that the entire world had been destroyed, just as in the generation of the flood.

2. A. "...Come, let us make our father drink wine, and we will lie with him, that we may preserve offspring through our father'" (Gen. 19:31):

    B. R. Tanhuma in the name of Samuel: "What is written is not, 'So that we may keep a child alive from our father,' but rather, 'so that we may preserve offspring through our father' (Gen. 19:31). That is to say, the king-messiah, who will come from another source."

3. A. "So they made their father drink wine that night, and the first-born went in and lay with her father, and he did not know when she lay down or when she arose" (Gen. 19:33):

    B. There are dots written over the word "when she arose," meaning that while he did not know when she lay down, he did know when she got up.

4. A. "And on the next day, the first-born said to the younger, ['Behold, I lay last night with my father;] let us make him drink wine [tonight also; then you go in and lie with him, that we may preserve offspring through our father']" (Gen., 19:34):

B. Where did they get wine in the cave?

C. Because the people of the area had a large supply of wine, they kept it in caves.

D. Said R. Yudan bar Samuel, "It was a foretaste of the world to come, in line with this verse: 'And it shall come to pass in that day that the mountains shall drop down sweet wine' (Joel 4:18)."

No. 1 explains why the daughters of Lot conducted themselves as they did. The point seems obvious. No. 2 reverts to the familiar point that Lot was the forefather of the Messiah. No. 3 explains a peculiarity of the text. No. 4 answers an obvious question.

LI:IX.

1. A. "Thus both the daughters of Lot were with child by their father" (Gen. 19:36):

B. Said R. Eleazar, "A woman never gets pregnant from the first act of sexual relations."

C. They raised an objection from the following statement: "Thus were both daughters of Lot with child by their father" (Gen. 19:36).

D. Said R. Tanhuma, "They exercised great self-control and removed their own virginity and so became pregnant by the first act of sexual relations."

2. A. Said R. Nahman bar Hanan, "Whoever lusts after fornication in the end will be fed with his own flesh [committing incest]."

B. R. Yudan of Galliah and R. Samuel bar Nahman, both in the name of R. Elijah Enene: "We do not know whether Lot lusted for his daughters, or his daughters lusted for him. On the basis of what is said in the following verse: 'He who separates himself seeks desire' (Prov. 18:1), it is clear that Lot lusted after his daughter."

3. A. R. Tanhum bar Hiyya in the name of R. Hoshaia, the public speaker: "There is not a Sabbath on which people do not read the passage dealing with Lot.

B. "What is the biblical evidence for that statement? 'At every [gathering of]= wisdom he is revealed' [but the Hebrew may be read: 'repelled'] (Prov. 18:1)."

C. Said R. Aha, "What is written is not 'they are repelled' but 'he is repelled.' That is, men are put off but women are attracted [by the story]."

No. 1 cites the base-verse in the service of its own syllogism. The interest of Nos 2 and 3 is to show the full complicity of Lot in his own degradation.

LI:X.

1. A. "I know his conception, says the Lord, that it was not so" (Jer. 48:30):

B. R. Hinena bar Pappa and R. Simon:

C. R. Hinena bar Pappa said, "In the beginning of the conception of Moab, it was not for the sake of fornication but for the sake of heaven. 'But his scions did not act thus' (Jer. 48:30), but rather for the sake of fornication, and so it says, 'And Israel abode in Shittim and the people began to commit harlotry with the daughters of Moab' (Num. 25:1). [What Lot's daughters did they did for an honorable motive, but what the descendants did at Shittim they did not do for an honorable motive.]"

D. R. Simon said, "In the beginning of the conception of Moab, it was not for the sake of heaven but for the sake of fornication. 'But his scions did not act thus' (Jer. 48:30), but rather for the sake of heaven, and so it says, 'And she went down to the threshing floor and did according to all that her mother-in-law had commanded her' (Ruth 3:6). [Reversing matters, we point to Ruth as the descendant.]"

E. Said R. Levi, "If the beginning of the conception was for the sake of fornication, so too in the end it was for the sake of fornication: 'But his scions did not act thus' (Jer. 48:30), 'And she went down to the threshing floor and did according to all that her mother-in-law had commanded her' (Ruth 3:6)."

The issue of Moab enters for obvious reasons. None of this has bearing on the passage at hand. But it does underline the relationship between Lot, through Moab, and Ruth.

LI:XI.

1. A. "The first-born bore a son and called his name Moab; he is the father of the Moabites to this day" (Gen. 19:37):

B. R. Yudan in the name of R. Aibu: "As to the first-born daughter, because she treated with contempt the respect that was owing to her father and called her child by the father, 'Moab,' meaning, 'by [from] my father,' Scripture commanded in her regard: 'Do not hate Moab, nor contend with them in battle' (Deut. 2:9). The meaning is that while one may not wage war against them, you may divert their streams and burn their barns.

C. "But as to the younger one, because she treated with regard the honor that was owing to her father, '[The younger also bore a son] and called his name Ben-ammi. [He is the father of the Ammonites to this day]' (Gen. 19:38), that is, 'he is a son of one who happened to be with me,' Scripture declared: 'Do not harass them or contend with them' (Deut. 2:19) in any way at all."

2. A. R. Judah and R. Hanan in the name of R. Yohanan: "The daughters of Lot went to commit a transgression but they were remembered [and became pregnant which is regarded as the sign of great merit].

B. "On account of what merit [did they get pregnant]? It was on account of the Moab, that is, on account of the 'one who is a father,' [of him concerning whom it is written,] 'For the father of a multitude of nations have I made you' Gen. 17:5), [that is, Abraham]."

The contrast between the first-born and the younger daughter is neatly drawn by reference to the names they give their sons. This seems to me a solid insight. No. 2 draws the story to a close with a reference to Abraham's contribution to the matter.

Chapter Twenty

Parashah Fifty-Two.   Genesis 20:1-18

LII:I.

1. A. "From there Abraham [journeyed toward the territory of the Negeb and dwelt between Kadesh and Shur; and he sojourned in Gerar]" (Gen. 20:1):

   B. "And surely the mountain falling crumbles away" (Job 14:18):

   C. "And surely the mountain falling" speaks of Lot, who fell from the mountain [that is, Abraham].

   D. "And the rock is removed out of its place" (Job 14:18) speaks of Abraham, for the destruction of the locale of Sodom meant the end of bypassers. So he said, "Am I going to stop handing out charity ['acts of righteousness'] from my house?" He went and pitched his tent at Gerar.

   E. "From there Abraham [journeyed toward the territory of the Negeb and dwelt between Kadesh and Shur; and he sojourned in Gerar]" (Gen. 20:1).

The contrast to Lot and the allusion to Abraham's hospitality serve to link the passage now closed to the one about to begin.

LII:II.

1. A. "A brother offended is harder to be won than a strong city" (Prov. 18:19):

   B. This speaks of Lot, who was Abraham's nephew [and who offended him].

   C. "...offended is harder to be won than a strong city" (Prov. 18:19):

   D. [Addressing Lot:] "You have sinned against Abraham, you denied him, you were false to him."

   E. And whom did he as a result cause [to be his enemies]?

   F. "And judges like the bars of a castle" (Prov. 18:19): He brought against him judges [who kept him out] like the bars of the house of the sanctuary.

   G. Just as elsewhere: "So that no one who was unclean in any aspect should come in" (2 Chr. 23:19), so here, 'An Ammonite or a Moabite [descended from Lot's daughters] shall not enter into the assembly of the Lord" (Deut. 23:4).

H. [That fact explains why Abraham left Lot:] "From there Abraham [journeyed toward the territory of the Negeb and dwelt between Kadesh and Shur; and he sojourned in Gerar]" (Gen. 20:1).

The net effect is to explain why Lot falls from the story and the focus now remains solely on Abraham. The exclusion of Lot further stands for the exclusion of the Ammonites from the Temple, and the whole thus links the story at hand to the history and law of the sanctuary later on.

LII:III.

1. A. "The wise in heart will take good deeds" (Prov. 10:8): refers to Abraham.

B. "...will take good deeds" (Prov. 10:8) for the destruction of the locale of Sodom meant the end of bypassers. Consequently Abraham's stores did not fall.

C. So he said, "Am I going to stop handing out charity [acts of righteousness] from my house?" He went and pitched his tent at Gerar.

D. "From there Abraham [journeyed toward the territory of the Negeb and dwelt between Kadesh and Shur; and he sojourned in Gerar]" (Gen. 20:1).

E. "But the foolish of tongue shall fall" (Prov. 10:8) refers to Lot, who was foolish in what he said. For he ought to have told his daughters, "Something on account of which the world was smitten we are coming to do."

F. What disaster did he bring on himself?

G. "He shall fall" (Prov. 10:8).

H. He brought on himself one fall after another.

I. Just as elsewhere: "So that no one who was unclean in any aspect should come in" (2 Chr. 23:19), so here, 'An Ammonite or a Moabite shall not enter into the assembly of the Lord" (Deut. 23:4).

J. [That fact explains why Abraham left Lot:] "From there Abraham [journeyed toward the territory of the Negeb and dwelt between Kadesh and Shur; and he sojourned in Gerar]" (Gen. 20:1).

There obviously is some repetition of earlier material, but the new proof-text serves as did the other to explain the same issue, namely, how the foolishness of Lot led Abraham to take his leave.

LII:IV.

1. A. "From there Abraham journeyed toward the territory of the Negeb, and dwelt between Kadesh and Shur, and he sojourned in Gerar" (Gen. 20:1):

   B. "From there Abraham journeyed" away from the bad odor, for people were saying, "Lot, Abraham's nephew, had sexual relations with his two daughters."

2. A. "...toward the territory of the Negeb, and dwelt between Kadesh and Shur, and he sojourned in Gerar" (Gen. 20:1):

   B. The Negeb has seven names: South, Dry Area, Teman, Yamin [the right], Hadar, Yam, and Sinin.

   C. This question was raised: "And lo, it is written, 'Nor yet from the wilderness, Harim' (Ps. 75:7)?"

   D. They said, "That too is the South."

3. A. Said R. Hiyya bar Abba, "I was walking by the synagogue of the Babylonians in Sepphoris. I heard the children in session and reciting Scripture there: 'From there Abraham journeyed.'

   B. "[Since the word for journey' can also be understood to mean 'split,' as in 'split the fowl in half,'] I said to myself, "How great are the words of the sages! For they have said, **"Take heed of their burning coals, lest you be burned, for their bite is the bite of a fox"** [M. Abot 2:10]. From the moment that our father, Abraham, left Lot, his separation was forever.'"

4. A. "And he sojourned in Gerar" (Gen. 20:1):

   B. It is the place now known as Geradike.

5. A. "And Abraham said of Sarah his wife, 'She is my sister'" (Gen. 20:2):

   B. This was against her will and consent.

Nos. 1, 3 carry forward the theme of Abraham's leaving Lot and the cause. No. 2 adds a piece of information, and likewise No. 4 identifies the place by its contemporary name. No. 5 is puzzling, but the abrupt introduction of the theme is no more surprising than Scripture's own shift in the narrative at this point.

LII:V.

1. A. "But God came to Abimelech in a dream by night [and said to him, 'Behold, you are a dead man, because of the woman whom you have taken, for she is a man's wife']" (Gen. 20:3):

   B. What is the difference between the prophets of Israel and those of the nations?

   C. R. Hama b. R. Haninah said, "The Holy One, blessed be he, is revealed to the prophets of the nations of the world only in partial speech, in line with the following verse of Scripture: 'And God called [WYQR, rather than WYQR' as at Lev. 1:1] Balaam' (Num. 23:16). [Lev. R. I:XIII.1.C adds: On the other hand, he reveals himself to the prophets of Israel in full and complete speech, as it is said, 'And the Lord called (WYR') to Moses' (Lev. 1:1).]"

   D. Said R. Issachar of Kepar Mandi, "[Lev. R. I:XIII.1.D adds: Should that prophecy, even in partial form, be paid to them as their wage? Surely not, in fact that is no form of speech to gentile prophets, who are frauds.] The connotation of the language, 'And God called to Balaam' (Num. 23:16) is solely unclean. That is in line with the usage in the following verse of Scripture: 'That is not clean, by that which happens by night' (Deut. 23:11). [So the root is the same, with the result that YQR at Num. 23:16 does not bear the meaning of God's calling to Balaam. God rather declares Balaam unclean.]

   E. "But the prophets of Israel are addressed in language of holiness, purity, clarity, in language used by the ministering angels to praise God. That is in line with the following verse of Scripture: 'And they called one to another and said, "Holy, holy, holy is the Lord of hosts"' (Is. 6:3)."

2. A. R. Yose said, "'The Lord is far from the evil, but the prayer of the righteous does he hear' (Prov. 5:29).

   B. "'The Lord is far from the wicked' refers to the prophets of the nations of the world.

   C. "'But the prayer of the righteous does he hear' refers to the prophets of Israel.

3. A. R. Yose b. Bibah said, "The Holy One, blessed be he, appears to the prophets of the nations of the world only by night, when people take leave of one another: 'Now a word was secretly brought to me...at the time of leave-taking, from the visions of the night, when deep sleep falls on men' (Job 4:12-13)."

4. A. Said R. Eleazar b. Menahem, "'The Lord is far from the evil' (Prov. 5:29) refers to the prophets of the nations of the world.

B. "'But the prayer of the righteous does he hear' (Prov. 5:29) speaks of the prophets of Israel.

C. "You furthermore find that the Holy One, blessed be he, appears to the prophets of the nations of the world only like a man who comes from some distant place. That is in line with the following verse of Scripture: 'From a distant land they have come to me, from Babylonia' (Is. 39:3).

D. "But in the case of the prophets of Israel, he is always near at hand: 'And he appeared [not having come from a great distance]' (Gen. 18:1). 'And the Lord called' (Lev. 1:1).' [These usages bear the sense that he was right nearby.]"

5. A. What is the difference between the prophets of Israel and those of the nations?

B. R. Hinena said, "The matter may be compared to a king who, with his friend, was in a hall, with a curtain hanging down between them. When the king speaks to his friend, he turns back the curtain and speaks to his friend."

C. And rabbis say, "The matter may be compared to the case of a king who had a wife and a concubine. When he walks about with his wife, he does so in full public view. When he walks about with his concubine, he does so discreetly. So too, the Holy One, blessed be he, is revealed to the prophets of the nations only at night,

D. "in line with that which is written:' And God came to Balaam at night' (Num. 22:20). 'And God came to Laban the Aramean in a dream of the night' (Gen. 31:24). 'And God came to Abimelech in a dream by night' (Gen. 19:3)."

6. A. "[But God came to Abimelech in a dream by night and said to him,] 'Behold, you are a dead man, because of the woman whom you have taken, for she is a man's wife'" (Gen. 20:3):

B. On the basis of God's behavior here, we see that it is not necessary to supply an admonition [of the consequence of a violation of the law] to a gentile [who may be punished without the procedure of admonition]. [Freedman, p. 455, n. 1: The next verse says that Abimelech had not come near here, whence it follows that if he had, death would have been the penalty, even before this was told him.]

7. A. "... for she is a man's wife" (Gen. 20:3):

B. Said R. Aha, "Her husband was crowned by her, but she was not crowned by her husband."

C. Rabbis say, "She is her husband's master. Ordinarily, it is the husband who gives the orders. But here: 'In all that Sarah has said to you, listen to her voice' (Gen. 21:12)."

What captures the compositor-exegetes' attention is the statement that God communicated with Abimelech. This arouses their interest, since it would seem to imply that gentiles can receive God's word and become prophets. The opening composition, Nos. 1-5, work out their own syllogism, to which the base verse is tangential. The passage is equally tangential at Lev. R. I:XIII and has been prepared to make its own point and not to contribute to the exegesis of the passage at hand. But it is a perfectly intelligible choice and does advance the argument of the compositor-exegetes as a whole. We note that there is a certain amount of rearranging, which makes the composition slightly more appropriate here, e.g., the proof texts at 5.D. No. 6 draws its own conclusion, hence a syllogistic composition. No. 7 turns to the verse at hand. Since the Hebrew is written so that it may be read, "a ruler to her husband," the conclusions stated here follow.

LII:VI.

1. A. "Now Abimelech had not approached her, so he said, 'Lord, will you slay an innocent nation?'" (Gen. 20:4):

B. He said, "Is this is how you judged the generation of the flood and the generation of the dispersion, then they were righteous!"

C. Said R. Berekhiah, "'If you kill this gentile [namely, me], you kill a righteous man [namely, Abraham, who misled me].'"

2. A. "Did he not himself say to me, 'She is my sister'? And she herself said too, 'He is my brother.' In the integrity of my heart and the innocence of my hands I have done this" (Gen. 20:5):

B. [Since the word "too" is used, it encompasses] her, her ass-drivers, camel drivers, her household.

3. A. "...In the integrity of my heart and the innocence of my hands I have done this" (Gen. 20:5):

B. Lo, [by mentioning his hands] he conceded that he had laid hands on her.

The several compositions lightly gloss the cited statements.

LII:VII.

1. A. "Then God said to him in the dream, ['Yes, I know that you have done this in the integrity of your heart, and it was I who kept you from sinning against me; therefore I did not let you touch her. Now then, restore the man's wife']" (Gen. 20:6-7):

    B. R. Isaac said, "'...from sinning against me.'"

    C. "...'therefore I did not let you touch her:'"

    D. Said R. Aibun, "The matter may be compared to the case of a soldier who was riding on a horse, and the horse was running full speed. He saw a child in the path and rained in the horse so that the child was not injured. Whom do all praise? The horse or the rider? One must say it is the rider who gets the praise.

    E. "'...therefore *I* did not let you touch her.' [God is the one to get the credit, not Abimelech.]"

The sense of B is not clear to me. C-E make an explicit point in interpreting the language of the verse."

LII:VIII.

1. A. "Now then restore the man's wife, for he is a prophet, and he will pray for you, and you shall live" (Gen 20:7):

    B. He said to him, "Who is going to appease him, convincing him that I never touched her?"

    C. He said to him, "'...for he is a prophet.'"

    D. "And who is going to tell everybody about it?"

    E. He said to him, "'...and he will pray for you, and you shall live' (Gen 20:7)."

2. A. "But if you do not restore her, know that you shall surely die, you and all that are yours" (Gen. 20:7):

    B. On the basis of God's behavior here, we see that it is not necessary to supply an admonition [of the consequence of a violation of the law] to a gentile [who may be punished without the procedure of admonition]. [Freedman, p. 455, n. 1: The next verse says that Abimelech had not come near her, whence it follows that if he had, death would have been the penalty, even before this was told him.]

The exposition of the verse at No. 1 supplies a colloquy between God and Abimelech and so makes sense of each detail in the larger context of that conversation. The narrative is enriched by the new dialogue. No. 2 is familiar.

LII:IX.

1. A. "And Abimelech rose early in the morning and called all his servants [and told them all these things, and the men were very much afraid]" (Gen. 20:8):

   B. Said R. Hanan, "Since they saw the smoke of Sodom rising as from a furnace, they said, 'Is it possible that those angels that were sent against Sodom have come here? Therefore: 'the men were very much afraid' (Gen. 20:8).'"

The exegete supplies a motive to the household staff.

LII:X.

1. A. "Then Abimelech called Abraham and said to him, ['What have you done to us? And how have I sinned against you, that you have brought on me and my kingdom a great sin? You have done to me things that ought not to be done']" (Gen. 20:9):

   B. What is the meaning of the statement, "What have you done to us?"

   C. "Behold, you are a dead man, because of the woman [whom you have taken, for she is a man's wife]" (Gen. 20:3).

   D. What is the meaning of the statement, "And how have I sinned against you"?

   E. "But if you do nor not restore her, know that you shall surely die, you and all that are yours" (Gen. 20:7).

   F. "...that you have brought one me and my kingdom a great sin? You have done to me things that ought not to be done" (Gen. 20:9).

   G. "For the Lord had closed all the wombs of the house of Abimelech because of Sarah, Abraham's wife" (Gen. 20:18).

2. A. "[...that you have brought on me and my kingdom a great sin? You have done to me] things that ought not to be done" (Gen. 20:9):

   B. Said R. Helbo, "In every place before you got there, prosperity [heralded your way], while here, there was famine.

   C. "'...You have done to me things that ought not to be done' (Gen. 20:9)."

No. 1 weaves together the several verses to supply a colloquy for Abimelech and produces the effect of tightening the fabric of the tale. No. 2 explains what it is that Abimelech found so unusual in Abraham's visit. He had expected to benefit but that had not happened.

LII:XI.

1. A. "And Abimelech said to Abraham, 'What were you thinking of, that you did this thing?' And Abraham said, 'I did it because I thought, There is no fear of God at all in this place, and they will kill me because of my wife. Besides she is indeed my sister, the daughter of my father but not the daughter of my mother, and she became my wife'" (Gen. 20:12):

   B. [It has been taught on Tannaite authority: In the case of a man who converted to Judaism and was married to his sister, whether it was his sister on the father's side or his sister on his mother's side, he must divorce her, in accord with the view of R. Meir. And sages say, "If it was his sister on the mother's side, he must divorce her, but if it was his sister on the father's side, he may remain wed to her, for there is no consideration of paternity in the case of a gentile." The following objection was raised: And is it not written, "And moreover she is my sister, the daughter of my father" (Gen. 20:12)? So here is a case of paternity in the discourse with a gentile. Abraham] replied to them in accord with their theory of matters [but that was not his personal view of the case].

2. A. "And when God caused me to wander from my father's house, [I said to her, 'This is the kindness you must do me, at every place to which we come, say of me, "He is my brother"']" (Gen. 20:13):

   B. Said R. Hanan, "Would that we might interpret this verse of Scripture in three ways and so carry out our obligation! [Freedman, p. 457, n. 4: The verse contains two difficulties. First, 'caused to wander' is in the plural, while verbs referring to God should be in the singular. Second, the verb, 'caused to wander' bears the meaning of, 'caused to err.' Hanan gives three different renderings of the verse to obviate these difficulties.]

   C. "'When the nations of the world came to engage with me while I was still in father's house, the Holy One, blessed be he, stood up for me. When the nations of the world wanted to mislead me, God revealed himself to me and commanded me, 'Get you out of your father's house' (Gen. 12:1). When the nations of the world wanted to depart from his ways, he produced two heroes out of my father's family, Shem and Eber, to warn them.'" [Freedman, p. 458, n. 1: These are his three renderings: "And it came to pass when *the nations* erred *by their idolatry and wished to slay me because I rejected it,* God *saved* me in my *father's* house, and it came to pass, when *the nations* tried to mislead *me, that* God *commanded me to get me gone* from my father's house, and it came to pass, when the nations erred, that God raised men out of my father's house *to teach them better*."]

No. 1 presents a fragment, as indicated. No. 2 takes up the exact wording of the verse at hand and irons out its theological difficulties, as explained by Freedman.

LII:XII.

1. A. "Then Abimelech took sheep and oxen, and male and female slaves, and gave them to Abraham and restored Sarah his wife to him. And Abimelech said, 'Behold, my land is before you. Dwell where it pleases you.'

    B. "And to Sarah he said, 'Behold, I have given your brother a thousand pieces of silver. It is for you a covering of the eyes [RSV: your vindication in the eyes] of all who are with you, and before every one you are righted'" (Gen. 20:14):

    C. Said R. Judah bar Ilai, "'You went down to Egypt and did business with her, you came here and did business with her. Now if it's money that you want, here's your money.'

    D. "'It is your vindication in the eyes [of all who are with you, and before every one you are righted'] (Gen. 20:14)."

2. A. "...It is for you a covering of the eyes:"

    B. Said R. Yohanan, "'Make a cloak for her, so that everyone will look at it and not at her beauty.

    C. "'"It is for you a covering of the eyes" so that the garment will attract peoples' eyes.'"

3. A. R. Berekhiah said, "He treated her like a noble lady:

    B. "'It is for you a covering of the eyes' so that the garment will cover her from peoples' eyes."

4. A. R. Simeon b. Laqish said, "He wanted to make her discontented on account of her husband, so that she might say that all those years that she was with him, he had not done a thing for her, and this one, during a single night, has done all this for her."

5. A. He said to them, "You have covered up my eyes. The son whom you will produce will have covered eyes [and suffer from blindness]."

6. A. "And before all men you are reproved" (Gen. 20:16) [RSV: "And before everyone you are righted"]:

B. He said to him, "The reproof of that man is already by his side."

C. For we have learned in the Mishnah: **If a woman refuses to have sexual relations with her husband, they deduct seven *denarii* a week from her marriage-settlement [M. Ket. 5:5].**

D. Why seven? It is on account of the seven forms of labor that a woman is to carry out for her husband, grinding grain, baking, laundering, cooking, suckling her child, preparing the bed, and working in wool, thus, seven.

E. And if a man refuses to have sexual relations with his wife, they add three *denarii* a week to her marriage settlement.

F. Why three? It is on account of the three forms of labor that a man is to carry out for his wife, food, clothing, and sexual relations, so three.

G. Now if she brought in to the marriage as part of her dowry slaves, she owes him nothing at all, and if he stipulated when the marriage-settlement was prepared that he will be free of the obligation of food, clothing, and sexual relations, he owes her nothing.

H. Said R. Yohanan, "When the sexual relations are denied, it affects a man more than a woman. So it is written, 'And it came to pass, when she pressed him daily with her words and urged him' (Judges 16:16). She is the one who slipped out from under him. And then, 'That *his* soul was vexed unto death' (Judges 16:16), but her soul was not vexed. Why not? Because she got sexual satisfaction elsewhere."

No. 1 reconstructs Abimelech's statement to Abraham, and No. 2 does the same for Sarah. No. 3 extends No. 2. No. 4 then provides an insight into Abimelech's true motive. No. 5 links the present story to what is to come. No. 6 ignores the base verse entirely. But Freedman, p. 459, n. 2, proposes: She was now assured that Abraham stood reproved, in the sense that if he now refused her her rights, the law had already provided that he should be fined, as the passage proceeds to spell matters out. The passage obviously has been lifted straight out of its original location elsewhere, since most of it has no bearing on our text.

LII:XIII.

1. A. "Then Abraham prayed to God, and God healed Abimelech and also healed his wife and female slaves so that they bore children" (Gen. 20:17):

B. Said R. Hama b. R. Hanina, "From the beginning of the book [of Genesis] to this passage we do not find this usage [that someone prayed to God to help someone else]. But when our father, Abraham, prayed in this way, the knot was untied [and people could pray for one another]."

2. A. "For the Lord had closed all the wombs of the house of Abimelech because of Sarah, Abraham's wife" (Gen. 20:18):

B. "The 'closing up' applied to the mouth, throat, eye, ear, above and below. And all knew that it was 'because of Sarah, Abraham's wife.'"

3. A. Said R. Berekhiah, "It was because he had the gall to come near even the shoe of that noble woman."

4. A. And that entire night Sarah lay prostrate in prayer, saying, "Lord of the ages, Abraham went forth on account of trust, and I went forth in good faith. Abraham is outside of prison, so should I be put in prison?"

B. Said to her the Holy One, blessed be he, "Whatever I am going to do will be on your account."

C. Everyone said, "It is 'because of Sarai, Abram's wife' (Gen. 12:17)."

5. A. Said R. Levi, "For that entire night the angel was standing by with a whip in hand. If she said to him, 'Hit,' it hit, and if she said to him, 'Leave off,' he left off."

B. And why all this? Because she had said to [Pharaoh], "I am a married woman," and he did not leave her alone.

6. A. R. Eleazar, and it has been taught in the name of R. Eliezer b. Jacob, "We have heard concerning Pharaoh that he was smitten with *saraat,* and in the case of Abimelech, that he was smitten with constipation.

B. "How do we know that what applied to the one applied to the other and vice versa?

C. "It is because the words 'for the sake of' occur in both cases, so serving to establish an analogy between them."

No. 1 makes a fresh point, and the remainder serves Gen. 12:12ff. It is included here because of No. 6.

Chapter Twenty-One

Parashah Fifty-Three.   Genesis 21:1-20

LIII:I.

1. A. "The Lord remembered Sarah as he had said [and the Lord did to Sarah as he had promised]" (Gen. 21:1):

   B. This is in line with the following statement of Scripture: "And all the trees of the field shall know that I the Lord have brought down the high tree, have exalted the low tree, have dried up the green tree, and have made the dry tree to flourish; I the Lord have spoken and done it" (Ez. 17:24).

   C. Said R. Yudan "He is not like those who say but do not do."

   D. Said R. Berekhiah, "'I the Lord have spoken and done it' (Ez. 17:24). Where did he speak? 'At the set time I shall return to you...and Sarah shall have a son' (Gen. 18:14).

   E. "'and done it' (Ez. 17:24). '...and the Lord did to Sarah as he had promised]' (Gen. 21:1).

2. A. "...And all the trees of the field shall know" refers to people in general, in line with this verse: 'For the tree of the field is man' (Deut. 20:19).

   B. "...that I the Lord have brought down the high tree" refers to Abimelech.

   C. "...have exalted the low tree" speaks of Abraham.

   D. "... have dried up the green tree" refers to the wives of Abimelech: "For the Lord had closed up all the wombs of the house of Abimelech" (Gen. 20:18).

   E. "...and have made the dry tree to flourish" alludes to Sarah."

   F. "I the Lord have spoken and done it"(Ez. 17:24):

   G. Said R. Yudan "He is not like those who say but do not do."

   H. Said R. Berekhiah, "'I the Lord have spoken and done it' (Ez. 17:24).

   I. "Where did he speak? 'At the set time I shall return to you...and Sarah shall have a son' (Gen. 18:14).

   J. "'...and done it' (Ez. 17:24). '...and the Lord did to Sarah as he had promised]' (Gen. 21:1)."

The base verse underlines that God did precisely what he had said he would do, and that is the theme of the present composition. The intersecting verse is systematically applied to Abraham and Abimelech, so joining the preceding theme to the present one. Again the net effect of the exegesis is to tighten the lines of the story and weave them together. Both Nos. 1 and 2 go over exactly the same ground.

LIII:II.

1. A. "Shall a man be more righteous than God, shall a man be purer than his maker" (Job 4:17):

B. Now is it possible for a mortal to be more righteous than his creator?

C. "...shall a man be purer than his maker" (Job 4:17).

D. Now is it possible for a mortal to be more pure than his creator? [We shall now see that Elisha's word was carried out, all the more so God's.]

E. What did Elisha say to the Shunamite? "At this season, when the time comes around, you shall embrace a son" (1 Kgs. 4:16).

F. She said to him, "No, my lord, you man of God, do not lie to your handmaid" (2 Kgs. 4:16).

G. Those angels who gave the good news to Sarah said this to her: "At the set time I will return to you" (Gen. 18:14).

H. He said to her, "Since those angels knew that they would live and endure forever, they said, 'At the set time I will return to you' (Gen. 18:14). But I [Elisha] am mortal, alive today and dead tomorrow. So, whether I am alive or dead: 'At this season you shall embrace a son' (2 Kgs. 4:16)." [Elisha did not say he would return at the set time.]

I. What is then written? "And the woman conceived and bore a son" (2 Kgs. 4:17).

J. So the statement of the mortal was carried out.

K. Now as to that of the Holy One, blessed be he, is it not an argument *a fortiori*?

L. "The Lord remembered Sarah as he had said [and the Lord did to Sarah as he had promised]" (Gen. 21:1).

Once more the emphasis is on God's carrying out what he has promised, simply expanding on the simple statement which makes the matter explicit. The comparison of the two stories proceeds apace.

LIII:III.

1. A. "For though the fig tree does not blossom" (Hab. 3:17):

B. This refers to Abraham, in line with the following verse: "I saw your fathers as the first ripe in the fig tree at her first season" (Hos. 9:10).

C. "Neither is there fruit in the vines" (Hab. 32:17) speaks of Sarah, in line with this verse: "Your wife shall be as a fruitful vine" (Ps. 128:3).

D. "The labor of the olive fails" (Hab. 3:17): the angels who brought the good news to Sarah made her face shine like an olive. Now did they tell lies?

E. No, but "The fields yielded no food" (Hab. 3:17) indicates that "the withered breast" [a play on the fact that the word for "fields" and the word for "breasts" use the same consonants] yielded no food.

F. "The flock is cut off from the fold" (Hab. 3:17) in line with this: "And you my flock, the flock of my pasture, are men" (Ez. 34:31).

G. "There is no herd in the stalls" (Hab. 3:17). "And Ephraim is a heifer well broken, that loves to thresh" (Hos. 10:11).

H. Now Sarah went and said, "Shall I then give up hoping in my creator? God forbid. I shall not give up hoping in my creator, 'For I will rejoice in the Lord, I will exalt in the God of my salvation' (Hab. 3:18)."

I. Said to her the Holy One, blessed be he, "You did not give up hope in me. So I shall not give up hope in you."

J. "The Lord remembered Sarah as he had said [and the Lord did to Sarah as he had promised]" (Gen. 21:1).

2. A. "The grass withers, the flower fades" (Is. 40:8):

B. The grass of Abimelech withers and his flower fades.

C. "But the word of our God shall stand forever" (Is. 40:8).

D. "The Lord remembered Sarah as he had said and the Lord did to Sarah as he had promised" (Gen. 21:1).

The intersecting verse of No. 1 is chosen for good reason. It shows that Sarah had kept the faith, and that accounts for God's remembering her. No. 2 goes over the ground of the relationship between the present story and the one just completed. The message to contemporary Israel cannot be missed.

LIII:IV.

1. A. "For ever, O Lord, your word stands fast in heaven" (Ps. 119:89):

B. But does God's word not stand fast on earth?

C. But what you said to Abraham in heaven, "At this season I shall return to you" (Gen. 18:14) [was carried out:]

D. "The Lord remembered Sarah as he had said and the Lord did to Sarah as he had promised" (Gen. 21:1).

2. A. R. Menahamah and R. Nahman of Jaffa in the name of R. Jacob of
Caesarea opened discourse by citing the following verse: "'O God of hosts,
return, we beseech you' (Ps. 80:15).

B. "'Return and carry out what you promised to Abraham: "Look from
heaven and behold" (Ps. 80:15). "Look now toward heaven and count the
stars"' (Gen. 15:5).

C. "'And be mindful of this vine' (Ps. 80:15). 'The Lord remembered Sarah
as he had said and the Lord did to Sarah as he had promised' (Gen. 21:1)."

3. A. R. Samuel bar Nahman opened discourse with this verse: "God is not a
man, that he should lie" (Num. 23:19).

B. Said R. Samuel bar Nahman, "The beginning of this verse does not
correspond to its end, and the end does not correspond to its beginning.

C. "'God is not a man that he should lie' (Num. 23:18), but the verse ends,
'When he has said, he will not do it, and when he has spoken, he will not
make it good' (Num. 23:18).

D. "[That obviously is impossible. Hence:] When the Holy One, blessed
be he, makes a decree to bring good to the world: 'God is not a man that he
should lie' (Num. 23:18).

E. "But when he makes a decree to bring evil on the world: 'When he has
said, he [nonetheless] will not do it, and when he has spoken, he will not
make it good' (Num. 23:18).

F. "When he said to Abraham, 'For through Isaac shall your descendants be
named,' 'God is not a man that he should lie' (Num. 23:18).

G. "When he said to him, 'Take your son, your only son' (Gen. 22:2),
'When he has said, he will not do it, and when he has spoken, he will not
make it good' (Num. 23:18).

H. "When the Holy One, blessed be he, said to Moses, 'I have surely
remembered you' (Ex. 3:16), 'God is not a man that he should lie' (Num.
23:18).

I. "When he said to him, 'Let me alone, that I may destroy them' (Deut.
9:14), 'When he has said, he will not do it, and when he has spoken, he will
not make it good' (Num. 23:18).

J. "When he said to Abraham, 'And also that nation whom they shall serve
will I judge' (Gen. 15:14), 'God is not a man that he should lie' (Num. 23:18).

K. "When he said to him, 'And they shall serve them and they shall afflict
them for four hundred years' (Gen. 15:13), 'When he has said, he will not do
it, and when he has spoken, he will not make it good' (Num. 23:18).

L. "When God said to him, 'I will certainly return to you' (Gen. 18:10,
'God is not a man that he should lie' (Num. 23:18).

M. "'The Lord remembered Sarah as he had said and the Lord did to Sarah as he had promised' (Gen. 21:1)."

The point of No. 1 is now familiar. No. 2 makes the same statement, now in a somewhat more complex composition. No. 3 presents a magnificent exposition of its simple syllogism, the relevance of which is self-evident. The main point is that God will always carry out his word when it has to do with a blessing, but God may well go back on his word when it has to do with punishment. The later events in the history of Israel are drawn together to make this important point.

LIII:V.

1. A. "Who has kept with your servant, David my father" (1 Kgs. 8:24):

B. This refers to Abraham [even though it speaks of David].

C. "That which you did promise him" (1 Kgs. 8:24) "At the set time I will return to you" (Gen. 18:14).

D. "Yes, you spoke with your mouth and have fulfilled it with your hand as it is this day" (1 Kgs. 8:24).

E. "And the Lord remembered Sarah" (Gen. 21:1).

2. A. "Who makes the barren woman dwell in her house" (Ps. 113:9):

B. That verse refers to Sarah: "And Sarai was barren" (Gen. 11:30).

C. "As a joyful mother of children" (Ps. 113:9).

D. "Sarah has given children suck" (Gen. 21:7).

3. A. "And the Lord remembered Sarah as he had said" (Gen. 21:1):

B. R. Judah said, "'And the Lord remembered Sarah as he had said' (Gen. 21:1). refers to what he had stated to her by an act of saying, while 'And he did to Sarah as he had spoken' (Gen. 21:1) alludes to statements that he made to her with an act of speaking."

C. R. Nehemiah said, "'And the Lord remembered Sarah as he had said' (Gen. 21:1). refers to what he had stated to her through an angel, while 'And he did to Sarah as he had spoken' (Gen. 21:1) alludes to statements that he made to her himself."

4. A. R. Judah says, "'And the Lord remembered Sarah' (Gen. 21:1) by giving her a son, 'and the Lord did to Sarah as he had promised' (Gen. 21:1) by giving her the blessing of milk."

B. Said to him R. Nehemiah, "And had she already been informed about the matter of milk? But this teaches that the Holy One, blessed be he, restored her youth to her."

5. A. R. Abbahu [in the name of R. Yose b. R. Hanina]: "'I shall place fear of her over all the nations of the world, so that they will not abuse her by calling her barren.'"

B. R. Yudan [in the name of R. Simeon b. Laqish]: "She had no ovary, so the Holy One, blessed be he, formed an ovary for her."

6. A. "The Lord remembered Sarah" (Gen. 21:1):

B. Said R. Aha, "The Holy One, blessed be he, takes care of [and remembers] bailments. Amalek entrusted to the Holy One bundles of thorns, so he returned him bundles of thorns: 'I remember what Amalek did to Israel' (1 Sam. 15:2).

C. "Sarah entrusted to the Holy One, blessed be he, the religious duties and good deeds that she had performed, and he returned to her the reward of doing religious duties and good deeds [namely giving birth and raising a son]: 'The Lord remembered Sarah' (Gen. 21:1)."

Nos. 1 and 2 present interweavings of verses, making points in an elegant way. No. 3 then reads the base verse in terms of its broader meaning. Judah wants to distinguish things God has said from those that he has spoken, and Nehemiah finds his own distinction for the same terms. What follows, however, has no place here. It has been revised from its original appearance, XLVII:II, at which point it made sense. No. 5 makes that certain, since it is completely irrelevant to the present context. We therefore see what the framers were willing to do to revise what they had received -- and what they were not willing to do. Overall they simply inserted whole compositions, even though only small parts of those compositions had a place. But where they did make changes, as here, we can readily discern what was original and what has emerged as the revised version. No. 6 draws its own contrast, resting on the usages of the word "remember" of Amalek and Sarah. It produces the effect of linking the life of Sarah to the history of Israel. The lives of the patriarchs and matriarchs therefore prefigure the life of israel, as we have seen throughout.

LIII:VI.

1. A. "R. Isaac said, "It is written, 'And if the woman be not defiled but is clean, then she shall be cleared and shall conceive seed' (Num. 5:28).

B. "Now this one went into the house of Pharaoh and got away clean, into the house of Abimelech and got away clean, and is it not reasonable to expect that she will be remembered [and become pregnant]?"

2. A. Said R. Judah, "Even though R. Huna said, 'There is an angel who is appointed to watch over lust,' Sarah, for her part, had no need for such matter. For God in his own person [took charge]: 'The Lord remembered Sarah' (Gen. 21:1)."

3. A. "And Sarah conceived and bore Abraham a son in his old age at the time of which God had spoken to him" (Gen. 21:2):

B. This teaches that she did not acquire the seed through theft from some other source. [Isaac really was Abraham's son.]

4. A. "...a son in his old age [at the time of which God had spoken to him]" (Gen. 21:2):

B. This teaches that the child's looked like him.

5. A. "...at the time of which God had spoken to him" (Gen. 21:2):

B. R. Yudan said, "He was born after a pregnancy of nine full months, so that people should not say that he was a scion of the house of Abimelech."

C. R. Hunia said, "He was born after a pregnancy of seven incomplete months."

D. R. Huna in the name of Hezekiah: "He was born at noon. 'Set time' is stated here, and the word bears that meaning of midday elsewhere: 'At the set time that you came forth out of Egypt' (Deut. 16:6)."

No. 1 once more explains the merit by which Sarah became pregnant, this time invoking the ordeal of the accused wife. No. 2 draws the discussion to a close with its emphasis that it was the Lord who did it, no one less. And it really was Abraham's son, a point repeatedly stressed. Nos. 3, 4 beginning the glossing of the next verse. No. 5 takes up the meaning of the word "set time," introducing two considerations, the one polemical, the other philological, A-B and C, respectively.

LIII:VII.

1. A. ""Abraham called the name of his son who was born to him, whom Sarah bore him, Isaac" (Gen. 21:3):

B. [The word Isaac, YSHQ] stands for "a law has come forth for the world" [YS' HQ], a gift has been given to the world."

C. R. Isaac Hippusheh said, "The letter Y stands for ten, for the Ten Commandments, the letter S for ninety, 'And shall Sarah, who is ninety years old, bear' (Gen. 17:17). The H stands for an eight, in line with this verse: 'And Abraham circumcised his son Isaac when he was eight days old, as God had commanded him' (Gen. 21:4). The letter Q stands for a hundred: 'Shall a child be born to him who is a hundred years old' (Gen. 17:17)."

The name of Isaac is given two meanings, B, C. In context, the passage is to be classified as philological.

LIII:VIII.

1. A. "And Sarah said, 'God has made joy for me; everyone who hears will rejoice with me'" (Gen. 21:6):

B. R. Berekhiah, R. Judah bar Simon, R. Hanan in the name of R. Samuel bar R. Isaac: "If Reuben is happy, what difference does it make to Simeon? So too, if Sarah was remembered, what difference did it make to anyone else?

C. "When our mother, Sarah, was remembered, with her many barren women were remembered, with her many of the deaf had their ears opened, with her many of the blind had their eyes opened, with her many of those who had lost their senses regained their senses.

D. "The word 'making' ['God has made joy'] is used here and also in the following verse: 'And he made a release to the provinces' (Est. 2:18).

E. "Just as the word 'making;' used there indicates that a gift had been given to the entire world, so the word 'making;' used there indicates that a gift had been given to the entire world."

F. [Explaining the source common joy,] R. Levi said, "She added to the lights of the heavens. The word 'making' ['God has made joy'] is used here and also in the following verse: 'And God made the two lights' (Gen. 1:16)."

The exegete now treats the sense of the cited verse as a whole. This he does through philological inquiry.

LIII:IX.

1. A. "And she said, 'Who will tell Abraham that Sarah would suckle children? Yet I have borne him a son in his old age'" (Gen. 21:7):

B. R. Phineas in the name of R. Hilqiah: "What is stated is not 'who will say' or 'who will speak' but 'who will tell' [using the verb MLL, the numerical value of the letters of which adds up to 100]. This contains the indication that he produced a child at a hundred years."

C. R. Phineas in the name of R. Hilqiah: "The use of that word further indicates that Abraham's 'standing grain' had dried up but now was turned into ripe ears of grain [MLYLWT]."

2. A. " ...that Sarah will suckle children..." (Gen. 21:7):

B. She suckled builders [which uses the same letters as the word for children].

3. A. Sarah was unusually modest. Our father, Abraham, said to her, "This is not a time for modesty, but show your breasts, so that everyone will know that the Holy One, blessed be he, has begun to make miracles. [This is time for the nations to accept God's dominion.]"

B. She showed her breasts and they began to spout milk like two fountains. The noble ladies came and suckled their children from her, saying, "We really do not enjoy the merit of having our children suckled by that righteous woman."

C. Rabbis say, "Whoever came for the sake of Heaven [to see the miracle] became God-fearing."

D. R. Aha said, "Even those [nations] who did not come for the sake of Heaven were given dominion in the world. Yet things did not work out, for when they separated themselves at Sinai and did not accept the Torah, that dominion was taken away from them: 'He looses the bonds of kings and binds their loins with a girdle' (Job 12:18)."

No. 1 interprets the odd word choice at hand. No. 2 plays on the correspondence of the word for "children" and "builders." I assume this yields the bridge to Israelite history later on. No. 3 then broadens discourse, explicitly linking Israel's history at Sinai to the true acceptance of the miracle of Sarah's milk.

LIII.X.

1. A. "And the child grew and was weaned, [and Abraham made a great feast on the day that Isaac was weaned]" (Gen. 21:8):

B. R. Hoshaia the Elder said, "He was weaned from the evil impulse."

C. Rabbis say, "He was weaned from relying upon milk."

2. A. "...and Abraham made a *great* feast on the day that Isaac was weaned" (Gen. 21:8):

    B. R. Judah said, "The *Great* One of the ages was there."

    C. R. Yudan in the name of R. Yose bar Haninah: "'The king made a great feast' (Est. 2:18). The *Great* One of the ages was there. That is in line with this verse: 'For the Lord will again rejoice over you for good' (Deut. 30:9), in the days of Mordecai and Esther, 'As he rejoiced over your fathers' (Deut. 30:9), in the days of Abraham, Isaac, and Jacob."

3. A. Said R. Judah, "'A great feast' refers to a feast for the great ones of the age. Og and all the great ones were there. They said to Og, 'Did you not say that Abraham was a barren mule, who cannot produce a child?'

    B. "He said to them, 'Now what is this gift of his? Is he not puny? If I put my finger out on him, I can crush him.'

    C. "Said to him the Holy One, blessed be he, 'Now are you treating my gift with contempt? By your life, you will see a thousand myriads of his children, and you will fall in the end to his children.'

    D. "So it is said: 'And the Lord said to Moses, "Fear him not, for I have delivered him into your hand"' (Num. 21:34)."

    E. [Freedman:] (R. Levi said, "The cradle was rocked for the first time in the house of our father Abraham.")

    F. [Continuing A-D,] for R. Joshua bar Nehemiah said, "Those thirty-one kings whom Joshua killed were all present at the feast made by Abraham."

    G. But there were not thirty-one. The matter accords with what R. Berekhiah and R. Helbo, R. Parnakh in the name of R. Yohanan [said], "'The king of Jericho, one' (Joshua 12:9). Scripture states, 'One,' meaning, 'he and his regent.'"

No. 1 contrasts figurative and literal interpretations of the verse. No. 2 explicitly links Isaac's feast with the miracle in the time of Esther, and, should we miss the point, further links the two matters explicitly. The recurrent appeal to the events of the Book of Esther should not be missed. No. 3 succeeds still more effectively in introducing the theme of Israel's history. So the feast for Isaac prefigures the redemption of Israel.

LIII:XI.

1. A. "But Sarah saw the son of Hagar the Egyptian, whom she had borne to Abraham, making sport " (Gen. 21:9):

    B. Said R. Simeon, "R. Aqiba would explain this matter [of making sport] in a way that deprecated Ishmael."

C. R. Aqiba interpreted the matter in this way: "'But Sarah saw the son of Hagar the Egyptian, whom she had borne to Abraham, making sport' (Gen. 21:9). The word 'making sport' bears only one meaning, namely, fornicating, in line with this verse: 'The Hebrew servant whom you brought me came in to me to make sport of me' (Gen. 39:17).

D. "This teaches, then, that Sarah saw Ishmael seducing 'gardens [virgins],' making love to married women and dishonoring them."

2. A. R. Ishmael taught on Tannaite authority, "The word 'making sport' refers only to idolatry, as it is said, 'And rose up to make sport' (Ex. 32:6).

B. "This teaches, then, that Sarah saw Ishmael building little altars, hunting locusts, and offering them up [on the altars, as a game]."

3. A. R. Eleazar says, "The word 'make sport' refers only to murder: 'Let the young men, I pray you, arise and make sport before us' (2 Sam. 2:15)."

B. [Showing just what murder is in mind,] R. Azariah in the name of R. Levi: "They said, 'Come and let's go see our portion of the fields. Then Ishmael took a bow and arrows and shot at Isaac and pretended to be making sport. That is in line with this verse: 'As a madman who casts fire-brands, arrows, and death, so is the man who deceives his neighbor and says, Am I not making sport?' (Prov. 22:18)."

4. A. [Reverting to Simeon, 1.B:] "But I say that the word 'making sport' refers only to inheritance.

B. "For when our father, Isaac, was born, everybody rejoiced. Ishmael said to them, 'You really are fools. I am the first born, and I shall take a double portion.'

C. "For from the answer that Sarah gave to Abraham, you learn what is at issue: '...for the son of this slave woman shall not be an heir with my son Isaac.'

D. "'...with my son' even if it were not Isaac, '...with Isaac' even if it were not my son. All the more so: '...with my son, Isaac.'"

The composition is unitary and powerful. It rings the changes on the conventional trilogy of mortal sins, fornication, idolatry, and murder, and then comes back to the main point. It is thoroughly persuasive.

LIII:XII.

1. A. "[So she said to Abraham, 'Cast out this slave woman with her son, for the son of this slave woman shall not be heir with my son Isaac.'] And the thing was very displeasing to Abraham on account of his son" (Gen. 21:11):

   B. That is in line with this verse: "And shuts his eyes from looking upon evil" (Is. 33:15). [Freedman, p. 471, n. 1: He shut his eyes from Ishmael's evil ways and was reluctant to send him away.]

2. A. "But God said to Abraham, 'Be not displeased because of the lad and because of your slave woman; whatever Sarah says to you, do as she tells you, for through Isaac shall your descendants be named'" (Gen. 21:12):

   B. Said R. Yudan bar Shillum, "What is written is not 'Isaac' but 'through Isaac.' [The matter is limited, not through all of Isaac's descendants but only through some of them, thus excluding Esau.]"

3. A. R. Azariah in the name of Bar Hutah" "The Hebrew letter B, [which means "through"] also stands for two, and so indicates that he who affirms that there are two worlds will inherit both worlds [this age and the age to come]."

   B. Said R. Yudan bar Shillum, "It is written, 'Remember his marvelous works that he has done, his signs and the judgments of his mouth' (Ps. 105:5). I have given a sign to anyone who gives the appropriate evidence through what he says. Specifically, he who affirms that there are two worlds will be called 'your seed.'

   C. "And he who does not affirm that there are two worlds will not be called 'your seed.'"

No. 1 makes "the matter" refer to Ishmael's misbehavior, not Sarah's proposal, so removing the possibility of disagreement between Abraham and Sarah. Nos. 2, 3 interpret the limiting particle, "in," that is, *among* the descendants of Isaac will be found Abraham's heirs, but not all the descendants of Isaac will be heirs of Abraham. No. 2 explicitly excludes Esau, that is Rome, and No. 3 makes the matter doctrinal in the context of Israel's inner life.

LIII:XIII.

1. A. "So Abraham rose early in the morning and took bread and a skin of water [and gave it to Hagar, putting it on her shoulder, along with the child, and sent her away, and she departed and wandered in the wilderness of Beer Sheba]" (Gen. 21:14):

B. Was the house of Abraham not generous, [that he should send her away with so little,] as it is said, "So Abraham rose early in the morning and took bread and a skin of water" (Gen. 21:14)?

C. The custom involving slaves was for them to carry water in their pitchers, [therefore Abraham was generous in giving her a skin of water]. [I follow Freedman, p. 471.]

2. A. "...putting it on her shoulder, along with the child" (Gen. 21:14):

B. He was twenty-seven years old, and you say, "...putting it on her shoulder, along with the child" (Gen. 21:14)?

C. This teaches that Sarah had put the evil eye in the child, so he got feverish [and had to be carried].

D. You may know that this was the case, for lo, it is said, "When the water in the skin was gone" (Gen. 21:15).

E. It is the way of a sick person to take a drink every hour [which is why the water was used up so quickly].

3. A. "And she cast the child under one of the shrubs (Gen. 21:15):

B. Said R. Meir, "[Freedman:] It was a juniper tree, which grow in the wilderness."

C. Said R. Issi, "[Since the word for 'shrub' uses consonants that can be read, 'conversation,' the sense is this:] It indicates that there the ministering angels spoke with her."

4. A. "Then she went and sat down over against him a good way off, [about the distance of a bowshot, for she said, 'Let me not look upon the death of the child.' And as she sat over against him, the child lifted up his voice and wept]" (Gen. 21:16):

B. Here you say, "A good way off, [about the distance of a bowshot]" and elsewhere: "Yet there shall be a space between you and it, about two thousand cubits by measure" (Joshua 3:4).

C. So we learn the sense of the word "against" from a further use of the same word, and the meaning of the word "a good way off" from a similar passage. [Freedman, p. 472, n. 6: By comparing these verses we learn that she sat at a distance of two thousand cubits.]

D. Said R. Isaac, "Two bowshots cover a *mil* ."

E. Said R. Berekhiah, "The expression at hand means that she was a woman who complained against the divinity: 'Yesterday you promised me, "I will greatly multiply your seed" (Gen. 16:10), and today he is dying of thirst!'"

Nos. 1, 2 explain the verse at hand, drawing upon the facts of nature, that is, the propensity of the sick to drink a lot, to explain the sense of the tale. No. 2 glosses the cited verse, but also finds a deeper meaning in the word choice. Nos. 3, 4 simply explain a detail, part of the large-scale interest in simply clarifying the facts of passages. Only Berekhiah's statement at the end, No. 4, leaves the commonplace realm of facts.

LIII:XIV.

1. A. "You have counted *nudi* " (Ps. 56:9), meaning, "You have counted my wanderings."

    B. "You have counted my wanderings."

    C. "Put my tears into your bottle" (Ps. 56:9): by that woman who had the bottle [namely, Hagar].

    D. "Are they not in your book" (Ps. 56:9): Just as it is written in the book of Psalms: "Hear my prayer, Lord, and give ear to my cry, do not keep silent at my tears" (Ps. 39:13). "You did not keep silent at the tears of Hagar, do not keep silent at my tears."

    E. "And if you should claim that it was because she was beloved by you as a convert, so I too: 'For I am a convert with you, a sojourner, as all my fathers were (Ps. 39:13).'"

2. A. "And the angel of God called to Hagar [from heaven and said to her, 'What troubles you, Hagar? Fear not, for God has heard the voice of the lad where he is. Arise and lift up the lad and hold him fast with your hand, for I will make him a great nation']" (Gen. 21:18-19):

    B. "And the angel of God called to Hagar" on account of the merit accumulated by Abraham.

    C. "...where he [personally] is" on account of the merit accumulated by the boy himself.

    D. The prayer of the sick person [because of Sarah's curse] is the best of all.

3. A. "...where he is:"

    B. Said R. Simon, "The ministering angels jumped to indict the boy, saying before him, 'Lord of all ages, a man who is destined to kill your children with thirst will you provide with a well?'

    C. "He said to them, 'What is he now?'

    D. "They said to him, 'He is a righteous man.'

E. "He said to them, 'I judge someone only 'where he is,' meaning, in his present condition.' 'Arise and lift up the lad and hold him fast with your hand' (Gen. 21:18).

4. A. "Then God opened her eyes" (Gen. 21:18):

B. R. Benjamin bar Levi and R. Jonathan bar Amram both said, "All people are assumed to be blind until the Holy One, blessed be he, opens their eyes. That is shown by this verse: 'Then God opened her eyes.'"

5. A. "[And she saw a well of water] and she went and filled the skin with water [and gave the lad a drink]" (Gen. 21:19):

B. [Her filling the bottle] indicates that she had little faith [and feared that the well would run dry, as Abraham's devotion to her had run dry].

No. 1 presents a somewhat complicated weaving of two intersecting verses, Ps. 56:9 and 39:13, alluding to our story but not citing any part of it. No. 2 prepares the way for No. 3. No. 2 indicates that Ishmael himself had attained merit. Then No. 3 explains why God acted rationally in saving Ishmael, despite what his descendants would do to Israel. He judges people as they are, since, whatever foresight anyone may have, people can change. Eilberg-Schwartz adds: He judges people as they are, even though he knows that they will subsequently change. No. 4 uses the fact supplied by the base verse to prove its own syllogism. No. 5 makes a wry comment.

LIII:XV.

1. A. "And God was with the lad [and he grew up. He lived in the wilderness and became an expert with the bow]" (Gen. 21:20):

B. R. Ishmael asked R. Aqiba, saying to him, "Because you studied with Nahum of Gimzu for twenty-two years, who maintains that the use of such words as 'only' and 'but' serve to exclude, while the use of the accusative particle 'T and the word 'also' serve to include, can you explain for me the meaning of the accusative particle used here, when the verse says, 'God was T the youth'?"

C. He said to him, "If it had said only, 'And God was the lad,' [i.e., leaving out the word 'with' altogether,] the meaning would be quite a problem. Therefore it says 'with' [using the accusative particle, T] the child.'"

D. He said to him, "'For it is not an empty thing from you' (Deut. 32:47), meaning that if it appears to be empty [of all meaning, as in the case of the accusative particle used here], it is because of your fault, since you cannot explain the Scripture in the correct way.

E. "'God was 'T the youth ' means to encompass his ass-drivers, his camel-drivers, and his household [indicating that God was with all of them]."

2. A. "He became an expert with the bow (RBH QST)" (Gen. 21:20):

B. [Freedman:] As he grew (RBH), so did his cruelty (QSYWT) grow with him.

C. [Interpreting the word for archer differently:] while he was young (RBH), he taught himself to use the bow (QST).

D. [Interpreting the word for archer differently:] He was master (RBH) of all who taught archery (MWRYM BQST).

3. A. "And he lived in the wilderness of Paran" (Gen. 21:21):

B. Said R. Isaac, "Throw a stick into the air, and it will fall back on its own spot. Since it is written, 'An Egyptian handmaiden, named Hagar' (Gen. 15:1), therefore: 'And his mother took a wife for him from the land of Egypt' (Gen. 21:21)."

No. 1 makes its own point, explaining the passage in line with an established exegetical principles. No. 2 takes up the language at hand and induces its meanings. No. 3 then links two verses to make sense of a stated fact.

Chapter Twenty-Two

Parashah Fifty-Four. Genesis 21:22-34

LIV:I.

1. A. "At that time Abimelech and Phicol the commander of his army said to Abraham, 'God is with you in all that you do'" (Gen. 21:22).

    B. "When a man's ways please the Lord, even his enemies are at peace with him" (Prov. 16:7).

    C. R. Yohanan said, "The reference to one's enemies speaks, in fact, of one's wife: 'A man's enemies are the people of his own house' (Mic. 7:6)."

    D. There was the case of a woman who complained against her husband to the government, and they cut off his head.

    E. And some say that they also cut off her head.

    F. R. Samuel bar Nahman said, "The cited verse refers to the snake."

    G. A Tannaite authority of the house of Halapta bar Saul taught, "The snake lusts for garlic."

    H. Said R. Samuel bar Nahman, "There was the case of a snake that went down into a house and found a bowl of garlic and ate it and vomited up into the bowl. There was a [second] snake in the house, and it could not withstand the intruder [and keep it out, being too weak]. But when the first snake left, the second snake went and filled the bowl with dirt [saving the life of the people of the house, who otherwise would have eaten the venom]."

    I. R. Joshua b. Levi said, "The cited verse refers to the impulse to do evil.

    J. "Under ordinary circumstances if someone grows up with a fellow for two or three years, he develops a close tie to him. But the impulse to do evil grows with someone from youth to old age, and, if one can, someone strikes down the impulse to do evil even when he is seventy or eighty.

    K. "So did David say, 'All my bones shall say, "Lord, who is like unto you, who delivers the poor from him who is too strong for him, yes, the poor and the needy from him who spoils him"' (Ps. 35:10)."

    L. Said R. Aha, "And is there a greater thief than this one? And Solomon said, 'If your enemy be hungry, give him bread to eat' (Prov. 25:21). The meaning is, the bread of the Torah [which will help a person resist the enemy that is the impulse to do evil], as it is said, 'Come, eat of my bread' (Prov. 9:5).

M. "'If he is thirsty give him water to drink' (Prov. 25:21), that is, the water of the Torah, as it is said, 'Ho, everyone who is thirsty come for water' (Is. 55:1)."

N. R. Berekhiah said, "The verse says, '...*also* his enemies' (Prov 16:7), with the word 'also' encompassing the insects of the house, vermin, flies and the like.'"

2.   A. Another view: "When a man's ways please the Lord, even his enemies are at peace with him" (Prov. 16:7):

B. "At that time Abimelech and Phicol the commander of his army said to Abraham, 'God is with you in all that you do'" (Gen. 21:22).

No. 2 of course makes the main point relevant to our chapter, and the point is so obvious that it is not even articulated. No. 1 presents a repertoire of other interpretations of the intersecting verse, the wife, the snake, and the impulse to do evil -- this reverting to the story of the Garden of Eden. But the net effect of joining Nos. 1 and 23 is to invoke a much broader range of themes than No. 2 alone suggests. If someone wanted to procede to a typological identification, e.g., of Abimelech and Phicol with the snake, the evil wife, and the like, the materials are in hand.

LIV:II.

1.   A. "And Phicol" (Gen. 21:22):

B. R. Judah and R. Nehemiah:

C. R. Judah says, "Phicol was his name."

D. R. Nehemiah said, "The name means, 'Everybody's mouth' (Phi is 'mouth,' Col is 'everybody'], for all of his army would kiss him on his mouth."

2.   A. "God is with you in all that you do" (Gen. 21:22):

B. People had been saying, "If he were a righteous man, would he not have produced a son?" Now, however, that he had produced a son, they said, "God is with you in all that you do" (Gen. 21:22).

C. And they further said, "If he were righteous, he would listen to the voice of his wife." When it had been said to him, "As to whatever Sarah says to you, listen to her voice" (Gen. 21;12), they said to him, "God is with you in all that you do" (Gen. 21:22).

D. And they further said, "If he were righteous, he would drive away his first born son. When they saw what he had done, they said, "God is with you in all that you do" (Gen. 21:22).

E. Since the place of Sodom had been destroyed and passersby had ceased to come along, and his stores no longer were diminished, therefore they said, "God is with you in all that you do" (Gen. 21:22).

3. A. "Now therefore swear to me here by God that you will not deal falsely with me or with my offspring or with my posterity" (Gen. 21:22):

B. To that extent do the mercies of the father extend, namely to his descendants [that is, to his grandson].

C. Said R. Abba bar Kahana, "To that extent do brothers in partnership go."

4. A. Said R. Yose b. Hanina, "'But my enemies are strong in health' (Ps. 38:20).

B. "What Abraham's descendant received only after seven generations [namely, the land, for seven generations after Abraham Israel entered the land] was given to Abimelech in three. Why did 'God lead them not by the way of the land of the Philistines' (Ex. 13:17)? Because the grandson of Abimelech was still alive. [So Abimelech was rewarded.]"

5. A. "As I have dealt mercifully with you, you will deal with me and with the land where you have sojourned" (Gen. 21:23):

B. Now just what sort of act of mercy had he shown to Abraham?

C. But he said to him, "Lo, my land is before you, live where you want" (Gen. 20:15).

D. But Abraham had not accepted this offer.

No. 1 provides a minor clarification of the cited name. No. 2 places the present story into its prior context, an important effort to weave the sequence of unrelated tales together as best as one can. Now we see reason to doubt God had been with Abraham, together with reason to affirm God's favor. No. 3 clarifies a minor point, using the cited verse as a fact for the syllogism at hand. No. 4 explains the full extent of the oath that Abraham took. No. 5 then answers an obvious question in the cited verse.

LIV:III.

1. A. "And Abraham complained to Abimelech about a well of water which Abimelech's servants had seized" (Gen. 21:25):

B. Said R. Yose bar Haninah, "Rebuke leads people to love: 'Rebuke a wise man and he will love you' (Prov. 9:8)."

C. That accords with the position of R. Yose b. Haninah, for he said, "Any form of love not accompanied by rebuke is not love [because it is not honest]."

D. Said R. Simeon b. Laqish, "Rebuke produces peace: 'And Abraham complained to Abimelech about a well of water which Abimelech's servants had seized' (Gen. 21:25)."

E. That accords with the position of R. Simeon b. Laqish, for he said, "Any form of peace not accompanied by rebuke is not peace [because it is not honest]."

2. A. "Because of a well of water which Abimelech's servants had seized" (Gen. 21:25):

B. What is the definition of a robber?

C. R. Eleazar bar Qappara: "It is one who steals in plain sight, in light of the following verse: 'And they robbed all that came along that way by them' (Judges 9:25). Just as the way is in plain sight, so an act of theft is in plain sight."

D. R. Simeon b. Yohai derives proof from the following verse: "'And you have brought that which was taken by force and the lame' (Mal. 1:13). Just as the lame beast reveals its defect in public, so the robber steals in plain sight."

E. R. Yose in the name of R. Abbahu, R. Hezekiah, R. Abbahu in the name of R. Simeon b. Laqish: "If the theft is before nine people, it is a mere thief [because this is considered not in public], but if it is in front of ten, he is a thief."

F. R. Tanhuma in the name of R. Huna: "One is a thief only if he siezes an object right from the hand of the victim. That is in line with this verse: 'And he plucked the spear out of the Egyptian's hand' (2 Sam. 23:21)."

3. A. "Abimelech said, 'I do not know who has done this thing; you did not tell me, and I have not heard of it until today'" (Gen. 21:26):

B. "...you did not tell me" through a messenger.

No. 1 makes its point, a syllogism, by citing the fact of the base verse. No. 2 is inserted because it defines a word in the base verse, but the composition in no way intersects with the base verse. No. 3 explains how Abraham was supposed to have informed Abimelech of his complaint.

LIV:IV.

1. A. "Abraham set seven ewe lambs of the flock apart" (Gen. 21:28):

B. Said the Holy One, blessed be he, to him, "You have given him seven ewe lambs. By your life I shall postpone the joy of your descendants for seven generations.

C. "You have given him seven ewe lambs. By your life matching them his descendants [the Philistines] will kill seven righteous men among your descendants, and these are they: Hofni, Phineas, Samson, Saul and his three sons.

D. "You have given him seven ewe lambs. By your life, matching them the seven sanctuaries of your descendants will be destroyed, namely, the tent of meeting, the altars at Gilgal, Nob, Gibeon, Shiloh, and the two eternal houses of the sanctuary.

E. "You have given him seven ewe lambs. [By your life, matching them] my ark will spend seven months in the fields of the Philistines."

2. A. R. Jeremiah in the name of R. Samuel bar R. Isaac: "If the mere chicken of one of them had been lost, would he not have gone looking for it by knocking on doors, so as to get it back, but my ark spent seven months in the field and you pay not mind to it. I on my own will take care of it: 'His right hand and his holy arm have wrought salvation for him' (Ps. 98:1).

B. "That is in line with this verse: 'And the kine took the straight way' (1 Sam. 6:12). They went straight forward, turning their faces to the ark and [since the word for 'straight forward' contains the consonants for the word for 'song'] singing."

C. And what song did they sing?

D. R. Meir said, " 'The song of the sea. Here it is said, 'They went along...lowing as they went' (1 Sam. 6:12), and in that connection: 'For he is highly exalted' (Ex. 15:1). [The word for lowing' and the word for 'exalted' share the same consonants.]"

E. R. Yohanan said, "'O sing to the Lord a new song' (Ps. 98:1)."

F. R. Eleazar said, "'O Give thanks to the Lord, call upon his name' (Ps. 105:1)."

G. Rabbis said, "'The Lord reigns, let the earth rejoice' (Ps. 97:1)."

H. R. Jeremiah said, "The three: 'O sing to the Lord a new song, sing to the Lord, all the earth' (Ps. 96:1). 'The Lord reigns, let the peoples tremble' (Ps. 99:1)."

I. Elijah taught, "[Freedman:] 'Rise, rise, you acacia, soar, soar, in your abundant glory, beautiful in your gold embroidery, extolled in the innermost shrine of the sanctuary, encased between the two cherubim.'"

J. Said R. Samuel bar. R. Isaac, "How much did [Moses,] son of Amram labor so as to teach the art of song to the Levites. But you beasts are able to sing such a song on your own, without instruction. All power to you!"

No. 1 reverts to the theme of indignation at Abraham's coming to an agreement with Abimelech, forcefully imposing the theme of the later history of Israel upon the story at hand. No. 2 is tacked on because of the concluding reference to No. 1. Once more we see that a composition was complete before selection for use here, and the materials in our hands indicate that the compositors were reluctant to change much that they had received.

LIV:V.

1. A. "He said, 'These seven ewe lambs you will take from my a hand, that you may be a witness for me that I dug this well'" (Gen. 21:30):

B. Rabbis say, "The shepherds of Abimelech argued with the shepherds of Abraham. These said, 'The well is ours.' The others said, 'The well is ours.' The shepherds of Abraham said to them, 'If the water of the well sees the flock of one [of us] and rises to meet that flock, then the well belongs to the owner of that flock.'

C. "When the water saw the flock of our father Abraham, forthwith it rose.

D. "Said the Holy One, blessed be he, to him, 'It is a sign for your children that the flock will rise for them. That is in line with this verse: 'Spring up, o well, sing you unto it' (Num. 21:17)."

E. Said R. Isaac bar Haqorah, "In this passage itself we do not lack proof for the same proposition. What is written is not, 'That [the rising of the water] *is* a witness for me' but 'That it *will be* a witness for me' (Gen. 21:30)."

No. 1 links the present incident to the history of Israel in the wilderness. The behavior of the water of the well testifies to Abraham's and Israel's status.

LIV:VI.

1. A. "Abraham planted a tamarisk tree in Beer Sheba and called there on the name of the Lord, the Everlasting God" (Gen. 21:33):

B. R. Judah said, "The word for tamarisk, *eshel*, means orchard, since the letters supply the word for 'ask' (*shaal*), hence, 'Ask for whatever you want, figs, grapes pomegranates.'"

C. R. Nehemiah said, ""The word for tamarisk, *eshel*, means inn, since the letters supply the word for 'ask' (*shaal*), hence, 'Ask for whatever you want, meat, wine, eggs.'"

D. R. Azariah in the name of R. Judah: "The word refers to the sanhedrin, in line with this verse: 'Now Saul was in session in Gibeah under the tamarisk tree in Ramah' (1 Sam. 22:6). [The session refers to a session of the court.]"

E. In the view of R. Nehemiah, identifying the tamarisk with an inn, [we have the following picture:]

F. "Abraham would receive passersby. When they had eaten and drunk, he would say to them, 'Say a blessing.'

G. "They said to him, 'What should we say?'

H. "He said, 'Blessed is the God of the world, whose food we have eaten.'"

I. That is in line with this verse:"...and called there on the name of the Lord, the Everlasting God" (Gen. 21:33).

2. A. "And Abraham sojourned many days in the land of the Philistines" (Gen. 21:24):

B. It was more than the time he spent in Hebron. In Hebron he spent twenty-five years, and here he spent twenty-six years.

The interpretation of the verse, No. 1, rests on the meaning of the word for tamarisk. In the now familiar way, the exegete finds analogies to the word by rearranging its letters. In doing so, the several exegetes at hand link the minor detail to important elements of Israelite life as they imagine it. No. 2 adds a detail.

Chapter Twenty-Three

Parashah Fifty-Five.   Genesis 22:1-3

LV:I.

1. A. "And it came to pass after these things God tested Abraham" (Gen. 22:1):

    B. "You have given a banner to those that fear you, that it may be displayed because of the truth, *selah* " (Ps. 60:6).

    C. [Since the word for "banner" shares the consonants of the word for "test," we interpret:] test after test, one attainment of greatness after another, so as to test them in the world and so as to endow them with greatness in the world, like the ensign of a ship.

    D. And all this why? "...because of the truth, *selah*" (Ps. 60:6).

    E. [Since the word for "truth" and the word for "validate" share the same consonants, we interpret:] it is so that the attribute of justice may be validated in the world.

    F. For if someone should say, "He gives riches to whomever he wishes, and he impoverishes whomever he wishes, and whomever he wishes he makes king [all this without justice], and so too as to Abraham, when he wanted, he made him rich, and when he wanted, he made him king [and all this without justice], you may reply to him, saying, "Can you do what Abraham did?"

    G. "Abraham was a hundred years old when Isaac, his son, was born to him" (Gen. 21:5). And after all that anguish, it was stated to him, "Take your son" (Gen. 22:2).

    H. And he did not demur.

    I. Accordingly: "You have given a banner to those that fear you, that it may be displayed because of the truth, selah" (Ps. 60:6).

    J. "And it came to pass after these things God tested [i.e., displayed] Abraham" (Gen. 22:1)

The intersecting verse serves because it highlights the key word of the base verse, "try" or "test." The power of the intersecting verse is to demonstrate that what God did in favoring Abraham rested on justice, not capriciousness. The two plays on words are secondary, since the main point flows from the sense of

the intersecting verse. The insistence that what man does matters constitutes the
main point of the exegesis.

LV:II.

1. A.   "The Lord tries the righteous, but the wicked and him who loves
violence his soul hates" (Ps. 11:5):

B.   Said R. Jonathan, "A potter does not test a weak utensil, for if he hits it
just once, he will break it. What does the potter test? He tests the strong
ones, for even if he strikes them repeatedly, they will not break. So the Holy
One, blessed be he, does not try the wicked but the righteous: 'The Lord tries
the righteous' (Ps. 11:5)."

C.   Said R. Yose bar Haninah, "When a flax maker knows that the flax is in
good shape, then the more he beats it,the more it will improve and glisten.
When it is not of good quality, if he beats it just once, he will split it. So the
Holy One, blessed be he, does not try the wicked but the righteous: 'The Lord
tries the righteous' (Ps. 11:5). "

D.   Said R. Eleazar, "The matter may be compared to a householder who has
two heifers, one strong, one weak. On whom does he place the yoke? It is on
the one that is strong. So the Holy One, blessed be he, does not try the
wicked but the righteous: 'The Lord tries the righteous' (Ps. 11:5).

What God did for Abraham was just, and we now are told that Abraham was
chosen for the test because of his strength. The sequence of statements produces
a coherent message, that of the compositors. Abraham was the right choice for
the test.

LV:III.

1. A.   Another interpretation: "The Lord tries the righteous, but the wicked and
him who loves violence his soul hates" (Ps. 11:5):

B.   The cited verse speaks of Abraham: "And it came to pass after these
things God tested Abraham" (Gen. 22:1).

2. A.   R. Abin commenced discourse by citing the following verse of
Scripture: "Forasmuch as the king's word has power, and who may say to
him, 'What are you doing?'" (Qoh. 8:4).

B.   Said R. Abin to Rab, "The matter may be compared to the case of a
master who instructs his disciple, saying to him, 'Do not lend money on
interest,' while the master himself lends money on interest.

C.   "So the disciple says to him, 'You tell me not to lend money on
interest, but you lend money on interest.'

D. "He says to him, 'I tell you not to lend money on interest to Israelites, but it is all right to do so to the nations of the world, as it is said, 'To a foreigner you may lend on interest, but to your brother you shall not lend on interest' (Deut. 23:21). [The result of learning is an accurate knowledge of what one must and must not do.]

E. "So the Israelites said before the Holy One, blessed be he, 'Lord of the ages, "You have written in the Torah, 'You shall not take vengeance nor bear any grudge' (Lev. 19:18), but you do it yourself: 'The Lord avenges and is full of wrath, the Lord takes vengeance on his adversaries and keeps wrath for his enemies' (Nah. 1:2).'"

F. "Said the Holy One, blessed be he, to them, 'I have written in the Torah, "You shall not take vengeance nor bear any grudge" (Lev. 19:18), with reference to Israel. But as to the nations of the world: "You shall avenge the children of Israel" (Num. 31:2).'"

G. Along these same lines, it is written, "You shall not try the Lord your God" (Deut. 6:16), yet: "And it came to pass after these things God tested Abraham" (Gen. 22:1).

The message of the composite is not made explicit, because it is obvious. Israel may not test God, but God may test Israel. But that point is not the principal polemic before us. In the established context, the testing of Abraham stands for the trials of Israel, and God's testing of Abraham, hence of Israel, marks Israel in its history as special and holy, just as (we have seen at LV:I, II) Abraham was suitable for testing because he was strong and worthy of it. So through a somewhat circuitous route, asking a superficially theological question of theodicy, the compositors make a stunning point in linking Abraham's life to Israel's.

LV:IV.

1. A. "After these things" (Gen. 22:1):

B. The "things" were misgivings [or second thoughts].

C. Who had misgivings? Abraham.

D. He said, "I rejoiced and I gave joy to everyone, but I did not set aside for the Holy One, blessed be he, an ox or a ram."

E. Said the Holy One, blessed be he, to him, "It was because if you were told to sacrifice your son to me, you would not hold him back."

F. In accord with the view of R. Eleazar, who has said, "Any passage in which it is said, 'And the Lord,' refers to him and his court," it was the ministering angels who said to him, "This Abraham has rejoiced and given joy to everyone, but he did not set aside for the Holy One, blessed be he, an ox or a ram."

G. Said the Holy One, blessed be he, to them, "It was because, if he were told to sacrifice his son to me, he would not hold him back."

2. A. Isaac and Ishmael were arguing with one another. One said, "I am more beloved than you, for I was circumcised when I was thirteen years old."

B. The other said, "I am more beloved than you, for I was circumcised sooner, namely, on the eighth day."

C. Ishmael said to him, "I am more beloved than you, because I could have objected but didn't."

D. At that moment Isaac said, "Would that the Holy One, blessed be he, appeared to me and told me to cut off one of my limbs. I would not object."

E. Said the Holy One, blessed be he, to him, "If I should tell you to offer yourself up to me, you would not refuse."

No. 1 goes over the same matter twice, making a single point. Abraham's devotion to God brought him to the limit. No. 2 gives Isaac an important role in what is about to happen. He no longer is a passive victim, so he gets merit for what is done. Both he and Abraham make the same statement, namely, each is prepared to give the life most precious to himself: Abraham Isaac's, Isaac his own.

LV:V.

1. A. "With. what shall I come before the Lord and bow myself before God on high...[Shall I give my firstborn for my transgression, the fruit of my body for the sin of my soul]?" (Mic. 6:6):

B. R. Joshua in the name of R. Levi: "Even though the statement was made with reference to Mesha, king of Moab, it speaks in fact about Isaac:

C. "'With what shall I come before the Lord and bow myself before God on high...Shall I give my firstborn for my transgression, the fruit of my body for the sin of my soul?' (Mic. 6:6)."

The direct parallel to what is condemned by the prophet is now drawn. The uncited portion of the verse, about God's wanting humanity to do justice and love mercy, may well resolve the tension introduced by the intersecting verse. The text as we have it, however, presents no problems.

LV:VI.

1. A. "That God tested Abraham" (Gen. 22:1):

B. R. Yose the Galilean said, "He made him great, like the ensign of a ship. [The use of the word ensign derives from the shared consonants for the words "test" and "ensign."]

C. R. Aqiba said, "The word bears its literal meaning of testing, so that people should not say that he confused him or perplexed him so that he would not know what to do. [The test consisted of the three days of journeying, which gave Abraham plenty of time to think about what he was going to do.]"

2. A. "And he said to him, 'Abraham!' And he said, 'Here I am'" (Gen. 22:1):

B. Said R. Joshua, "In two passages Moses compared himself to Abraham.

C. "God said to him, "'Do not glorify yourself in the presence of the king and do not stand in the place of great men'" (Prov. 25:6).

D. "Abraham said, 'Here I am.' 'Here I am, ready for the priesthood, here I am, ready for the monarchy.'

E. "He had the merit of attaining the priesthood: 'The Lord has sworn and will not repent, you are a priest for ever after the manner of Melchizedek' (Ps. 110:4).

F. "He also had the merit of attaining the monarchy: 'You are a mighty prince among us' (Gen. 23:5).

G. "Moses for his part also said, 'Here I am' (Ex. 3:4). 'Here I am, ready for the priesthood, here I am, ready for the monarchy.'

H. "But the Holy One, blessed be he, said to him, 'Do not draw nigh hither' (Ex. 3:5). 'Drawing nigh' speaks of the priesthood: 'And the common man who draws nigh shall be put to death' (Num. 1:51). 'Hither' refers to the monarchy, as it is said, 'You have brought me thus far' (2 Sam. 7:18)."

No. 1 juxtaposes two unrelated comments, Yose's interpretation of the word, "test," familiar from LV:I, and Aqiba's observation about the three days' journey. No. 2 proceeds to link Abraham to Moses, a routine and important exercise. But Abraham was greater than Moses. The upshot is to link Abraham to Moses and to show how the biography of the patriarch prefigures the life of the founder of the nation. Since Moses is usually represented as meek and mild, the comparison presents a certain irony.

LV:VII.

1. A. "And he said , 'Take, I pray you, your son, your only son, Isaac, whom you love, and go to the land of Moriah, and offer him there as a burnt offering upon one of the mountains of which I shall tell you'" (Gen. 22:3):

B. He said to him, "Take, I pray you," meaning, "By your leave."

C. "...your son."

D. He said to him, "Which son?"

E. He said to him, "...your only son."

F. "This one is the only son of his mother, and that one is the only son of his mother."

G. "...whom you love."

H. "Where are the dividing walls within the womb? [I love them both.]"

I. "Isaac."

J. Why did he not tell him to begin with? It was so as to make Isaac still more precious in his view and so to give him a reward for each exchange.

K. This accords with the view of R. Yohanan, for R. Yohanan said, "'Go from your country"(Gen. 12:1), refers to your hyparchy.

L. "'From your birthplace' refers to your neighborhood.

M. "'From your father's house' refers literally to the house of your father.

N. "'To the land that I will show you:'" but why did he not inform him [in advance where that would be]?

O. "It was so as to make it still more precious in his view and to give him a reward for each step that he took [in perfect faith and reliance on God]."

P. Said R. Levi bar Haytah, , "'Go, go' (Gen. 12:1) is repeated twice [once in the present context, the other at Gen. 22:1, in going to offer up Isaac at Mount Moriah].

Q. "We do not know which of them is more precious, the first or the second. On the basis of that which is written, 'And take yourself to the land of Moriah' (Gen. 22:2), I know that the second was more precious than the first. [Mount Moriah is the holiest place in the Land of Israel.]"

2. A. "And take yourself to the land of Moriah" (Gen. 22:2):

B. R. Hiyya the Elder and R. Yannai:

C. One of them said, "[The meaning of the name, Moriah, which shares the consonants of the word for instruction] is, 'to the place from which instruction goes forth to the world, [namely, the Temple].'"

D. The other said, "It is the place from which awe goes forth to the world [since the word 'Moriah' and the word for 'awe' likewise share the same consonants.]"

E. Along these same lines, we deal with the matter of the word for ark [aron]:

F. R. Hiyya the Elder and R. Yannai:

G. One of them said, "It is the place from which light [orah] enters the world."

H. The other said, "It is the place from which reverence [*morah*] [for God] enters the world.

I. Along these same lines we deal with the matter of the word for sanctuary [DBYR]:

J. R Hiyya and R. Yannai:

K. One of them said, "It is the place from which divine speech (*dibbur*) goes forth to the world."

L. The other one said, "It is the place from which pestilence [as retribution] [*deber*] goes forth to the world."

M. Said R. Joshua b. Levi, "Moriah is so called because that is the place from which the Holy One, blessed be he, shoots [using the same consonants as appear in the word Moriah] at the nations of the world and brings them down to Gehenna."

N. R. Simeon b. Yohai says, "To the place that matches [using the same letters as Moriah] the house of the sanctuary that is above."

O. R. Yudan b. Palya said, "It is the place that he will show you [the consonants of the word for 'show' and of 'Moriah" being common]."

P. R. Phineas said, "It is to the seat of the dominion of the world."

Q. Rabbis said, "It is the place at which the incense will be offered: 'I will get me to the mountain of myrrh' (that is, *mor*) (Song 4:6)."

3. A. "...and offer him there as a burnt offering" (Gen. 22:2):

B. Said R. Yudan, "He said before him, 'Lord of all ages, is it possible to make an offering without a priest?'

C. "He said to him, 'I have already appointed you as priest: 'The Lord has sworn and will not repent, you are a priest for ever after the manner of Melchizedek' (Ps. 110:4)."

4. A. "...on one of the mountains of which I shall tell you" (Gen. 22:2):

B. That is in line with what R. Huna said in the name of R. Eliezer, "He whom the Holy One, blessed be he, puts in doubt and holds in suspense, namely, the righteous, he then informs, explaining the meaning of the matter.

C. "Thus: 'To the land that I will show you' (Gen. 12:1). 'On one of the mountains which I shall tell you' (Gen. 22:2). 'And make to it the proclamation that I shall tell you' (Jonah 3:2). 'Arise, go forth to the plain, and there I will speak with you' (Ez. 3:22)."

The phrase by phrase exegesis of the verse, at No. 1, produces an important syllogism. No. 2 provides a series of plays on the word Moriah. The point is to identify Moriah with the Temple, Abraham's binding of Isaac with the consecration of the Temple, and the Temple with the place from his sanctification, instruction, and authority radiate to the world. No. 3 supplies a missing detail and obviates an objection. No. 4 draws the present discourse in line with others.

LV:VIII.

1. A. "And Abraham rose early in the morning, [saddled his ass, and took two of his young men with him, and his son Isaac, and he cut the wood for the burnt offering and arose and went to the place which God had told him]" (Gen. 22:3):

B. Said R. Simeon b. Yohai, "Love disrupts the natural order of things, and hatred disrupts the natural order of things.

C. "Love disrupts the natural order of things we learn from the case of Abraham: '...he saddled his ass.' But did he not have any number of servants? [Why then did a slave not saddle the ass for him? Out of his dedication to his son, Abraham performed that menial task.] That proves love disrupts the natural order of things.

D. "Hatred disrupts the natural order of things we learn from the case of Balaam: 'And Balaam rose up early in the morning and saddled his ass' (Num. 22:21). But did he not have any number of servants? That proves hatred disrupts the natural order of things.

E. "Love disrupts the natural order of things we learn from the case of Joseph: 'And Joseph made his chariot ready' (Gen. 46:29). But did he not have any number of servants? But that proves love disrupts the natural order of things.

F. "Hatred disrupts the natural order of things we learn from the case of Pharaoh: 'And he made his chariot ready' (Ex. 14:6). But did he not have any number of servants? But that proves hatred disrupts the natural order of things."

2. A. Said R. Simeon b. Yohai, "Let one act of saddling an ass come and counteract another act of saddling the ass. May the act of saddling the ass done by our father Abraham, so as to go and carry out the will of him who spoke and brought the world into being counteract the act of saddling that was carried out by Balaam when he went to curse Israel.

B. "Let one act of preparing counteract another act of preparing. Let Joseph's act of preparing his chariot so as to meet his father serve to counteract Pharaoh's act of preparing to go and pursue Israel."

C. R. Ishmael taught on Tannaite authority, "Let the sword held in the hand serve to counteract the sword held in the hand.

D. "Let the sword held in the hand of Abraham, as it is said, 'Then Abraham put forth his hand and took the knife to slay his son' (Gen. 22:10) serve to counteract the sword taken by Pharaoh in hand: 'I will draw my sword, my hand shall destroy them' (Ex. 15:9)."

3. A. "...and took two of his young men with him, and his son Isaac" (Gen. 22:3):

B. Said R. Abbahu "Two men behaved most appropriately, Abraham and Saul.

C. "Abraham: '...and took two of his young men with him.'

D. "And Saul: 'And Saul...went, he and two men with him' (1 Sam. 28:8)."

4. A. "... and he cut the wood for the burnt offering [and arose and went to the place which God had told him]" (Gen. 22:3):

B. R. Hiyya bar Yose said the following in the name of R. Miasha, while it has been taught on Tannaite authority in the name of R. Benaiah, "[Since the word for wood is written in the plural, we know that Abraham cut up two logs. Hence] on account of the reward of the two acts of wood-cutting that our father, Abraham, carried out in preparing wood for the burnt offering, he received the merit that the Holy One, blessed be he, would cut the Sea in half before his children, as it is said: 'And the waters were divided' (Ex. 14:21)."

C. Said R. Levi, "Enough for you. This is as far [as we can go]. In point of fact, Abraham did what he could do, and the Holy One, blessed be he, did what he could do. [The comparison of Abraham's chopping wood to God's chopping the Sea in half is not appropriate.]"

5. A. "...and arose and went to the place which God had told him" (Gen. 22:3):

B. To him was given a reward for the act of rising and a reward for the act of going [which is why both acts are stated explicitly].

Abraham's action prefigured the salvation of Israel. In response to each gesture of Abraham, God produced a counterpart in saving Israel from its enemies. No. 1 executes a striking syllogism, with a beautifully balanced articulation. No. 2 goes over the ground of No. 1, giving somewhat different statement of the same idea. No. 3 has its own syllogism. The contribution of Nos. 2-3 is to link Israel's history to Abraham's biography, a familiar notion. It is proper to go with companions when making such a trip. No. 4 reverts to the polemic of Nos. 1-2. No. 5 makes a minor observation.

Chapter Twenty-Four

Parashah Fifty-Six. Genesis 22:4-19

LVI:I.

1. A. "On the third day Abraham lifted up his eyes and saw the place afar off" (Gen. 22:4):

    B. "After two days he will revive us, on the third day he will raise us up, that we may live in his presence" (Hos.16:2).

    C. On the third day of the tribes: "And Joseph said to them on the third day, 'This do and live'" (Gen. 42:18).

    D. On the third day of the giving of the Torah: "And it came to pass on the third day when it was morning" (Ex. 19:16).

    E. On the third day of the spies: "And hide yourselves there for three days" (Josh 2:16).

    F. On the third day of Jonah: "And Jonah was in the belly of the fish three days and three nights" (Jonah 2:1).

    G. On the third day of the return from the Exile: "And we abode there three days" (Ezra 8:32).

    H. On the third day of the resurrection of the dead: "After two days he will revive us, on the third day he will raise us up, that we may live in his presence" (Hos. 16:2).

    I. On the third day of Esther: "Now it came to pass on the third day that Esther put on her royal apparel" (Est. 5:1).

    J. She put on the monarchy of the house of her fathers.

    K. On account of what sort of merit?

    L. Rabbis say, "On account of the third day of the giving of the Torah."

    M. R. Levi said, "It is on account of the merit of the third day of Abraham: 'On the third day Abraham lifted up his eyes and saw the place afar off' (Gen. 22:4)."

2. A. "...lifted up his eyes and saw the place afar off" (Gen. 22:4):

B. What did he see? He saw a cloud attached to the mountain. He said, "It would appear that that is the place concerning which the Holy One, blessed be he, told me to offer up my son."

The third day marks the fulfillment of the promise, at the end of time of the resurrection of the dead, and, at appropriate moments, of Israel's redemption. The reference to the third day at Gen. 22:2 then invokes the entire panoply of Israel's history. The relevance of the composition emerges at the end. Prior to the concluding segment, the passage forms a kind of litany and falls into the category of a liturgy. Still, the recurrent hermeneutic which teaches that the stories of the patriarchs prefigure the history of Israel certainly makes its appearance.

LVI:II.

1. A. He said, "Isaac, my son, do you see what I see?"

   B. He said to him, "Yes."

   C. He said to the two lads, "Do you see what I see?"

   D. They said to him, "No."

   E. He said, "Since you do not see, 'Stay here with the ass' (Gen. 22:5), for you are like an ass."

   F. On the basis of this passage we learn that slaves are in the category of asses.

   G. Rabbis derive proof [that slaves are like livestock] from the matter of the giving of the Torah: "Six days you shall labor and do all your work, you...your daughter, your man-servant, your maid-servant, your cattle" (Ex. 20:10). [The slave is grouped next to the cattle.]

2. A. Said R. Isaac, "Will this place [the Temple mount] ever be distant from its owner [God]? Never, for Scripture says, 'This is my resting place for ever; here I will dwell, for I have desired it' (Ps. 132:14).

   B. "It will be when the one comes concerning whom it is written, 'Lowly and riding upon an ass' (Zech. 1:9)."

3. A. "I and the lad will go thus far [and worship and come again to you]" (Gen. 22:5):

   B. Said R. Joshua b. Levi, "[He said,] 'We shall go and see what will be the end of "thus."'" [Freedman, p. 492, n. 5: God had said, "Thus shall your seed be" (Gen. 15:5). So the sense is, "We will see how that can be fulfilled, now that I am to lose my son."]

4. A. "...and we will worship [through an act of prostration] and come again to you" (Gen. 22:5):

B. He thereby told him that he would come back from Mount Moriah whole and in peace [for he said that *we* shall come back].

5. A. Said R. Isaac, "And all was on account of the merit attained by the act of prostration.

B. "Abraham returned in peace from Mount Moriah only on account of the merit owing to the act of prostration: '...and we will worship [through an act of prostration] and come [then, on that account] again to you' (Gen. 22:5).

C. "The Israelites were redeemed only on account of the merit owing to the act of prostration: And the people believed...then they bowed their heads and prostrated themselves' (Ex. 4:31).

D. "The Torah was given only on account of the merit owing to the act of prostration: 'And worship [prostrate themselves] you afar off' (Ex. 24:1).

E. "Hannah was remembered only on account of the merit owing to the act of prostration: 'And they worshipped before the Lord' (1 Sam. 1:19).

F. "The exiles will be brought back only on account of the merit owing to the act of prostration: 'And it shall come to pass in that day that a great horn shall be blown and they shall come that were lost...and that were dispersed...and they shall worship the Lord in the holy mountain at Jerusalem' (Is. 27:13).

G. "The Temple was built only on account of the merit owing to the act of prostration: 'Exalt you the Lord our God and worship at his holy hill' (Ps. 99:9).

H. "The dead will live only on account of the merit owing to the act of prostration: 'Come let us worship and bend the knee, let us kneel before the Lord our maker' (Ps. 95:6)."

No. 1 explains both how Abraham knew it was the place and also why he left the lads behind. No. 2 then takes up the language of "seeing the place from afar," and by a play on the words, asks whether this place will ever be made far from its owner, that is, God. The answer is that it will not. No. 3 draws a lesson from the use of "thus" in the cited verses.

The sizable construction at No. 4 makes a simple point, to which our base verse provides its modest contribution. But its polemic is hardly simple. The entire history of Israel flows from its acts of worship ("prostration") and is unified by a single law. Every sort of advantage Israel has ever gained came about through worship. Hence what is besought, in the elegant survey, is the law of history. The Scripture then supplies those facts from which the governing law is derived.

LVI:III.

1. A. "And Abraham took the wood of the burnt offering and laid it on Isaac, his son; [and he took in his hand the fire and the knife]" (Gen. 22:6):

    B. It is like one who carries his own cross on his shoulder.

2. A. "...and he took in his hand the fire and the knife" (Gen. 22:6):

    B. Said R. Haninah, "Why is a knife called in Hebrew by a word that means 'the eater'? Because it turns food into edibles."

    C. Rabbis say, "Whatever acts of eating Israelites do in this world is on account of the merit attained through that 'eater,' [namely, that knife]."

3. A. "So they went both of them together" (Gen. 22:6):

    B. This one went to tie up and the other to be tied up, this one went to slaughter and the other to be slaughtered.

The successive units gloss the cited language. The force of No. 3 is to show that both parties concurred, thus Isaac gained merit from his agreement, as much as Abraham did. Isaac knew just what was going to happen.

LVI:IV.

1. A. "And Isaac said to his father Abraham, 'My father'" (Gen. 22:7):

    B. Samuel came to our father, Abraham. He said to him, "What sort of nonsense is troubling your heart? The son that was given to you at the age of a hundred are you going to slaughter?"

    C. He said to him, "Indeed so."

    D. He said to him, "And if he tests you still further than this, can you stand the test? 'If a thing be put to you as a trial, will you be wearied' (Job 4:2)?"

    E. He said to him, "And still more."

    F. He said to him, "Tomorrow he will [reverse himself and], tell you that you are a murderer, and you are liable."

    G. He said to him, "Indeed so."

    H. When he saw that he could accomplish nothing with him, he came to Isaac. He said to him, "Oh son of a miserable mother. He is going to slaughter you."

I. He said to him, "Indeed so.":

J. He said to him, "If so, all those lovely cloaks which your mother made will be the inheritance of Ishmael, the hated one of her house."

K. If a word does not make its way entirely, it makes its way in part. That is in line with this verse: "And Isaac said to his father Abraham, 'My father'" (Gen. 22:7). [That is, Isaac began to waver in his faith.]

L. Why does the verse state, "And Isaac said to Abraham *his* father and said, '*My* father'"? Why thus: "his father...my father"?

M. It was so that he should be filled with mercy for him.

N. And he said, "Behold the fire and the wood, but where is the lamb for a burnt offering?"

O. Abraham said, "May that man who incited you drown."

P. In any event: "'God will provide himself the lamb for a burnt offering,' and if not, then: 'the lamb for the burnt offering will be my son'" (Gen. 21:8).

Q. "So they went both of them together" (Gen. 22:6):

R. This one went to tie up and the other to be tied up, this one went to slaughter and the other to be slaughtered.

The sustained narrative turns the laconic description of the event into a dialogue, in which Isaac engages Abraham in a difficult conversation. I am inclined to see the whole as a unity. The main point recurs: Isaac, though troubled, accepted the decision.

LVI:V.

1. A. "When they came to the place of which God had told him, Abraham built an altar there" (Gen. 22:9):

B. Where was Isaac?

C. Said R. Levi, "He took him and hid him away. He thought, 'Lest that one who tried to seduce him throw a stone at him and render him unfit for use as an offering.'"

2. A. "...[and laid the wood in order] and bound Isaac his son [and laid him on the altar, upon the wood]" (Gen. 22:9):

B. R. Hinenah bar Isaac said, "All the time that Abraham was binding his son below, the Holy One, blessed be he, was binding the [heavenly] Princes of the nations above. [Hence the merit of the binding of Isaac served to protect Israel from the angelic patrons of the nations at large. They were bound and made powerless by God.] But they did not remain so."

C. "For when the Israelites separated themselves [from God] in the time of Jeremiah, the Holy One, blessed be he, said, 'Do you think that those bonds still endure?'

D. "So it is said, 'For shall they be liked tangled thorns for ever?' (Nahum 1:10).

E. "That is to say, 'For are the Princes bound for ever?'

F. "No, for 'When the Israelites are drunk according to their drink' (Nahum 1:10), then their bonds are released, as it is written, 'They shall be devoured as stubble fully dry' (Nahum 1:10)."

3. A. Now at the moment at which our father, Abraham, stretched out his hand to take up the knife to slaughter his son, the ministering angels wept. That is in line with this verse: "Behold, their valiant ones cry outside" (Is. 33:7).

B. What is the meaning of "outside"?

C. R. Azariah said, "It is outside the realm of the normal. It is not normal for him to slay his son with his own hand."

4. A. [We return to the exposition of Is. 33:7 in line with the binding of Isaac.] And what is it that the angels were saying? "'The highways lie waste" (Is. 33:7). Abraham is no longer receiving wayfarers.

B. "The wayfaring man ceases" (Is. 33:7), as in the verse, "It had ceased to be with Sarah" (Gen. 18:11).

C. "He has broken the covenant" (Is. 33:7). "But my covenant will I establish with Isaac" (Gen. 17:21).' [That covenant is being broken.]

D. "He has despised the cities" (Is. 33:7). "And Abraham dwelled between Kadesh and Shur" (Gen. 20:1).

E. "He does not regard man" (Is. 33:7). "Does Abraham have no merit in his favor?"

F. Now who will tell you that this passage does not speak only of the ministering angels? For here it is said, "Above the wood" (Gen. 22:9), and elsewhere: "Above him stood the seraphim" (Is. 6:2). [Accordingly, the use of the word "above," or "upon," invites the allusion to the angelic plea.]

No. 1 answers an obvious question. No. 2 reverts to a somewhat more sophisticated inquiry, once more relating the events in the lives of the patriarchs to the life of Israel later on. The justification of No. 2 comes only at 4.F. After the brief interpolation of No. 3, No. 4 takes the base-verse of Is. 33:7 and reads it in terms of the angels' plea to God for Isaac's life.

LVI:VI.

1: A. "Then Abraham put forth his hand and took the knife to slay his son" (Gen. 22:10):

B. Rab asked before R. Hiyya the Elder, "In the view of the Rabbi [Judah the Patriarch], how on the basis of Scripture do we know that the act of slaughter is to be carried out with an object that is movable?"

C. He said to him, "From the verse at hand: 'Then Abraham put forth his hand and took the knife' (Gen. 22:10)."

D. "Did he report this to you as a matter of lore, in which case he may change his mind, or was it on the basis of formal teaching that he told it to you, in which case he will not change his mind?

E. "For R. Levi repeated on Tannaite authority, 'If [sharp flints] were held fast [to the ground and not movable]', they are unfit. If they were dug up and then affixed to the ground, lo, they are valid.

F. "'For we have learned in the Mishnah: **If one slaughters with a hand-sickle, flint, or reed, the act of slaughter is valid [M. Hul. 1:2].**"

G. Said R. Yose bar Abin, "There are five teachings that have been stated with regard to a reed stalk: With it one may not slaughter, circumcise, cut meat, wipe the hands, or pick the teeth, because an evil spirit rules over it."

The base verse merely provides a fact for the stated syllogism.

LVI:VII.

1. A. "But the angel of the Lord called to him from heaven and said, 'Abraham, Abraham!' [And he said, 'Here am I']" (Gen. 22:11).

B. R. Hiyya repeated on Tannaite authority, "The repeated name represents an expression of affection and eagerness."

C. R. Eliezer said, "It means that he spoke both to him and to coming generations.

D. "You have not got a single generation in which there is no one of the standing of Abraham, and you have not got a single generation in which there is no one of the standing of Jacob, Moses, and Samuel."

2. A. "He said, 'Do not lay your hand on the lad or do anything to him, for now I know that you fear God, seeing you have not withheld your son, your only son, from me'" (Gen. 22:12):

B. Where was the knife ["Do not lay your *hand* "]?

C. Tears from the ministering angels had fallen on it and dissolved it.

D. Then he said, "So I shall strangle him."

E. He said to him, "Do not lay your hand on the lad."

F. Then he said, "Then let us at least draw a drop of blood [symbolic of the offering]."

G. He said to him, "'...or do anything to him.'"

H. "...for now I know [that you fear God]:"

I. "Now I am telling everybody that you love me: 'seeing you have not withheld your son, your only son, from me' (Gen. 22:12).

J. "And do not claim, 'Whatever sickness does not affect one's own body is no sickness,' for I credit the merit to you for this action as though I had said to you, 'Offer me yourself,' and you did not hold back."

No. 1 allows the exegete to make the important point that each generation lives out the lives of the patriarchs. No. 2 constructs a dialogue for God and Abraham. Out of the angel's statement Abraham's answers are worked out.

LVI:VIII.

1. A. Said R. Aha, "[Abraham said to God,] 'Are there jokes even before you? Yesterday you said to me, "For in Isaac shall seed be called to you" (Gen. 21:12). And then you went back on your word and said, "Take your son" (Gen. 22:2). And now: "Do not lay your hand on the lad or do anything to him." [What's next?]

B. "Said the Holy One, blessed be he, to him, 'Abraham, "My covenant I will not profane" (Ps. 89:35). "And I *will* establish my covenant with Isaac" (Gen. 17:21).

C. "'True, I commanded you, "Take now your son" (Gen. 33:2). "I will not alter what has gone out of my lips" (Ps. 89:35). Did I ever tell you to kill him? No, I told you, 'Bring him up.'

D. "'Well and good! You did indeed bring him up. Now take him down.'"

No. 1 raises the obvious question of how God can have changed his mind and given so many conflicting promises and instructions to Abraham. The exegete shows that he did not contradict himself. The underlying polemic favors God's faithfulness and reliability.

LVI:IX.

1. A. "And Abraham lifted up his eyes and looked, and behold, behind him was a ram, [caught in a thicket by his horns. And Abraham went and took the ram and offered it up as a burnt offering instead of his son]" (Gen. 22:13):

B. What is the meaning of the word for "behind"?

C. Said R. Yudan, "'Behind' in the sense of 'after,' that is, after all that happens, Israel nonetheless will be embroiled in transgressions and perplexed by sorrows. But in the end, they will be redeemed by the horns of a ram: 'And the Lord will blow the horn' (Zech. 9:14)."

D. Said R. Judah bar Simon, "'After' all generations Israel nonetheless will be embroiled in transgressions and perplexed by sorrows. But in the end, they will be redeemed by the horns of a ram: 'And the Lord God will blow the horn' (Zech. 9:14)."

E. Said R. Hinena bar Isaac, "All through the days of the year Israelites are embroiled in transgressions and perplexed by sorrows. But on the New Year they take the ram's horn and sound it, so in the end, they will be redeemed by the horns of a ram: 'And the Lord God will blow the horn' (Zech. 9:14)."

F. R. Abba bar R. Pappi, R. Joshua of Siknin in the name of R. Levi: "Since our father, Abraham, saw the ram get himself out of one thicket only to be trapped in another, the Holy One, blessed be he, said to him, 'So your descendants will be entangled in one kingdom after another, struggling from Babylonia to Media, from Media to Greece, from Greece to Edom. But in the end, they will be redeemed by the horns of a ram: 'And the Lord God will blow the horn...the Lord of Hosts will defend them' (Zech. 9:14-5)."

2. A. "... And Abraham went and took the ram and offered it up as a burnt offering instead of his son]" (Gen. 22:13):

B. R. Yudan in the name of R. Benaiah: "He said before him, 'Lord of all ages, regard the blood of this ram as though it were the blood of Isaac, my son, its innards as though they were the innards of Isaac my son.'"

C. That [explanation of the word "instead"] accords with what we have learned in the Mishnah: "Lo, this is instead of that, this is in exchange for that, this is in place of that" -- lo, such is an act of exchanging [one beast for another in the sacrificial rite, and both beasts then are held to be sanctified] [M. Tem.   5:5].

D. R. Phineas in the name of R. Benaiah: "He said before him, 'Lord of all ages, regard it as though I had offered up my son, Isaac, first, and afterward had offered up the ram in his place.'"

E. That [sense of the word "instead"] is in line with this verse: "And Jothan his son reigned in his stead" 2 Kgs. 15:7).

F. That accords with what we have learned in the Mishnah: [If one says, "I vow a sacrifice] like the lamb," or "like the animals of the Temple stalls" [it is a valid vow] [M. Ned. 1:3].

G. R. Yohanan said, "That is in the sense of 'like the lamb of the daily whole offering.'" [One who made such a statement has vowed to bring a lamb.]

H. R. Simeon b. Laqish said, "...'like the ram of Abraham, our father.'" [One who has made such a statement has vowed to bring a ram.]

I. There they say, "...'like the offspring of a sin-offering.'"

J. Bar Qappara taught on Tannaite authority, "...'like a lamb which has never given suck [thus, a ram].'"

The power of No. 1 is to link the life of the private person, affected by transgression, and the history of the nation, troubled by its wandering among the kingdoms. From the perspective of the Land of Israel, the issue is not Exile but the rule of foreigners. In both cases the power of the ram's horn to redeem the individual and the nation finds its origin in the Binding of Isaac. The exegetical thrust, linking the lives of the patriarchs to the life of the nation, thus brings the narrative back to the paradigm of individual being, so from patriarch to nation to person. The path leads in both directions, of course, in a fluid movement of meaning. No. 2 works on the language of "instead," a technical term in the cult, and so links the Binding of Isaac to the Temple cult.

LVI:X.

1. A. "So Abraham called the name of that place 'The Lord will provide,' [as it is said to this day, 'On the mount of the Lord it shall be provided']" (Gen. 22:14):

B. R. Bibi the Elder in the name of R. Yohanan: "He said before him, 'Lord of all ages, from the time that you said to me, "Take your son, your only son" (Gen. 22:2), I could have replied to you, "Yesterday you said to me, 'For in Isaac shall seed be called to you' (Gen. 21:12), and now you say, 'Take your son, your only son' (Gen. 22:2)." God forbid, did I not do it? But I suppressed my love so as to carry out your will. May it always please you, Lord our God, that, when the children of Isaac will come into trouble, you remember in their behalf that act of binding and be filled with mercy for them.'"

2. A. [Jerusalem had various names.] Abraham called it "will provide." "So Abraham called the name of that place 'The Lord will provide,' [as it is said to this day, 'On the mount of the Lord it shall be provided']" (Gen. 22:14).

B. Shem called it "Salem." "And Melchizedek, king of Salem" (Gen. 14:18).

C. Said the Holy One, blessed be he, "If I call the place '...will provide,' as Abraham called it, Shem, a righteous man, will have a legitimate complaint.

D. "If I call it '...Salem,' as Shem did, then Abraham, a righteous man, will have a legitimate complaint.

E. "So therefore I will call it by the name that both of them have given it, thus: *'Yireh Shalem* ,' or Jerusalem ['He will see peace']."

3. A. R. Berekhiah in the name of R. Helbo: "While the place was still called Salem, the Holy One, blessed be he, made a tabernacle and prayed in it: 'In Salem also is set his tabernacle and his dwelling-place in Zion' (Ps. 76:3).

B. "And what did he say there? 'May it be pleasing for me to witness the building of the house of the sanctuary.'"

4. A. ["So Abraham called the name of that place 'The Lord will provide,' as it is said to this day, 'On the mount of the Lord it shall be provided'" (Gen. 22:14)]: This teaches that the Holy One, blessed be he, showed him the house of the sanctuary as it was built, wiped out, and built once more:

B. "So Abraham called the name of that place 'The Lord will provide'" refers to the house of the sanctuary when it was built, in line with this verse: "Three times in the year will all your males be seen...in the place where he shall choose" (Gen. 16:16).

C. "as it is said to this day, 'On the mount of the Lord'" refers to the Temple in its hour of destruction, in line with this verse: "For the mountain of Zion, which is desolate" (Lam. 5:18).'

D. "...it shall be provided" [refers to the Temple] rebuilt and restored in the coming age, in line with this verse: "When the Lord has built up Zion, when he has been seen in his glory" (Ps. 102:17).

No. 1 explains the future tense of "the Lord will provide," or "see to it," emphasizing once more the future tense of the action. No. 2 explains the name of the spot in terms of the twin etiology. No. 3 pursues the same line of thought. No. 4 reverts to the overriding theme of the correspondence of the life of the patriarch to the history of Israel, now explicitly linked. The history of the Temple is contained in Abraham's name for the place.

LVI:XI.

1. A. "And the angel of the Lord called to Abraham a second time from heaven and said, 'By myself I have sworn, [says the Lord, because you have done this thing, and have not withheld your son, your only son, I will indeed bless you and I will multiply your descendants as the stars of heaven and as the sand which is on the seashore. And your descendants shall possess the gate of their

enemies, and by your descendants shall all the nations of the earth bless themselves, because you have obeyed my voice']" (Gen. 22:15-17):

B. What need was there for taking such an oath?

C. He said to him, "Take an oath to me that you will never again test me or Isaac my son."

2. A. What need was there for taking such an oath?

B. R. Levi in the name of R. Hama bar Hanina, "He said to him, 'Take an oath to me that you will never again test me.'

C. "The matter may be compared to the case of a king who was married to a noble lady. She produced a first son from him, and then he divorced her, [remarried her, so she produced] a second son, and he divorced her again, a third son, and he divorced her again. When she had produced a tenth son, all of them got together and said to him, 'Take an oath to us that you will never again divorce our mother.'

D. "So when Abraham had been tested for the tenth time, he said to him, 'Take an oath to me that you will never again test me.'"

3. A. Said R. Hanan, "'...because you have done this thing...'! It was the tenth trial and he refers to it as '...this [one] thing...'? But this also is the last, since it outweighs all the rest.

B. "For if he had not accepted this last trial, he would have lost the merit of all that he had already done."

4. A. "...I will indeed bless you [and I will multiply your descendants as the stars of heaven and as the sand which is on the seashore. And your descendants shall possess the gate of their enemies, and by your descendants shall all the nations of the earth bless themselves, because you have obeyed my voice]" (Gen. 22:17):

B. [Since the Hebrew makes use of the verb, "bless," two times, translated "indeed bless," we explain the duplicated verb to mean] a blessing for the father, a blessing for the son.

C. [Similarly, the duplicated verb for "multiply" means] myriads for the father and myriads for the son.

5. A. "...And your descendants shall possess the gate of their enemies...:"

B. Rabbi said, "This refers to Palmyra. Happy is he who will witness the fall of Palmyra, since it participated in both destructions of the Temple."

C. R. Yudan and R. Hanina:

D. One of them said, "At the destruction of the first Temple it provided eighty thousand archers."

E. The other said, "At the destruction of the Temple it supplied eight thousand archers."

6. A. "So Abraham returned to his young men[and they arose and went together to Beersheba and Abraham dwelt at Beersheba]" (Gen. 22:19):

B. And where was Isaac?

C. R. Berekhiah in the name of Rabbis over there [in Babylonia]: "He had sent him to Shem to study Torah with him. [Why the emphasis on Torah-study?]

D. "The matter may be compared to the case of a woman who got rich from her spinning. She said, 'Since it is from this spindle that I got rich, it will never leave my hand.'"

E. R. Yose bar Haninah said, "He sent him away by night, on account of the evil eye."

F. For from the moment that Hananiah, Mishael, and Azariah came up out of the fiery furnace, their names are not mentioned again in the narrative. So where had they gone?

G. R. Eleazar said, "They died in spit."

H. R. Yose bar Haninah said, "They died on account of the evil eye."

I. R. Joshua b. Levi said, "They changed their residence and went to Joshua b. Yehosedeq to study Torah, in line with this verse: 'Hear now, O Joshua the high priest, you and your fellows that sit before you, for they are men that are a sign' (Zech. 3:8)."

J. R. Tanhum bar Abina in the name of R. Hinena: "It was on that stipulation that Hananiah, Mishael, and Azariah descended to the fiery furnace, namely, that he should turn them into a sign."

No. 1 spells out the matter of the oath, which is an unusual and weighty procedure. No. 2 then carries forward a statement made in No. 1, though it has no bearing upon the larger issue. No. 3 and No. 4 gloss the base verse. No. 5 answers a basic question left open by the narrative. F-J were included in the composition before the whole was inserted here, and hence the syllogism preceded the exegesis.

Chapter Twenty-Five

Parashah Fifty-Seven. Genesis 22:20-24

LVII:I.

1. A. "And it came to pass after these things it was told Abraham,'Behold, Milcah also has borne children to your brother Nahor'" (Gen. 22:20):

    B. "A tranquil heart is the life of the flesh" (Prov. 14:30):

    C. While he was still standing on Mount Moriah, he was given the good news that his son's mate had been born [that is, Rebecca]: "Behold, Milcah also has borne children to your brother Nahor" (Gen. 22:20). ["Uz, the first born, Buz his brother, Kemuel the father of Aram. Chesed, Hazo, Pildash, Jidlaph, and Bethuel. And Bethuel became the father of Rebekah" (Gen. 22:24).]

The point of the inclusion of the genealogical pericope is spelled out. The question cannot be avoided. The answer certainly is not farfetched.

LVII.II.

1. A. "As cold waters to a faint soul, so is good news from a far country" (Prov. 25:25):

    B. Just as for good news, one says, "Blessed is he who is good and does good," so for cool water one says, "Blessed is he who is good and does good."

    C. "As cold waters to a faint soul, so is good news from a far country" (Prov. 25:25).

    D. While he was still standing on Mount Moriah, he was given the good news that his son's mate had been born [that is, Rebecca]: "Behold, Milcah also has borne children to your brother Nahor" (Gen. 22:20).

We have a restatement of the foregoing pericope.

LVII:III.

1. A. "And it came to pass after these things" (Gen. 22:20):

B. There were misgivings then [for the word for "things" can also mean "thoughts" or "misgivings"].

C. On whose part? On Abraham's.

D. Abraham said, "Had [Isaac] died on Mount Moriah, would he have not died without children? Now I shall quickly marry him off to the daughters of Aner, Eshkol, or Mamre, all of them righteous women. For to me what difference does the matter of genealogy matter?"

E. Said to him the Holy One, blessed be he, "You do not have to do so: Your son's mate has already been born [that is, Rebecca]: 'Behold, Milcah also has borne children to your brother Nahor' (Gen. 22:20)."

2. A. What is the meaning of "also"?

B. Just as in this case, there were eight children for the mistress and four to the concubine, so in the case of this one, the mistress will have eight children, and the concubine four.

No. 1 restates the basic notion, now in a richer version. No. 2 links details of distinct stories to form a single tapestry.

LVII:IV.

1. A. Another matter: Abraham was concerned about suffering [so, as stated above, "And it came to pass after these things" (Gen. 22:20) means that there were misgivings then. On whose part? On Abraham's.]

B. Said the Holy One, blessed be he, "You do not have to worry. The one who is going to receive suffering has now been born, namely, 'Uz [who is Job], the first born and Buz his brother.'"

2. A. [Since Uz is the same as Job, a contemporary of Abraham, we proceed to discuss Job.] When did Job live?

B. R. Simeon b. Laqish in the name of Bar Qappara: "He lived in the time of Abraham: 'Uz, the first born and Buz his brother' (Gen. 22:20). It is written, 'There was a man in the land of Uz. His name was Job' (Job 1:1)."

C. R. Abba bar Kahana said, "Job lived in the time of Jacob."

D. For R. Abba bar Kahana said, "Dinah was the wife of Job."

E. R. Levi said, "Job lived in the time of the tribes [Reuben and Judah, who confessed their sins to Jacob (Freedman, p. 506, n. 2)], in line with this verse: 'Which wise man have told and have not hid it from their fathers' (Job 15:18).

F. "And what reward did they receive on that account? 'Unto them alone the land was given' (Job 15:19)."

G. R. Yose bar Halputa said, "When the Israelites went down to Egypt he was born, and when they came up from Egypt, he died. You find that the period in which Job flourished was two hundred and ten years, and the Israelites spent two hundred and ten years in Egypt. What happened was that Satan came to condemn Israel, and God sicked him on Job."

H. R. Hinena bar Aha and R. Hama bar Haninah:

I. R. Hinena bar Aha said, "The matter may be compared to the case of a shepherd who was standing and watching his flock. A wolf came along and attacked him. He said, 'Throw him a he-goat on which to spend his wrath.'"

J. R. Hama bar Haninah said, "The matter may be compared to the case of a king who was sitting at a banquet and a dog came along and attacked him. He said, 'Give him a bone on which to spend his wrath.'"

K. [Reverting to G:] "That is in line with this verse: 'God delivers me to the ungodly and throws me into the hands of the wicked' (Job 16:11), and would that people were righteous, but they are indeed wicked."

L. R. Yose bar Judah said, "He lived in the time that the judges ruled, in line with this verse: 'Behold, all you yourselves have seen it, why then are you altogether vain' (Job 27:12). That is to say, 'You have seen my deeds, you have seen the deeds of my contemporaries.' 'You have seen my deeds, which are the performance of religious duties and of good deeds.' 'You have seen the deeds of my contemporaries, who want to pay whores right out of the granaries, while righteous men do not pay whores right out of the granaries,' as it is said, 'You have loved a harlot's hire out of every grain-floor' (Hos. 9:1)."

M. R. Samuel bar Nahman said, "He lived in the time of the Chaldeans: 'The Chaldeans set themselves in three bands' (Job 1:17)."

N. R. Nathan said, "He lived in the time of the Queen of Sheba: 'And the Sabeans made a raid and took them away' (Job 1:15)."

O. R. Joshua said, "He lived in the days of Ahasuerus: 'Let there be sought for the king young virgins, fair to look on' (Est. 2:2), and it is written, 'And there were no women found so fair as the daughters of Job' (Job 42:15)."

P. R. Simeon b. Laqish said, "Job never lived at all."

Q. Opinions attributed to R. Simeon b. Laqish are contradictory. For there R. Simeon b. Laqish in the name of Bar Qappara said, "He lived in the time of Abraham: ['Uz, the first born and Buz his brother' (Gen. 22:20). It is written, 'There was a man in the land of Uz' (Job 1:1).]"

R. But here, [Simeon b. Laqish] said, "He did not live at all."

S. [In this context, Simeon b. Laqish did not mean that Job had not lived at all.] But the point is that he did not live through the sufferings that are written in his regard.

T. Then why are they written in his regard? To indicate that if they had come upon him, he would have been able to endure them.

U. R. Yohanan said, "He was among those who came back up from the Exile, and he was an Israelite. Therefore the laws of mourning are derived from his example."

V. Thus it is written, "Then Job arose and tore his cloak" (Job 1:20), on the basis of which we derive the rule that one must tear his cloak while standing up.

W. R. Haninah said, "He was a gentile."

X. R. Hiyya taught on Tannaite authority: "[God speaks,] 'There was one righteous man who arose among the nations of the world, and I paid off his reward and dismissed him. Who was this? It was Job.'"

3. A. "Uz, the first born, [Buz his brother, Kemuel the father of Aram. Chesed, Hazo, Pildash, Jidlaph, and Bethuel. And Bethuel became the father of Rebekah. These eight Milcah bore to Nahor, Abraham's brother. Moreover, his concubine, whose name was Reumah, bore Tebah, Gaham, Tahash, and Maacah]" (Gen. 22:24):

B. R. Yudan and R. Judah bar Simon in the name of R. Joshua: "Laban and Kemuel are the same person. Why then was he called Kemuel? Because he rose up (kam) against the nation of God (el)."

4. A. "...his concubine, whose name was Reumah, [bore Tebah, Gaham, Tahash, and Maacah]" (Gen. 22:24):

B. Said R. Isaac, "All of these names mean one thing, which is punishment:

C. "'Tebah' is slaughter, 'Gaham' is burn, 'Tahash' is silence, and 'Maacah' is crush.' [In all cases, these are things they do to others]."

Since No. 1 introduces Job, No. 2 is tacked on, the whole joined before selection for use here. No. 3 provides glosses on the names, so too No. 4. But the relevance of Job is more than merely redactional. In fact the testing of Abraham and the testing of Job bear deep points of correspondence, and the theme is what joins the two. So the redactors' interest in Job is hardly routine or formal.

Chapter Twenty-Six

Parashah Fifty-Eight.   Genesis 23:1-19

LVIII:I.

1. A. "Sarah lived a hundred and twenty-seven years. These were the years of the life of Sarah" (Gen. 23:1):

    B. "The Lord knows the days of those who are without blemish, and their inheritance shall be for ever" (Ps. 37:18):

    C. Just as they are without blemish, so their years are without blemish.

    D. The one who is twenty-years old is like the one who is seven years old as to beauty, the one who is a hundred years old is like the one who is twenty-years old as to sin.

2. A. Another interpretation: "The Lord knows the days of those who are without blemish" refers to Sarah.

    B. "... and their inheritance shall be for ever." "These were the years of the life of Sarah" (Gen. 23:1).

    No. 1 does not necessarily refer to Sarah. No. 2 links the intersecting verse to the base verse. The praise of Sarah derives from the intersecting verse, as proved by the fact that the years of Sarah are carefully enumerated.

LVIII:II.

1. A. "The sun rises and the sun goes down" (Qoh. 1:5):

    B. Said R. Abba, "Now do we not know that the sun rises and the sun sets? But the sense is this: before the Holy One, blessed be he, makes the sun of one righteous man set, he brings up into the sky the sun of another righteous man.

    C. "On the day that R. Aqiba died, Our Rabbi [Judah the Patriarch] was born. In his regard, they recited the following verse: 'The sun rises and the sun goes down' (Qoh. 1:5).

D. "On the day on which Our Rabbi died, R. Adda bar Ahbah was born. In his regard, they recited the following verse: 'The sun rises and the sun goes down' (Qoh. 1:5).

E. "On the day on which R. Ada died, R. Abin was born. In his regard, they recited the following verse: 'The sun rises and the sun goes down' (Qoh. 1:5).

F. "On the day on which R. Abin died, R. Abin his son was born. In his regard, they recited the following verse: 'The sun rises and the sun goes down' (Qoh. 1:5).

G. "On the day on which R. Abin died, Abba Hoshaiah of Taraya was born. In his regard, they recited the following verse: 'The sun rises and the sun goes down' (Qoh. 1:5).

H. "On the day on which Abba Hoshaiah of Taraya died, R. Hoshaiah was born. In his regard, they recited the following verse: 'The sun rises and the sun goes down' (Qoh. 1:5).

I. "Before the Holy One, blessed be he, made the sun of Moses set, he brought up into the sky the sun of Joshua: 'And the Lord said to Moses, Take you Joshua, the son of Nun' (Num. 27:18).

J. "Before the Holy One, blessed be he, made the sun of Joshua set, he brought up into the sky the sun of Othniel, son of Kenaz: 'And Othniel the son of Kenaz took it' (Joshua 15:17).

K. "Before the Holy One, blessed be he, made the sun of Eli set, he brought up into the sky the sun of Samuel: 'And the lamp of God was not yet gone out, and Samuel was laid down to sleep in the Temple of the Lord' (1 Sam. 3:3)."

L. Said R. Yohanan, "He was like an unblemished calf."

M. [Reverting to K:] "Before the Holy One, blessed be he, made the sun of Sarah set, he brought up into the sky the sun of Rebecca: 'Behold Milcah also has borne children' (Gen. 22:20). 'Sarah lived a hundred and twenty-seven years. These were the years of the life of Sarah' (Gen. 23:1)."

One rule of Israel's history is yielded by the facts at hand. Israel is never left without an appropriate hero or heroine. The relevance the long discourse becomes clear at the end. We in point of fact take up exactly where the preceding *Parashah* has left off, and the bridge from one passage to the next has been constructed.

LVIII:III.

1. A. "A hundred and twenty-seven years" (Gen. 23:1):

B. R. Aqiba was giving an exposition and the community dozed. He wanted to wake them up. He said, "On what account did Esther rule over one hundred twenty-seven provinces? But it was to indicate that Esther, who was the daughter of Sarah's daughter, who lived a hundred and twenty-seven years, should rule over one hundred twenty-seven provinces."

The nonsense-statement produces the effect of linking Sarah's life to Esther's. But the salvific theme thus reenters the tale: Esther and Mordecai at the end, like the patriarchs and matriarchs at the outset.

LVIII:IV.

1. A. "And Sarah died in Kiriath Arba (that is Hebron) in the land of Canaan, [and Abraham went in to mourn for Sarah and to weep for her]" (Gen. 23:2):

B. That place [Kiriath Arba, city of four] had four names, Eshkol, Mamre, Kiriath Arba, and Hebron.

C. Why was it called Kiriath Arba [city of four]?

D. Because of the fact that four righteous ones lived there, Aner, Eshkol, Mamre, and Abraham.

E. Furthermore, four righteous men were circumcised there, Aner, Eshkol, Mamre, and Abraham.

F. Furthermore, four righteous men were buried there, the first man, Abraham, Isaac, and Jacob.

G. Not only so, but the four matriarchs were buried there: Eve, Sarah, Rebecca, and Leah.

H. It is also because it had four owners, Anak and his three sons.

I. Said R. Azariah, "It is because Abraham, our father, went forth from there and pursued four kings, rulers of the world."

J. It is furthermore because it came up as the lot for four, first, Judah, then Caleb, then the priests, and finally, the Levites.

K. It is furthermore because it is one of the four least impressive places in the land of Israel.

L. What are they?

M. R. Isaac said, "Dor, Nofeth Dor, Timnath Serah, and Hebron."

N. Rabbis said, "Dannah, Kiriath-Sannah, Timnath-Serah, and Hebron."

The passage answers an obvious question, with no bearing upon the exegesis of the passage. I see no polemic linking the story of Abraham to the later history of Israel. It is simply a catalogue of holy names associated with the place, a different thing entirely.

LVIII:V.

1. A. "...and Abraham went in to mourn for Sarah [and to weep for her]" (Gen. 23:2):

   B. Whence did he come?

   C. R. Levi said, "From the grave of Terah he came to that of Sarah."

   D. Said to him R. Yose, "But is it not the case that from the burial of Terah to the burial of Sarah there was an interval of two years? Hence, whence did he come? He came from Mount Moriah."

The verse at hand receives a light gloss.

LVIII:VI.

1. A. "And Abraham rose up from upon the face of his dead" (Gen. 23:3):

   B. This [silence about the name of the deceased] teaches that he saw the angel of death defying him."

2. A. Said R. Yohanan, "From whence do we derive scriptural support for that which we have learned in the Mishnah: **He who has yet to bury his deceased is exempt from the requirement of reciting the Shema [M. Ber. 3:1]**?

   B. "It is from this passage: 'And Abraham rose up from upon the face of his dead and [without reciting his prayers, he turned directly to the business of the burial, for] he said...' (Gen. 23:3)."

3. A. "[...and said to the Hittites,] 'I am a stranger and a sojourner among you; [give me property among you for a burying place, that I may bury my dead out of my sight]'" (Gen. 23:4):

   B. [The terms "stranger" and "sojourner" are mutually contradictory, in the way in which] one cannot be both a tenant and a landlord.

   C. [So he said to him,] "If I want, I am a tenant, and if not, I am the landlord.

   D. "For so did the Holy One, blessed be he, say to me, 'To your seed will I give this land' (Gen. 15:18)."

4. A. "...give me property among you for a burying place, that I may bury my dead out of my sight" (Gen. 23:4):

   B. "Enough for one corpse."

5. A. "The Hittites answered Abraham, 'Hear us, my lord, you are a mighty prince among us'" (Gen. 23:5):

B. "You are prince over us, you are God over us, 'bury your dead in the choicest of our sepulchres, [none of us will withhold from you his sepulchre or hinder you from burying your dead]' (Gen. 23:6), even many deceased."

6. A. "Abraham rose and bowed to the Hittites, the people of the land" (Gen. 23:7):

B. On the basis of this statement we learn that people are expected to give thanks for good news.

No. 1 imposes an incomplete thought on the verse at hand. No. 2 derives from it a scriptural basis for a rule. No. 3 introduces the paradox of Abraham's buying real estate in a country the whole of which God has already given him. This sifts the sense of the discourse and brings it into line with God's promises. No. 4 contributes a minor gloss. No. 5 augments the statement of the Hittites. No. 6 falls into the same category is No. 2.

LVIII:VII.

1. A. "[And he said to them,] 'If you are willing that I should bury my dead [out of my sight, hear me,] and entreat for me [Ephron the son of Zohar that he may give me the cave of Machpelah, which he owns; it is at the end of his field']" (Gen. 23:8-9):

B. "Let me meet him, or you serve as go-between for me, or if not, then beg him for me."

2. A. "Now Ephron was sitting among the Hittites" (Gen. 23:10):

B. R. Isaac said, "The word for sitting is written defectively, meaning that it was on that very day that they had appointed him to be chief commander.

C. "It was so that a great man should not have to do business with an unimportant person."

3. A. "And Ephron the Hittites answered Abraham in the hearing of the Hittites, of all those who went in at the gate of his city" (Gen. 23:10):

B. Said R. Phineas, "This teaches that everyone locked his door and went to pay their respects to Sarah."

4. A. "[No, my lord, hear me, I give you the field, and I give you the cave that is in it; in the presence of the sons of my people I give it to you; bury your dead. Then Abraham bowed down before the people of the land. And he said to Ephron in the hearing of the people of the land, 'But if you will, hear me; I will give the price of the field; accept it from me, that I may bury my dead there.' Ephron answered Abraham, 'My lord, listen to me; a piece of land worth four hundred shekels of silver, [what is that between you and me? Bury your dead.' Abraham agreed with Ephron; and Abraham weighed out for Ephron the silver which he had named in the hearing of the Hittites, four hundred shekels of silver, according to the weights current among the merchants]" (Gen. 23:11-16):

B. Said R. Haninah, "All references to shekels in the Torah speak of *selas*, in the Prophetic books speak of *litras*, and in the Writings, speak of a *centenarium* ."

C. R. Abba bar Yudan in the name of R. Judah bar Simon: "Except for the shekels paid out to Ephron, which were *centenarii* .

D. "So it is written: 'He who has an evil eye hastens after riches' (Prov. 28:22).

E. "'He who has an evil eye hastens after riches' refers to Ephron, who was jealous of the wealth of Abraham.

F. "'And does not know that want shall come upon him' (Prov. 28:22): for the Torah took away a letter from his name, specifically an O [i.e., a *vav*].

G. "Specifically, it is written, 'Abraham agreed with Ephron; and Abraham weighed out for Ephrn...' The second reference to Ephron is written without the O {i.e., the *vav*]."

5. A. "...according to the weights current among the merchants" (Gen. 23:16):

B. R. Abba bar Abina said, "It was acceptable legal tender."

No. 1 imposes a light gloss on Abraham's statement. Nos. 2 and 3 do the same. No. 4 moves on to make its own point and supply an intersecting verse. No. 5 glosses lightly.

LVIII:VIII.

1. A. "So the field of Ephron in Machpelah, [which was to the east of Mamre, the field with the grave which was in it, and all the trees that were in the field, throughout its whole area, was made over to Abraham as a possession in the presence of the Hittites before all who went in at the gate of his city]" (Gen. 23:17-18):

B. [The verb for "made over" bears the meaning of "rose," because] it had fallen in status and now rose. For it had belonged to an unimportant person but now passed into the hands of a significant person.

C. "...in Machpelah" [a word which bears the consonants meaning "double"]: This usage teaches that it doubled in value in everyone's view. For whoever was buried there was now assured that his reward was doubled and redoubled.

D. Said R. Abbahu, "[Since the word bears consonants that can mean double over] the meaning is that the Holy One, blessed be he, had doubled the length of the first man so as to bury him in that cave."

2. A. "...the field with the grave which was in it, and all the trees that were in the field, throughout its whole area:"

B. Said Rabbi, "How do we know on the basis of Scripture the rule that we have learned in the Mishnah: He who sells a field has to write in the deed marks that characterize the field [M. B.B. 4:5]?

C. "It is from this verse: '...the field with the grave which was in it, and all the trees that were in the field, throughout its whole area.'"

3. A. "... was made over to Abraham as a possession in the presence of the Hittites before all who went in at the gate of his city]" (Gen. 23:17-18):

B. Said R. Eleazar, "How much ink has been poured out, how many quills broken, so as repeatedly to write the words, 'the Hittites,' who occur ten times in the passage at hand. It is a counterpart to the Ten Commandments.

C. "This serves to teach you that whoever clarifies a dealing for a righteous person is as though he kept all of the Ten Commandments."

D. Said R. Yudan, "'The sons of Barzillai' is written five times, as a counterpart to the five scrolls of the Torah.

E. "This serves to teach you that whoever gives a piece of bread to a righteous person is as if he fulfilled the teachings of the entire Torah."

No. 1 investigates the meaning of the name of the cave. No. 2 links the cited verse to a Mishnah-rule. The syllogism of No. 3 invokes the cited verse, among others, to make its point.

LVIII:IX.

1. A. "After this, Abraham buried [Sarah his wife in the cave of the field of Machpelah east of Mamre, that is Hebron, in the land of Canaan]" (Gen. 23:19):

B. "He who follows after righteousness and love finds life, prosperity, and honor" (Prov. 21:21).

C. "He who follows after righteousness" refers to Abraham, as it is said, "That they make keep the way of the Lord, to do righteousness and justice" (Gen. 18:19).

D. "...and love:" for he dealt lovingly with Sarah [in burying her].

E. "...finds life, [prosperity, and honor]" (Prov. 21:21): 'And these are the days of the years of Abraham's life, which he lived, a hundred and seventy-five years' (Gen. 25:7).

F. "...prosperity, and honor:"

G. Said R. Samuel bar R. Isaac, "Said the Holy One, blessed be he, to him, 'My profession is to practice acts of love. Since you have taken over my profession, put on my cloak as well [as a fellow-craftsman, wearing the same signifying clothing]: 'And Abraham was old, well advanced in age' (Gen. 24:1)." [God dresses in the garment of old age, so Dan. 7:13 (Freedman, p. 515, n. 1)]."

The intersecting verse leads to a stunning climax at G. In redactional terms the framer has built a bridge from story to story, joining the burial of Sarah to the beginning of the next account, Gen. 24:1. In theological terms he has linked Abraham to God. In moral terms he has made the principal trait of God, hence of the human being like God, the practice of acts of lovingkindness, that is, those acts of *hesed*, translated here, "love," that God does as the divine profession.

Chapter Twenty-Seven

Parashah Fifty-Nine. Genesis 24:1-11

LIX:I.

1. A. "Now Abraham was old, well advanced in years; and the Lord had blessed Abraham in all things" (Gen. 24:1):

B. "The hoary head is a crown of glory, it is found in the way of righteousness" (Prov. 16:31).

C. R. Meir went to Mamala. He saw that everyone there had black hair [so there were no old people]. He said to them, "What family do you come from? Could it be that you come from the family of Eli, concerning whom it is written, 'And all the increase of your house shall die as young men' (1 Sam. 2:33)?"

D. They said to him, "Rabbi, pray for us."

E. He said to them, "Go and carry out works of righteousness [charity], and you will gain the merit of enjoying old age.

F. "What is the biblical verse that indicates it? 'The hoary head is a crown of glory, it is found in the way of righteousness' (Prov. 16:31).

G. "From whom do you learn that lesson? It is from Abraham. Because concerning him it is written, 'To do righteous deeds' (Gen. 18:19), he had the merit of attaining old age: 'Now Abraham was old, well advanced in years.'"

The intersecting verse is brought into relationship to the life of Abraham, which itself is clarified. Abraham had the merit of reaching a ripe old age because of the acts of righteousness (charity) that he had performed.

LIX:II.

1. A. "Strength and dignity are her clothing, and she laughs at the time to come" (Prov. 31:25):

B. "Strength and dignity are her clothing," namely, the clothing of the Torah.

C. When is that the case? When "she makes a person laugh at the time to come." [That is, the Torah makes a person unafraid of death.]

D. When does God give the reward for Torah[-study]? In the age to come.

E. From whom do you derive that lesson? From Abraham.

F. Since it is written concerning him, "That they may keep the way of the Lord, to do righteousness and justice" (Gen. 18:19), he had the merit of attaining old age: "Now Abraham was old, well advanced in years."

2. A. "Length of days are in her right hand" (Prov. 33:16) in the world to come.

B. "In her left hand are riches and honor" (Prov. 3:16) in this world.

C. From whom do you derive that lesson? From Abraham.

D. Since it is written concerning him, "That they may keep the way of the Lord, to do righteousness and justice" (Gen. 18:19), he had the merit of attaining old age: "Now Abraham was old, well advanced in years."

No. 1 makes the same point as the foregoing. No. 2 proceeds to go over the same ground.

LIX:III.

1. A. R. Aha commenced discourse [by citing the following verse:] "And even unto old age and hoary hairs, O God, do not forsake me" (Ps. 71:18).

B. Said R. Aha, "Do not 'old age' and 'hoary hairs' add up to the same thing? But the sense is that if you have given me old age, give me hoary hairs."

C. From whom do you derive that lesson? From Abraham.

D. Since it is written concerning him, "That they may keep the way of the Lord, to do righteousness and justice" (Gen. 18:19), he had the merit of attaining old age: "Now Abraham was old, well advanced in years."

We go over familiar ground.

LIX:IV.

1. A. R. Samuel bar R. Isaac commenced discourse by citing the following verse: "He who follows after righteousness and mercy finds life, prosperity and honor" (Prov. 21:21).

B. When R. Samuel bar R. Isaac died, winds and cyclones came and tore up all the splendid trees of the Land of Israel. Why so? Because he would take branches from them and walk before the bride [to celebrate her marriage].

C. And rabbis would say, "Why does he do this and so bring disrepute to the Torah"

D. Said R. Zeira, "Let him be. He knows just what he is doing."

E. When he died, they went out to pay their respects. A tongue of flame came forth and appeared like a branch of a myrtle and took a position between his bier and the community. The people said, "See how the branches interpose between the old man [Freedman:] in good stead]."

2. A. Another teaching:

B. "He who follows after righteousness and love finds life, prosperity, and honor" (Prov. 21:21).

C. "He who follows after righteousness" refers to Abraham, as it is said, "That they make keep the way of the Lord, to do righteousness and justice" (Gen. 18:19).

D. "...and love:" for he dealt lovingly with Sarah [in burying her].

E. "...finds life, [prosperity, and honor]" (Prov. 21:21): ""And these are the days of the years of Abraham's life, which he lived, a hundred and seventy-five years" (Gen. 25:7).

F. "...prosperity, and honor:"

G. Said R. Samuel bar R. Isaac, "Said the Holy One, blessed be he, to him, 'My profession is to practice acts of love. Since you have taken over my profession, put on my cloak as well [as a fellow-craftsman, wearing the same signifying clothing]: 'And Abraham was old, well advanced in age' (Gen. 24:1)." [God dresses in the garment of old age, so Dan. 7:13 (Freedman, p. 515, n. 1)]."

The composite is inserted because of No. 2, which goes over familiar ground in linking the intersecting verse to the case of Abraham. No. 1 presents some textual problems.

LIX:V.

1. A. "You are fairer than the children of men" (Ps. 45:3):

B. You have found praise among the beings of the upper world,

C. as it says, "Behold, their valiant ones cry without" (Is. 33:7).

D. You have been praised among the beings of the lower world,

E. as it says, "You are a mighty prince among us"(Gen. 23:6).

F. "Therefore God has blessed you forever" (Ps. 45:3).

G. "Now Abraham was old, well advanced in years; and the Lord had blessed Abraham in all things" (Gen. 24:1).

2. A. "Who shall ascend into the mountain of the Lord, and who shall stand in his holy place? [He who has clean hands and a pure heart, who has not taken his life without cause, and who has not sworn deceitfully. He shall receive a blessing from the Lord]" (Ps. 24:3-5):

B. "Who shall ascend into the mountain of the Lord" speaks of Abraham, as it is said, "For now I know that you fear God" (Gen. 22:12).

C. "...and who shall stand in his holy place" speaks of Abraham, as it is said, "And Abraham got up early in the morning, to the place where he had stood before the Lord" (Gen. 19:27).

D. "He who has clean hands," as it is said, "I will not take a thread or a shoe latchet" (Gen. 14:23).

E. "...and a pure heart." "Far be it from you to do such a thing" (Gen. 18:25).

F. "...who has not taken his life without cause," the life of Nimrod.

G. "...who has not sworn deceitfully." "I have lifted up my hand to the Lord, God most high, maker of heaven and earth" (Gen. 14:22).

H. "He shall receive a blessing from the Lord." "Now Abraham was old, well advanced in years; and the Lord had blessed Abraham in all things" (Gen. 24:1).

3. A. Abraham blessed everyone, as it is said, "And through you will all the families of the earth be blessed" (Gen. 12:3). But who blesses Abraham? The Holy One, blessed be he, blesses him, as it is said, "...and the Lord had blessed Abraham in all things" (Gen. 24:1).

B. Moses was the ensign of Israel, as it is said, "Why strive you with me? Why do you make me the ensign before the Lord" (Ex. 17:2). But who was the ensign of Moses? It was God: "And Moses built an altar and called the name of it, 'The Lord is my ensign'" (Ex. 17:14).

C. David was the shepherd of Israel, as it says, "'You shall shepherd my people, Israel'" (1 Chr. 11:2). But who was the shepherd of David? It was the Holy One, blessed be he, as it is said, "The Lord is *my* shepherd, I shall not want" (Ps. 23:1).

D. Jerusalem is the light of the world, as it is said, "And nations shall walk in your light" (Is. 60:3). But who is the light of Jerusalem? It is God, as it is written, "But the Lord shall be for you an everlasting light" (Is. 60:3).

No. 1 simply interweaves a number of verses to indicate that the cited intersecting verse speaks of Abraham. No. 2 follows the same pattern. What we are given is summaries of the life and virtues of Abraham, as these illustrate passages of Psalms and are illustrated by them. No. 3 goes along its own way, making one point through three examples. It is included because it makes use of our base verse. Its basic point is that the lives of the patriarchs prefigure the entire history of Israel.

LIX:VI.

1.   A. "Now Abraham was old" (Gen. 24:1):

    B. [Since the word for "old" contains the consonants that can mean, "this" and "acquired," we interpret the statement as follows:] "This one has acquired both ages, [this age and the age to come]."

2.   A. "...well advanced in years..." (Gen. 24:1):

    B. Said R. Aha, "You can find someone who enjoys the status of old age [that is, authority in the community] but not the years, or the years but not the status of old age.

    C. "But here we find the status of old age matching the years, and the years matching the status: '...well advanced in years.'"

3.   A. [Since the Hebrew reads, "coming along in years," we wish to know to what "coming" refers.] R. Yudan in the name of R. Judah bar Simon: "He had come into both worlds."

    B. R. Berekhiah in the name of R. Abba: "He entered the gateway to the life of the age to come."

    C. R. Isaac: "He came into those days concerning which it is written, 'Before the evil days come' (Qoh. 12:1)."

The exegesis of the base verse follows two paths, Nos. 1, 2 and No. 3. The former deals with the reference to both age and advanced years. The later focuses on the philological problem.

LIX:VII.

1.   A. "And the Lord had blessed Abraham in all things" (Gen. 24:1):

    B. R. Judah said, "It is because he gave him a girl-child."

    C. Said R. Nehemiah, "Then the focus of the king's household [was this daughter] but no blessing is recorded for her? Rather, the sense of the verse, 'And the Lord had blessed Abraham in all things' is that he did not give him a girl-child."

D. [Explaining the meaning of "all things,"] R. Levi said, "There were three matters. [God] gave him rule over his impulse to do evil, Ishmael repented, and his storehouse lacked for nothing."

E. R. Levi in the name of R. Hama bar Hanina: "That he did not go and put him to the test again [was the blessing to which reference is made]."

The base verse is subjected to a careful analysis. A number of details complete the incomplete thought of Scripture.

LIX:VIII.

1. A. "And Abraham said to his servant, the oldest of his house, [who had charge of all that he had, 'Put your hand under my thigh, and I will make you swear by the Lord, the God of heaven and of the earth, that you will not take a wife for my son from the daughters of the Canaanites, among whom I dwell, but will go to my country and to my kindred and take a wife for my son Isaac']" (Gen. 24:2-4):

B. [He was called "the oldest of his house:"] because his face resembled Abraham's [a play on the word "oldest"].

2. A. "...who had charge of all that he had:" because like Abraham he had dominion over his impulse to do evil.

3. A. "...Put your hand under my thigh:"

B. Said R. Berekhiah, "Because it was given to them by it [namely, the mark of circumcision], therefore he took his oath by it."

4. A. "... and I will make you swear by the Lord, the God of heaven and of the earth:"

B. Said R. Phineas, "Before I made him known to his creatures, 'the God of heaven.'

C. "and now that I have made him known to his creatures, 'and of the earth.'"

5. A. "...that you will not take a wife for my son from the daughters of the Canaanites, among whom I dwell:"

B. He admonished him against choosing a wife from among the daughters of Aner, Eshcol, and Mamre.

6. A. "...but will go to my country and to my kindred and take a wife for my son Isaac" (Gen. 24:2-4):

B. Said R. Isaac, "Though the grain of your locale is mediocre, sow seed out of that grain."

The systematic glossing of the cited verse presents no problems. The basic interest is to link the servant to Abraham and to explain the intent of the passage.

LIX:IX.

1. A. "The servant said to him, 'Perhaps [the woman may not be willing to follow me to this land; must I then take your son back to the land from which you came?]'" (Gen. 24:5):

B. That is in line with this verse: "Canaan, the balances of deceit are in his hand" (Hos. 12:8).

C. "Canaan" refers to Eliezer.

D. "... the balances of deceit are in his hand" (Hos. 12:8): For he sat and weighed the prospects of his own daughter, "Is she suitable or not suitable [to be married to Isaac]?"

E. "To rob the beloved one" (Hos. 12:8): to rob the one whom the world loves, Isaac.

F. He spoke to him in this way until he came to the word "perhaps," [which can be read, "to me." Thus he indicated that he had in mind a marriage between Isaac and his own family. Then his statement's sense was,] "Perhaps I may give him my daughter."

G. Abraham said to him, "You are cursed and my son is blessed, and a curse cannot cleave to a blessing."

Once more a close reading of the verse yields fresh dimensions for the dialogue at hand. The exegete has an interest in what Eliezer was thinking and provides a more detailed picture of the transaction between the two men. Eliezer is now shown to have been duplicitous.

LIX:X.

1. A. "Abraham said to him, 'See to it that you do not take my son back there. The Lord, the God of heaven, who took me from my father's house and from the land of my birth and who spoke to me and swore to me, "To your descendants I will give this land," [will send his angel before you, and you shall take a wife for my son from there]'" (Gen. 24:7):

B. "...from my father's house" refers to the house of his father.

C. "...and from the land of my birth" refers to his neighborhood.

D. "... and who spoke to me" in Haran.

E. "...and swore to me" between the parts.

F. "...will send his angel before you:"

G. R. Dosa says, "Lo, this refers to a particular angel. When Abraham said, 'He will send his angel before you,' the Holy One, blessed be he, appointed two angels, one to bring Rebecca out, the other to accompany Eliezer."

H. "But if the woman is not willing to follow you, then you will be free from this oath of mine. Only my son you must not take back there" (Gen. 24:8):

I. The word "only" serves as exclusionary. "My son may not go back there, but the son of my son [Jacob] may go back there."

The exegete glosses the cited verses, item by item. I see no substantial polemic.

LIX:XI.

1. A. "Then the servant took ten of his master's camels and departed, [taking all sorts of choice gifts from his master, and he arose and went to Mesopotamia, to the city of Nahor]" (Gen. 24:10):

B. The camels of our father, Abraham, were well known everywhere, because they went forth muzzled [so as not to steal other peoples' crops].

2. A. "...taking all sorts of choice gifts from his master:"

B. Said R. Helbo, "This refers to a deed of gift [from Abraham to Isaac, handing over his estate to him]."

3. A. "... and he arose and went [to Mesopotamia, to the city of Nahor]" (Gen. 24:10):

B. R. Berekhiah in the name of R. Isaac, "He made the trip in one day."

C. That accords with the view of R. Berekhiah in the name of R. Isaac, "'And I came this day to the fountain' (Gen. 24:42) means, 'Today I left and today I arrived.'"

4. A. [In line with the foregoing, we now list others who made miraculously speedy trips.] "You have made the land to shake, you have cleft it. Heal its breaches, for it totters" (Ps. 60:4):

B. "You have made the land to shake..." in the days of Abraham [by shortening the journey of Eliezer].

C. "...you have cleft it" in the time of Eliezer.

D. "Heal its breaches" in the days of Jacob.

E. "...for it totters" in the days of the inhabitants of Nob.

5. A. That is in line with this verse: "And Ishbi-benob, who was of the sons of the giant" (2 Sam. 21:16) raised up his shield [to attack David], so David jumped back eighteen cubits.

B. This one was afraid of that one, and that one was afraid of this one.

C. This one was afraid of that one, thinking, "If this one can jump eighteen cubits backward in this way, how far frontward can he leap?"

D. That one was afraid of this one: "If he can raise up a shield so lightly, how can I withstand him?"

E. At that moment David said, "Would that one of the sons of my sister would come and help me." Forthwith: "But Abishai, son of Zeruiah, helped him" (2 Sam. 21:17).

F. Now was he standing right behind the gate? [Obviously not, he had to make the trip very rapidly.]

G. Rabbis say, "Even if he had been standing at the other end of the world, the Holy One, blessed be he, could carry him and bring him in the blink of an eye, so that righteous man should not have to stand in distress.

H. "That is in line with this verse: 'But Abishai, son of Zeruiah, helped him, and he smote the Philistine and killed him. Then the men of David swore to him' (2 Sam. 21:17)."

Nos. 1, 2, 3 gloss the verse. No. 1 explains the reference to the well-known camels of his master. Nos. 4-5 then are tacked on because of the substance of No. 2. Obviously Nos. 4-5 reached their present state before inclusion here.

LIX:XII.

1. A. "[And he made the camels kneel down outside the city by the well of water] at the time of evening, the time when women go out to draw water" (Gen. 24:11):

B.   Said R. Huna, "When someone goes to find a wife and hears dogs barking, does he have the ability to know what they are saying? [How did Eliezer know what was going on] '...at the time of evening, the time when women go out to draw water'?"

The sense of the passage is not self-evident to me.

Chapter Twenty-Eight

Parashah Sixty.   Genesis 24:12-67

LX:I.

1. A. "And he said, 'O Lord, God of my master, Abraham, grant me success today, I pray you, and show steadfast love to my master Abraham'" (Gen. 24:12):

    B. "Who is among you who fears the Lord, who hears the voice of his servant, who walked in darkness and has no light? Let him trust in the name of the Lord and rely upon his God." (Is. 50:10).

    C. "Who is among you who fears the Lord" refers to Abraham.

    D. "...who hears the voice of his servant" (Is. 50:10): Who hears the voice of the Holy One, blessed be he, to his servant.

    E. "...who walked in darkness" in Mesopotamia and its environs.

    F. "...and has no light" And who gave light to him? The Holy One, blessed be he, gave light to him wherever he travelled.

    G. "...Let him trust in the name of the Lord and rely upon his God." (Is. 50:10). "And you have found his heart faithful before you" (Neh. 9:8).

2. A. Another interpretation of the verse, "Who is among you who fears the Lord, who hears the voice of his servant, who walked in darkness and has no light? Let him trust in the name of the Lord and rely upon his God" (Is. 50:10):

    B. "Who is among you who fears the Lord" speaks of Eliezer.

    C. "who hears the voice of his servant," for he was the servant of Abraham.

    D. "...who walked in darkness" when he went to bring Rebecca.

    E. "...and has no light" for who was there to give light for him? It was the Holy One, blessed be he, who gave light for him through lightning and meteors.

    F. "Let him trust in the name of the Lord and rely upon his God" (Is. 50:10).

G. "And he said, 'O Lord, God of my master, Abraham, grant me success today, I pray you, and show steadfast love to my master Abraham'" (Gen. 24:12).

In the present composition both halves of the presentation of the intersecting verse fit together, since we speak first of Abraham, then of Eliezer. The base verse finds a fresh perspective as Eliezer's trip is brought into relationship with Abraham's life, the former a microcosm of the latter.

LX:II.

1. A. "A servant who deals wisely shall have rule over a son who brings shame and shall have part of the inheritance among the brothers" (Prov. 17:2).

B. "A servant who deals wisely" speaks of Eliezer.

C. What marked his wise dealing?

D. He said, "The curse that has applied to that man [me] still pertains [since, as a Canaanite, I must be a slave to someone]. Perhaps an Ethiopian or a barbarian will come and enslave me. It is better for me to be a slave in this household and not in some other household."

E. "...shall rule over a son who brings shame" speaks of Isaac, who [by his devotion to God] shamed the entire world when he was bound on the altar.

F. "...and shall have part of the inheritance among the brothers" (Prov. 17:2): For among the brothers he will share out the inheritance.

G. Just as these [Israelites] call to mind the merit accrued by the patriarchs, so this one [namely, Eliezer] called to mind the merit accrued by the patriarchs:

H. "And he said, 'O Lord, God of my master, Abraham, [grant me success today, I pray you, and show steadfast love to my master Abraham']" (Gen. 24:12).

2. A. "...grant me success today, I pray you, and show steadfast love to my master Abraham" (Gen. 24:12):

B. "Today you began the work. Now finish it 'and show steadfast love to my master Abraham.'"

C. Said R. Haggai in the name of R. Isaac, "Everyone needs steadfast love from God, even Abraham, who had ridiculed [the capacities of the servant], saying, 'He will send his angel before you' (Gen. 24:7), needs steadfast love from God, as it is said, 'and show steadfast love to my master Abraham' (Gen. 24:12)."

No. 1 explains the base verse by calling attention to the Canaanite's invocation of the God of Abraham and explaining his doing so. No. 2 moves on to construct a dialogue for Eliezer.

LX:III.

1. A. "Behold, I am standing by the spring of water, and the daughters of the the men of the city are coming out to draw water. Let the maiden to whom I shall say, 'Pray let down your jar that I may drink,' and who shall say, 'Drink, and I will water your camels' -- let her be the one whom you have appointed for your servant Isaac. By this I shall know that you have shown steadfast love to my master" (Gen. 24:13-14):

B. Four asked for what they wanted in an improper way. To three what they asked was given in a proper way, and to the fourth what was asked was not given in the proper way.

C. These are they: Eliezer, Caleb, Saul, and Jephthah.

D. Eliezer: "Let the maiden to whom I shall say, 'Pray let down your jar that I may drink,' and who shall say, 'Drink, and I will water your camels' -- let her be the one whom you have appointed for your servant Isaac. By this I shall know that you have shown steadfast love to my master" (Gen. 24:13-14).

E. [What made this statement improper?] Would that apply even to a serving girl?

F. But the Holy One, blessed be he, designated Rebecca for him, so in a proper way he gave him what he had asked.

G. Caleb: "And Caleb said, 'Whoever smites Kiriath Sepher and takes it, to him will I give Achsah, my daughter, as wife'" (Joshua 15:16).

H. Is it possible that he would give her even to a slave? The Holy One, blessed be he, designated Othniel for him.

I. Saul: "And the men of Israel said, 'Have you seen this man who has come up? Surely he has come up to defy Israel, and the man who kills him the king will enrich with great riches and will give him his daughter'" (1 Sam. 17:25).

J. Is it possible that he would give her even to a slave? The Holy One, blessed be he, designated David for him.

K. Jephthah asked not in a proper way, and it was not in a proper way that the Holy One, blessed be he, responded to him.

L. He asked not in a proper way, as it is said, "And Jephthah made a vow to the Lord and said, 'If you will give the Ammonites into my hand, then whoever comes forth from the doors of my house to meet me when I return victorious from the Ammonites shall be the Lord's, and I will offer him up for a burnt offering'" (Judges 11:30-31).

M. Said to him the Holy One, blessed be he, "If a camel or an ass or a dog should come forth from your house, would you then offer him up as a burnt offering before me?"

N. What did the Holy One, blessed be he, do to him?

O. He responded to him not in a proper way and designated his daughter, as it is said, "Then Jephthah came to his home at Mizpah, and behold, his daughter came out to meet him with timbrels and with dances; she was his only child; beside her he had neither son nor daughter. And when he saw her, he tore his clothes and said, 'Alas my daughter, you have brought me very low and you have become the cause of great trouble to me'" (Judges 11:34-35):

P. R. Yohanan and R. Simeon b. Laqish:

Q. R. Yohanan said, "He was liable to pay off his statement of sanctification by paying the monetary worth involved."

R. R. Simeon b. Laqish said, "He was not even liable to pay off his statement of sanctification by paying the monetary worth involved."

S. "For we have learned in the Mishnah: "If one has made a statement concerning an unclean beast or a beast that was blemished and unfit for the altar, 'Lo, this one is in the status of a burnt-offering,' he has said nothing, 'Lo, this is for the purpose of a burnt-offering,' then the thing is to be sold and a burnt offering purchased with the proceeds" [M. Temurah 5:6]."

T. But was Phineas not there, who could have released him from his vow?

U. Phineas said, "Lo, he needs me, and should I go to him? And not only so, but I am high priest and the son of a high priest, and should I go to an ordinary person?"

V. Jephthah said, "I am the head of the rulers of Israel, and should I go to Phineas?"

W. [Due to the stubbornness of] this one and that one, the girl perished.

X. In a proverb people say, "Between the midwife and the woman in travail, the poor woman's baby is going to die."

Y. Both of them, therefore, were punished on account of her blood.

Z. Jephthah's limbs fell off of him limb by limb, and he therefore was buried in many places. That is in line with the following verse of Scripture: "And Jephthah died and was buried in the cities of Gilead" (Judges 12:7). What is written is not, "in a city of Gilead" but rather, "In the cities of Gilead." [This teaches that a limb would fall off from him here and was buried where it fell, and a limb would fall off of him in another place and was buried where it fell.]

AA. From Phineas the Holy Spirit was taken away, as it is said, "Phineas, the son of Eleazar, was ruler over them; in times past the Lord was with him" (1 Chr. 9:20). What is written is not, "...is ruler over them," but rather, "...was ruler over them, i. e. in times past."

BB. He had been with him in times past, but not now.

The composition draws upon the base verse in the work of establishing its own syllogism. Its illustration of how not to ask, and of God's mode of answering nonetheless, follows its own program and logic of composition.

LX:IV.

1. A. "Before he had done speaking, behold, Rebecca, who was born to Bethuel, the son of Milcah, the wife of Nahor, Abraham,'s brother, came out with her water jar upon her shoulder" (Gen. 24:15):

B. R. Simeon taught on Tannaite authority, "There were three who were answered while they were still speaking, and these are they: Eliezer, the slave of Abraham, Moses, and Solomon.

C. "Eliezer: 'Before he had done speaking, behold, Rebecca, who was born to Bethuel, the son of Milcah, the wife of Nahor, Abraham,'s brother, came out with her water jar upon her shoulder' (Gen. 24:15).

D. "Moses: 'And it came to pass, as he made an end of speaking all these words, that the ground did cleave asunder' (Num. 16:31).

E. "Solomon: 'Now when Solomon had made an end of praying, the fire came down from heaven' (2 Chr. 7:1)."

The composition once again draws upon the base verse in the work of establishing its own syllogism. These exemplify God's willingness to respond promptly to prayer.

LX:V.

1. A. "The maiden was very fair to look upon, a virgin, whom no man had known" (Gen. 24:16):

B. We have learned in the Mishnah:

C. **"The marriage-settlement owing to a girl who had lost her virginity by the blow of a piece of wood is two hundred,"** the words of R. Meir.

D. And sages say, **"As to a girl who had lost her virginity by the blow of a piece of wood, it is a maneh [one hundred]"** [M. Ket. 1:3].

E. R. Abbahu in the name of R. Eleazar: "The scriptural basis for the position of R. Meir is as follows: '... whom no man had known.' Lo, if she had lost her virginity by the blow of a piece of wood, she remains a virgin.

F. "The scriptural basis for the position of sages is as follows: '... a virgin.' Lo, if she had lost her virginity by the blow of a piece of wood, she would not have been regarded as a virgin."

2. A. Said R. Yohanan, "No woman prior to Rebecca had ever had sexual relations with someone who had been circumcised on the eighth day."

B. Said R. Simeon b. Laqish, "The daughters of the gentiles had been careful to protect the virginity of their vaginas but they were quite free with themselves at other orifices. But this one was 'a virgin' as to the vagina, and 'no man had known' her under any other circumstances either."

C. Said R. Yohanan, "Since it is said, 'a virgin,' do I not know that 'no man had known her'? But a man had not even propositioned her, in line with this verse: 'The rod of wickedness shall not rest upon the lot of the righteous' (Ps. 125:3)."

3. A. "She went down to the spring and filled her jar and came up" (Gen.24:16):

B. All of the other women would go down and draw water from the spring. And, as to this one, when the water saw her, the water forthwith rose to meet her.

C. Said the Holy One, blessed be he, to her, "It is a sign for your children. Just as the water rose to meet you as soon as it saw you, so with your descendants, as soon as the well sees them, it will rise to meet them. That is in line with this verse: 'Spring up, o well, sing you unto it' (Num. 21:17)."

No. 1 makes its own point, utilizing the cited verse in connection with the stated dispute. No. 2 presents a close reading of the base verse, making an obvious point. No. 3 contributes a miracle, but the basis for 3.B is not entirely clear.

LX:VI.

1. A. "Then the servant ran to meet her and said, 'Pray, give me a little water to drink from your jar.' She said, 'Drink my lord,' and she quickly let down her jar upon her hand and gave him a drink" (Gen. 24:18):

B. "Then the servant ran to meet her" to respond to her good deeds.

C. "... and said, 'Pray, give me a little water:'" a sip.

2. A. "[When she had finished giving him a drink, she said, 'I will draw for your camels also, until they have done drinking.' So she quickly emptied her jar into the trough and ran again to the well to draw, and she drew for all his camels.] The man gazed at her in silence to learn whether the Lord had prospered his journey or not" (Gen. 24:19-21).

   B. R. Phineas in the name of R. Hanan of Sepphoris: "He sipped the water and stared at her, asking 'whether the Lord had prospered his journey or not.'"

3. A. "When the camels had done drinking, the man took a gold ring, [weighing a half shekel, and two bracelets for her arms weighing ten gold shekels and said, 'Tell me whose daughter you are. Is there room in your father's house for us to lodge in?]'" (Gen. 24:22-23).

   B. R. Huna in the name of R. Joseph, "There was a precious stone in it, weighing a half a shekel."

4. A. "...and two bracelets for her arms:" corresponding to the two tablets.

   B. "weighing ten gold shekels:" corresponding to the ten commandments.

5. A. "...and said, 'Tell me whose daughter you are. Is there room in your father's house for us to lodge in?'" (Gen. 24:22-23):

   B. [He requested] only one place of lodging [as indicated by the fact that the Hebrew uses a Y instead of a W in the word to lodge].

   C. "She said, 'We have both straw and provender enough and room to lodge in'" (Gen. 24:24-25): [she offered him] several rooms for lodging [as indicated by the presence of the W in the word to lodge].

6. A. "The man bowed his head and worshipped the Lord and said, ['Blessed be the Lord, the God of my master Abraham, who has not forsaken his steadfast love and his faithfulness toward my master. As for me, the Lord has led me in the way to the house of my master's kinsmen']" (Gen. 24:26-27)):

   B. On the basis of this verse, we learn that one must give thanks for good news.

7. A. "'Blessed be the Lord, the God of my master Abraham, who has not forsaken his steadfast love and his faithfulness toward my master. [As for me, the Lord has led me in the way to the house of my master's kinsmen']" (Gen. 24:26-27)):

   B. "On account of the fact that the road folded up before me, I knew that 'As for me, the Lord has led me in the way to the house of my master's kinsmen'."

The systematic glossing of the verse amplifies here and there but does not greatly shift the thrust of the narrative, so far as I can see.

LX:VII.

1. A. "Then the maiden ran and told her mother's household [about these things. Rebecca had a brother whose name was Laban, and Laban ran out to the man, to the spring. When he saw the ring and the bracelets on his sister's arms and when he heard the words of Rebecca, his sister, 'Thus the man spoke to me,' he went to the man, and behold, he was standing by the camels at the spring]" (Gen. 24:28-31):

B. Said R. Yohanan, "A woman feels at home only in the house of her mother."

C. This objection was raised: "And she told her *father's* house" (Gen. 29:12).

D. He said to them, "It was because her mother was dead, so to whom would she report the matter if not to her father?"

2. A. "Rebecca had a brother whose name was Laban:"

B. R. Isaac said, "He was an albino [hence his name, meaning 'white,' was appropriate]."

C. R. Berekhiah said, "He was painted white by his wickedness."

3. A. "...and Laban ran out to the man, to the spring. When he saw the ring and the bracelets on his sister's arms and when he heard the words of Rebecca, his sister, 'Thus the man spoke to me,' he went to the man, and behold, he was standing by the camels at the spring" (Gen. 24:28-31):

B. [Since the consonants for the word for "spring" also bear the meaning of "examine,"] he was examining himself.

4. A. "He said, 'Come in, blessed of the Lord, [why do you stand outside? For I have prepared the house and a place for the camels']" (Gen. 24:31):

B. [Explaining why Laban called Eliezer, "blessed:"] For he thought that he was Abraham, for he looked like Abraham.

5. A. Said R. Yose bar Dosa, "Eliezer was a Canaanite, and because he served the righteous man with loyalty, he emerged from the category of the cursed and entered into the category of the blessed, as it is said, 'He said, "Come in, blessed of the Lord."'"

B. R. Jacob bar Yohai in the name of R. Yohanan of Beth Gubrin closed his remarks with this statement, "Now if because he served the righteous man with loyalty, he emerged from the category of the cursed and entered into the category of the blessed, Israelites, who treat their great men in a loving way through their own deeds, how much the more so [are they blessed]!"

6. A. "...why do you stand outside? [For I have prepared the house and a place for the camels]" (Gen. 24:31):

B. "It is not appropriate to your status for you to wait outside."

7. A. "...For I have prepared the house [and a place for the camels]" (Gen. 24:31):

B. ["I have prepared the house by removing] the pollution of idolatry and made 'a place for the camels.'"

Once more we have a sustained glossing of the base verses, with little substantial result.

LX:VIII.

1. A. "So the man came into the house, and Laban ungirded the camels [and gave him straw and provender for the camels and water to wash his feet and the feet of the men who were with him]" (Gen. 24:32):

B. He released the camels' muzzles. [They were kept muzzled so as to keep them from taking fodder that did not belong to their master, a mark of the scrupulous honesty of their master.]

2. A. R. Hiyya, R. Jeremiah asked R. Huna bar Rabbah, "Were the camels of our father, Abraham, not like the ass of R. Phineas b. Yair? [If they were in the same category, then there should have been no need to muzzle them, since the beasts would not eat untithed produce, just as Phineas's ass would not do so. We now follow up on that matter.]"

B. The ass of R. Phineas b. Yair was taken by bandits. The beast worked for them for three days but would not eat anything. They said, "In the end this beast is going to die and stink up our house." They sent it off and it returned to the house of its master.

C. When it got there, it brayed, and he recognized the sound. He said, "Open the gate for that poor beast and give it food, for it has not tasted a thing in three days."

D. They gave it barley and it would not take a taste of it. The master said to them, "Has the grain been properly tithed?"

E. They said to him, "Yes."

F. "Has the doubtfully tithed produce been removed from it?"

G. They said to him, "No. But has not the master taught us, 'He who purchases seed fodder for a beast, flour for tanning hides, oil for the lamp and for anointing utensils is exempt from having to separate doubtfully tithed produce.'"

H. He said to them, "But what can we do with this beast, which imposes an especially strict rule on itself."

3. A. R. Jeremiah sent to R. Zeira a basket of figs. R. Jeremiah thought, "It is not possible that R. Zeira will eat them without suitably removing the necessary tithes." R. Zeira said to himself, "It is not possible for R. Jeremiah to send them without properly tithing them." Between this one and that one, the figs were eaten in totally untithed state.

B. On the next day R. Jeremiah encountered R. Zeira, and asked him, "Did you remove the tithes from those figs?"

C. He said to him, "No."

D. R. Abba bar Zamina in the name of R. Eleazar the Younger: "If the former masters were angels, we are mortals. If they were mortals, we are asses."

E. Said R. Mana, "We are not even asses. For the ass of R. Phineas b. Yair, when given untithed barley, would not taste it, while we have eaten totally untithed figs."

4. A. "...and gave him straw and provender for the camels [and water to wash his feet and the feet of the men who were with him]" (Gen. 24:32):

B. Said R. Aha, "Better is the idle conversation of the slaves of the houses of the patriarchs than the Torah-talk of their descendents.

C. "The story of Eliezer fills up two or three columns, stated and amplified. But while the uncleanness attaching to a dead creeping thing is one of the principles of the Torah, the fact that its blood does not impart uncleanness as its flesh does derives only from the interpretation of an amplificatory particle of Scripture.

D. "[Here are the exegetical bases for that rule.] R. Simeon b. Yohai says, 'The word is given with the definite article, where as merely saying, "unclean," without the definite article, would have been enough. [That indicates that the stated rule is in the mind of the Torah's authority.]'

E. "R. Eleazar b. R. Yose says, '[The principle derives from the use of the] definite article with the word "this," rather than stating the word "this" without the definite article.'"

5. A. "...and water to wash his feet and the feet of the men who were with him:"

B. Said R. Aha, "Better is merely washing the feet of the slaves of the houses of the patriarchs than the Torah-talk of their descendents.

C. "For even the fact that their feet were washed had to be spelled out, while the uncleanness attaching to a dead creeping thing is one of the principles of the Torah, and the fact that its blood does not impart uncleanness as its flesh does derives only from the interpretation of an amplificatory particle of Scripture.

D. "[Here are the exegetical bases for that rule:] R. Simeon b. Yohai says, 'The word is given with the definite article, where as merely saying, "unclean," without the definite article, would have been enough.

E. "R. Eleazar b. R. Yose says, '[The principle derives from the use of the] definite article with the word "this," rather than stating the word" this" without the definite article.'"

Nos. 2, 3 explain why Abraham's camels were muzzled, No. 1. That is a far-fetched excuse for inserting what is a totally independent composition. Nos. 4, 5 make a point autonomous of the exegesis of the cited verse.

LX:IX.

1. A. "Then food was set before him to eat, but he said, 'I will not eat until I have told my errand.' He said, 'Speak on.' So he said, 'I am Abraham's servant'" (Gen. 24:33-34):

B. Said R. Isaac, "If there is something that bothers you, you be the first to say it."

2. A. "Now, then, if you will deal loyally and truly with my master, tell me, and if not, tell me, that I may turn to the right hand or to the left" (Gen. 24:49):

B. "The right hand" refers to Ishmael.

C. "The left hand" refers to Lot, as it is written, "If you will take the left hand, then I will go to the right, or if you take the right hand, then I will go to the left" (Gen. 12:9).

No. 1 presents a lesson illustrated by the conduct of Eliezer. No. 2 glosses lightly. Why the sizable passage from Gen. 24:34 through 24:48 is ignored I do not know, though the prolixity of the narrative, with its sizable repetition, has already drawn comment.

LX:X.

1. A. "Then Laban and Bethuel answered, 'The thing comes from the Lord. [We cannot speak to you bad or good. Behold, Rebecca is before you. Take her and go, and let her be the wife of your master's son, as the Lord has spoken]'" (Gen. 24:50-51):

    B. Whence did the thing come forth?

    C. "From Mount Moriah," the words of R. Joshua b. R. Nehemiah in the name of R. Hinena bar Isaac.

    D. Rabbis say, "Whence did the thing come forth? From: '...Take her and go, and let her be the wife of your master's son, as the Lord has spoken.' [It is from God.]"

The verse draws an expected gloss, explaining "whence" the matter had come, meaning, on the basis of what merit or whose decision.

LX:XI.

1. A. "[When Abraham's servant heard their words, he bowed himself to the earth before the Lord.] And the servant brought forth jewelry of silver and gold and raiment and gave them to Rebecca; he also gave to her brother and to her mother various goodies" (Gen. 24:52-53):

    B. R. Huna said, "He gave them pearls."

    C. Rabbis said, "He gave them dried ears of corn and nuts."

    D. And [since they were cited last on the list,] were dried ears of corn the most valuable things of all?

    E. This teaches that if someone goes on a trip without the food that he has to have, he will be in a bad way.

    F. Along these same lines: "But every woman shall ask of her neighbor...jewels of silver and jewels of gold and clothing" (Ex. 3:22):

    G. And [since they were cited last on the list,] is clothing the most valuable thing of all?

    H. This teaches that if someone goes on a trip without the clothing that he has to have, he will be in a bad way.

    I. Along these same lines: "And all they that were round about them strengthened their hands with vessels of silver with gold and with goodies" (Ezra 1:6):

    J. And [since they were cited last on the list,] were dried ears of corn the most valuable things of all?

K. This teaches that if someone goes on a trip without the food that he has to have, he will be in a bad way.

The syllogism is proved three times; our verse simply supplies its fact.

LX:XII.

1. A. "[When they arose in the morning, he said, 'Send me back to my master.'] Her brother and her mother said, 'Let the maiden remain with us a while, at least ten days; after that she may go'" (Gen. 24:55):

B. Where was Bethuel?

C. He wanted to hold things back, so he was smitten that night.

D. It is in line with this verse: "The righteousness of the sincere shall make straight his way. But the wicked shall fall by his own wickedness" (Prov. 11:5):

E. "The righteousness of the sincere" speaks of Isaac.

F. "...shall make straight his way" speaks of Eliezer.

G. "But the wicked shall fall by his own wickedness" (Prov. 11:5) alludes to Bethuel, who wanted to hold things back, so he was smitten that night.

2. A. "Let the maiden remain with us a while, at least ten days; after that she may go'" (Gen. 24:55):

B. "...a while" speaks of seven days of mourning [for Bethuel].

C. "...at least ten days" alludes to the twelve months that are assigned to a virgin to get herself ready for the consummation of a marriage.

3. A. ["But he said to them, 'Do not delay me, since the Lord has prospered my way; let me go that I may go to my master.'] They said, 'We will call the maiden and ask her'" (Gen. 24:56-57):

B. On the basis of this incident we learn that people may marry off an orphan girl [that is, a girl not subject to the authority of her father] only with her consent.

4. A. "And they called Rebecca and said to her, 'Will you go with this man?' She said, 'I will go'" (Gen. 24:58):

B. R. Hanania son of R. Ada in the name of R. Isaac: "They gave her an indication of the answer they wanted, in saying to her, "Will you go with this man?'

C. "'She said, "I will go"' [meaning] 'against your will and without your consent.'"

No. 1 introduces an intersecting verse to answer an obvious question. The other segments supply light glosses of one sort of another. Rebecca comes forth as a strong-willed person.

LX:XIII.

1. A. "And the sent away Rebecca, their sister, and her nurse, and Abraham's servant and his men. And they blessed Rebecca and said to her, ['Our sister, be the mother of thousands of ten thousands, and may your descendants possess the gate of those who hate them']" (Gen. 24:60):

   B. Said R. Aibu, "They were impoverished and poor, and had nothing to give her as a dowry but words."

2. A. "...'Our sister, be the mother of thousands of ten thousands, and may your descendants possess the gate of those who hate them'" (Gen. 24:60):

   B. R. Berekhiah and R. Levi in the name of R. Hama bar Hanina: "On what account was Rebecca not visited [with children] until Isaac prayed for her? It was so that the nations of the world should not say, 'It was our prayer [through her brother] that was fruitful. [The prayer of Laban and Rebecca's mother is meant.] Rather: 'And Isaac prayed to the Lord for his wife' (Gen. 25:21)."

3. A. R. Berekhiah in the name of R. Levi: "It is written, 'The blessing of the destroyer came upon me' (Job 29:13).

   B. "'The blessing of the destroyer' refers to Laban the Syrian: 'An Aramean tried to destroy my father' (Deut. 26:5).

   C. "'...came upon me' refers to Rebecca. This is the blessing: 'Our sister, be the mother of thousands of ten thousands, and may your descendants possess the gate of those who hate them.'"

4. A. "Our sister, be the mother of thousands of ten thousands, and may your descendants possess the gate of those who hate them:"

   B. From her came forth thousands from Esau and tens of thousands from Jacob.

   C. "Thousands from Esau:" "The thousands of Teman, the thousands of Omar" (Gen. 36:15).

D. "...and tens of thousands from Jacob:" "I made you into ten thousands, even as the growth of the field" (Ez. 16:7).

E. Some say, "Both derived from Israel: 'And when it rested, he said, "Return O Lord unto the ten thousands of the thousands of Israel"' (Num. 10:36)."

After a minor gloss, the principal problem of the cited verse moves to the fore. It is the fact that the gentiles blessed their sister, with the question of whether they had the power of giving such a blessing. So the first point is that when Rebecca was blessed with children, it was on account of Isaac, not the blessing of her brother and mother. Further, the blessing was unbalanced, so Esau was less than Jacob.

LX:XIV.

1. A. "Then Rebecca and her maids arose and rode upon the camels [and followed the man; thus the servant took Rebecca and went his way]" (Gen. 24:61):

B. Said R. Levi, "[It was quite normal over there for women to ride on camels,] for that is the way of camels bred in the east [to bear women. In the Land of Israel it was regarded as unusual.]"

C. Rabbis say, "Just as a camel has one signification that it is unclean but another that it is clean [since it chews the cud but does not have a cloven hoof] so Rebecca produced one wicked [unclean] and one righteous [clean] son [Esau and Jacob, respectively]."

2. A. "...and followed the man:"

B. Said R. Yohanan, "For it is improper for a man to walk behind a woman."

3. A. "Now Isaac had come [from Beer lahai roi and was dwelling in the Negeb. And Isaac went out to meditate in the field in the evening, and he lifted up his eyes and looked and behold, there were camels coming]" (Gen. 24:62-63):

B. [Since the verb for "come" is doubled, it means] he came from bringing someone.

C. And where had he gone? To Beer lahai roi [the well of life...of seeing]. He had gone to bring Hagar, the one who had sat by the *well* and had said to the *One Who Lives for All Ages*, "*Look* [thus explaining the name of the well] at my distress."

4. A. "And Isaac went out to meditate in the field in the evening, and he lifted up his eyes and looked and behold, there were camels coming" (Gen. 24:63):

B. The meaning of "meditate" is only "prayer," in line with this verse: "A prayer of the afflicted when he faints and pours out his meditation before the Lord" (Ps. 102:1).

C. So too: "Evening and morning and at noonday will I pray and moan" (Ps. 55:18).

No. 1 explains a detail that elicited special interest. Rabbis pursue the same matter in a more figurative way so linking the story to Israel's present condition. No. 3 then fills out a detail. No. 4 explains the sense of the word "meditate" by referring to passages in which the same word means prayer.

LX:XV.

1. A. "...and he lifted up his eyes and looked and behold, there were camels coming. And Rebecca lifted up her eyes, and when she saw Isaac, she fell off the camel and said to the servant, 'Who is the man yonder, walking in the field to meet us?' The servant said, 'It is my master'" (Gen. 24:62-65):

B. Said R. Huna, "She saw that he had stretched out his hand" [following Freedman].

C. "...she fell off the camel" in the sense that she got off the camel. [She did not actually fall.] That is in line with this usage: "Though he fall , he shall not be utterly cast down" (Ps. 37:24).

2. A. "She said to the servant, 'Who is the man yonder, walking in the field to meet us?'"

B. R. Berekhiah in the name of R. Hiyya, his father: "She saw that, [since he is described with the word 'yonder,'] he was handsome, in line with the meaning of the same word [when applied to Joseph] in the following verse: 'Behold, yonder dreamer comes' (Gen. 37:19)."

C. Rabbis said, "The usage refers to his guardian, with the word 'yonder' bearing the sense, 'This one is for his service.'"

3. A. "The servant said, 'It is my master.' And she took her veil and covered herself" (Gen. 24:65):

B. Two covered themselves with a veil and produced twins, Rebecca and Tamar.

C. Rebecca: "...And she took her veil and covered herself."

D. Tamar: "And she covered herself with her veil" (Gen. 38:14).

4. A. "And the servant told Isaac all the things that he had done" (Gen. 24:66):

B. Said R. Eleazar, "The general principles of the Torah are more encompassing than the narrative of the details. For if he had wanted, he could have written out two or three columns."

C. Rabbis say, "He told him the good parts, about how the road had doubled up so as to make the journey quicker."

The glosses clarify the meanings of words and phrases. I see no sustaining polemic.

LX:XVI.

1. A. "Then Isaac brought her into the tent of Sarah, his mother, and took Rebecca and she became his wife, and he loved her. So Isaac was comforted after his mother's death" (Gen. 24:67):

B. You find that as long as Sarah was alive, a cloud hung over her tent. When she died, the cloud went away. When Rebecca came, it came back.

C. So long as Sarah was alive, her doors were open in prosperity. When Sarah died, that prosperity ceased. When Rebecca came, it came back.

D. So long as Sarah was alive, a blessing was in dough, and the lamp gave light in her tent from the night on the Sabbath until the following Sabbath night. When Sarah died, it all came to an end. When Rebecca came, it came back.

E. When Isaac saw that he did the same sort of deeds as did his mother, preparing her dough in a state of cultic cleanness, cutting off her dough-offering in a state of cultic cleanness, forthwith: "Then Isaac brought her into the tent of Sarah, his mother."

2. A. Said R. Yudan, "The Torah teaches you the right way to do things. For if a man has grown up sons, he should first marry them off, and then take a wife for himself. From whom do you learn that rule? From Abraham.

B. "First: 'Then Isaac brought her into the tent of Sarah, his mother.' Then: And Abraham took another wife, and her name was Keturah' (Gen. 25:1)."

No. 1 links the rules of cultic rites in the home to the practice of the matriarchs. No. 2 presents a syllogism based on the story at hand.

Chapter Twenty-Nine

Parashah Sixty-One. Genesis 25:1-6

LXI:I.

1. A. "Abraham took another wife, and her name was Keturah [and she bore him Zimran, Jokshan, Medan, Midian, Ishbak, and Shuah]"(Gen. 25:1).

    B. "Happy is the man who has not walked in the counsel of the wicked, [nor stood in the way of sinners, nor sat in the seat of the scornful. But his delight is in the Torah of the Lord, and in his Torah does he meditate day and night. And he shall be like a tree planted by streams of water, that brings forth its fruit in its season, and whose leaf does not wither, and in whatsoever he does, he shall prosper]" (Ps. 1:1-3):

    C. "Happy is the man" speaks of Abraham.

    D. "...has not walked in the counsel of the wicked" speaks of the generation of the dispersion.

    E. "...nor stood in the way of sinners" refers to the men of Sodom, as it is said, "The men of Sodom were evil and sinful" (Gen. 13:13).

    F. "...nor sat in the seat of the scornful" refers to Abimelech, who said to him, "Lo, my land is before you" (Gen. 20:15), but Abraham did not accept the offer.

    G. "But his delight is in the Torah of the Lord." "For I have known him, to the end that he may command his children that they may keep the way of the Lord" (Gen. 18:19).

    H. "...and in his Torah does he meditate day and night:"

    I. Said R. Simeon b. Yohai, "His father did not teach him, he never had a master. Whence did he learn Torah? The Holy One, blessed be he, designated his two kidneys like two rabbis, and they flowed and taught him wisdom, in line with the following verse: 'I will bless the Lord, who has given me counsel, yes, in the night seasons my kidneys instruct me' (Ps. 16:7)."

    J. " And he shall be like a tree planted by streams of water." For the Holy One, blessed be he, planted him in the land of Israel.

    K. "...that brings forth its fruit in its season" refers to Ishmael.

    L. "...and whose leaf does not wither" refers to Isaac.

M. "...and in whatsoever he does, he shall prosper." This refers to the sons of Keturah: "Abraham took another wife, and her name was Keturah [and she bore him Zimran, Jokshan, Medan, Midian, Ishbak, and Shuah]"(Gen. 25:1).

The systematic exposition of the intersecting verse in line with the life of Abraham succeeds admirably. I see no false step and no forced point. But apart from the rather exultant praise of Abraham, I also see no point. The fact that Abraham studied the Torah before it was given of course is taken for granted.

LXI:II.

1. A. "They shall still bring forth fruit in old age, [they shall be full of sap and richness]" (Ps. 92:15):

B. This refers to Abraham.

C. "...they shall be full of sap and richness:"

D. "Abraham took another wife, and her name was Keturah [and she bore him Zimran, Jokshan, Medan, Midian, Ishbak, and Shuah]"(Gen. 25:1).

2. A. "For there is hope of a tree. [If it be cut down, that it will sprout again. And that his tender branch will not cease. Though his root wax old in the earth, and his stock die in the ground, yet through the scent of water he will blossom, and put forth boughs like a plant]" (Job 14:7-9):

B. "For there is hope of a tree" refers to Abraham, who has hope.

C. "If it be cut down, that it will sprout again." If concerning him it is said that he has entered the covenant [using the same verb as serves to mean "cut down,"] "it will sprout again." He shall produce more actions in conformity with religious requirements as well as good deeds.

D. "And that his tender branch will not cease." That is, his semen.

E. " Though his root wax old in the earth..." "And Abraham was old" (Gen. 24:1).

F. "...and his stock die in the ground...." ""And Sarah died" (Gen. 23:2).

G. "... yet through the scent of water he will blossom." That is, from the scent of the religious duties and good deeds, he will blossom.

H. "...and put forth boughs like a plant."

I. What is said is not, "...put forth a plant like boughs," but rather, "boughs like a plant," in that the further growth was more than the original.

J. "Abraham took another wife, and her name was Keturah and she bore him Zimran, Jokshan, Medan, Midian, Ishbak, and Shuah"(Gen. 25:1).

The same exercise succeeds with a intersecting verse at No. 1. No. 2 is still more successful in making the same point, which is that Abraham even in old age remained virile.

LXI:III.

1. A. "In the morning sow your seed and in the evening do not withhold your hand, for you do not know which will prosper, whether this or that, or whether they both shall alike be good" (Qoh. 11:6):

    B. R. Eliezer and R. Joshua:

    C. R. Eliezer says, "If you have sown in the early planting season, sow again in the later season, for you do not know which of the crops will survive, the first fruits or the later harvest: 'for you do not know which will prosper, whether this or that, or whether they both shall alike be good' (Qoh. 11:6)."

    D. R. Joshua says, "If a poor man comes to you in the morning, give him something, if one comes in the evening, give again, for you do not know which of them the Holy One, blessed be he, will inscribe in your behalf, 'for you do not know which will prosper, whether this or that, or whether they both shall alike be good' (Qoh. 11:6)."

2. A. R. Ishmael and R. Aqiba:

    B. R. Ishmael says, "If you have studied the Torah when you are young, study the Torah when you are old, for you do not know which of them will endure: 'for you do not know which will prosper, whether this or that, or whether they both shall alike be good' (Qoh. 11:6)."

    C. R. Aqiba says, "If you have raised up disciples in your youth, raise up more disciples in your old age, for you do not know which of them the Holy One, blessed be he, will inscribe in your behalf, 'for you do not know which will prosper, whether this or that, or whether they both shall alike be good' (Qoh. 11:6)."

3. A. R. Aqiba had twelve thousand pairs of disciples, living from Gabbath to Antipatris. All of them died in a single season. Why? Because they were envious of one another. In the end he raised up exactly seven: R. Meir, R. Judah, R. Yose, R. Simeon, R. Eleazar b. Shamua, R. Yohanan Hassandlar, and R. Eliezer b. Jacob.

    B. Some say, "R. Judah, R. Nehemiah, R. Meir, R. Yose, R. Simeon b. Yohai, R. Hananiah b. Hakhinai, and R. Yohanan Hassandlar."

    C. He said to them, "My sons, the first disciples of mine died because they were envious of one another in Torah-study. Do you pay heed not to act like them." They went and filled up the entire Land of Israel with knowledge of the Torah.

4. A. R. Dosetai and R. Yannai in the name of R. Samuel bar Nahman: "If you have children when you are young, take a wife when you are old and produce more children. From whom do you learn that lesson? It is from our father, Abraham, who had children when he was young and took a wife in his old age and produced more children.

B. "That is in line with this verse: 'Abraham took another wife, and her name was Keturah and she bore him Zimran, Jokshan, Medan, Midian, Ishbak, and Shuah' (Gen. 25:1)."

The same point is made several times, sometimes with tales, other times with the appeal to an intersecting verse, always reverting to the example of Abraham. The repertoire of intersecting verses is fully exploited.

LXI:IV.

1. A. "Abraham took another wife" (Gen. 25:1):

B. R. Judah said, "This refers to Hagar."

C. Said to him R. Nehemiah, "And lo, it is written, 'Abraham took another wife.'"

D. [He said to him,] "This was on instructions of a statement from God, in line with this statement: 'And the Lord spoke to me yet again' (Is. 8:5). [Freedman, p. 543, n. 1: The same word, again, occurs in both verses, since in the case of Isaiah it refers to God's speech, in the case of Abraham it shows that he took Keturah because God told him.]"

E. [He said to him,] "But it is written, 'and her name was Keturah' [so how can you hold her name was Hagar]?"

F. He said to him, "[It was the same person, but she was called Keturah] because she united [using the same letters as the name] the practice of doing religious duties with the work of doing good deeds."

G. "But is it not written, 'But to the sons of his concubines, Abraham gave gifts' (Gen. 25:6). [How can this be only Hagar, when there is a reference to several concubines.]"

H. He said to him, "It is written defectively, so as to read 'concubine' in the singular, specifically, it was the one who had sat down by the well and wept to him who is the life of all ages, 'See my sorrow.'"

2. A. Said R. Berekhiah [who took the view that Keturah was the same as Hagar], "Even though it is written, 'And she went and wandered...' (Gen.

21:14), do not imagine that anyone ever was suspect of having immoral relations with her,

B. "for Scripture states, 'Her name was Keturah,' meaning, that such a one as this served as the seal of a treasure, and she produced the treasure with its seal. [Freedman, p. 543, n. 5: Deriving Keturah from *katar* , to tie, hence to seal up.]"

3. A. R. Simeon b. Laqish in the name of Bar Qappara: "The addition that the Holy One, blessed be he, supplies is greater than the principal. Cain was the principal and Abel, mentioned as a second, was born together with his two twin sisters.

B. "Joseph was principal and Benjamin, because he was mentioned as an addition, produced ten sons: 'And the sons of Benjamin, Bela, Becher, Ashbel, Gera' (Gen. 46:21).

C. "Er was principal and Shelah, because he was mentioned as an addition, yielded ten [*sic*] law courts: 'The sons of Shelah, the son of Judah: Er the father of Lecah, Ladah the father of Mareshah, and the families of those who wrought fine linen of the house of Ashea' (1 Chr. 4:21).

D. "The principal years assigned to Job were only two hundred and ten, but a hundred and forty more were added to his life: 'And after this Job lived a hundred and forty years' (Job. 42:16).

E. "The principal period of the rule of Hezekiah was only fourteen years, but an additional fifteen years were given to him: 'Behold, I will add to your days fifteen years' (Is. 38:5).

F. "Ishmael was the principal, and the sons of Keturah, because they are spoken of as addition, are specified as sons as well: '...and she bore him Zimran, Jokshan, Medan, Midian, Ishbak, and Shuah' (Gen. 25:1)."

No. 1 conducts an inquiry into the relationship between Hagar and Keturah. No. 2 follows up on the same matter. The main point comes at No. 3, the view that the sons of Keturah were superior to Ishmael. This removes the possibility that Ishmael in any way takes precedence over any other son of Abraham.

LXI:V.

1. A. "...and she bore him Zimran, Jokshan, Medan, Midian, Ishbak, and Shuah]"(Gen. 25:1):

B. Ammi bar Ezekiel and rabbis:

C. Ammi bar Ezekiel said, "Zimran, because they produced destruction in the world, Jokshan, because they were cruel in the world."

D. Rabbis say, "Zimran, because they would make music with a cymbal for idolatry, and Jokshan, because they would beat out a rhythm with a cymbal for idolatry."

2. A. "And Jokshan was father of Sheba and Dedan. And the sons of Dedan were Asshurim, and Letushim, and Leummim" (Gen. 25:3):

B. R. Samuel bar Nahman said, "Even though the translators render these as [Freedman:] 'merchants, artificers, and heads of people,' in point of fact all were heads of peoples."

The names are given meaning, No. 1, and, by the way, Abraham,'s treatment of the sons is justified. No. 2 spells out the meaning of the names, a philological note.

LXI:VI.

1. A. "Abraham gave all that he had to Isaac" (Gen. 25:2):

B. R. Judah, R. Nehemiah, and rabbis:

C. R. Judah said, "The sense is that what he gave to Isaac was the birthright [as first born]."

D. R. Nehemiah said, "It was the power to give a blessing."

E. Rabbis say, It was the ownership of the sepulchre at Hebron and [the inheritance through] donation."

2. A. R. Judah bar Simon and R. Berekhiah and R. Levi in the name of R. Hama bar Hanina: "He did not bless him but only gave him gifts. [This is now explained.]

B. "The matter may be compared to the case of a king who had an orchard, which he handed over to a sharecropper. There were two trees in the orchard, intertwined with one another, one of which produced an elixir of life, the other a deadly poison. Said the sharecropper, 'If I water the one that produces the elixir of life, the one that produces the deadly poison will live with it, but if I do not water the one that produces the deadly poison, how will the one that produces the elixir of life live?'

C. "Then he went and said, 'I am a sharecropper. I'll do my job, and whatever pleases the owner of the orchard to do he will do in due course.'

D. "So too Abraham said, 'If I give a blessing to Isaac, then the children of Ishmael and the children of Keturah will be covered by the blessing. And if I do not give a blessing to the children of Ishmael and the children of Keturah, how shall I give a blessing to Isaac?'

E. "Then he went and said, 'I am merely mortal. I shall do what is my job, and what the Holy One, blessed be he, wants to do in his world, let him do.'

F. "[So to Isaac he gave no blessing.] When our father, Abraham, died, the Holy One, blessed be he, appeared to Isaac and blessed him.

G. "That is in line with this verse: 'And it came to pass after the death of Abraham that God blessed Isaac his son' (Gen. 25:11)."

The explanation of giving "all that he had to Isaac" is worked out in two distinct approaches. No. 1 is fairly straight-forward. No. 2 finds that Abraham did not give a blessing to Isaac, but God made it up afterward. What is evidently striking is the absence of a reference to Abraham's blessing Isaac.

LXI:VII.

1. A. "But to the sons of his concubines, Abraham gave gifts, and while he was still living, he sent them away from his son Isaac, eastward to the east country" (Gen. 25:6):

B. In the time of Alexander of Macedonia the sons of Ishmael came to dispute with Israel about the birthright, and with them came two wicked families, the Canaanites and the Egyptians.

C. They said, "Who will go and engage in a disputation with them."

D. Gebiah b. Qosem [the enchanter] said, "I shall go and engage in a disputation with them."

E. They said to him, "Be careful not to let the Land of Israel fall into their possession."

F. He said to them, "I shall go and engage in a disputation with them. If I win over them, well and good. And if not, you may say, 'Who is this hunchback to represent us?'"

G. He went and engaged in a disputation with them. Said to them Alexander of Macedonia, "Who lays claim against whom?"

H. The Ishmaelites said, "We lay claim, and we bring our evidence from their own Torah: 'But he shall acknowledge the firstborn, the son of the hated' (Deut. 21;17). Now Ishmael was the firstborn. [We therefore claim the land as heirs of the first-born of Abraham.]"

I. Said to him Gebiah b. Qosem, "My royal lord, does a man not do whatever he likes with his sons?"

J. He said to him, "Indeed so."

K. "And lo, it is written, 'Abraham gave all that he had to Isaac' (Gen. 25:2)."

L. [Alexander asked,] "Then where is the deed of gift to the other sons?"

M. He said to him, "'But to the sons of his concubines, Abraham gave gifts, [and while he was still living, he sent them away from his son Isaac, eastward to the east country]' (Gen. 25:6)."

N. [The Ishmaelites had no claim on the land.] They abandoned the field in shame.

O. The Canaanites said, "We lay claim, and we bring our evidence from their own Torah. Throughout their Torah it is written, 'the land of Canaan.' So let them give us back our land."

P. Said to him Gebiah b. Qosem, "My royal lord, does a man not do whatever he likes with his slave?"

Q. He said to him, "Indeed so."

R. He said to him, "And lo, it is written, 'A slave of slaves shall Canaan be to his brothers' (Gen. 9:25). So they are really our slaves."

S. [The Canaanites had no claim to the land and in fact should be serving Israel.] They abandoned the field in shame.

T. The Egyptians said, "We lay claim, and we bring our evidence from their own Torah. Six hundred thousand of them left us, taking away our silver and gold utensils: 'They despoiled the Egyptians' (Ex. 12:36). Let them give them back to us."

U. Gebiah b. Qosem said, "My royal lord, six hundred thousand men worked for them for two hundred and ten years, some as silversmiths and some as goldsmiths. Let them pay us our salary at the rate of a *denar* a day."

V. The mathematicians went and added up what was owing, and they had not reached the sum covering a century before the Egyptians had to forfeit what they had claimed. They abandoned the field in shame.

W. [Alexander] wanted to go up to Jerusalem. The Samaritans said to him, "Be careful. They will not permit you to enter their most holy sanctuary."

X. When Gebiah b. Qosem found out about this, he went and made for himself two felt shoes, with two precious stones worth twenty thousand pieces of silver set in them. When he got to the mountain of the house [of the Temple], he said to him, "My royal lord, take off your shoes and put on these two felt slippers, for the floor is slippery, and you should not slip and fall."

Y. When they came to the most holy sanctuary, he said to him, "Up to this point, we have the right to enter. From this point onward, we do not have the right to enter."

Z. He said to him, "When we get out of here, I'm going to even out your hump."

AA. He said to him, "You will be called a great surgeon and get a big fee."

2. A. "[But to the sons of his concubines, Abraham gave gifts, and while he was still living,] he sent them away from his son Isaac, eastward to the east country]' (Gen. 25:6):

B. He said to them, "Go as far to the east as you can, so as not to be burned by the flaming coal of Isaac."

C. But because Esau came to make war with Jacob, he took his appropriate share on his account: "Is this your joyous city, whose feet in antiquity, in ancient days, carried her afar off to sojourn? Who has devised this against Tyre, the crowning city" (Is. 23:7).

D. Said R. Eleazar, "Whenever the name of Tyre is written in Scripture, if it is written out [with all of the letters], then it refers to the province of Tyre. Where it is written without all of its letters [and so appears identical to the word for enemy], the reference of Scripture is to Rome. [So the sense of the verse is that Rome will receive its appropriate reward.]"

E. [As to the sense of the word for] "the crowning city,"

F. R. Abba bar Kahana said, "It means that they surrounded the city like a crown."

G. R. Yannai, son of R. Simeon b. R. Yannai, said, "They surrounded it with a fence of thorns."

No. 1 is deposited here because of the case of the Ishmaelites, Abraham's children, deprived as they were of their inheritance. That issue pressed on the consciousness of the exegete-compositors. No. 2 carries forward the eschatological reading of the incident. Israel's later history is prefigured in the gift to Isaac and the rejection of the other sons. The self-evidence that Esau's reward will be recompense for his evil indicates that the passage draws upon sarcasm to make its point.

Chapter Thirty

Parashah Sixty-Two. Genesis 25:7-18

LXII:I.

1. A. "These are the days of the years of Abraham's life, a hundred and seventy-five years" (Gen. 25:7):

    B. "The Lord knows the days of them who are whole hearted and their inheritance shall be forever" (Ps. 37:18).

    C. "The Lord knows the days of them who are whole hearted" speaks of Abraham.

    D. "... and their inheritance shall be forever" (Ps. 37:18): "These are the days of the years of Abraham's life, a hundred and seventy-five years" (Gen. 25:7).

Since the base verse refers to the word "years," the consonants of which can be read, "two," the exegete finds the base verse to refer to the "two lives" of Abraham, with the understanding that one is in this world, the other in the age to come. Hence the reference to the "inheritance forever," meaning that Abraham enjoys eternal life.

LXII:II.

1. A. "Abraham breathed his last and died in a good old age, an old man and full of years, and was gathered to his people" (Gen. 25:8):

    B. Said R. Judah bar Ilai, "The earlier pious men would suffer from belly aches ten to twenty days, showing that illness purifies."

    C. R. Judah says, "Any figure concerning whose death the word 'breathed his last' is written is someone who died of an intestinal ailment."

2. A. "Strength and dignity are her clothing, and she laughs at the time to come" (Prov. 31:25):

    B. The whole of the reward of the righteous is readied for them in the age to come, but the Holy One, blessed be he, shows it to them while they are yet in this world. Since he shows them their full recompense in the world to come while they are yet in this world, their soul is satisfied and they go to sleep peacefully.

C. Said R. Eleazar, "The matter may be compared to the case of a king who called a banquet and invited guests and showed them in advance what they were going to eat and drink, so their souls were satisfied and they fell asleep. So the Holy One, blessed be he, shows the righteous while they are yet in this world the coming recompense that he is going to give to them in the age to some, and their souls are satisfied and they fall asleep.

D. "What scriptural verse indicates it? 'For now I should have lain still and been quiet, I should have slept, then I had been at rest' (Job 3:13). Thus when the righteous leave, the Holy One, blessed be he, shows them the recompense that is coming."

3. A. When R. Abbahu was dying, they showed him thirteen rivers of balsam. He said to them, "To whom do these belong?"

B. They said to him, "To you."

C. He said to them, "These belong to Abbahu? And I had thought, 'I have labored in vain, I have spent my strength for nought and vanity, yet surely my right is worth the Lord, and my recompense with my God' (Is. 44:4). [But I was wrong.]"

4. A. Zabedi b. Levi, R. Joshua b. Levi and R. Yose b. Petros: each of them recited a verse as he lay dying.

B. One of them said, "For this let every one who is godly pray to you in a time when you may be found" (Ps. 32:6). "For in him does our heart rejoice, because we have trusted in his holy name" (Ps. 33:21).

C. One of them said, "You prepare a table before me in the presence of my enemies" (Ps. 23:5). "So shall all those who take refuge in you rejoice" (Ps. 5:12).

D. The third said, "For a day in your courts is better than a thousand" (Ps. 84:11).

E. Rabbis said, "Oh how abundant is your goodness, which you have laid up for those who fear you" (Ps. 31:20).

F. This indicates that when the righteous leave, the Holy One, blessed be he, shows them the recompense that is coming.

5. A. Ben Azzai says, "'Precious in the sight of the Lord is the death of his saints' (Ps. 116:15). When does the Holy One, blessed be he, show them the recompense that is coming? Right near their death.

B. "That is in line with this verse: '... is the death of his saints.' Therefore: 'She laughs at the time to come' (Prov. 31:25)."

6. A. What is the difference between the death of the young and the death of the old?

B. R. Judah and R. Abbahu:

C. R. Judah said, "When a lamp goes out on its own, it is good for the lamp and good for the wick, but when it goes out not on its own, it is bad for it and bad for the wick."

D. R. Abbahu said, "When figs are picked in season, it is good for them and good for the fig-tree, and when not picked in season, it is bad for them and bad for the fig-tree."

7. A. There is this story. R. Hiyya and his disciples, and some say, R. Aqiba and his disciples, were accustomed to get up early and to go into session under a fig tree. And the owner of the fig tree would get up early and pick off the figs. They said, "Is it possible that he suspects us [of stealing his figs]? We should change our place."

B. What did they do? They changed their place. He went to them and said to them, "My lords, the merit of one religious duty that you would study under my fig tree has accrued to me, and now you have taken it away."

C. They said to him, "We wondered, Is it possible that you suspect us [of stealing his figs]? [We therefore changed our place.]"

D. He assured them [that that was not the case], and they went back to their original place.

E. What did he then do? He ceased to gather his figs at dawn. The figs then began to rot [on the tree].

F. They said, "The owner of the fig-tree knows when the season of each fig has come, and that is when he picks it. [That is why he picked the figs early in the morning.] So too, the Holy One, blessed be he, knows the season of the righteous, and he then gathers them. What is the scriptural basis for this view? 'My beloved has gone down to his garden' (Song 6:2)."

8. A. Another version of the same story: R. Hiyya the Elder and and his disciples, and some say, R. Hoshaia and his disciples, were accustomed to get up early and to study under a fig tree. And the owner of the fig tree day by day would get up early and pick off the figs. They said, "Is it possible that he suspects us [of stealing his figs? We should change our place."

B. [What did they do?] They changed their place. The owner of the fig tree got up early to pick off his figs and did not find them there. He went looking for them. He said to them, "My lords, the merit of one religious duty that you would carry out [to my benefit] you now withhold from me."

C. They said to him, "God forbid!"

D. He said to them, "On what account did you abandon your place and go into session somewhere else?"

E. They said to him, "We said, we should change our place, for it may be that you suspect us [of stealing his figs]. [We therefore changed our place.]"

F. He said to them, "God forbid. Let me tell you why I would get up early in the morning and go to my fig tree to collect the ripe figs. Once the sun has shown on them, they start rotting."

G. [He relieved their doubts, and] they went back to their original meeting place.

H. On that day he left them alone and did not gather his figs, and the sun shown on the figs, and they split some of them and found that they had rotted.

I. They said, "The owner of the fig-tree knows when the season of each fig has come, and that is when he picks it. So too, the Holy One, blessed be he, knows the season of the righteous, and he then gathers them. What is the scriptural basis for this view? 'My beloved has gone down to his garden' (Song 6:2)."

9. A. "In a good old age" (Gen. 25:8):

B. Said R. Simeon b. Laqish, "There are three concerning whom 'good old age' is stated, Abraham , and he had it coming, David, and he had it coming, [and Gideon,] but Gideon did not have it coming.

C. "Why not? Because 'Gideon made an ephod thereof' (Judges. 8:27) for idolatry."

No. 1 is included because of its philological interpretation of a word in the base verse. Nos. 2, 3-5 then work on the theme that the righteous die happy, because they know what is coming to them, a generally relevant message for the theme of Abraham's death. The disparate materials of Nos. 2-5 conclude with the intersecting verse with which No. 2 commences, a mark that, at some point, an author has drawn the whole together into a single composition. The remainder form a topical miscellany, through No. 9. But the net effect is to underline the fact that God knows when it is time for a particular person to die, and that point illuminates the story of Abraham's death.

LXII:III.

1. A. "Isaac and Ishmael his sons buried him [in the cave of Machpelah, in the field of Ephron the son of Zohar the Hittite, east of Mamre, the field which

Abraham purchased from the Hittites. There Abraham was buried and Sarah his wife]" (Gen. 25:9-10):

B. In this case, the son of the handmaiden paid respect to the son of the mistress [who took precedence as the cited verse is framed].

2. A. "...[in the cave of Machpelah, in the field of Ephron the son of Zohar the Hittite, east of Mamre,] the field which Abraham purchased [from the Hittites. There Abraham was buried and Sarah his wife]" (Gen. 25:9-10):

B. Said R. Tanhuma, "And was there not a span of thirty-eight years from the burial of Abraham back to the burial of Sarah? And yet you say, 'There Abraham was buried and Sarah his wife.'

C. "This teaches that whoever did honor to Sarah [by helping to mourn for her] had the merit of doing honor for Abraham."

3. A. Said R. Samuel bar Nahman, "Shem and Eber went before her bier, and they saw which burial niche [kokh] was open for our father, Abraham, and they buried her in his compartment [accounting for the statement that Abraham was buried right along with Sarah]."

The glossing of the verse takes two problems, one the order of the names, No. 1, and the second, the reference to Abraham's being buried right with Sarah, which yields two explanations, Nos. 2, 3.

LXII:IV.

1. A. "And it came to pass after the death of Abraham that God blessed Isaac his son. [And Isaac dwelt at Beer-lahai-roi]" (Gen. 25:11):

B. Said R. Simon, "In every passage in which it is said, 'And it came to pass after,' the meaning is that the world returned to its former condition.

C. "For example: 'And it came to pass after the death of Abraham,' forthwith: 'All the wells which his father's servants had dug in the days of Abraham, his father, the Philistines stopped them up' (Gen. 26:15, 18).

D. "'And it came to pass after the death of Moses' (Joshua 1:1) forthwith the well went dry, and the mana and the clouds of glory disappeared.

E. "'And it came to pass after the death of Joshua' (Judges 1:1). Forthwith the strong men of the land rose up against them.

F. "'And it came to pass after the death of Saul' (2 Sam. 1:1) 'And the Philistines fought against Israel' (1 Sam. 31:1)."

G. His colleagues raised this objection to the statement of R. Simon, "But is it not written, 'And it came to pass after the death of Jehoiada, the princes of Judah came and prostrated themselves before the king' (2 Chr. 24:17)?"

H. Said R. Tanhuma, "R. Simon's statement speaks only of the phrase, 'And it came to pass after.'"

I. [Offering a different view of the meaning of the same clause,] R. Yudan said, "The sense is, 'If the Holy One, blessed be he, had not brought others to take their place, the world would have reverted to its former condition.

J. "For it is written, 'And it came to pass after the death of Abraham,' forthwith: 'All the wells which his father's servants had dug in the days of Abraham, his father, the Philistines stopped them up' (Gen. 26:15, 18). 'And Isaac again dug the wells of water' (Gen. 26:18).

K. "'And it came to pass after the death of Moses, the servant of the Lord, that the Lord spoke to Joshua' (Joshua 1:1).

L. "'And it came to pass after the death of Joshua...and the Lord said, "Judah shall go up"' (Judges 1:1).

M. "'And it came to pass after the death of Saul' (2 Sam. 1:1). 'When David had returned from the slaughter of the Amalekites...Now David was the son of that Ephrathite' (1 Sam. 17:12)."

The dispute is beautifully articulated, point by point. The syllogism does not derive from our verse in particular, but is constructed with its own focus.

LXII:V.

1. A. "These are the descendants of Ishmael, Abraham's son, [whom Hagar, the Egyptian, Sarah's maid, bore to Abraham]" (Gen. 25:12):

B. There is this case. R. Hama bar Uqba and rabbis were in session and seeking a reason that the Scripture took the trouble here of spelling out the genealogy of that wicked man.

C. R. Levi came by. They said, "Lo, here comes the master of traditions. Let us ask him."

D. R. Levi in the name of R. Hama bar Hanina produced [the following explanation]: "It is to let you know how old your ancestor [Jacob] was when he was blessed [by Isaac].

E. "'These are the years of the life of Ishmael, [a hundred and thirty-seven years; he breathed his last and died and was gathered to his kindred]' (Gen. 25:17):

F. "How come the Scripture took the trouble here of spelling out the age of that wicked man? It was he came from the depths of the wilderness to pay his respects to his father."

2. A. "And they dwelt from Havilah to Shur, which is opposite Egypt in the direction of Assyria. Over against all his brethren he fell" (Gen. 25:18):

B. Here you use the word"fell" and elsewhere "dwell" (Gen. 16:12).

C. So long as Abraham was alive, "he shall dwell." Once he died, "he fell [from glory]."

D. Before he laid hands on the Temple, "he shall dwell." After he laid hands on the Temple, "he fell."

E. In this world "he shall dwell." In the world to come, "he fell."

No. 1 asks an obvious question about the narrative, so requiring the narrator to express on the events at hand the established polemic concerning Israelite history. Along these same lines No. 2 compares the formulation of two relevant verses and draws a lesson from them, so linking the biographies of the patriarchs to the history of Israel.

Chapter Thirty-One

Parashah Sixty-Three. Genesis 25:19-34

LXIII:I.

1. A. "These are the generations of Isaac, Abraham's son" (Gen. 25:19).

   B. "The father of the righteous will greatly rejoice [and he who fathers a wise child will have joy in him]" (Ps. 23:24).

   C. There is rejoicing when the righteous one is born.

2. A. "And it came to pass in the days of Ahaz" (Is. 7:1):

   B. Said R. Hoshaiah, "The ministering angels said before the Holy One, blessed be he, 'Lord of all ages, woe that Ahaz reigns. [The word 'and it came to pass' bears the consonants that can be read 'woe.']

   C. "He said to them, 'He is the son of Jotham, and his father is a righteous man, so I cannot put my hands on him.'"

3. A. "...and he who fathers a wise child will have joy in him" (Ps. 23:24):

   B. R. Huna in the name of R. Aha: "On the basis of what biblical verse do you maintain that whoever has a son who labors in the Torah will be filled with mercy for him?

   C. "Scripture states, 'My son, if your heart be wise, my heart will be glad, mine also' (Prov. 25:15)."

   D. R. Simeon b. Menassia said, "I know only that that is the case of the heart of a mortal father. How do I know that even the Holy One, blessed be he, is filled with mercy for him when he labors in the Torah? Scripture says, 'my heart will be glad, mine also.'

   E. "There is rejoicing after rejoicing when it is a righteous one who is son of a righteous one: 'These are the generations of Isaac, Abraham's son' (Gen. 25:19)."

The thrust of the composition becomes clear only at the end, a mark that whatever the prior history of the components, the whole was put together in a purposeful way. No. 1 introduces the theme, No. 2 expands on it to show that the merit of the father protects the son, and then No. 3 makes the main point, which is that when there is a righteous son of a righteous father, there is no limit to the joy. That then points to the sense of the cited verse, with its stress on Isaac, Abraham's son.

LXIII:II.

1. A. "Children's children are the crown of old men, and the glory of children are their fathers" (Prov. 17:6):

B. Fathers are a crown for children, children are a crown for fathers.

C. Fathers are a crown for children, as it is written, "...the glory of children are their fathers."

D. And children are a crown for fathers, as it is written, "...children's children are the crown of old men."

2. A. R. Huna and R. Jeremiah in the name of R. Samuel b. R. Isaac: "Abraham was saved from the fiery furnace only on account of the merit of Jacob, our father.

B. "The matter may be compared to the case of someone who was on trial before the ruler, and the decision came forth from the ruler to have him put to death by burning. But the ruler foresaw through his astrology that that man was destined to produce a daughter who would be married to a king. He said, 'That man is worthy of being given a reprieve on account of the merit of his daughter.'

C. "So the Holy One, blessed be he, said, Abraham is worthy of being given a reprieve on account of the merit of his Jacob.'

D. "'Therefore the Lord says concerning the house of Jacob, who redeemed Abraham' (Isa. 29:22). The sense then is that it was Jacob who redeemed Abraham."

3. A. Another point: "Children's children are the crown of old men, and the glory of children are their fathers" (Prov. 17:6).

B. "These are the descendants of Isaac, Abraham's son: Abraham was the father of Isaac" (Gen. 25:19).

The composite as a whole goes over the point familiar from the foregoing. The notion that merit works backwards as well as forwards is new.

LXIII:III.

1. A. "These are the descendants of Isaac, Abraham's son: Abraham was the father of Isaac" (Gen. 25:19):

    B. Abram was called Abraham: "Abram, the same is Abraham" (1 Chr. 1:27).

    C. Isaac was called Abraham: "These are the descendants of Isaac, Abraham's son, Abraham."

    D. Jacob was called Israel, as it is written, "Your name shall be called more Jacob but Israel" (Gen. 32:29).

    E. Isaac also was called Israel: "And these are the names of the children of Israel, who came into Egypt, Jacob and his" (Gen. 46:8).

    F. Abraham was called Israel as well.

    G. R. Nathan said, "This matter is deep: 'Now the time that the children of Israel dwelt in Egypt' (Ex. 12:40), and in the land of Canaan and in the land of Goshen 'was four hundred and thirty years' (Ex. 12:40)." [Freedman, p. 557, n. 6: They were in Egypt for only 210 years. Hence their sojourn in Canaan and Goshen must be added, which means, from the birth of Isaac. Hence the children of Israel commence with Isaac. And since he was Abraham's son, it follows that Abraham was called Israel.]

The polemic at hand, linking the patriarchs to the history of Israel, claiming that all of the patriarchs bear the same names, derives proof, in part, from the base verse. But the composition in no way rests upon the exegesis of the base verse. Its syllogism transcends the case at hand.

LXIII:IV.

1. A. "And Isaac was forty years old [when he took to wife Rebecca, the daughter of Bethuel, the Aramaean of Paddan-aram, the sister of Laban the Aramean]" (Gen. 25:20:

    B. Said R. Isaac, "[What purpose is there in specifying that Laban came from Paddan-Aram?] If it was for the purpose of indicating that he came from Paddan-Aram, then why specify, 'Sister of Laban the Aramaean'?

    C. "But it serves to indicate that her father was deceitful and her brother deceitful [a play on the letters for the word Aramaean], and even the townsfolk of her place were deceitful. Yet that righteous woman come forth from them. What is she like? A rose among the thorns."

    D. R. Phineas in the name of R. Simon: "It is written, 'And Isaac sent away Jacob, and he went to Paddan-Aram, to Laban, son of Bethuel the Aramaean' (Gen. 28:5). That formulation indicates that every single one of them was complicit as a rogue."

The close reading of the formulation of the verse at hand serves to make the main point, which is that Rebecca came from poor stock.

LXIII:V.

1. A. "And Isaac prayed [to (or: entreated) the Lord for his wife, because she was barren, and the Lord granted his prayer, and Rebecca his wife conceived]" (Gen. 25:21):

B. R. Yohanan and R. Simeon b. Laqish:

C. R. Yohanan said, "He poured out prayers in proliferation."

D. R. Simeon b. Laqish said, "He overturned the decree. On that account they call a pitchfork by the letters of the same word as is used for 'prayer,' to indicate that [just as prayer overturns the decree,] so the pitchfork overturns the grain."

2. A. "...for his wife:"

B. This teaches that Isaac was prostrate on one side, and she was prostrate on the other.

C. He said before the Holy One, blessed be he, "Lord of the age, all of the children which you are going to give to me should come from that righteous woman. [I do not want children from a concubine.]"

D. And she said the same thing.

3. A. "...because she was barren:"

B. R. Yudan in the name of R. Simeon b. Laqish: "She had no ovary, so the Holy One, blessed be he, formed an ovary for her."

4. A. "and the Lord granted his prayer:"

B. [Since the Hebrew may be translated, "and the Lord let himself be entreated,"] R. Berekiah in the name of R. Levi said, "It may be compared to the prince who was digging [so Freedman] to the king to receive a *litra* of gold, and this one dug from inside and that one dug from outside. [God wanted to be entreated.]"

Each of the clauses is subjected to a close reading. The interesting observation is that Isaac wanted his children to come from Rebecca, thus linking the present matter to the story of Abraham, not to mention Jacob.

LXIII:VI.

1. A. "And the children struggled together [within her, and she said, 'If it is thus, why do I live?' So she went to inquire of the Lord. And the Lord said to her, 'Two nations are in your womb, and two peoples, born of you, shall be divided; the one shall be stronger than the other, and the elder shall serve the younger'] " (Gen. 25:22-23):

   B. R. Yohanan and R. Simeon b. Laqish:

   C. R. Yohanan said, "[Because the word, 'struggle,' contains the letters for the word, 'run,'] this one was running to kill that one and that one was running to kill this one."

   D. R. Simeon b. Laqish: "This one releases the laws given by that one, and that one releases the laws given by this one" [because the word struggle can be rearranged to produce "release the laws"].

2. A. R. Berekhiah in the name of R. Levi said, "It is so that you should not say that it was only after he left his mother's womb that [Esau] contended against [Jacob].

   B. "But even while he was yet in his mother's womb, his fist was stretched forth against him: 'The wicked stretch out their fists [so Freedman] from the womb' (Ps. 58:4)."

3. A. "And the children struggled together within her:"

   B. [Once more referring to the letters of the word "struggled," with special attention to the ones that mean, "run,"] they wanted to run within her.

   C. When she went by houses of idolatry, Esau would kick, trying to get out: "The wicked are estranged from the womb" (Ps. 58:4).

   D. When she went by synagogues and study-houses, Jacob would kick, trying to get out: "Before I formed you in the womb, I knew you" (Jer. 1:5)."

4. A. "...and she said, 'If it is thus, why do I live?'"

   B. R. Haggai in the name of R. Isaac: "This teaches that our mother, Rebecca, went around to the doors of women and said to them, 'Did you ever have this kind of pain in your life?'"

   C. "[She said to them,] "'If thus:" If this is the pain of having children, would that I had not gotten pregnant.'"

   D. Said R. Huna, "If I am going to produce twelve tribes only through this kind of suffering, would that I had not gotten pregnant."

5. A. It was taught on Tannaite authority in the name of R. Nehemiah, "Rebecca was worthy of having the twelve tribes come forth from her. That is in line with this verse:

B. "'Two nations are in your womb, and two peoples, born of you, shall be divided; the one shall be stronger than the other, and the elder shall serve the younger.' When her days to be delivered were fulfilled, behold, there were twins in her womb. The first came forth red, all his body like a hairy mantle, so they called his name Esau. Afterward his brother came forth...' (Gen. 25:23-24).

C. "'Two nations are in your womb:' thus two.

D. "'and two peoples:'thus two more, hence four.

E. "'...the one shall be stronger than the other:' two more, so six.

F. "'...and the elder shall serve the younger:' two more, so eight.

G. "'When her days to be delivered were fulfilled, behold, there were twins in her womb:' two more, so ten.

H. "'The first came forth red:' now eleven.

I. "'Afterward his brother came forth:' now twelve."

J. There are those who say, "Proof derives from this verse: 'If it is thus, why do I live?' Focusing on the word for 'thus,' we note that the two letters of that word bear the numerical value of seven and five respectively, hence, twelve in all."

6. A. "So she went to inquire of the Lord:"

B. Now were there synagogues and houses of study in those days [that she could go to inquire of the Lord]?

C. But is it not the fact that she went only to the study of Eber?

D. This serves to teach you that whoever receives an elder is as if he receives the Presence of God.

Nos. 1-3 take for granted that Esau represents Rome, and Jacob, Israel. Consequently the verse underlines the point that there is natural enmity between Israel and Rome. Esau hated Israel even while he was still in the womb. Jacob, for his part, revealed from the womb those virtues that would characterize him later on, eager to serve God as Esau was eager to worship idols. The text invites just this sort of reading. No. 4 and No. 5 relate Rebecca's suffering to the birth of the twelve tribes. No. 6 makes its own point, independent of the rest and tacked on.

LXIII:VII.

1. A. "And the Lord said to her, 'Two nations are in your womb, and two peoples, born of you, shall be divided; the one shall be stronger than the other, and the elder shall serve the younger'" (Gen. 25:23):

B. R. Judah [bar Simon] and R. Yohanan in the name of R. Eleazar bar Simon: "On no occasion did the Holy One, blessed be he, ever find it necessary to enter into a conversation with a woman, except with that righteous woman [Sarah] alone, and even on that occasion there was a special reason." [In the case of the woman in the garden, it is alleged in a parallel version, God used an intermediary. We now review other possible cases, in addition to the one involving Eve, as these cases unfold in the book of Genesis.]

C. R. Abba bar Kahana in the name of R. Biri: "How many roundabout routes did he take in order to enter into conversation with her: 'And he said, "No, but you did laugh"' (Gen. 18:15)."

D. But it is written, "And she called on the name of the Lord who had spoken with her" (Gen. 16:13) [speaking of Hagar]!

E. R. Joshua bar Nehemiah in the name of R. Idi: "It was through an angel."

F. And is it not written, "And the Lord said to her [Rebecca]" (Gen. 25:23)?

G. R. Levi in the name of R. Hama bar Hanina: "It was through an angel."

H. R. Eleazar in the name of R. Yose b. Zimri: "It was through Shem."

2. A. "Two nations are in your womb, [and two peoples, born of you, shall be divided; the one shall be stronger than the other, and the elder shall serve the younger]" (Gen. 25:23):

B. There are two proud nations in your womb, this one takes pride in his world, and that one takes pride in his world.

C. This one takes pride in his monarchy, and that one takes pride in his monarchy.

D. There are two proud nations in your womb.

E. Hadrian represents the nations, Solomon, Israel.

F. There are two who are hated by the nations in your womb. All the nations hate Esau, and all the nations hate Israel.

G. [Following Freedman's reading:] The one whom your creator hates is in your womb: "And Esau I hated" (Mal. 1:3).

3. A. "and two peoples, born of you, shall be divided:"

B. Said R. Berekhiah, "On the basis of this statement we have evidence that [Jacob] was born circumcised."

4. A. "...the one shall be stronger than the other, [and the elder shall serve the younger]" (Gen. 25:23):

B. R. Helbo in the name of the house of R. Shila: "Up to this point there were Sabteca and Raamah, but from you will come Jews and Romans." [Freedman, p. 561, n. 8: "Hitherto even the small nations such as Sabteca and Raamah counted; but henceforth all these will pale into insignificance before the two who will rise from you.]

5. A. "...and the elder shall serve the younger" (Gen. 25:23):

B. Said R. Huna, "If he has merit, he will be served, and if not, he will serve."

The syllogism invokes the base-verse as part of its repertoire of cases. No. 2 augments the statement at hand, still more closely linking it to the history of Israel. Nos. 3, 4, and 5 gloss minor details.

LXIII:VIII.

1. A. "When her days to be delivered were fulfilled, [behold, there were twins in her womb. The first came forth red, all his body like a hairy mantle, so they called his name Esau. Afterward his brother came forth, and his hand had taken hold of Esau's heel, so his name was called Jacob. Isaac was sixty years old when she bore them]"(Gen. 25:24-26):

B. [At Gen. 38:28, we have in the case of Tamar, "And it came to pass, when she was being delivered," without reference to the days being fulfilled. Nothing is said about her days being fulfilled (Freedman, p. 562, n. 2). Hence we ask:] In that later case, the period was abbreviated, but here it was complete.

2. A. "...behold, there were twins in her womb:"

B. The word for "twins" here is written defectively while in the case of Tamar, it is fully spelled out. .

C. The reason is that Perez and Zerah [whom Tamar produced] were both righteous, while here we have a case in which Jacob was a righteous and Esau was wicked.

3. A. "The first came forth red:"

B. R. Haggai in the name of R. Isaac: "On account of the merit attained by obeying the commandment, 'You will take for yourself on the first day...,' (Lev. 23:40),

C. "I shall reveal myself to you as the First, avenge you on the first, rebuild the first, and bring you the first.

D. "I shall reveal myself to you the First: 'I am the first and I am the last' (Is. 44:6).

E. "...avenge you on the first: 'Esau, 'The first came forth red.'

F. "...rebuild the first: that is the Temple, of which it is written, 'Your throne of glory, on high from the first, the place of our sanctuary' (Jer. 17:12).

G. "...and bring you the first: that is, the messiah-king: 'A first unto Zion will I give, behold, behold them, and to Jerusalem' (Is. 41:27)."

4. A. "The first came forth red:"

B. Why did Esau come out first?

C. It was so that he would come forth and bring with him all the slop.

D. Said R. Abbahu, "It is comparable to the case of the bath-attendant who cleans out the bath and then washes the prince. So too, why did Esau come out first?

E. "It was so that he would come forth and bring with him all the slop."

5. A. A noble lady asked R. Yose bar Halapta, "Why did Esau come out first?"

B. He said to her, "The first drop of semen went to Jacob. [Thus he was inside first and came out last.]"

C. He said to her, "The matter may be compared to this case. If you put two pearls into a single tube [and then pour them out from the same end of the tube], will not the one that you put in first come out last? So too, the first drop of semen went to Jacob. [Thus he was inside first and came out last.]"

6. A. "The first came forth red:"

B. R. Abba bar Kahana, "[He was red] because he was entirely a shedder of blood.

C. "When Samuel saw that David was red, as it is written, 'And he sent and brought him in. Now he was ruddy' (1 Sam. 16:12), he feared, saying, perhaps this one too is a shedder of blood.

D. "Said the Holy One, blessed be he, to him, 'Withal of beautiful eyes' (1 Sam. 16:12), that is to say, Esau killed out of his own will and consent, but this one puts people to death only upon the decision of the sanhedrin."

7. A. Diocletian the king was originally a swineherd in Tiberias. When he came near a school, the children would go out and beat him up. After some time he was made king. He came and took up residence near Paneas and he sent letters to Tiberias just before the eve of the Sabbath, giving this command: "I command the rabbis of the Jews to appear before me on Sunday morning." He gave orders to the messenger, telling him not to give the command to them until the last light on Friday evening. [It would not be possible for the rabbis to keep the order unless they traveled on the Sabbath day.]

B. R. Samuel bar Nahman went down to bathe. He saw Rabbi standing before his school, and his face was white. He said to him, "Why is your face white?"

C. He said to him, "Thus and so were the orders that were sent to me in letters from King Diocletian."

D. He said to him, "Go and bathe, for our creator will do miracles for you."

E. He went in to bath and a bath sprite came along, joking and dancing toward them. Rabbi wanted to rebuke him. Said to him R. Samuel bar Nahman, "Leave him alone, for there are times that they appear because of miracles."

F. He said to the sprite, "Your master is in distress, and you are laughing?"

G. He said to them, "Go, eat and celebrate a happy Sabbath, for your creator is doing miracles, and I will place you on Sunday morning where you wish to be."

H. At the end of the Sabbath, when the session ended, he went out and set them before the gates of Paneas. They went in and said to Diocletian, "Lo, they are standing before the gates."

I. He said to them, "Then close the gates."

J. He took them and set them on the rampart of the town.

K. They went in and told Diocletian. He said to them, "I order that you heat the baths for three days, then let them go in and bathe and come before me."

L. They went and heated the baths for three days, and the sprite went and cooled off the heat for them, so the rabbis went in, bathed, and appeared before him.

M. He said to them, "Because you people know that your God does miracles for you, you ridicule the king!"

N. They said to him, "True enough, we ridiculed Diocletian the swineherd, but to Diocletian the King we are loyal subjects."

O. He said to them, "Nonetheless, do not insult even an unimportant Roman or a soldier of the lowest rank."

8. A. "...all his body like a hairy mantel:"

B. Said R. Hinena bar Isaac, "All of him is worthy of a mantel. [Freedman, p. 5674, n. 2: Every Roman, no matter how humble might attain to the royal mantle, as in the case of Diocletian.]

C. Rabbis of the south in the name of R. Alexandri, and Rahbah in the name of R. Abba bar Kahana, "This one came forth entirely like chaff in the threshing floor: 'Then was the iron...broken in pieces together and became like the chaff of the summer threshing floors' (Dan. 2:35)." [Freedman, p. 564, n. 3: Mantle is connected with the word for threshing floor, while the word for hair is read as the word for whirlwind, which scatters the chaff.]

D. Said R. Hinena bar Isaac, "How come they will be entirely like chaff in the threshing floor? Because they attacked noble ones." [Freedman, p. 564, n. 4: That refers to Israel: "They are the excellent in whom is all my delight" (Ps. 16:3). This comment is a play on the words for mantle and threshing floor, the latter word now connected with the word, sharing the same letters, that means strong or distinguished.]

9. A. "So they called his name Esau" (Gen. 25:25):

B. [Connecting the Hebrew name of Esau, *esav* , with the word for worthless, *shav* :] "Lo, this one is worthless, whom I have created my world."

C. Said R. Isaac, "You have given a name to your pig, so I shall name my firstborn: 'Thus says the Lord, Israel is my son, my firstborn' (Ex. 4:22)."

10. A. "And afterward his brother came forth, [and his hand had taken hold of Esau's heel, so his name was called Jacob. Isaac was sixty years old when she bore them]" (Gen. 25:26):

B. An official posed a question to one of the members of the house of Silna, saying to him, "What nation will hold power after us?"

C. He produced a blank piece of paper, took his pen, and wrote on it: "And afterward his brother came forth, and his hand had taken hold of Esau's heel. [After Esau, that is Rome, comes Israel, holding on to the heel.]"

D. They said, "See how old words from an elder become new: this verse serves to tell you how much suffering troubled that righteous man [Jacob]."

Nos. 1, 2 present minor philological clarifications. No. 3 provides a kind of litany, now built on "the first," to which our base verse makes a tangential contribution. The exegesis of the sense of the verse itself then begins with No.

4's special interest in the sense of the passage. Nos. 5, 6 make their own points, to which the facts of the verse make a modest contribution. No. 5 answers an obvious question, and No. 6 makes something of the fact that both Esau and David are described as ruddy. I assume that No. 7 is inserted because Esau stands for Rome. Then 8.A. accounts for the item. I can think of no other explanation for its inclusion. No. 9 explains the name of Esau, with the two-pronged polemic. First, naming Esau is like naming a pig. Second, in any event Israel, not Esau, is called firstborn. No. 10 presents the stunning claim that after Rome comes the rule of Israel. No effort is spared to link the present passage to Israelite history.

LXIII:IX.

1. A. "When the boys grew up, [Esau was a skillful hunter, a man of the field, while Jacob was a quiet man, dwelling in tents]" (Gen. 25:27):

    B. R. Phineas in the name of R. Levi: "The matter may be compared to the case of a myrtle and a wild rose, growing side by side. When they had grown up, the one gave forth its scent, the other its thorns.

    C. "So too, all thirteen years [of immaturity] the two of them would go to school and come home from school, but after thirteen years, the one went to the study houses, and the other to temples of idolatry."

    D. Said R. Eleazar b. R. Simeon, "A person has to take responsibility for his son for thirteen years. From that time on, he has to say, 'Blessed is he who has relieved me from the penalties coming for the misdeeds of this one, [since he is now responsible for himself]."

The exegete yields a detail on the youth of the lads. The recurrent insistence on Esau's engagement with idolatry recurs.

LXIII:X.

1. A. "[When the boys grew up,] Esau was a skillful hunter, [a man of the field, while Jacob was a quiet man, dwelling in tents]" (Gen. 25:27):

    B. He hunted people through snaring them in words [as the Roman prosecutors do:] "Well enough, you did not steal. But who stole with you? You did not kill, but who killed with you?"

2. A. R. Abbahu said, "He was a trapper and a fieldsman, trapping at home and in the field.

    B. "He trapped at home: 'How do you tithe salt?' [which does not, in fact, have to be tithed at all!]

C. "He trapped in the field: 'How do people give tithe for straw?' [which does not, in fact, have to be tithed at all!]"

3. A. R. Hiyya bar Abba said, "He treated himself as totally without responsibility for himself, like a field [on which anyone tramples].

B. "Said the Israelites before the Holy One, blessed be he, 'Lord of all ages, is it not enough for us that you have subjugated us to the seventy nations, but even to this one, who is subjected to sexual intercourse just like a woman?'

C. "Said to them the Holy One, blessed be he, 'I too will exact punishment from him with those same words: 'And the heart of the mighty men of Edom at that day shall be as the heart of a woman in her pangs' (Jer. 49:22)."

4. A. "...while Jacob was a quiet man, dwelling in tents" (Gen. 25:27):

B. There is a reference to two tents, that is, the school house of Shem and the school house of Eber.

5. A. "Now Isaac loved Esau, because he ate of his game:"

B. It was first rate meat and wine for Isaac's eating.

6. A. "...but Rebecca loved Jacob" (Gen. 25:28):

B. The more she heard his voice, the more she loved him.

Nos. 1-3 deal with the description of Esau, explaining why he was like the field, Nos. 2, 3. No. 2 follows up on No. 1, that is, hunting people and trapping them with words. In the one case Esau is compared to a Roman prosecutor, in the other, to a critic of the law. No. 3 then moves on to fresh material. Now Esau/Rome is condemned for yet another reason. The final items, Nos. 4-6, present light glosses.

LXIII:XI.

1. A. "Once when Jacob was boiling pottage,[Esau came in from the field, and he was famished]" (Gen. 25:29):

B. He said to him, "What is this dish for?"

C. He said to him, "It is because that elder [grandfather, Abraham] has died [and I am preparing a meal for the mourners."

D. He said to him, "Has the attribute of justice smitten that elder? Then there is no possibility either of reward or of the resurrection of the dead."

2. A. And the Holy Spirit says, "'Do not weep for the dead, do not mourn for him' (Jer. 22:10).

B. "'Do not weep for the dead' refers to Abraham.

C. "'But weep for the one who goes' (Jer. 22:10) speaks of Esau."

The incident now is placed in the larger context of the narrative, namely, the death of Abraham, Gen. 25:8. No. 1 has the meal prepared by Jacob intended for the mourners' meal, and No. 2 compares the death of Abraham to the fall of Esau. The effect is to tighten the narrative.

LXIII:XII.

1. A. "Esau came in from the field, and he was famished" (Gen. 25:29):

B. R. Phineas in the name of R. Levi and rabbis in the name of R. Simon: "You find that Abraham lived one hundred seventy-five years, while Isaac lived one hundred eighty. Those five years that the Holy One, blessed be he, deducted from the life of Abraham were because Esau both had sexual relations with a betrothed girl and also killed someone.

C. "That is in line with this verse: 'Esau came in from the field.' That means, he had sexual relations with a betrothed girl, in line with this verse: 'But if the man find the damsel that is betrothed in the field and the man take hold of her and lie with her' (Deut 22:25).

D. "'That he was famished' means that he murdered someone: 'For my soul faints before the murderers' (Jer. 4:31)."

E. R. Berekhiah and R. Zakkai the Elder: "He also stole, in line with this verse: 'If thieves came to you, if robbers by night' (Obad. 1:5). [The word for field is linked to the word for robbers, both of which use the same letters.]

F. "Said the Holy One, blessed be he, 'Thus did I promise Abraham, saying to him, "And you shall go to your fathers in peace, you shall be buried in a good old age" (Gen. 15:15). Now is it good old age to have to see your grandson worshipping idols, committing acts of fornication, and murdering? It is better for him to pass away in peace, as it is said, "For your lovingkindness is better than life" (Ps. 63:4).' [So just as we saw, earlier, that Abraham died in peace, so the story now goes on to explain why Abraham died prematurely.]"

2. A. "And Esau said to Jacob, 'Let me swallow some of that red pottage, for I am famished'" (Gen. 25:30):

B. Said R. Isaac bar Zeira, "That wicked man opened up his mouth like a camel. He said to him, 'I'll open up my mouth, and you just toss in the food.'

C. "That is in line with what we have learned in the Mishnah: **People may not stuff a camel or force food on it, but may toss food into its mouth [M. Shab. 24:3]."**

3. A. "Of that red pottage" (Gen. 25:29):

B. R. Yohanan and R. Simeon b. Laqish:

C. R. Yohanan said, "He wanted his own and his master's [namely, what belonged to Edom, for *edom* is the word for red, hence the red pottage of Edom]."

D. R. Simeon b. Laqish said, "He wanted what belonged to him and people like him."

4. A. He was red, his food was red, his land was red, his mighty men were red, their clothing was red, his avenger will be red, and dressed in red. [Red symbolizes war.]

B. He was red: "And the first came forth ruddy" (Gen. 25:25).

C. ...his food was red: "Let me swallow some of that red pottage, for I am famished"' (Gen. 25:30).

D. ...his land was red: "To Esau his brother to the land of Seir, the field of red" (Gen. 32:4).

E. ...his mighty men were red: "The shield of his mighty men is made red" (Nahum 2:4).

F. ...their clothing was red: "The valiant men are in scarlet" (Nahum 2:4).

G. ...his avenger will be red: "My beloved is white and ruddy" (Song 5:10).

H. ...and dressed in red: "Wherefore is your apparel red" (Is. 63:2).

No. 1 again links Esau's behavior to the mortal sins of murder, idolatry, fornication, and the like, and further explains why Abraham died prematurely. Thus Abraham is set into opposition to Esau, that is Rome. No. 2 stresses Esau's animal-like behavior. No. 3 takes up the correspondence of the word for "red" and for "Edom." No. 4 exploits that correspondence to create a striking litany, identifying Rome with all sorts of red symbols.

LXIII:XIII.

1. A. "Jacob said, 'First sell me your birthright.' Esau said, 'I am about to die, of what use is a birthright to me?'"

B. He said to him, "Sell me one day that is yours."

C. Said R. Aha, "Whoever knows how to reckon [the exile] will discover that for only one day Jacob did live under the shadow of Esau." [Freedman, p.

568, n. 4: The verse is translated as symbolically alluding to Israel in the diaspora, with Jacob demanding, "Sell me...yours," "leave me in peace if only for a short while," and R. Aha observes that that indeed has been the case.]

2. A. "Esau said, 'I am about to die, of what use is a birthright to me?'"

    B. R. Simeon b. Laqish said, "He began to revile and blaspheme. What do I need it for: '...of what use is a birthright to me?'"

3. A. Another explanation: "I am about to die:"

    B. For Nimrod was looking for him to kill him on account of the garment that had belonged to the first man, for at the moment that Esau put it on and went out to the field, all of the wild beasts and fowl in the world came and gathered around him [and that is why he was such a good hunter].

4. A. "Jacob said, 'Swear to me first.' So he swore to him and sold his birthright to Jacob" (Gen. 25:33):

    B. Why did Jacob risk his life for the right of the firstborn?

    C. For we have learned in the Mishnah: **Before the tabernacle was set up, the high places were permitted, and the rite of offering was carried out by the first born. Once the tabernacle was set up, the high places were forbidden, and the rite of offering was carried out by the priests**[M. Zebahim 14:4].

    D. He said, "Should that wicked man stand and make offerings?" Therefore Jacob risked his life for the right of the firstborn.

5. A. That is in line with the following verse: "I will prepare you for blood, and blood shall pursue you, surely you have hated blood, therefore shall blood pursue you" (Ez. 35:6).

    B. But did Esau hate blood?

    C. R. Levi in the name of R. Hama bar Hanina: "This is the blood of circumcision [which Esau did hate]."

    D. R. Levi in the name of R. Samuel b. Nahman,"This refers to the blood of the offerings by the firstborn."

    E. Rabbis say, "You have hated the blood of man when it is in his body, in line with this verse: 'Yes, he loved cursing and it came to him and he did not delight in blessing' (Ps. 109:17)."

    F. R. Levi in the name of R. Hama bar Hanina, "He did not take pleasure in the birthright."

G. R. Huna said, "This refers to the blood of the offerings, which are called a blessing, in line with this verse: 'An altar of earth you shall make for me...I will come to you and bless you' (Ex. 20:21)."

No. 1 makes explicit what is at stake in the sale, namely, Israel's life under Esau's rule. Nos. 2, 3 revert to the body of the story and gloss details. No. 4 shows that what was at stake was a considerable issue. No. 5 takes up the cited intersecting verse, continuing the foregoing, the matter of the offerings. Esau had no right to make offerings, he had no respect for the Temple and its cult.

LXIII:XIV.

1. A. "Then Jacob gave Esau bread and pottage of lentils [and he ate and drank and rose and went away. Thus Esau despised his birthright]" (Gen. 25:34):

B. Just as a lentil is shaped like a wheel, so the [mourning in this] world is like a wheel.

C. Just as a lentil has no mouth, so mourning has no mouth. How so? The mourner is forbidden to speak.

D. Just as a lentil is subject to mourning and joy [being served on both occasions] so the mourning of our father, Abraham, contained some joy, since Jacob took the birthright.

2. A. "...and he ate and drank:"

B. He brought with him a gang of thugs. They said, "We will eat Jacob's food and ridicule him."

C. But the Holy Spirit said, "They prepare the table" (Is. 21:5). They arrange the table.

D. "They light the lamps" (Is. 21:5). They kindle the lights.

E. R. Abba b. Kahana said, "In some places a lamp is called by the word at hand."

F. "Rise up, you princes" (Is. 21:5). This refers to Michael and Gabriel.

G. "Anoint the shield" (Is. 21:5). "Write over the birthright to Jacob."

H. Bar Qappara taught on Tannaite authority, "It was because they were making fun of him.

I. "And how do we know that the Holy One, blessed be he, concurred with them [that is, the gang was ridiculing Jacob in selling the birthright, but God took it very seriously]? Since it says, 'Thus says the Lord, Israel is my son, my firstborn' (Ex. 4:22). [Thus God confirmed the sale of the right of the firstborn to Jacob, who is Israel.]"

3. A. "...and rose and went away:"

    B. R. Levi said, "His world went with him. [He lost his portion in the world to come.]"

4. A. "Thus Esau despised his birthright" (Gen. 25:34):

    B. What did he despise right along with the birthright [that there should be the inclusionary use of the accusative particle *T* which indicates that there was something more subject to his contempt]?

    C. Said R. Levi, "The resurrection of the dead is what he despised along with the birthright."

5. A. "When the wicked comes, there comes also disgrace, and with ignominy, reproach" (Prov. 18:3):

    B. "When the wicked comes" refers to Esau, in line with this verse: "And they shall be called the border of wickedness'" (Mal. 1:4, which speaks of Esau).

    C. "...there comes also disgrace," for his disgrace came right with him.

    D. "..., and with ignominy, reproach," for the reproach of famine accompanied him.

    E. The word reproach speaks of famine: "And I will no more make you a reproach of famine among the nations" (Cf. Joel 2:19, Ez. 36:30) [Freedman, p. 571, n. 4).]

    F. "Now there was a famine in the land" (Gen. 16:1).

No. 1 reverts to the direct connection of Jacob to Abraham. No. 2 fills out the story of Esau's sale. He brought friends and pretended to go along with Jacob, all the while ridiculing him. But God affirmed his action. The intersecting verse is particularly effective here. Nos. 3, 4 make the same point. No. 5 builds a stunning bridge to the next story.

Chapter Thirty-Two

Parashah Sixty-Four. Genesis 26:1-32

LXIV:I.

1. A. "Now there was a famine in the land, besides the former famine that was in the days of Abraham" (Gen. 26:1):

   B. "The Lord knows the days of those who are whole-hearted, and their inheritance shall be forever. They shall not be ashamed in the time of evil, and in the days of famine they shall be satisfied" (Ps. 37:18-19).

   C. "The Lord knows the days of those who are whole-hearted" refers to Isaac.

   D. "...and their inheritance shall be forever." "Sojourn in this land and I will be with you" (Gen. 26:3).

   E. "They shall not be ashamed in the time of evil" refers to the time of the evil of Abimelech.

   F. "...and in the days of famine they shall be satisfied." "Now there was a famine in the land, besides the former famine that was in the days of Abraham" (Gen. 26:1).

   The intersecting verse weaves tightly into the fabric of the base verse, embracing, as it does, two of the base verses, Gen. 26:1 and 3. The key to the selection of the intersecting verse, of course, is its reference to famine. The main point is that Isaac survived the famine because God was with him.

LXIV:II.

1. A. "The Lord will not suffer the soul of the righteous to famish, but he thrusts away the desire of the wicked" (Prov. 10:3):

   B. "The Lord will not suffer the soul of the righteous" refers to Isaac, as it is said, "Sojourn in this land and I will be with you" (Gen. 26:3).

   C. "...but he thrusts away the desire of the wicked" (Ps. 37:19) speaks of Abimelech.

   D. "They shall not be ashamed in the time of evil" refers to the time of the evil of Abimelech.

E. "... and in the days of famine they shall be satisfied" (Ps. 37:19) "Now there was a famine in the land, besides the former famine that was in the days of Abraham" (Gen. 26:1).

2. A. R. Levi commenced discourse by citing the following verse: "'When the wicked comes, there comes also disgrace, and with ignominy, reproach' (Prov. 18:3):

B. "'When the wicked comes' refers to the wicked Esau.

C. "'...there comes also disgrace,' for his disgrace came right with him.

D. "'...and with ignominy, reproach,' for the reproach of famine accompanied him. [So Esau brought the famine.]

E. "The word reproach speaks of famine: 'And I will no more make you a reproach of famine among the nations' (Cf. Joel 2:19, Ez. 36:30) [Freedman, p. 571, n. 4].

F. "'Now there was a famine in the land' Gen. 16:1)."

3. A. "Now there was a famine in the land" Gen. 16:1):

B. Ten famines came into the world.

C. One was in the time of Adam: "Cursed is the ground for your sake" (Gen. 3:17).

D. One was in the time of Lamech: "Out of the ground which the Lord has cursed" (Gen. 5:29).

E. One was in the time of Abraham: "And there was a famine in the land" (Gen. 12:10).

F. One was in the time of Isaac: "And there was famine in the land, beside the first famine that was in the time of Abraham" (Gen. 26:1).

G. One was in the time of Jacob: "For these two years has the famine been in the land" (Gen. 45:6).

H. One was in the time of the rule of judges: "And it came to pass in the days when the judges ruled, that there was a famine in the land" (Ruth 1:1).

I. One was in the time of Elijah: "As the Lord, the God of Israel, lives, before whom I stand, there shall not be dew or rain these years" (1 Kgs. 17:1).

J. One was in the time of Elisha: "And there was a great famine in Samaria" (2 Kgs. 6:25).

K. There is one famine which moves about the world.

L. One famine will be in the age to come: "Not a famine of bread nor a thirst for water but of hearing the words of the Lord" (Amos 8:11).

M. R. Huna and R. Jeremiah in the name of Samuel bar R. Isaac: "In point of fact its principal appearance should have come not in the time of David. It was supposed to come only in the time of Saul, but because Saul was a shoot of a sycamore tree, the Holy One, blessed be he, postponed the famine and assigned it to the time of David."

N. Will Shilah sin and Yohanan be punished? [Why punish David for what Saul did?]

O. Said R. Hiyya, "The matter may be compared to the case of a glass maker who had a basket full of cups and cut glass. When he wanted to hang up the basket, he would bring a peg and drive it in and first suspend himself from the peg [to test it] and only then would suspend his basket.

P. "That is why all of the famines came not in the time of unimportant men but in the time of heroes, who could withstand the test."

Q. R. Berekhiah recited in their regard the following verse of Scripture: "He gives power to the faint" (Is. 40:29).

R. R. Berekhiah in the name of R. Helbo: "Two famines came in the time of Abraham." [This would then take Lamech off the list of heroes.]

S. R. Huna in the name of R. Aha: "One indeed was in the time of Lamech, the other in the time of Abraham."

T. The famine that came in the time of Elijah was one of [Freedman:] scarcity, one year yielding and one year not yielding. [Freedman p. 208, n. 5: There was food, but not enough to satisfy.]

U. The famine that came in the time of Elishah was one of panic: "Until an ass's head was sold for fourscore pieces of silver" (2 Kgs. 6:25).

V. As to the famine that came in the time of the judges:

W. R. Huna in the name of R. Dosa: "From two *seah*s of wheat for a *sela* the price went up to one *seah* of wheat per *sela*."

X. And lo, it has been taught on Tannaite authority: [Since it is a religious duty to dwell in the holy land,] someone should go abroad, leaving the land, only if two *seah*s of wheat go for a *sela*. [How then could the family have left Bethlehem and gone abroad, if the price was not at the level that justified emigration?]

Y. Said R. Simeon, "When does this rule apply? It is when one cannot find any to buy [at such a high price], but if one can find some to buy, then even if the price is a *seah* for a *sela*, one should not abandon the land and go abroad."

The choice of the intersecting verse, No. 1, rests upon the verb for "suffer," which uses the same consonants as the word for famine. The repetition of the materials of Ps. 37:18 obviously is an error, since it is uncommon for an intersecting verse to shift in the middle of a composition. No. 2 goes over familiar ground. Its location at the end of LXIII is preferable. It appears to blame the famine on Esau. But this point is undeveloped. No. 3 intersects in using our base-verse as a proof-text; the syllogistic composition is interchangeable in a number of locations. At issue is the rule governing when famine comes, an inquiry into the laws of history.

LXIV:III.

1. A. "And Isaac went to Gerar, to Abimelech, king of the Philistines"(Gen. 26:1):

    B. Gerar is the same as Geradike.

    C. R. Dosetai in the name of R. Samuel bar Nahman: "On what account did sages decree for the air-space of Geradike the status of uncleanness? It is because it is bad air."

    D. And to what extent did they impose that status?

    E. R. Hanan in the name of R. Samuel bar R. Isaac: "To the brook of Egypt."

2. A. "And the Lord appeared to him and said, 'Do not go down to Egypt; dwell in the land [of which I shall tell you. Sojourn in this land, and I will be with you and will bless you; for to you and to your descendants I will give all these lands, and I will fulfil the oath which I swore to Abraham, your father']" (Gen. 26:2-3):

    B. [As to the meaning of the verb "dwell," the sense is this:] Make a dwelling [cultivate] in the land, be a sower of seed, be a planter.

    C. Another meaning of the statement, "Sojourn in this land" [invokes the consonants for the word for the Presence of God, which are the same as for the verb "dwell," thus:] "Dwell in the land, make a dwelling for the Presence of God."

3. A. "...for to you and to your descendants I will give all these lands:" [The word for "these" is written as "the strong," hence, even the strong lands (Freedman)].

    B. [The same construction also bears the sense of "these lands and not others," hence] only part of them.

    C. "When shall I give you the rest? In the age to come."

No. 1 contributes a minor gloss. No. 2 does the same. No. 3 introduces a messianic dimension to the discourse.

LXIV:IV.

1. A. "[I will multiply your descendants as the stars of heaven and will give to your descendants all these lands; and by your descendants all the nations of the earth shall bless themselves,] because Abraham obeyed my voice and kept my charge, my commandments, my statutes, and my laws" (Gen. 26:4-5):

   B. Both R. Hanina and R. Yohanan said, "At the age of forty-eight, Abraham came to recognize his creator."

   C. R. Levi in the name of R. Simeon b. Laqish: "He was three years old."

   D. "How do we know? It is stated, 'because Abraham obeyed my voice and kept my charge,' that is, he listened to the voice of his creator and kept his charge [for the years numbered by the numerical value of the consonants in the word] 'because' [and since he lived 175 years, and the letters of the word for 'because' bear the numerical value of 172, he was three years of age when he converted]."

2. A. R. Aha in the name of R. Alexandri, R. Samuel b. Nahman in the name of R. Jonathan: "Even the laws governing the commingling of domain in courtyards [for purposes of creating a single domain for carrying on the Sabbath] did Abraham know."

   B. R. Phineas, R. Hilqiah, R. Simon in the name of R. Samuel: "Even the new name that the Holy One, blessed be he, is destined to assign to Jerusalem: 'On that day they will call Jerusalem "the throne of God"' (Jer. 3:17) Abraham knew."

   C. R. Berekhiah, R. Hiyya, the rabbis of the other place [Babylonia] in the name of R. Judah: "There is not a single day on which the Holy One, blessed be he, does not create a new law in the court above. What is the scriptural verse that shows it? 'Hear attentively the noise of his voice and the meditation that goes out of his mouth' (Job 37:2). The word meditation speaks only of the Torah, as it is said, 'But you shall meditate therein day and night' (Joshua 1:8). [Even those new laws Abraham knew.]"

The polemic repeats the claim that Abraham kept the entire Torah even before it was given. The base-verse surely invites that judgment. No. 1 makes a point to which our base verse supplies a piece of information. No. 2 is tacked on because it accounts for the reference to Abraham here.

LXIV:V.

1. A. "And it came to pass, when he had been there a long time, [Abimelech, king of the Philistines, looked out of a window and saw Isaac fondling Rebecca, his wife]" (Gen. 26:8):

B. Said R. Yohanan, "[With reference to the passage of time, to which the base verse refers,] a bad dream, a bad prophecy, and a pathological mourning all are in the end annulled by the passage of time.

C. "As to a bad dream and a bad prophecy: 'The days are prolonged and every vision fails' (Ez. 12:22).

D. "As to pathological mourning: 'And it came to pass, when he had been there a long time, Abimelech, king of the Philistines, looked out of a window and saw Isaac fondling Rebecca, his wife' (Gen. 26:8). [Isaac thus had resumed sexual relations with his wife.]"

2. A. R. Huna and R. Jeremiah in the name of R. Hiyya bar Ba: "It was because much time had passed that he did this thing [that is, had sexual relations after a period of cessation in grief at his father's death]."

B. [But how could they have had sexual relations in daylight?] Did not R. Yohanan say, "He who has sexual relations by day, lo, this is an inappropriate practice."

C. For R. Yohanan said, "Sexual relations should be carried on only by night: 'In the evening she came' (Est. 2:14).

D. "Job cursed 'the day' of his birth and 'the night' of his conception: 'Let the day perish on which I was born and the night on which it was said, "A man has been conceived"' (Job 3:3)."

E. Said R. Marinos b. Hoshaia, "Said Job, 'Would that his mother was in her menstrual period when his father came to have sexual relations with her, so that she should say to him, "Does a man kill? Would a man make me conceive?"'"

F. [Taking up the discourse left off at D:] "Jeremiah cursed the day on which he was born and the day on which he was conceived: 'Cursed be the day on which I was born, the day on which my mother bore me' (Jer. 20:14).

G. "'...the day on which I was born' refers to the day on which he came forth.

H. "'...the day on which my mother bore me' refers to the day on which he was conceived."

I. But how is it possible that a righteous man like Hilqiah should have had sexual relations by day?

J. Since Jezebel was killing the prophets, he came and had sexual relations by day and then he fled.

No. 1 invokes the base verse as part of its repertoire of facts. No. 2 carries forward the topic and discourse of No. 1.

LXIV:VI.

1. A. "And Isaac sowed in that land and reaped in the same year a hundredfold" (Gen. 26:12):

   B. Said R. Helbo, "The text stresses 'that land,' 'that year,' thus the land was hard and the year difficult. But if it had been a good year, how much the more so [would the crop have prospered]!"

2. A. "...and reaped in the same year a hundredfold" (Gen. 26:12):

   B. The reference to a hundredfold means, a hundred *kor*.

   C. The reference to a hundredfold also teaches that they made an estimate of what it would yield, and the crop was a hundred times more than the estimate.

   D. But how is it possible to have made such an estimate, since what is weighed, measured, or counted will not produce a blessing?

   E. The measurement was taken on account of tithing.

The verse is lightly glossed. The sense of a hundredfold is enriched.

LXIV:VII.

1. A. "So Abimelech commanded [warned] [all the people, saying, 'Whoever touches this man or his wife shall be put to death']" (Gen. 26:11):

   B. Said R. Aibu, No one should do so much as to toss a pebble at them: 'They gather themselves together, they hide themselves, they mark my steps, according as they have waited for my soul' (Ps. 56:7). [That is why such orders had to be given.]"

2. A. "And the man became rich and gained more and more until he became very wealthy. [He had possessions of flocks and herds and a great household, so that the Philistines envied him] (Gen. 26:11):

   B. Said R. Hanan, "It reached the point that people said, 'I'd rather have the manure of the mules of Isaac than the gold and silver of Abimelech.'"

3. A. "He had possessions of flocks and herds and a great household, so that the Philistines envied him" (Gen. 26:11):

   B. Daniel the tailor said, "The word for "household" is written so as to be pronounced 'service.'

   C. "If a man does not become a slave to his slave, he does not acquire possession of him."

4. A. "And Abimelech said to Isaac, 'Go away from us, for you are much mightier than we'" (Gen. 26:16):

B. [Since the word for "mightier than we," may be read "might derives from us,"] he said to him, "All of the power that you have gained, does it not come from us to you? In the past you had only one sheep, and now you have many."

Nos. 1, 2, and 4 gloss the cited verses. No. 3 uses the verse at hand to demonstrate its own syllogism. The main point is that the others envied Isaac for his wealth, which God had given him.

LXIV:VIII.

1. A. "And Isaac dug again the wells of water [which had been dug in the days of Abraham his father; for the Philistines had stopped them after the death of Abraham; and he gave them the names which his father had given them. But when Isaac's servants dug in the valley and found there a well of springing water, the herdsmen of Gerar quarreled with Isaac's herdsmen, saying, 'The water is ours.' So he called the name of the well Esek, because they contended with him. Then they dug another well, and they quarreled over that also, so he called its name Sitnah. And he moved from there and dug another well and over that they did not quarrel, so he called its name Rehoboth, saying 'For now the Lord has made room for us, and we shall be fruitful in the land'" (Gen. 26:18-22). "That same day Isaac's servants came and told him about the well which they had dug and said to him, 'We have found water.' He called it Shibah, therefore the name of the city is Beer Sheba to this day" (Gen. 26:32-33)]:

B. How many wells did our father Isaac dig in Beer Sheba?

C. R. Judah bar Simon said, "Four, corresponding to the four standards in the wilderness that marked off his descendants."

D. And rabbis said, "Five, corresponding to the five scrolls of the Torah."

E. "'So he called the name of the well Esek, because they contended with him:' this one corresponds to the scroll of Genesis, in which the Holy One, blessed be he, is contending in the creation of his world.

F. "'Then they dug another well, and they quarreled over that also, so he called its name Sitnah:' this one corresponds to the scroll of Exodus, on the count that they embittered their lives with harsh labor.

G. "'But when Isaac's servants dug in the valley and found there a well of springing water:' this corresponds to the book of Leviticus, which is full of many laws.

H. "'He called it Shibah:' this one corresponds to the book of Numbers, which completes the number of the seven scrolls of the Torah."

I. But are they not only five, not seven?!

J. [No, indeed there were seven, as will now be explained:] Bar Qappara treated the first part of the book of Numbers until the verse, "And it came to pass, when the ark set forward" (Num. 10:35), as one book. [And the portion beginning with the verse,] "And it came to pass, when the ark set forward" until the end of the book of Numbers, he treated as another book.

2. A. "And he moved from there and dug another well and over that they did not quarrel, so he called its name 'Room' [Rehoboth],"

B. on account of the following explanation: "saying 'For now the Lord has made room for us, and we shall be fruitful in the land'" (Gen. 26:18-22). 2-33).

No. 1 works out a detailed reading of the verse. But the introduction of the points of correspondence between the deeds of the patriarchs and the history of Israel moves the interpretation away from a simple work of glossing. No. 2 explains the obvious.

LXIV:IX.

1. A. "Then Abimelech went to him from Gerar [with Ahuzzath his adviser and Phicol the commander of his army]" (Gen. 26:26):

B. He was wounded [Freedman, p. 579, n. 2: the word for wounded, *megorar*, is a play on the letters used to say "from Gerar."]

C. This teaches that thugs got into his house and beat him up all night.

2. A. Another matter: [Since the same letters yield the word] "scrape," it teaches that scabs came up on him. [He kept scraping himself.]

3. A. "...with Ahuzzath his adviser:"

B. R. Judah and R. Nehemiah:

C. R. Judah said, "His name was 'Ahuzzath-his-adviser.'"

D. R. Nehemiah said, "The words refer to a whole company of his friends."

4. A. "And Phicol" (Gen. 21:22):

B. R. Judah and R. Nehemiah:

C. R. Judah says, "Phicol was his name."

D. R. Nehemiah said, "The name means, 'Everybody's mouth' (Pi is 'mouth,' Col is 'everybody'], for all of his army would kiss him on his mouth."

Each of the clauses is given its gloss. Apart from an interest in denigrating Abimelech and his crew, I see no polemical charge.

LXIV:X.

1. A. "They said, 'We see plainly that the Lord is with you; [so we say, 'Let there be be an oath between you and us, and let us make a covenant with you, that you will do us no harm, just as we have not touched you and have done to you nothing but good and have sent you away in peace. You are now the blessed of the Lord']" (Gen. 26:29):

B. ["We have seen plainly that the Lord is with you] on the basis of the fact that we have seen your deeds and the deeds of your fathers.

C. "...'so we say, 'Let there be be an oath between you and us, and let us make a covenant with you.'"

2. A. "[...so we say,'Let there be be an oath between you and us, and let us make a covenant with you,] that you will do us no harm, just as we have not touched you and have done to you nothing but good:'"

B. [As to the meaning of the words, "nothing but good,"] the word for "nothing but" constitutes an exclusionary usage, bearing the meaning that in point of fact, they did not do them a complete favor.

3. A. In the time of R. Joshua b. Hananiah the government decreed that the house of the sanctuary should be rebuilt. Pappus and Lulianus set up money changing tables from Acco to Antioch to provide what was needed for those who came up from the Exile in Babylonia.

B. The Samaritans went and reported to him, "Let it be known to the king that if this rebellious city is rebuilt and the walls are finished, they will not pay tribute (*mindah*), impost (*belo*) or toll (*halak*)" (Ezra 4:13).

C. The words *mindah, belo,* and *halak,* respectively, mean land tax, poll tax, and a tax on crops [Freedman, p. 580, n. 2].

D. He said to them, "What shall we do? For the decree has already been issued [for the rebuilding to go forward]."

E. They said to him, "Send orders to them either to change its location or to add five cubits to it or to cut it down by five cubits, and they will give up the project on their own."

F. The community was assembled on the plain of Beth Rimmon, when the royal orders arrived they began to weep. They had the mind to rebel against the government.

G. They said, "Let one wise man go and calm the community down." They said, "Let R. Joshua b. Hananiah do it, because he is a scholar [Hebrew: *askolostiqah*] of the Torah."

H. He went up and expounded as follows: "A wild lion killed a beast and got a bone stuck in his throat. The lion said, 'To whoever will come and remove it I shall give a reward.' An Egyptian heron with a long beak came and removed the bone, then asked for his fee. The lion answered, 'Go. Now you can boast that you stuck your head into the lion's mouth whole and pulled it out whole.'

I. "So it is enough for us that we entered into dealings with this nation whole and have come forth whole." [Likewise it was enough for Isaac to have gotten out as well as he did.]

4. A. "That same day Isaac's servants came and told him about the well which they had dug and said *to him* , 'We have found water.' [He called it Shibah, therefore the name of the city is Beer Sheba to this day]" (Gen. 26:32-33):

B. On the basis of this statement, ["to him," which may be spelled to mean, "to him," or to mean "not,"] we do not know whether or not they found anything.

C. On the analogy to the verse, "...and found there a well of living water" (Gen. 26:19), we know that they found water.

No. 1 contributes a minor gloss, explaining the conversation. No. 2 is inserted as a bridge to No. 3, underlining that the dealings with Abimelech in no way were so harmonious as the narrative suggests on the surface. This yields, at No. 3, the story, quite *a propos*, that Israel should be glad to emerge from such dealings whole and unscathed, and should expect nothing more. No. 4 clarifies the ambiguous matter of the word at hand, which, spelled one way, means "to him," and the other, "not," hence, in the latter, "we have not found...." The diverse composition yields the simple point that what is at the surface of the story cannot dictate the real meaning. There is no good to be derived from dealings with the gentiles.

Chapter Thirty-Three

Parashah Sixty-Five. Genesis 26:34-27:27

LXV:I.

1. A. "When Esau was forty years old, he took to wife Judith, the daughter of Beeri, the Hittite, and Basemath the daughter of Elon the Hittite; and they made life bitter for Isaac and Rebecca" (Gen. 26:34-35):

 B. "The swine out of the wood ravages it, that which moves in the field feeds on it" (Ps. 80:14).

 C. R. Phineas and R. Hilqiah in the name of R. Simon: "Among all of the prophets, only two of them spelled out in public [the true character of Rome, represented by the swine], Asaf and Moses.

 D. "Asaf: 'The swine out of the wood ravages it.'

 E. "Moses: 'And the swine, because he parts the hoof' (Deut. 14:8).

 F. "Why does Moses compare Rome to the swine? Just as the swine, when it crouches, puts forth its hoofs as if to say, 'I am clean,' so the wicked kingdom steals and grabs, while pretending to be setting up courts of justice.

 G. "So Esau, for all forty years, hunted married women, ravished them, and when he reached the age of forty, he presented himself to his father, saying, 'Just as father got married at the age of forty, so I shall marry a wife at the age of forty.'

 H. "'When Esau was forty years old, he took to wife Judith, the daughter of Beeri, the Hittite, and Basemath the daughter of Elon the Hittite.'"

The exegesis of course identifies Esau with Rome. The round-about route linking the fact at hand, Esau's taking a wife, passes through the territory of Roman duplicity. Whatever the government does, it claims to do in the general interest. But it really has no public interest at all. Esau for his part spent forty years pillaging women and then, at the age of forty, pretended, to his father, to be upright. That, at any rate, is the parallel clearly intended by this obviously unitary composition. The issue of the selection of the intersecting verse does not present an obvious solution to me; it seems to me only the identification of Rome with the swine accounts for the choice.

LXV:II.

1. A. R. Yudan bar Simon commenced [discourse by citing the following verse: "God makes the solitary to dwell in a house" (Ps. 78:7).

B. That accords with the view of R. Judah bar Simon, who has said, "Even if there is a *mamzer* at one end of the world, and a female-*mamzer* at the other end of the world, the Holy One, blessed be he, brings them together and matches them up. What is the Scriptural proof of that view? '...God makes the solitary to dwell in a house' (Ps. 78:7). [A *mamzer* -man and woman can only marry someone in that same status, otherwise they must remain solitary.]

C. "So, since it is written, 'You shall utterly destroy them: the Hittite...' (Deut. 20:17), therefore let this man [Esau], may his name be wiped out, come and marry this woman [Judith the Hittite], may her name be blotted out.

D. "'When Esau was forty years old, he took to wife Judith, the daughter of Beeri, the Hittite, and Basemath the daughter of Elon the Hittite.'"

The point is that Esau married the one woman in the world who was suitable for him, namely, a Hittite woman. His name and hers likewise were to be blotted out. This then illustrates God's unerring aim in mating up those who should marry, just as he matches the male-*mamzer*, who cannot marry an acceptable Israelite woman, with a female *mamzer*. Thus they do have a chance to marry, just as Esau married someone suitable for him.

LXV:III.

1. A. "Every raven after its kind" (Lev. 11:15):

B. In the time of R. Hiyya the Elder, the starling came to the Land of Israel. They brought it to him to examine it and asked him whether it might be eaten. He said, "Go, put it on a roof. Any bird that comes to light with it is of its kind. [Find the correct classification, and we shall know the answer. It will follow the rule of the classification into which it falls.]"

C. They went and put it up on a roof, and an Egyptian raven came and lighted by it.

D. He said, "It is unclean, for it is of the same category [as the Egyptian raven]. That is in line with this verse: 'Every raven after its kind' (Lev. 11:15)."

E. They said: The raven came to the starling only because it is its kind.

F. "So, since it is written, 'You shall utterly destroy them: the Hittite...' (Deut. 20:17), therefore let this man [Esau], may his name be wiped out, come and marry this woman [Judith the Hittite], may her name be blotted out.

G. "'When Esau was forty years old, he took to wife Judith, the daughter of Beeri, the Hittite, and Basemath the daughter of Elon the Hittite.'"

The same point is now made, that Esau married exactly the sort of person he should have married.

LXV:IV.

1. A. "And they made life bitter for Isaac and Rebecca" (Gen. 26:35):

B. Why is Isaac mentioned first? Because, since Rebecca was the daughter of priests of idolatry, she paid no attention to the pollution of idolatry. But he was the son of holy parents, therefore he paid attention to it.

C. Therefore Isaac came first.

2. A. Another matter: Why Isaac first? Because she was responsible [for Esau's character]. For it is said, "And the Lord said to her, 'Two nations are in your womb'" (Gen. 25:23).

3. A. Another matter: Why Isaac first?

B. Because a woman ordinarily stays home and a man goes out to the market and acquires understanding by circulating in public.

C. But this one, since his eyes were weak, stayed in the house, therefore, it was Isaac first.

4. A. Said R. Joshua b. Levi, "He was responsible that the Holy Spirit left [Isaac]."

The question at hand focuses upon the exposition of the framing of the base-verse. Why Isaac realized the problem before Rebecca did generates a variety of explanations, each based on a distinct analogy. At the same time we have a link to what is to follow. For Isaac was ready to bless Esau instead of Jacob, even though he realized the corruption of the household. So Isaac appears to be a fool. He should have known better -- that is the lesson at hand. The larger polemic favors Jacob over Esau, one need hardly add.

LXV:V.

1. A. "When Isaac was old, [and his eyes were dim, so that he could not see, he called Esau his older son, and said to him, 'My son,' and he answered, 'Here I am']" (Gen. 27:1):

B. R. Isaac opened discourse by citing the following verse: "That justify the wicked because of a bribe and take away the righteousness of the righteous from him (Is. 5:23)." [The bribe is the venison.]

C. R. Isaac said, "Whoever takes a bribe and therefore justifies the wicked 'because of a bribe' therefore 'takes away the righteousness of the righteous from him (Is. 5:23)."

2. A. ["That justify the wicked because of a bribe and take away the righteousness of the righteous from him (Is. 5:23):"] "the righteous" refers to Moses.

B. "...and take away the righteousness of the righteous from him" (Is. 5:23) refers to Isaac. Because he justified the wicked man, his eyes became weak: "When Isaac was old, and his eyes were dim, so that he could not see, [he called Esau his older son, and said to him, 'My son,' and he answered, 'Here I am']" (Gen. 27:1).

No. 1 expounds the intersecting verse in its own terms. The bribe is the venison; because of that, Isaac was ready to give Esau what he had already sold to Jacob. No. 2 blames Isaac for his own condition. It was because he justified Esau. Here again Isaac is at fault, having taken a bribe, and Jacob is exculpated. He took what was coming to him, even by deceit.

LXV:VI.

1. A. "He who justifies the wicked and he who condemns the righteous, even though they both are an abomination to the Lord" (Prov. 17:15):

B. Said R. Joshua b. Levi, "It was not because Rebecca loved Jacob more than Esau that she did what she did.

C. "But she said, 'Let him not enter and mislead that old man, on the count of: 'they both are an abomination to the Lord.'

D. "Because he justified the wicked man, his eyes became weak: 'When Isaac was old, and his eyes were dim, so that he could not see, [he called Esau his older son, and said to him, "My son," and he answered, "Here I am"'] (Gen. 27:1)."

The composition repeats the point of the foregoing.

LXV:VII.

1. A. R. Isaac commenced, "You shall take no gift, for a gift blinds those that have sight" (Ex. 23:8).

B. Said R. Isaac, "Now if Isaac took a gift from someone who owed it to him [since his son was liable to provide the venison], and his eyes grew dim, someone who takes such a thing from someone who does not owe it to him, all the more so [will lose his sight]!"

C. "When Isaac was old, and his eyes were dim, so that he could not see" (Gen. 27:1).

The reference to taking bribes to justify the wicked now becomes more *a propos*. It is because of the present intersecting verse, which indicates that someone becomes blind who takes a bribe. So, working backward, since Isaac was blind, he presumably took bribes. The working of the moral law, as stated by the Torah, now explains the facts of the case.

LXV:VIII.

1. A. R. Hinena bar Papa opened discourse by citing the following verse: "Many things have you done, O Lord my God, even your wondrous works and your thoughts toward us" (Ps. 40:6).

B. Said R. Hinena bar Pappa, "All the deeds and thoughts which you have done were 'toward us,' that is, for our sake.

C. "Why then did Isaac's eyes grow dim? So that Jacob should come and receive the blessings.

D. "'When Isaac was old, and his eyes were dim, so that he could not see.'"

Now we move forward with a fresh explanation for Isaac's blindness. We move from the moral to the national-historical category of reasons. It is no longer Isaac's fault, but a different consideration altogether. Isaac lost his sight so that he would give the birthright to Jacob, a different explanation of his blindness.

LXV:IX.

1. A. "When Isaac was old, and his eyes were dim, so that he could not see, he called Esau his older son, and said to him, 'My son,' and he answered, 'Here I am'" (Gen. 27:1):

B. Said R. Judah bar Simon, "Abraham sought [the physical traits of] old age [so that from one's appearance, people would know that he was old]. He said before him, 'Lord of all ages, when a man and his son come in somewhere, no one knows whom to honor. If you crown a man with the traits of old age, people will know whom to honor.'

C. "Said to him the Holy One, blessed be he, 'By your life, this is a good thing that you have asked for, and it will begin with you.'

D. "From the beginning of the book of Genesis to this passage, there is no reference to old age. But when Abraham our father came along, the traits of old age were given to him, as it is said, 'And Abraham was old' (Gen. 24:1).'

E. "Isaac asked God for suffering. He said before him, 'Lord of the age, if someone dies without suffering, the measure of strict justice is stretched out against him. But if you bring suffering on him, the measure of strict justice will not be stretched out against him. [Suffering will help counter the man's sins, and the measure of strict justice will be mitigated through suffering by the measure of mercy.]'

F. "Said to him the Holy One, blessed be he, 'By your life, this is a good thing that you have asked for, and it will begin with you.'

G. "From the beginning of the book of Genesis to this passage, there is no reference to suffering. But when Isaac came along, suffering was given to him: his eyes were dim.'

H. "Jacob asked for sickness. He said before him, 'Lord of all ages, if a person dies without illness, he will not settle his affairs for his children. If he is sick for two or three days, he will settle his affairs with his children.'

I. "Said to him the Holy One, blessed be he, 'By your life, this is a good thing that you have asked for, and it will begin with you.'

J. "That is in line with this verse: 'And someone said to Joseph, "Behold, your father is sick"' (Gen. 48:1)."

K. Said R. Levi, "Abraham introduced the innovation of old age, Isaac introduced the innovation of suffering, Jacob introduced the innovation of sickness.

L. "Hezekiah introduced the innovation of chronic illness. He said to him, 'You have kept a man in good condition until the day he dies. But if someone is sick and gets better, is sick and gets better, he will carry out a complete and sincere act of repentance for his sins.'

M. "Said to him the Holy One, blessed be he, 'By your life, this is a good thing that you have asked for, and it will begin with you.'

N. "'The writing of Hezekiah, king of Judah, when he had been sick and recovered of his sickness' (Is. 38:9)."

O. Said R. Samuel b. Nahman, "On the basis of that verse we know that between one illness and another there was an illness more serious than either one."

The syllogism that the suffering, old age, sickness, and the like come to benefit humanity leads to the inclusion of the base verse. But obviously the syllogism makes no effort to clarify the present verse or its context.

LXV:X .

1. A. "[When Isaac was old, and his eyes were dim,] so that he could not see, [he called Esau his older son, and said to him, 'My son,' and he answered, 'Here I am']" (Gen. 27:1):

B. R. Eleazar b. Azariah said, "'...so that he could not see' the wickedness of the wicked person.

C. "Said the Holy One, blessed be he, 'Should Isaac go out to the market and have people say, "Here is the father of that wicked man."

D. "'It is better that I make his eyes dim, so he will stay home.'

E. "So it is written, 'When the wicked rise, men hide themselves' (Prov. 28:28).

F. "On the basis of this verse, they have said, 'Whoever raises a wicked son or a wicked disciple will have his eyes grow dim.

G. "The case of the wicked disciple derives from Ahijah the Shilonite, who raised up Jeroboam, so his eyes grew dim: 'Now Ahijah could not see, for his eyes were set by reason of his old age' (1 Kgs. 14:4). It was because he had produced Jeroboam, the wicked disciple.

H. "As for a wicked son, that is shown by the case of Isaac."

2. A. Another matter: "So that he could not see..."

B. It was on account of that spectacle [at Moriah].

C. Now at the moment at which our father, Abraham, bound Isaac his son, the ministering angels wept. That is in line with this verse: "Behold, their valiant ones cry outside" (Is. 33:7).

D. The tears fell from their eyes into his and made a mark on them, so when he got old, his eyes dimmed: "When Isaac was old, and his eyes were dim, so that he could not see..."

3. A. Another matter: "So that he could not see..."

B. It was on account of that spectacle.

C. Now at the moment at which our father, Abraham, bound Isaac his son, he looked upward and gazed upon the Presence of God.

D. They made a parable. The case may be compared to that of a king who was strolling in the gate of his palace, and he looked up and saw the son of his ally peeking in and gazing at him through a window. He said, "If I put him to death, I shall alienate my ally. But I shall give a degree that his windows be stopped up [so he will not do this again].

E. Now at the moment at which our father, Abraham, bound Isaac his son, he looked upward and gazed upon the Presence of God. Said the Holy One, blessed be he, "If I put him to death, I shall alienate Abraham, my ally. But I shall give a degree that his eyes should be stopped up [so he will not do this again]."

F. "When Isaac was old, and his eyes were dim, so that he could not see...."

No. 1 explains Isaac's blindness in the familiar framework; he tolerated Esau's wicked ways or at least had to be protected from them. Nos. 2, 3 then link the blindness to something he saw when he was bound on the altar. The parable is striking, since it presents the blindness as an act of mercy on God's part.

LXV:XI.

1. A. "When Isaac was old, and his eyes were dim, so that he could not see, he called Esau his older son, and said to him, 'My son,' and he answered, 'Here I am'" (Gen. 27:1):

B. Said R. Eleazar b. R. Simeon, "The matter may be compared to the case of a town that was collecting a bodyguard for the king. There was a woman there, whose son was a dwarf. She called him 'Tallswift' [Freedman]. She said, 'My son is "Tallswift," so why do you not take him?'

C. "They said to her, 'If in your eyes he is "Tallswift," in our eyes he is a dwarf.'

D. "So his father called him 'great:' '...he called Esau his great son.' So too his mother called him 'great:' 'Then Rebecca took the best garments of Esau, her great son.'

E. "Said the Holy One, blessed be he, to them, 'If in your eyes he is great, in my eyes he is small: 'Behold, I make you small among the nations' (Obad. 1:2) [speaking of Edom/Esau/Rome].'"

2. A. Said R. Abbahu said R. Berekhiah, "In accord with the size of the ox is the stature of the slaughterer.

B. "That is in line with the following verse: 'For the Lord has a sacrifice in Bozrah, and a great slaughter in the land of Edom' (Is. 34:6)."

C. Said R. Berekhiah, "The sense is, 'There will be a great slaughterer in the land of Edom. [Freedman, p. 587, n. 2: Since Esau is called great, his slaughterer, God, will likewise be great.]"

3. A. "...he called Esau his older son, and said to him, 'My son,' and he answered, 'Here I am'" (Gen. 27:1):

B. That [credulity on the part of Isaac] is in line with this verse: "When he speaks fair, do not believe him [for there are seven abominations in his heart]" (Prov. 26:25). [Isaac should never have believed Esau.]

C. Hezekiah the translator said, "'For there are seven abominations in his heart' (Prov. 26:25.

D. "You find that while the Torah speaks of a single abomination, in point of fact ten abominations are stated in that connection.

E. "It is written, 'There shall not be found among you any one who makes his son or his daughter pass through the fire...or a charmer or one who consults a ghost or a familiar spirit or a necromancer. For whoever does these things is an abomination to the Lord' (Deut. 18:11).

F. "Here in a case [referring to Esau, as stated above] in which seven are mentioned, how much the more so is it the case : 'For there are seven abominations in his heart' (Prov. 26:25) means that in fact there are seventy abominations in his heart."

The parable powerfully makes the point of the exegete: only in the parents' eyes was Esau "great." Thus at No. 1 the reference to the older son is explained away. In no way was Esau the elder, and Jacob's action was justified. No. 2 works out a different meaning for the same reference. No. 3 moves on to the exchange in which Esau responds faithfully to Isaac, making the point that Isaac should never have believed Esau on any terms, as Scripture says.

LXV:XII.

1. A. "...he called Esau his older son, and said to him, 'My son,' and he answered, 'Here I am.' He said, 'Behold I am old; I do not know the day of my death'" (Gen. 27:1):

   B. Said R. Joshua b. Qorhah, "If someone has come to within five years of the age at which his parents died, for the period before and afterward he himself should fear death.

   C. "For so Isaac said, 'If I am going to reach the age to which my father lived, I am still far short. If I am to reach the age to which mother lived, "Behold I am old. [Freedman, p. 587, n. 5: Isaac was 122 years old then, five years short of Sarah's age at death.]"

2. A. It has been taught on Tannaite authority:

   B. Seven matters are hidden away from mortals and these are they: the day of death, the day of consolation, the full depth of divine judgment, and a person does not know what will bring him a benefit, and he does not know what his fellow is thinking, and he does not know the character of a woman's foetus, nor does he know when the wicked kingdom will fall.

C. The day of death: "For man also does not know his time" (Qoh. 9:12).

D. ...the day of consolation: "I the Lord will hasten it in its time" (Is. 60:22).

E. ...the full depth of divine judgment: "For the judgment is God's" (Deut.; 1:17).

F. ...and a person does not know what will bring him a benefit: "It is the gift of God" (Qoh.3:13).

G. ...and he does not know what his fellow is thinking: "I the Lord search the heart" (Jer. 17:10).

H. ...and he does not know the character of a woman's foetus: "Nor how the bones do grow in the womb of her that is with child" (Qoh. 9:5).

I. ...nor does he know when the wicked kingdom will fall: "For the day of vengeance is in my heart" (Is. 63:4).

3. A. Said R. Joshua b. Qorhah, "If someone has come to within five years of the age at which his parents died, for the period before and afterward he should fear death himself.

B. "For so Isaac said, 'If I am going to reach the age to which my father lived, I am still far short. If I am to reach the age to which mother lived, "Behold I am old."

No. 1 explains why Isaac thought he was old. No. 2 is inserted because of its thematic relevance, underlining the point that the compositor wishes to make. No. 3 is an obvious mistake.

LXV:XIII.

1. A. "[He said, 'Behold I am old; I do not know the day of my death.] Now then take your weapons, [your quiver and your bow, and go out to the field and hunt game for me, and prepare for me savory food, such as I love, and bring it to me that I may eat; that I may bless you before I die']" (Gen. 27:2-4):

B. "Sharpen your hunting gear, so that you will not feed me carrion or an animal that was improperly slaughtered.

C. "Take your *own* hunting gear, so that you will not feed me meat that has been stolen or grabbed."

2. A. "Your quiver:"

B. [Since the word for "quiver" and the word for "held in suspense" share the same consonants, we interpret the statement as follows:] he said to him, "Lo, the blessings [that I am about to give] are held in suspense. For the one who is worthy of a blessing, there will be a blessing."

3. A. Another matter: "Now then take your weapons, your quiver and your bow and go out to the field:"

B. "Weapons" refers to Babylonia, as it is said, "And the weapons he brought to the treasure house of his god" (Gen. 2:2).

C. "Your quiver" speaks of Media, as it says, "So they suspended Haman on the gallows" (Est. 7:10). [The play on the words is the same as at No. 2.]

D. "And your bow" addresses Greece: "For I bend Judah for me, I fill the bow with Ephraim and I will story up your sons, O Zion, against your sons, O Javan [Greece]" (Zech. (9:13).

E. "and go out to the field" means Edom: "Unto the land of Seir, the field of Edom" (Gen. 32:4).

4. A. "And prepare for me savory food:"

B. R. Eleazar in the name of R. Yose b. Zimra: "Three statements were made concerning the tree, that it was good to eat, a delight to the eyes, and that it added wisdom,

C. "and all of them were stated in a single verse:

D. "'So when the woman saw that the tree was good for food,' on which basis we know that it was good to eat;

E. "'and that it was a delight to the eyes', on which basis we know that it was a delight for the eyes,

F. "'and that the tree was to be desired to make one wise,' on which basis we know that it added to one's wisdom.

G. "That is in line with the following verse of Scripture: 'A song of wisdom of Ethan the Ezrahite' (Ps. 89:1)" [and the root for "song of wisdom" and that for "to make one wise" are the same].

H. "So did Isaac say, '"And prepare for me savory food." I used to enjoy the appearance [of food], but now I get pleasure only from the taste.'

I. "And so did Solomon say, 'When goods increase, those who eat them are increased, and what advantage is there to the owner thereof, saving the beholding of them with his eyes' (Qoh. 5:10).

J. "The one who sees an empty basket of bread and is hungry is not equivalent to the one who sees a full basket of bread and is satisfied."

5. A. "And Rebecca was listening when Isaac spoke to his son Esau. So when Esau went to the field to hunt for game and bring it..." (Gen. 27:5):

   B. If he found it, well and good.

   C. And if not, "...to bring it" even by theft or violence.

No. 1 begins with the imputation of some deeper meanings for Isaac's statement, showing him to be more perspicacious than the narrative before us. No. 2 broadens the range of meaning, making the matter of the blessing more conditional than the narrative suggests. Isaac now is not sure who will get the blessing; his sense is that it will go to whoever deserves it. No. 3 then moves from the moral to the national, making the statement a clear reference to the history of Israel (as though, by this point, it were not obvious). What the author of the item at hand contributes, then, is the specific details. What the compositor does is move the reader's mind from the philological to the moral to the national dimension of exegesis of the statements at hand. No. 4 works out the meaning of the request for tasty food; the main point is that Isaac wants highly spiced food, since he cannot see what he is eating. If one knows he has something to eat, that often satisfies; not seeing is not knowing. No. 5 contributes a familiar motif. But the point becomes clear at LXV:XIV.2.B. Esau steals, but Jacob takes only what is lawful.

LXV:XIV.

1. A. "And Rebecca said to her son, Jacob, 'I heard your father speak to your brother Esau, "Bring me game and prepare me savory food, that I may eat it and bless you before the Lord before I die." Now therefore my son, obey my word as I command you. Go to the flock [and fetch me two good kids, that I may prepare for from them savory food for your father, such as he loves; and you shall bring it to your father to eat, so that he may bless you before he dies']" Gen. 27:6-10):

   B. Said R. Levi, "Go and prefigure before the nation [compared to a flock], in line with this verse: 'And you my sheep, the sheep of my pasture' (Ez. 34:31)."

2. A. "...and fetch me two good kids:"

   B. Said R. Helbo, "If you find them [in your father's flock], well and good, and if not, bring them for me out of my dowry. [But do not seize them by theft or violence, like your brother, Esau.]"

   C. For R. Helbo said, "That was the case, since Isaac had written over to her in her marriage-agreement that he would provide her with two lambs every day."

3.   A. R. Berekhiah in the name of R. Helbo: "'...two good kids' means 'good for you and good for your descendants.'

B. "...'good for you,' for on their account you will receive the blessings.

C. "...'good for your descendants,' for on their account [Israel] will achieve atonement for themselves on the Day of Atonement, as it is written, 'For on this day shall atonement be made for you' (Lev. 16:30)."

No. 1 links Jacob's life to Israel's history. No. 2 contrasts Jacob's lawfulness with Esau's violence. No. 3 further links Jacob's life to Israel's cult. The next composite goes over the same themes.

LXXV:XV.

1.   A. "But Jacob said to Rebecca his mother, 'Behold, my brother Esau is a hairy man, [and I am a smooth man. Perhaps my father will feel me, and I shall seem to be mocking him, and bring a curse upon myself and not a blessing.' His mother said to him, 'Upon me be your curse, my son; only obey my word and go, fetch them to me']" (Gen. 27:11-13):

B. [Since the word for "hairy" may be read as "demonic,"] he is a demonic man, as in this verse: "And satyrs [using the same letters for 'satyr' and for the word 'hairy'] shall dance there" (Is. 13:21).

2.   A. "...and I am a smooth man:"

B. That is in line with this verse: "For the portion [the word 'portion' and the word 'smooth' share the same consonants] of the Lord is his people" (Deut. 32:9).

3.   A. R. Levi and R. Isaac:

B. R. Levi said, "The matter may be compared to the case of a man with a full head of hair and a bald man who were standing at the edge of the threshing floor, and the chaff got caught in the hair of the man with the full head of hair, becoming entangled in it. But when the chaff flew onto the head of the bald one, he just passed his hand over his bald head and wiped it away.

C. "So the wicked Esau is made filthy through sin all year long, and he has no means of atonement. But Jacob is made filthy with sin all year long and he has a means of atonement, for the Day of Atonement achieves atonement for him."

D. R. Isaac said, "[Freedman:] This interpretation is farfetched. [Rather derive it as follows:]

E. "'And the goat shall bear upon him all their iniquities unto a land which is cut off' (Lev. 16:22). [The word for 'goat' and the word for 'hairy' share the same consonants, thus:] 'the goat shall bear upon him' speaks of Esau, as it says, 'Behold, my brother Esau is a hairy man.'

F. "'...all their iniquities unto a land which is cut off' refers to the iniquities of the 'quiet man' [splitting up the word 'their iniquities' into two parts, 'iniquities' and 'their,' with the letters for 'their' spelling the word 'quiet, hence] 'Jacob was a quiet man' (Gen. 25:27)."

4. A. "'...Perhaps my father will feel me, and I shall seem to be mocking him, [and bring a curse upon myself and not a blessing.' His mother said to him, 'Upon me be your curse, my son; only obey my word and go, fetch them to me']" (Gen. 27:11-13):

B. [Since the word for "mock" bears the consonants for the word for "err," the sense is this:] "Like one who errs in idolatry."

5. A. "'...and bring a curse upon myself and not a blessing.' [His mother said to him, 'Upon me be your curse, my son; only obey my word and go, fetch them to me']" (Gen. 27:11-13):

B. "Even the blessing which he was planning to give me in the end he will not bestow upon me."

6. A. "His mother said to him, 'Upon me be your curse, my son; only obey my word and go, fetch them to me'" (Gen. 27:13):

B. R. Abba bar Kahana said, "[What she said to him is this:] 'When someone commits a sin, is not his mother cursed? "Cursed is the ground for your sake" (Gen. 3:17). So you too: "Upon me be your curse.""'

C. Said R. Isaac, "[What she said was this:] 'Upon me is the task of going in and telling your father that Jacob is a righteous man and Esau is wicked.'"

7. A. "So he went and took them and brought them to his mother" (Gen. 27:14):

B. He went under constraint, bent over and weeping.

No. 1 plays on the words for "hairy" and smooth. No. 2 carries the matter still further, again successfully linking Jacob's life to Israel's cult. No. 3 improves Isaac's image. No. 4 expands on Jacob's concern. No. 5 then spells out Rebecca's message. No. 6 totally exonerates Jacob. The thrust of the compositors' interest proves obvious.

LXV:XVI.

1.   A. "Then Rebecca took the choicest garments of Esau her older son, [which were with her in the house, and put them on Jacob her younger son; and the skins of the kids she put upon his hands and upon the smooth part of his neck; and she gave the savory food and the bread which she had prepared into the hand of her son Jacob]" (Gen. 27:15-17):

B. They were the ones that he had chosen from Nimrod: "The wicked covet the prey of evil men" (Prov. 12:12).

2.   A. "...which were with her in the house:"

B. For he would serve his father wearing those garments.

C. Said Rabban Simeon b. Gamaliel, "I served father all my life, and I did not give him one one-hundredth of the service that Esau gave his father. For I would serve him in dirty clothes, and when I would go out to the market, I would put on clean clothes. But as to Esau, when he would serve his father, he would serve him in royal garments. He said, 'The honor owing to father is attained only in by my wearing royal garments.'"

3.   A. "...which were with her in the house:"

B. How many wives did he have, and you say, "Which were with *her* "?

C. But he was the one who knew the ways of the others [and trusted only her].

D. Said R. Abba bar Kahana, "There was the case of a group of servants in Kefar Hatayyah, who had the habit of eating together in a synagogue every Friday evening. When they had eaten, they would throw the bones at the school-teacher. But when one of them was dying, they asked him, 'To whom do you entrust your children?' He said, 'To the school-teacher.' They said, 'How many friends he had, and yet he said, "To the school-teacher." But in fact he knew the deeds of the others.'"

E. Along these same lines: How many wives did he have, and you say, "Which were with her"?

F. But he knew the ways of the others [and trusted only her].

No. 1 identifies the garments, a familiar motif linking Esau to Nimrod, both of them hunters. No. 2 then explains why the garments were kept at home and makes sensible Isaac's appreciation of Esau. No. 3 makes its own point. I take this to be a comment on Esau's wives. Even Esau did not trust them.

LXV:XVII.

1.   A.   "...and the skins of the kids [she put upon his hands and upon the smooth part of his neck; and she gave the savory food and the bread which she had prepared into the hand of her son Jacob]" (Gen. 27:15-17):

    B.   Said R. Yohanan, "The two arms of Jacob, our father, were like two pillars, and you say, 'and the skins of the kids [she put upon his hands'? [How could they have been sufficiently large to cover such a space?] But she sowed them together [to make them fit]."

    C.   R. Huna in the name of R. Joseph: "The two daily whole-offerings which the Israelites offered up on the Festival of Tabernacles [were so large that] they were carried on two young camels, and, nonetheless, their legs would drag on the ground. [Accordingly, there could be hides large enough for the task at hand.]"

    D.   R. Huna in the name of R. Joseph: "The cinnamon tree would grow in the Land of Israel, and the goats and deer would eat of it [at the very top, and that is how large they were]."

    E.   Said R. Haninah, "Calves were slaughtered, olives were cut down, dirt was left on the mountains -- these things were really miracles [if the goats were so large]."

    F.,   Said R. Mana, "Everything is a matter of miracles."

2.   A.   "...and she gave the savory food and the bread which she had prepared into the hand of her son Jacob]" (Gen. 27:17):

    B.   She accompanied him right to the door, saying to him, "Up to this point, I was responsible to you. From this point onward, your creator will stand up for you."

No. 1 raises an exegetical question. No. 2 amplifies that narrative.

LXV:XVIII.

1.   A.   "So he went in to his father and said, 'My father,' and he said, 'Here I am. Who are you, my son?" And Jacob said to his father, 'I am Esau your first born. [I have done as you told me;' now sit up and eat of my game, that you may bless me']" (Gen. 27:18-19):

    B.   Said R. Levi, "'I' am the one who will receive the Ten Commandments, but Esau is indeed your first born.'"

2.   A.   "... now sit up:"

B. Said R. Yohanan, "Said the Holy One, blessed be he, to Jacob, "You have said, "...now sit up." By your life with that same language I shall pay you your just reward: "Rise up, O Lord, and let your enemies be scattered"' (Num. 10:35)."

3.   "But there is he who is swept away by want of righteousness" (Prov. 13:23) refers to Esau. Said the Holy One, blessed be he, to Esau, "You have said, 'Let my father arise' (Gen. 27:31). By the fortune of my idol I adjure you to arise.' By your life I shall pay you I shall pay you back with that very same language: 'Rise up, O Lord, and let your enemies be scattered' (Num. 10:35)."

Nos. 1, 2 amplify the discourse, redirecting the statements of Jacob to the history of Israel in the future. Each statement then bears a deeper meaning, drawn from that history. No. 3 builds on the point of No. 2, using the same verse to Esau's disadvantage that has served as praise for Jacob.

LXV:XIX.

1.   A.   "But Isaac said to his son, 'How is it that you have found it so quickly, my son?' [He answered, 'Because the Lord your God God granted me success']" (Gen. 27:20):

B.   "How come you found the blessing so quickly, my son. Your father was blessed at the age of seventy-five years, while you are only sixty-three."

2.   A.   "He answered, 'Because the Lord your God granted me success'" (Gen. 27:20):

B.   R. Yohanan and R. Simeon b. Laqish:

C.   One of them said, "If to provide a sacrifice for you the Holy One, blessed be he, provided what was required promptly, as it is written, 'And Abraham lifted up his eyes and looked and behold behind him a ram' (Gen. 22:13), how much the more so will he promptly provide food for you!"

D.   The other of them said, "If to provide a mate for you, the Holy One, blessed be he, provided what was required promptly, as it is written, 'And he saw, and behold, there were camels coming' (Gen. 24:63), how much the more so will he promptly provide food for you!"

3.   A.   "He answered, 'Because the Lord your God granted me success'" (Gen. 27:20):

B.   Said R. Yohanan, "The matter may be compared to the case of a raven bringing fire to his nest. [Freedman: He was courting disaster.] When he said, "'Because the Lord your God God granted me success,'" Isaac said, 'I know that Esau does not make mention of the Name of the Holy One, blessed be he, while this one does make mention of God's name. This cannot be Esau but can only be Jacob.'"

C. "So when Jacob said this, he said, 'Come near, that I may feel you my son, to know whether you are really my son Esau or not' (Gen. 27:22)."

4. A. Said R. Hoshaiah, "When Isaac said, 'Come near, that I may feel you my son, to know whether you are really my son Esau or not' (Gen. 27:22), sweat poured down Jacob's thighs, and his heart melted like wax. So the Holy One, blessed be he, appointed two angels, one at his right hand, one at the left, to hold him up by his elbows, so that he would not fall.

B. "Thus it is written, 'Do not be dismayed' (Is. 41:10), meaning, 'Do not be like wax' [since the words 'dismay' and 'wax' share the same consonants]."

Nos. 1, 2 amplify Jacob's colloquy with Isaac. No. 3 begins the process of showing that Isaac knew just what he was doing. He realized that Esau would not talk that way, but he allowed the charade to proceed. No. 4 shows that Jacob was a poor liar, but that God helped him lie.

LXV:XX.

1. A. "And Jacob went near to Isaac his father, who felt him and said, 'The voice is Jacob's voice, but the hands are the hands of Esau'" (Gen. 27:22):

B. "It is the sound of the voice of a wise man, but the hands are those of one who strips corpses."

2. A. "The voice is Jacob's voice:"

B. Jacob rules only by his voice [through reasoned argument].

C. "...but the hands are the hands of Esau:"

D. and Esau rules only by the power of his hands [by force].

3. A. "'The voice is Jacob's voice:'"

B. Said R. Phineas, "When the voice of Jacob is drawn mute, then: 'the hands are the hands of Esau.' He is called and comes."

4. A. "The voice is Jacob's voice, but the hands are the hands of Esau:"

B. Said R. Berekhiah, "When Jacob uses his voice to express anger [against God], then the hands of Esau take control, but when his voice speaks clearly, then the hands of Esau do not take control."

5. A. Said R. Abba bar Kahana, "No philosophers in the world ever arose of the quality of Balaam ben Beor and Abnomos of Gadara. All of the nations of the world came to Abnomos of Gadara. They said to him, 'Do you maintain that we can make war against this nation?'

B. "He said to them, 'Go and make the rounds of their synagogues and the study houses. If you find there children chirping out loud in their voices [and studying the Torah], then you cannot overcome them. If not, then you can conquer them, for so did their father promise them: "The voice is Jacob's voice," meaning that when Jacob's voice sounds forth in synagogues, Esau has no power.'"

6. A. "The voice is Jacob's voice:" In the incident of the concubine of Gibeah.

B. "Cursed is he who gives a wife to Benjamin" (Judges 21:18).

C. "The voice is Jacob's voice:"

D. In the days of Jeroboam: "Neither did Jeroboam recover strength again in the days of Abijah, and the Lord smote him and he died" (2 Chr. 13:20).

E. Said R. Samuel bar Nahman, "Do you think that Jeroboam was smitten? But in fact Abijah was smitten."

F. Why was Abijah smitten?

G. Said R. Abba b. Kahana, "Because he removed the identifying marks of the faces of the Israelites, as it is written, 'The show of their countenance does witness for them' (Is. 3:9)."

H. Said R. Assi, "Because he set up guards over them for three days until the features of their faces were disfigured.

I. "For so we have learned in the Mishnah: **People give testimony to the identity of a corpse only through the features of the face together with the nose, and that is the case even if there are other marks of identification on the body and the garments; and one may give testimony only within three days of death [beyond which point the face is disfigured]** [M. Yeb. 16:3].

J. "And it says, 'The widows are increased to me above the sands of the seas' (Jer. 15:8)."

K. R. Yohanan said, "It was because he treated with contempt Ahijah the Shilonite: 'And there were gathered to him vain men, base fellows' (2 Chr. 13:7). So he treated Ahijah as worthless."

L. R. Simeon b. Laqish said, "It was because he humiliated them in public: 'And you are a great multitude and there are with you the golden calves' (2 Chr. 13:7)."

M. Rabbis said, "It was because an idol came into his possession and he did not nullify it: 'And Abijah pursued after Jeroboam and took cities from him, Bethel and the towns thereof, and Jeshonah and the towns thereof' (2 Chr. 13:19), and further: 'And he set the one [golden calf] in Bethel and the other in Dan' (1 Kgs. 12:29).

N. "Now is it not an argument *a fortiori* : if, in the account of Scripture, because a king insulted a king like himself and therefore was smitten, if an ordinary person insults an ordinary person, how much the more so!"

Nos. 1-5 present a series of interpretations of Isaac's statement which yield a single notion. Jacob rules through measured, calm, and reasoned discourse. Jacob rules through study of the Torah. The nations of the world have no power over Jacob when Jacob studies Torah. The voice of Jacob prevails but when Jacob does not speak up, then Esau prevails. This single message comes in a number of forms and versions. Why the materials of No. 6 are introduced I do not know. At some prior stage in the agglutination of the composite, they were joined to expand on an available point, then never detached when no longer relevant.

LXV:XXI.

1. A. "'The voice is Jacob's voice, but the hands are the hands of Esau'" (Gen. 27:22):

    B. This is the voice that brings silence both above and on earth.

2. A. [We shall now have an account of how Israel's voice silences the angels.] R. Phineas in the name of R. Abin: "'When they stood, they let down their wings' (Ez. 1:24)."

    B. Now do the creatures up above ever sit down?

    C. And did not R. Haninah bar Andaray in the name of R. Samuel ben Sitir say, "The creatures up above never sit down: 'And their feet were straight feet' (Ez. 12:7). They have no joints: 'I came near to one of them that stood by' (Dan. 7:16), and the word for 'stand by' means, 'those who stand [all the time]. Further, 'Above him stood the seraphim' (Is. 6:2), and, 'And all the host of heaven standing by him on his right hand and on his left' (1 Kgs. 22:19)"?

    D. So how can you say "When they stood"?

    E. What is the meaning of the word that reads "when they stood"?

    F. It means, "When the people is silent" [with the Hebrew letters of the word "when they stood" broken apart to yield three words, "when," "people," and "silent"].

G. That is to say, When Israel recite, "Hear, O Israel," they are silent, and then, "when the people is silent," they let down their wings. And what do they then say? "Blessed is the name of the glory of his kingdom for ever and ever."

H. R. Phineas in the name of R. Levi and Rabbis in the name of R. Simon: "It is written, 'When the morning stars sang together and all the sons of God shouted for joy' (Job 38:7).

I. "The meaning is this: when the children of Jacob, who are compared to stars, as it is written, 'And they who turn many to righteousness shall shine as the stars' (Dan. 12:3), have given praise, then: 'And all the sons of God shout for joy.' This refers to the ministering angels.

J. "And what do the angels say? 'Blessed be the glory of the Lord from his place' (Ez. 3:12)."

K. R. Berekiah in the name of R. Samuel: "It is written, 'And I heard behind me the voice of a great rushing' (Ez. 3:12). What is meant by 'after me'? After my companions and I had given praise, then: 'I heard behind me the voice of a great rushing.'

L. "And what do the angels say? 'Blessed be the glory of the Lord from his place' (Ez. 3:12)."

3. A. Said R. Judah bar Ilai, "Rabbi would give the following exposition:

B. ""The voice is Jacob's voice," that is, the voice of Jacob crying out on account of what "the hands of Esau" have done to him."'

C. Said R. Yohanan, "It is the voice of Hadrian, may his bones be pulverized, killing in Betar eighty thousand myriads of people."

No. 2 is tacked in because No. 1 refers to how the voice of Jacob silences the heavenly creatures. No. 3 provides an interpretation that is more *a propos.* The insistence upon reading the history of Israel into the biography of Jacob stands behind No. 3. Nos. 1-2 have their own point to make, seeing Israel in the cosmic dimension.

LXV:XXII.

1. A. ["And he did not recognize him, because his hands were hairy like his brother Esau's hands, so he blessed him. He said, 'Are you really my son Esau?' He answered, 'I am.' Then he said, 'Bring it to me, that I may eat of my son's game and bless you.' So he brought it to him and he ate, and he brought him wine, and he drank. Then his father Isaac said to him,'Come near and kiss me my son.' So he came near and kissed him; he smelled the smell

of his garments, and blessed him, and said...'" (Gen. 27:23-27)] "And he did not recognize him:"

B. When wicked people came forth from him [Esau], he did not recognize that fact.

2. A. "Then his father Isaac said to him,'Come near and kiss me my son:'"

B. He said to him, "You will kiss me in the grave [being buried next to me] and no one else."

3. A. "So he came near and kissed him; he smelled the smell of his garments, and blessed him:"

B. Said R. Yohanan, "You have nothing with a more pungent odor than hides stripped from goats, and you you say, 'he smelled the smell of his garments, and blessed him'?

C. "When Jacob came into his father, the Garden of Eden came in with him: 'as the smell of a field which the Lord has blessed.'"

4. A. "See the smell of my son is as the smell of a field which the Lord has blessed:"

B. For example, Joseph Meshitha and Yaqim of Serorot.

C. As to Yose, when the time came that the enemies wanted to enter the mountain of the house [of the sanctuary], they said, "Let one of them go in first."

D. They said to Yose, "Go in. Whatever you take out will belong to you."

E. He went in and took out the golden candelabrum.

F. They said to him, "It is not proper for an ordinary person to make use of such a thing, so go in a second time, and what you take out will belong to you."

G. But he did not agree to do so.

H. Said R. Phineas, "They offered him the taxes for three years, but he did not agree to go in."

I. He said, "It is not enough for you that I have made my God angry once, should I now outrage him yet a second time?"

J. What did they do to him? They put him on a carpenter's vice and they sawed him in two, and he cried out, "Woe, woe that I angered my creator!"

K. Yaqim of Serurot was the son of the sister of R. Yose b. Yoezer of Seridah. He was riding on his horse. He passed before the beam on which [Yose] was to be hanged. He said to him, "Look at the horse on which my master has set me riding and look at the horse on which your master has set you riding!"

L. He said to him, "If that is what he does for those who spite him, how much the more will he do for those who do his will!"

M. He said to him, "And has anyone done his will more than you have?"

N. He said to him, "And if that is what happens to those who do his will [that they are tortured to death], all the more so will he do for those who spite him."

O. That statement penetrated into his heart like the venom of a snake, and he went and applied to himself the four modes of the death penalty applied by a court, namely, stoning, burning, decapitation, and strangulation.

P. How did he accomplish it? He brought a beam and stuck it into the ground, and put up a wall of stones around it, then tied a cord to it. He made a fire in front of the beam and put a sword in the middle of the post. He first hung himself on the post. The cord burned through, and he was strangled. Then the sword caught his body, and the wall of stones fell on him, and he burned up.

Q. Yose b. Yoezer of Seredah dozed off and he saw the bier of the other flying through the air. He said, "By a brief interval he reached the Garden of Eden before me."

Nos. 1-3 present minor glosses of various types. In both cases of No. 4 we deal with people who have proved treacherous to God, hence, "his clothing" is read, by providing the same consonants with different vowels, as "those who are treacherous to him" (Freedman, p. 599, n. 3). The stories themselves have no bearing on our exegetical program.

LXV:XXIII.

1. A. ["See the smell of my son is as the smell of a field which the Lord has blessed" (Gen. 27:27):] Another matter: this teaches that the Holy One, blessed be he, showed him the house of the sanctuary as it was built, wiped out, and built once more.

B. "See the smell of my son:" This refers to the Temple in all its beauty, in line with this verse: "A sweet smell to me shall you observe" (Num. 28:2).

C. "...is as the smell of a field:" This refers to the Temple as it was wiped out, thus: "Zion shall be ploughed as a field" (Mic. 3:12).

D. "...which the Lord has blessed:" This speaks of the Temple as it was restored once more in the age to come, as it is said, "For there the Lord commanded the blessing, even life for ever" (Ps. 133:3).

The conclusion explicitly links the blessing of Jacob to the Temple throughout its history. The concluding proof-text presumably justifies the entire identification of the blessing at hand with what was to come.

Chapter Thirty-Four

Parashah Sixty-Six. Genesis 27:28-32

LXVI:I.

1. A. "May God give you of the dew of heaven [and of the fatness of the earth, and of plenty of grain and wine. Let peoples serve you and nations bow down to you. Be lord over your brothers and may your mother's sons bow down to you. Cursed be everyone who curses you, and blessed be every one who blesses you]" (Gen. 27:27-29):

   B. "My root was spread out to the waters, and the dew lay all night on my branch" (Job 29:19).

   C. Said Job, "It was because my doors were wide open that when everybody reaped dried ears, I reaped ears full of sap."

   D. What is the scriptural basis for that statement?

   E. "My root was spread out to the waters, and the dew lay all night on my branch" (Job 29:19).

   F. Jacob said, "Because I engaged in study of the Torah, which is compared to water, I had the merit of being blessed with dew."

   G. "May God give you of the dew of heaven."

The reference to dew in the intersecting verse accounts for its inclusion with the base verse, and then the two verses are drawn together in a solid link. The main point is to introduce the theme of Torah-study.

LXVI:II.

1. A. R. Berekhiah opened [discourse by citing the following verse:] "'Return, return, O Shulamite, return, return that we may look upon you' (Song 7:1):

   B. "The verse at hand refers to 'return' four times, corresponding to the four kingdoms in which Israel enters in peace and from which Israel comes forth in peace.

   C. "'O Shulamite:' the word refers to the nation who every day is blessed with a blessing ending with peace [which shares the consonants of the word at hand], as it is said, 'And may he give you peace' (Num. 7:26).

D. "It is the nation in the midst of which dwells the Peace of the ages, as it is said, 'And let them make me a sanctuary that I may dwell among them' (Ex. 25:8).

E. "It is the nation to which I am destined to give peace: 'And I will give peace in the land' (Lev. 26:6).

F. "It is the nation over which I am destined to spread peace: 'Behold, I will extend peace to her like a river' (Is. 66:12)."

G. R. Samuel bar Tanhum, R. Hanan bar Berekiah in the name of R. Idi: "It is the nation that makes peace between me and my world. For if it were not for that nation, I would destroy my world."

H. R. Hana in the name of R. Aha [cited the following verse in support of this statement]: "'When the land and all the inhabitants thereof are dissolved' (Ps. 75:4), as in the statement, 'All the inhabitants of Canaan are melted away' (Ex. 15:15).

I. "'I' (Ps. 75:4), that is, when they accepted upon themselves [the Ten Commandments, beginning,] 'I am the Lord your God' (Ex. 20:2), I established the pillars of it' (Ps. 75:4), and the world was set on a solid foundation."

J. Said R. Eleazar bar Merom, "This nation preserves [makes whole] the stability of the world, both in this age and in the age to come."

K. R. Joshua of Sikhnin in the name of R. Levi: "This is the nation on account of the merit of which whatever good that comes into the world is bestowed. Rain comes down only for their sake, that is, 'to you' [as in the base verse], and the dew comes down only 'to you.'

L. "May God give you of the dew of heaven."

The point of this rather sizable composition comes at the end, but the intersecting verse is worked out in its own terms. We have a philosophy of Israel among the nations, stating in one place every component. We begin with a reference to the four kingdoms, but then we move out of that item to the name of the Shulamite, and, third, we proceed to work on the theme of Israel as the nation of peace. Once the praise of Israel forms the focus, we leave behind the issue of peace and deal with the blessings that come to the world on Israel's account. Only at that point does the base verse prove relevant. I could not begin to speculate on the origins of this complex composition -- unitary or incremental. What is important to us is the reason for its selection and inclusion on the part of those responsible for the document before us, and their interest is self-evident. But whether they took existing materials and tacked on their point, or whether the composition existed in this form prior to its selection and inclusion, we cannot now know.

LXVI:III.

1. A. May God give you [of the dew of heaven and of the fatness of the earth, and plenty of grain and wine] (Gen. 27:28):

   B. "May he give you and go and give you again.

   C. "May he give you blessings and may he give you [Freedman:] the means of holding them.

   D. "May he give you what belongs to you and may he give you what belongs to your father.

   E. "May he give you what belongs to you and may he give you what belongs to your brother."

   F. R. Aha: "May he give you what belongs to you and may he give you [Freedman:] of his own divine strength.

   G. "When? When you need it, in line with this verse, 'And Samson called to the Lord and said, "O Lord, remember me, I pray you, and strengthen me, I pray you, only this once, O God" (Judges 16:28).'   H. "He said, 'Lord of the age, Remember in my behalf the blessing with which my ancestor blessed me, "May he give you [Freedman:] of his own divine strength."'"

2. A. "of the dew of heaven:"

   B. This refers to mana: "Then said the Lord to Moses, Behold I will cause to rain bread from heaven for you" (Ex. 216:4).

3. A. "and of the fatness of the earth:"

   B. This refers to the well, which produced diverse fat fish.

4. A. "...and plenty of grain" refers to young men: "Grain shall make the young men flourish" (Zech. 9:17).

   B. "and wine:" refers to maidens: "And new wine for the maids" (Zech. 9:17).

5. A. Another interpretation: "May God give you of the dew of heaven:" speaks of Zion: "Like the dew of Hermon that comes down on the mountains of Zion" (Ps. 133:3).

   B. "and of the fatness of the earth:" speaks of the offerings.

   C. "and plenty of grain:" alludes to firstfruits.

   D. " and wine:" these are the drink offerings.

6. A. Another interpretation: "May God give you of the dew of heaven:" this is Scripture.

    B. "and of the fatness of the earth:" this is Mishnah.

    C. "and plenty of grain :" this is Talmud.

    D. "and wine:" this is lore.

No. 1 works out the first clause, on giving. No. 2 proceeds to the dew, No. 3, 4, 5 to the other parts of the composition. We proceed in the concluding units to rework the same matter in a more figurative way, ending, of course, with the imputation of the symbols critical to the sages' own world. Nos. 5, 6 draw the recurrent parallel between Temple offerings and Torah-study.

LXVI:IV.

1. A. "Let peoples serve you" (Gen. 27:29): this refers to the seventy nations.

    B. "and nations bow down to you:" these are the children of Ishmael and the children of Keturah: "And the sons of Dedan were Asshurim and Letushim and Lerummim" (Gen. 25:3).

    C. "Be lord over your brothers:" speaks of Esau and his chiefs.

2. A. "and may your mother's sons bow down to you:"

    B. Here you say "and may your *mother's* sons bow down to you," and elsewhere: "Your *father's* sons will down down before you" (Gen. 49:8).

    C. Since Jacob took four wives, Leah and Rachel, Zilpah and Bilah, it says, "Your father's sons," but since Isaac was married only to Rebecca, it is, "and may your mother's sons bow down to you."

3. A. "Cursed be everyone who curses you, and blessed be every one who blesses you" (Gen. 27:29):

    B. By contrast: "Blessed be everyone who blesses you and cursed be everyone who curses you" (Num. 24:9). [Why the difference in the precedence of blessing and curse in the two formulations?]

    C. Since Balaam hated Israel, he begins with a reference to a blessing and ends with a reference to a curse, but since Isaac loves Israel, he begins with a reference to a curse so as to conclude with a reference to a blessing.

    D. Said R. Isaac bar Hiyya, "Since the wicked begin in prosperity and end in suffering, they begin with a blessing and conclude with a curse, but since the righteous begin with suffering and end with prosperity, they begin with a curse and end with a blessing."

No. 1 glosses the cited verse, and Nos. 2, 3 compare the present formulation to its parallel and harmonize the difference.

LXVI:V.

1. A. "As soon as Isaac had finished [blessing Jacob, when Jacob had scarcely gone out from the presence of Isaac his father]" (Gen. 27:30):

    B. R. Aibu said, "The tent of our father Isaac was open at both sides [so one went in the one side as the other left by the other side]."

    C. Rabbis say, "The doors were hinged and could be folded backwards [Freedman]. Jacob stood behind the door while Esau came in, and then he went out. That is in line with this verse: 'When Jacob had scarcely gone out from the presence of Isaac his father, Esau his brother came in from his hunting' (Gen. 27:31). He seemed to have gone out, but he had not gone out."

2. A. "Esau his brother came in from his hunting" (Gen. 27:30:

    B. He came armed.

Both entries provide minor glosses. No. 1 explains the slightly curious formulation.

LXVI:VI. The text of Theodor-Albeck omits LXVI:VI.

LXVI:VII.

1. A. "He also prepared savory food and brought it to his father" (Gen. 27:31):

    B. "The spider you can take with the hands" (Prov. 30:28).

    C. Said R. Hama bar Hanina, "On account of what merit does the spider grasp [interpreting the cited verse to mean the spider can grasp with the hand]?

    D. "It is on account of the merit of him concerning whom it is written, 'He also prepared savory food and brought it to his father.'"

2. A. " And he said to his father, 'Let my father arise and eat of his son's game, that you may bless me'" (Gen. 27:31):

    B. [Said R. Yohanan,] "Said the Holy One, blessed be he, to Jacob, "You have said, "...now sit up." By your life with that same language I shall pay you your just reward: "Rise up, O Lord, and let your enemies be scattered"' (Num. 10:35)."

C. "But there is he who is swept away by want of righteousness" (Prov. 13:23) refers to Esau. Said the Holy One, blessed be he, to Esau, "You have said, 'Let my father arise' (Gen. 27:31).' [That is to say,] 'By the fortune of my idol I adjure you to arise.' By your life I shall pay you back with that very same language: 'Rise up, O Lord, and let your enemies be scattered' (Num. 10:35)."

As to No. 1, Esau is represented here by the spider. Its grasp of its imperial web is on account of that merit that Esau attained in serving his father. Freedman, p. 605, n. 2: Hama takes the verb in an active sense, "The spider seizes with its hands." No. 2 goes over familiar ground.

Chapter Thirty-Five

Parashah Sixty-Seven. Genesis 27:33-28:9

LXVII:I.

1. A. "Then Isaac trembled violently [and said, 'Who was it then that hunted game and brought it to me, and I ate it all before you came, and I have blessed him? yes, and he shall be blessed]'" (Gen. 27:33):

    B. "The trembling on account of man brings a snare, but whoever puts his trust in the Lord shall be set up on high" (Prov. 29:25):

    C. The trembling that Ruth caused to Boaz, as it is said, "And the man trembled and turned himself" (Ruth 3:8).

    D. "...brings a snare:" for he could have cursed her. [He might have done the wrong thing, but he avoided the trap.]

    E. "...but whoever puts his trust in the Lord shall be set up on high:" for [God] put in his heart [the impulse to bless her] and he blessed her: "Blessed are you of the Lord, my daughter" (Ruth 3:10).

    F. Along these same lines, the trembling that Jacob caused Isaac was such that he could have cursed him,

    G. "...but whoever puts his trust in the Lord shall be set up on high," for [God] put in his heart [the impulse to bless him] and he blessed him: "...yes, and he shall be blessed."

The intersecting verse is chosen because of its reference to trembling, with the further reference to the passage in Ruth allowing for the introduction of the notion of a blessing. Here again it is impossible to know whether this complex composition, with its deft reversion to our base verse, has been made up all at once or brought into being piece by piece. The net effect is very powerful, since it introduces God's action into Isaac's blessing of Jacob. It further links the story at hand to the coming of the Messiah through Ruth and Boaz. God made the men make the right choice, so he had a part in the blessing.

LXVII:II.

1. A. "Then Isaac trembled violently and said, 'Who was it then that hunted game and brought it to me, and I ate it all before you came, and I have blessed him? yes, and he shall be blessed'" (Gen. 27:33):

   B. Said R. Hama bar Haninah, "'...violently,' even more violently than he had trembled on the altar.

   C. "He said, "'Who was it then" who served as an intermediary between me and the Omnipresent, that Jacob should take away the blessings?"

   D. "He indicated that it was Rebecca, his mother."

2. A. Said R. Yohanan, "If someone has two sons, and it happens that one goes in and the other comes out, is there any reason for him to tremble?

   B. "But when Esau came in, Gehenna came in with him."

   C. R. Nathan in the name of R. Aha: "The walls of the house began to sweat.

   D. "That is in line with this verse: 'Who then' [in the sense of the word using the same consonants as the word for 'then,' namely, 'roast'] in this way: 'Who is the one who is going to be roasted here in Gehenna, my son [Jacob] or I?'

   E. "Said to him the Holy One, blessed be he, 'Neither you nor your son but 'he who has that hunted game and brought it.'"

3. A. "He hunted the hunter" [another way of reading the Hebrew that is translated, "he who has hunted game:]

   B. Said R. Eleazar bar Simeon, "'O trapper, how have you been entrapped? O you who break gates, how has your gate been broken and destroyed?'

   C. "That is in line with this verse: 'The deceitful man shall not roast his prey. But the substance of the man of glory is determined' (Prov. 12:27)."

   D. Rabbis said, "[The word for 'roast' can be sounded as 'postpone' or 'protract' in the transitive sense, hence] 'He will not last long, [for] the Holy One will not postpone matters either for a deceitful man or for his prey.'"

   E. R. Eliezer son of R. Yose the Galilean: "[The word for 'roast' can be read 'postpone' or 'protract' in the transitive sense, hence] 'He will not last long, [for] the Holy One will not postpone matters either for a deceitful man or for his pray.'"

   F. For R. Joshua b. Levi, "For that entire day Esau went hunting deer and tied them up, but the angel came and freed them;

   G. "he caught birds and bound them up, and the angel came and set them free. Why so?

H. "'But the substance of the man of glory is determined' (Prov. 12:27), that is, it was so that Jacob would came and take the blessings, which in principle from the beginning of the world had been assigned to him."

4.   A.   R. Hinena bar Pappa asked R. Aha, saying to him, "What is the meaning of the verse, 'But the substance of the man of glory is determined'?"

B. He said to him, "It is determined that the righteous in this world shall not receive any of the honor or glory that is coming to them in the world to come."

5.   A.   "...and I ate of all [before you came, and I have blessed him? yes, and he shall be blessed]'" (Gen. 27:33):

B.   R. Judah and R., Nehemiah:

C.   R. Judah said, "'I ate of all things that were created in the six days of creation.'"

D.   R. Nehemiah said, "'I ate of all the good that is made ready for the righteous in the age to come.'"

6.   A.   [Esau] said to [Isaac], "The main point is, what in fact did he give you to eat?"

B.   He said to him, "I do not know, but I tasted the taste of bread, meat, fish, locusts, and every sort of good food in the world."

C.   Said R. Berekhiah, "When he mentioned the taste of meat, he wept. He said, 'As for me, he fed me a bowl of lentils and took my birthright. As for you, he fed you meat -- how much the more so!'"

7.   A.   Said R. Levi, "Our father Isaac was fearful, saying, 'Perhaps I did not do the right thing when I treated the one who is not the firstborn as the first born.'

B.   "But when Esau said, 'He took away my birthright' (Gen. 27:36), he realized that he had done the right thing in blessing him."

No. 1 amplifies Isaac's statement and gives some sense to it. No. 2 develops a rather striking reading of the verse at hand, finding in the statements the sense that Gehenna had opened up for Esau. I am not sure that the translation does justice to the subtlety of the Hebrew. No. 3 takes up the delay of Esau in coming back and develops the idea that he was held back and not given a chance to come back promptly. That is the force of the play on word, reading "delay," in place of "roast." No. 4 simply expands on the exegesis of the intersecting verse. No. 5 supplies Isaac with further dialogue. The point is that

Jacob gave Isaac food of cosmic meaning, and that leads directly into No. 6. No. 6 then links the story of Jacob's purchase of the birthright and his theft of the blessing. No. 7 then provides a good piece of dialogue for Isaac and Esau, in line with Gen. 27:34-36. But, as expected, Isaac now realizes he really did the right thing, a point the biblical narrator fails to register.

LXVII:III.

1. A. ["Then Isaac trembled violently and said, 'Who was it then that hunted game and brought it to me, and I ate it all before you came, and I have blessed him? yes, and he shall be blessed'" (Gen. 27:33):] Said R. Eleazar, "The validation of a writ is effected only through the confirmation of the signatures of the witnesses.

    B. "So, if you might imagine that, had Jacob not deceived his father, he would not have taken the blessings, Scripture states explicitly, '...yes, and he shall be blessed.'"

2. A. Said R. Isaac, "He was coming to curse him. Said the Holy One, blessed be he, to him, 'Be careful, for if you curse him, you curse yourself.

    B. "For lo, you have said to him, 'Those who curse you will be cursed, and those who bless you will be blessed' (Gen. 27:29)."

3. A. Said R. Levi,"There are six things that serve a person, over three of which a person is in charge, and over three of which a person is not in charge.

    B. "Over the eye, ear, and nose, a person is not in charge, for a person sees, hears, and smells what one does not necessarily want to see, hear or smell.

    C. "Over the mouth, hand, and foot a person is in charge. As to the mouth, if someone wants, the person will study the Torah, and if someone wants, the person will slander others or blaspheme or revile.

    D. "As to the hand, if someone wants he may give out charity, and if someone wants, he may rob or murder.

    E. "As to the feet, if someone wants, he may walk to theaters or circuses, and if someone wants, he may walk to synagogues or houses of study.

    F. "But in a moment at which a potential victim has sufficient merit, the Hoy One, blessed be he, takes those limbs of which a person is in charge and removes them from his power.

    G. "As to the hand: 'And his hand, which he put forth against him, dried up' (1 Kgs. 13:45).

    H. "As to the mouth: 'Yes, and he shall be blessed.'

    I. "As to the feet: 'My son, do not walk in the way with them, for their feet run to evil' (Prov. 1:15)."

No. 1 makes an important point about the interpolation at Gen. 27:33. No. 2 adds an interesting point of its own, now revising the view of Isaac. The syllogism of No. 3 rests on the notion that if the victim of a person's mouth, hand, or foot has sufficient merit, God will not permit a wicked person free use of his mouth, hand, or foot. The syllogism draws on our base verse, which is why the passage is inserted here.

LXVII:IV.

1. A   "When Isaac heard the words of his father, he cried out with an exceedingly great and bitter cry [and said to his father, 'Bless me, even me also, O my father!']" (Gen. 27:34):

B. Said R. Hanina, "Whoever says that the Holy One, blessed be he, is lax, may his intestines become lax. While he is patient, he does collect what is coming to you.

C. "Jacob made Esau cry out one cry, and where was he penalized? It was in the castle of Shushan: 'And he cried with a loud and bitter cry' (Est. 4:1)."

2. A.   "But he said, 'Your brother came with guile and he has taken away your blessing'" (Gen. 33:35):

B. R. Yohanan said, "[He came] with the wisdom of his knowledge of the Torah."

3. A.   "Esau said, 'Is he not rightly named Jacob? [For he has supplanted me these two times. He took away my birthright and behold, now he has taken away my blessing.' Then he said, 'Have you not reserved a blessing for me?']" (Gen. 27:36):

B. "'He took away my birthright, and I kept silence, and now he has taken away my blessing.'"

4. A.   "Then he said, 'Have you not reserved a blessing for me?'" (Gen. 27:36):

B. --even an inferior one?

The point of No. 1 is to link the present passage to the history of Israel's redemption later on. In this case, however, the matter concerns Israel's paying recompense for causing anguish to Esau. No. 2 introduces Jacob's knowledge of torah in place of Esau's view of Jacob as full of guile. The remainder of the entries provides minor glosses.

LXVII:V.

1. A. "Isaac answered Esau, ['Behold I have made him your lord and all his brothers I have given to him for servants, and with grain and wine I have sustained him. What then can I do for you, my son?']" (Gen. 27:37):"

   B. Said R. Berekhiah, ""Behold I have made him your lord and all his brothers I have given to him for servants' is the seventh of the blessings Isaac passed out [to Jacob].

   C. "Why then does he mention it first?

   D. "The sense is this: 'I made him king over you, and your blessings belong to him.'"

   E. "A slave and everything he owns belongs to his master: all his brothers I have given to him for servants, and with grain and wine I have sustained him.'"

2. A. "... What then can I do for you, my son?'" (Gen. 27:37): [Since the word for "now" uses the consonants of the word for "bread," we interpret:] "Indeed for you the bread is baked [in that you will have prosperity also]."

   B. R. Yohanan said, "Leave him alone, for his bread is baked for him everywhere."

   C. R. Simeon b. Laqish said, "Leave him alone, for anger [which shares the consonants used for the word "now"] and wrath are handed over to him."

3. A. R. Simlai, and some say it in the name of R. Abbahu, "Said the Holy One, blessed be he, 'You have said, "What then can I do for you, my son?"

   B. "[Isaac replied,] '"Yet let favor be shown to him" (Is. 26:10).'

   C. "[God said,] '"He is wicked" (Is. 26:10).'

   D. ""Has he not learned righteousness?"'

   E. "'Did he not honor his parents?'

   F. ""In the land of uprightness will he deal wrongfully."'

   G. "He said to him, 'He is destined to lay his hands on the sanctuary.'

   H. "He said to him, 'If so, give him prosperity in this world: "and let him not behold the majesty of the Lord" in the world to come.'"

No. 1 amplifies the discourse between Isaac and Esau. No. 2 works on the word "now," which yields consonants bearing diverse meanings. The passage falls into the category of philological exegesis. Employing the cited verse of Isaiah, No. 3 then constructs a colloquy between Isaac and God. Now Esau's future destruction of the Temple enters the picture.

LXVII:VI.

1. A. "Then Isaac his father answered him, 'Behold of the fat places of the earth [shall your dwelling be, and of the dew of heaven from above. By your sword you shall live, and you shall serve your brother, but when you break loose, you shall break his yoke from your neck]'" (Gen. 27:39-40):

   B. "Then Isaac his father answered him, 'Behold of the fat places of the earth shall your dwelling be" refers to Italy.

   C. "...and of the dew of heaven from above" refers to Bet Gubrin.

2. A. "...'Behold of the fat places of the earth shall your dwelling be" refers to the fat-pursed people of the earth.

   B. Antoninus sent to Our Master [Judah the Patriarch], saying to him, "Since our treasury lacks funds, what should we do to fill it up?"

   C. He took the messenger and brought him into his vegetable patch. He began to pull up big radishes and to plant little ones in their place.

   D. He said to him, "Give me the answer in writing."

   E. He said to him, "You do not need it."

   F. He went back and said the king said to him, "Where is your answer?"

   G. He said to him, "He did not give me anything.?

   H. "What did he say to you?"

   I. "He did not say anything to me, but he took me and brought me into his vegetable patch and began to pull up big radishes and to plant little ones in their place."

   J. He began to remove officers and bring in officers, until his treasury was filled [with the bribes people paid for high office].

No. 1 lightly glosses the base text. No. 2 is tacked on; I see no clear relationship between the base verse and the story. But the comment on Rome bears its own polemic.

LXVII:VII.

1. A. "By your sword you shall live, [and you shall serve your brother, but when you break loose, you shall break his yoke from your neck']" (Gen. 27:39-40):

   B. Said R. Levi, "Pull out your sword and you will live."

2. A. "...and you shall serve your brother:"

B.   Said R. Huna, "If he has merit, you will serve, and if not, you will destroy him."

3.   A.   "...but when you break loose, you shall break his yoke from your neck:'"

B.   [Since the words for "break loose" and "fair" share the same consonants, the comment is as follows:] He said to him, "As to you, you have fairs, and he too has fairs. You have laws, and he has laws." [Israel and Rome enjoy parity with one another.]

4.   A.   Said R. Yose bar Halputa, "If you see your brother breaking the yoke of the Torah from his neck, decree persecution and you will rule over him."

B.   "For you are our father, for Abraham knows us not, and Israel does not acknowledge us" (Is. 63:16):

C.   Now where is Isaac?

D.   One who has said, "...decree persecution and you will rule over him" is not going to be associated with the patriarchs!

Nos. 1, 2 gloss the cited clauses. Nos. 3, 4 present two meanings for the base verse's reference to "you shall break...yoke." Once more therefore we have far more than an exercise in philological exegesis.

LXVII:VIII.

1.   A.   "Now Esau hated Jacob [because of the blessing with which his father had blessed him, and Esau said to himself, 'The days of mourning for my father are approaching; then I will kill my brother Jacob]'" (Gen. 27:41):

B.   Said R. Eleazar b. R. Yose, "He turned into a vengeful and vindictive enemy of his, just as even today they are called 'senators' in Rome [with the word for 'senator' bearing the consonants that appear in the words for enemy and vindictive]."

2.   A.   "...and Esau said to his heart:"

B.   [Reading the word "to his heart" to refer to someone in control of his heart, we interpret as follows:] The wicked exist subject to the domain of their heart.

C.   "The fool has said *in* his heart" (Ps. 14:1). "And Esau said *in* his heart" (Gen. 27:41). "And Jeroboam said in *his* heart" (1 Kgs. 12:25). "Now Haman said *in* his heart" (Est. 6:6).

D. But the righteous maintain their heart subject to their domain [speaking *to* their heart, as God does, and telling their heart what to do, rather than be governed by their heart's impulses, thus]:

E. "Now Hannah spoke upon her heart" (1 Sam. 1:13). "And David said to his heart" (1 Sam. 27:1). "But Daniel placed upon his heart" (Dan. 1:8).

F. "And the Lord said to his heart" (Gen. 8:21).

3. A. "The days of mourning for my father are approaching; then I will kill my brother Jacob:"

B. R. Judah said, "Esau was entirely calculating. He said, 'Why should I give grief to my father? Rather: "The days of mourning for my father are approaching; then I will kill my brother Jacob."'"

C. R. Nehemiah said, "Many young foals have died and their hides have served as saddles on the backs of their mothers."

D. Rabbis say, "'If I kill him, Shem and Eber will go into session and try me. Rather, I shall go and marry the daughter of Ishmael. Then he will come and dispute with Jacob about the birthright and kill him, and I shall then rise against him as the avenger of the blood and kill him and inherit the estates of two families."

E. "That is in line with this verse: 'Because you have said, "These two nations and these two countries shall be mine, and we will possess it," whereas the Lord was there' (Ez. 35:10)."

4. A. ["The days of mourning for my father are approaching; then I will kill my brother Jacob:"] Who reported that Esau made such a statement?

B. Said R. Yudan, "The Holy One, blessed be he: 'Whereas the Lord was there' (Ez. 35:10)."

C. Said R. Berekhiah, "Esau denied it and said, 'I made no such statement.'

D. "Said the Holy One, blessed be he, to him, 'Do you not know that I am the one who searches out all hearts, as it says, 'I the Lord search the heart' (Jer. 17:10)."

No. 1 presents a philological contribution, and No. 2, a syllogism to which our base verse makes its expected contribution. Nos. 3-4 form a single protracted statement, as shown by the occurrence of Ez. 35:10 in both parts. The statement of Esau is fully worked out, with the rabbis, 3.D, supplying a full account of Esau's plan and motivation. For the fact is that, as the narrative unfolds, Esau does nothing at all.

LXVII:IX.

1. A. "But the words of Esau her older son were told to Rebecca, [so she sent and called Jacob her younger son and said to him, 'Behold your brother Esau comforts himself by planning to kill you. Now therefore my son, obey my voice; arise, flee to Laban my brother in Haran, and stay with him a while, until your brother's fury turns away; until your brother's anger turns away, and he forgets what you have done to him; then I will send and fetch you from there. Why should I be bereft of you both in one day?']" (Gen. 27:42-45):

   B. R. Haggai in the name of R. Isaac, "The matriarchs were prophets, and Rebecca was one of the matriarchs [and that is how she knew what Esau was thinking of doing]."

   C. R. Berekhiah in the name of R. Isaac: "Even a common person will not plough one furrow within another. Will the prophets do so? And yet you find: 'Do not touch my anointed ones and do no harm to my prophets' (Ps. 105:15)."

2. A. "...so she sent and called Jacob her younger son and said to him, 'Behold your brother Esau comforts himself by planning to kill you:'"

   B. "It is as though he is desolate on your account, as if you were dead.

   C. " He is accepting condolences on your account as if you were dead.

   D. "He is already drinking the cup of consolation on your account, as if you were dead."

No. 1 answers the question of who told Rebecca what she knew. She is represented as a prophet. I cannot explain 1.C. No. 2 provides a vivid amplification of Rebecca's sarcastic word-choice about Esau's comforting himself.

LXVII:X.

1. A. "Now therefore my son, obey my voice; arise, flee to Laban my brother in Haran, and stay with him a few days, [until your brother's fury turns away; until your brother's anger turns away, and he forgets what you have done to him; then I will send and fetch you from there. Why should I be bereft of you both in one day?']" (Gen. 27:42-45):

   B. "And Jacob served seven years for Rachel, and they seemed to him like just a few days" (Gen. 29:20).

   C. Said R. Hinena bar Pazzi, "The word 'a few' is written both in the present case and in the later one. Just as the reference to 'a few' written later on means seven years, so 'a few' stated here means seven years."

2. A. "...until your brother's fury turns away:"

B. His mother, righteous woman that she was, said, "Until your brother's fury turns away" [because she could not imagine that he would bear a grudge forever].

. C. But Esau, for his part, was not that way: "And his anger raged perpetually and he kept his wrath for ever" (Amos 1:11).

D. R. Simeon b. Laqish said, "His anger and his wrath did not move from his mouth."

No. 1 clarifies Rebecca's meaning. No. 2 underlines the naivete of the assumption of Rebecca.

LXVII:XI.

1. A. "'Why should I be bereft of you both in one day?' Then Rebecca said to Isaac, 'I am weary of my life because of the Hittite women. If Jacob marries one of the Hittite women such as these, one of the women of the land, what good will my life be to me?'" (Gen. 27:46):

B. Said R. Huna, "She began to [Freedman:] make gestures of utter abhorrence."

C. "If Jacob marries one of the Hittite women such as these" -- striking at this one, that one, and the other.

The glosses embellish the statement.

LXVII:XII.

1. A. "Then Isaac called Jacob and blessed him [and charged him, 'You shall not marry one of the Canaanite women. Arise, go to Paddan-aram, to the house of Bethuel, your mother's father, and take as wife form there one of the daughters of Laban your mother's brother']" (Gen. 28:1-2):

B. [Isaac blessed Jacob,] said R. Abbahu, "Because the blessings were still unsteady in his possession. When did the blessings become securely in his hand? 'Then Isaac called Jacob and blessed him.'"

C. Said R. Eleazar, "The validation of a writ is effected only through the confirmation of the signatures of the witnesses.

D. "So, if you might imagine that, had Jacob not deceived his father, he would not have taken the blessings, Scripture states explicitly, 'Then Isaac called Jacob and blessed him.'"

E. R. Berekiah [in the name of R. Levi] said, "It may be compared to the case of a prince who was digging toward the king to receive a *litra* of gold.

The king said to him, 'Why do in it in secret? Come and take it for yourself in public.'

F. "So it is said, 'Then Isaac called Jacob and blessed him.'" [Thus he confirmed the original blessing and showed it was entirely by intention.]

2. A. "...and charged him, 'You shall not marry one of the Canaanite women:'"

B. He charged him concerning the daughters of Aner, Eshcol, and Mamre.

3. A. "Jacob obeyed his father and his mother [and went to Paddan-aram]" (Gen. 28:6):

B. "The way of a fool is straight in his own eyes, but he who is wise heartens to counsel" (Prov. 21:2):

C. "The way of a fool is straight in his own eyes" refers to Samson, who said, "Get her for me, for she pleases me very much" Judges 143:3).

D. "...but he who is wise heartens to counsel" refers to Jacob: "Jacob obeyed his father and his mother and went to Paddan-aram."

The thrust of No. 1 is to prove that Jacob really received the blessings from Isaac, and that Isaac knew just what he was doing. No. 2 glosses, and No. 3 draws a parallel between Samson, who ordered his parents to select a woman of his choice, and Jacob, who accepted his parents' judgment.

LXVII:XIII.

1. A. "So when Esau saw that the Canaanite women did not please Isaac his father, Esau went to Ishmael and took to wife, besides the wives he had, Mahalath, the daughter of Ishmael, Abraham's son, the sister of Nebaioth" (Gen. 28:7):

B. R. Joshua b. Levi said, "He decided to reform. 'Mahalath' is so-called because the Holy One, blessed be he, forgave him all his sons. Basemath is so called because [Freedman:] his mind was now satisfied."

C. Said to him R. Eleazar, "If he had divorced his first wives, you would have stated matters correctly. But what it says is, 'besides the wives he had.' What he did was add grief to grief, an addition to what was already a full house."

2. A. R. Yudan in the name of R. Aibu [commenced discourse by citing the following verse]: "'In the transgression of the lips is a snare to the evil man, but the righteous comes out of trouble' (Prov. 12:13):

B. "On account of the rebellion of Esau and Ishmael against the Holy One, blessed be he, their downfall came.

C. "'But the righteous comes out of trouble' (Prov. 12:13) refers to Jacob: 'Jacob left Beer Sheba' (Gen. 28:10)."

No. 1 considers whether Esau is to be praised for his new wives. No. 2 then draws a conclusion from the whole, and, in a recurrent pattern, links the present discussion to what is to follow, summarizing the whole.

Index

Aaron, 39, 105

Abba, 10, 28, 40, 41, 46, 47, 51, 53, 55, 68, 104, 114, 117, 120, 123, 137, 141, 143-45, 149, 152, 155, 161, 172, 174, 175, 193, 201, 204, 205, 208, 211, 213, 233, 261, 285, 292, 295, 296, 300, 307, 322, 339, 355, 357, 359, 361, 365, 392, 393, 397

Abbahu, 70, 170, 184, 248, 262, 275, 301, 318, 342, 343, 357, 360, 386, 414, 419

Abel, 9, 335

Abimelech, 89, 146, 234-45, 249, 259-64, 331, 367, 370-77

Abraham, 8, 20, 39, 48, 50, 54, 55, 59-75, 77-81, 83-85, 89, 90, 92-96, 99, 101, 102, 106-108, 110-112, 113-17, 119-22, 124-38, 141-44, 151-54, 157-63, 169-71, 173-88, 190-93, 195-210, 211, 212, 214-17, 220, 221, 226, 230-33, 236, 238-47, 249-57, 259-65, 267-71, 274, 275, 277, 279-89, 291-94, 297-311, 313-15, 317, 319-21, 323, 324, 326, 329, 331-39, 341, 344-47, 349-52, 361-63, 365-71, 374, 383-86, 395, 416, 420

Adam, 3, 79, 158, 198, 368

Aha, 11, 23, 62, 63, 69, 80, 89, 97, 102, 103, 110, 141, 142, 153, 159, 162, 169, 186, 196, 198, 199, 203, 204, 206, 229, 235, 248, 251, 259, 284, 293, 304, 307, 322, 323, 349, 363, 364, 369, 371, 404, 405, 410, 411

Ahaz, 39, 102, 103, 131, 349

Ahbah, 296

Ahitophel, 45

Aibu, 2, 5, 108, 131, 155, 173, 211, 229, 326, 373, 407, 420

Albeck, Ch., 117, 407

Alexander (the Great), 337, 338

Amorites, 41, 95, 109, 110, 144

Amos, 79, 196, 368, 419

Antoninus, 10, 415

Aqiba, 16, 143, 160, 252, 253, 257, 271, 295, 297, 333, 343

Arpachshad, 41, 46, 47, 52, 67

Arvadites, 41

Assyria, 32, 39, 40, 347

Azariah, 8, 14, 16, 48, 61, 62, 65, 81, 82, 93, 97, 110, 112, 135, 137, 148, 190, 199, 206, 253, 254, 265, 282, 289, 297, 385

Azzai, 16, 342

Ba, 372

Babylonia, 14, 34, 39, 40, 43, 61, 62, 73, 88, 101, 107, 136, 139, 183, 198, 235, 285, 289, 371, 376, 389

Balaam, 90, 234, 235, 274, 397, 406

275, 278, 279, 281, 282, 285-87,
293, 296, 297, 304, 306, 307,
315, 316, 327, 328, 331, 334,
337-39, 345, 347, 351, 354-56,
359, 360, 364, 365, 368, 375,
377, 380, 390-92, 394, 395, 398,
399, 403, 404, 406, 413, 416

Izates, 164

Jacob, 6, 8, 31, 72, 77, 79, 83, 89,
97, 103, 121, 122, 126, 127,
131, 134, 143, 144, 147, 157,
159, 162, 163, 195, 242, 246,
252, 283, 292, 297, 310, 311,
321, 326, 327, 333, 339, 346,
350-54, 356, 357, 359-66, 368,
381-84, 387, 390-400, 402, 403,
406, 407, 409-14, 416-21

Jastrow, 209

Jebusites, 41, 144

Jeremiah, 20, 71, 79, 83, 91, 114,
133, 149, 179, 201, 263, 282,
321, 322, 350, 368, 372

Jeroboam, 9, 114, 385, 397, 398,
416

Jesus, 120

Joab, 202

Job, 4, 10, 25-27, 49, 50, 70, 108,
124, 177, 178, 182, 198, 201,
202, 204-7, 212, 226, 231, 234,
244, 251, 280, 292-94, 326, 332,
335-37, 342, 371, 372, 399, 403

Jonathan, 1, 12, 21, 82, 110, 131,
179, 198, 203, 225, 257, 268,
371

Joseph, 4, 33, 42, 69, 72, 94, 105,
134, 274, 277, 319, 328, 335,
384, 394, 400

Joshua, 8, 12, 20-22, 38, 69, 71,
72, 75, 78, 99, 105, 119, 133,
138, 142, 143, 150, 155, 158,
161, 163, 169, 171, 172, 175,

187, 193, 197, 198, 200, 202,
203, 205, 207, 216, 220, 226,
252, 255, 259, 270, 271, 273,
278, 285, 289, 293, 294, 296,
315, 324, 333, 342, 345, 346,
355, 371, 376, 377, 381, 382,
387, 388, 404, 410, 420

Josiah, 103, 153

Judah, 3, 4, 12, 19, 21, 30, 33, 43,
47, 50, 52, 64, 72, 81, 93, 95,
96, 104, 110-112, 113, 116, 121-
24, 133, 137, 145, 149, 155,
167, 170, 171, 179, 180, 192,
193, 195, 197-99, 202, 205, 207,
211, 220, 224, 230, 240, 247-50,
252, 260, 264, 265, 283, 285,
292-95, 297, 300, 307, 333-36,
341, 343, 346, 355, 371, 374,
375, 380, 383, 384, 389, 399,
411, 415, 417

Judah bar Simon, 4, 30, 116, 179,
197, 205, 207, 211, 220, 250,
285, 294, 300, 307, 336, 374,
380, 383

Kahana, 28, 40, 41, 46, 53, 55,
117, 120, 137, 145, 155, 161,
172, 175, 193, 201, 261, 292,
339, 355, 357, 359, 365, 392,
393, 397

Kenite, 144, 190

Kenizzite, 144

Kittim, 37

Laban, 235, 294, 320, 321, 324,
326, 351, 418, 419

Lamech, 79, 80, 224, 368, 369

Laqish, 17, 38, 88, 111, 114, 132,
141, 146, 147, 154, 158, 170,
171, 173, 175, 183, 225, 240,
248, 262, 286, 292-94, 316, 318,
335, 344, 352, 353, 363, 364,
371, 395, 397, 414, 419

Made in the USA
San Bernardino, CA
08 December 2017